UNIT 18
BUSINESS TAX

(FA 2006)

Technician (NVQ/SVQ Level 4)

British Library Cataloguing-in-Publication Data

A catalogue record for this book is available from the British Library.

Published by
Kaplan Publishing Foulks Lynch
Unit 2, The Business Centre
Molly Millars Lane
Wokingham
RG41 2QZ

ISBN 10: 1 84710 132 1
ISBN 13: 978 1 84710 132 7

© FTC Kaplan Limited, October 2006

Printed and bound in Great Britain.

We are grateful to HM Revenue and Customs for the provision of tax forms, which are Crown Copyright and are reproduced here with kind permission from the Office of Public Sector Information.

We are grateful to the Association of Accounting Technicians for the permission to reproduce pass assessment materials. The solutions have been prepared by Kaplan Publishing Foulks Lynch.

CONTENTS

CONTENTS

CONTENTS

CONTENTS

PREFACE

STUDY TEXT

The Study Text is written in a practical and interactive style:
- key terms and concepts are clearly defined
- all topics are illustrated with practical examples with clearly worked solutions
- frequent practice activities throughout the chapters ensure that what you have learnt is regularly reinforced
- 'pitfalls' and 'examination tips' help you avoid commonly made mistakes and help you focus on what is required to perform well in your examination.

WORKBOOK

The Workbook comprises three main elements:

A question bank of key techniques to give additional practice and reinforce the work covered in each chapter. The questions are divided into their relevant chapters and students may either attempt these questions as they work through the textbook, or leave some or all of these until they have completed the Study Text as a sort of final revision of what they have studied.

Two mock examinations which closely reflect the type of examinations they may expect.

The AAT specimen paper.

STANDARDS OF COMPETENCE

Unit commentary

This unit is about preparing tax computations for businesses and completing the relevant tax returns. There are four elements in this unit.

The first element requires you to prepare capital allowances computations, including adjustments for private use by the owners of a business.

In the second element you must prepare assessable business income computations for partnerships and self-employed individuals. This includes identifying the National Insurance Contributions payable.

The third element is concerned with preparing capital gains computations for companies and unincorporated businesses.

The final element requires you to prepare Corporation Tax computations for UK resident companies.

Throughout the unit you must show that you take account of current tax law and HMRC practice and make submissions within statutory timescales. You also need to show that you consult with HMRC in an open and constructive manner, give timely and constructive advice to business clients and maintain client confidentiality.

> **Elements contained within this unit are:**
>
> **Element 18.1**
>
> **Prepare capital allowances computations**
>
> **Element 18.2**
>
> **Compute assessable business income**
>
> **Element 18.3**
>
> **Prepare capital gains computations**
>
> **Element 18.4**
>
> **Prepare Corporation Tax computations**

Knowledge and Understanding

To perform this unit effectively you will need to know and understand:

	The business environment	Chapter
1	The duties and responsibilities of the tax practitioner (Elements 18.1, 18.2, 18.3 & 18.4)	25
2	The issues of taxation liability (Elements 18.1, 18.2, 18.3 & 18.4)	Throughout
3	Relevant legislation and guidance from HM Revenue and Customs (Elements 18.1, 18.2, 18.3 & 18.4)	Throughout

Taxation principles and theory

4	Basic law and practice relating to all issues covered in the range and referred to in the performance criteria (Elements 18.1, 18.2, 18.3 & 18.4)	Throughout
5	Availability and types of capital allowance: · first year allowance · writing down allowance · balancing allowance and charge (relevant to industrial buildings and plant and machinery including computers, motor vehicles and short life assets) (Element 18.1)	4, 5
6	Treatment of capital allowances for unincorporated businesses including private use adjustments (Element 18.1)	14
7	Adjustments of trading profits and losses for tax purposes (Element 18.2)	3, 14
8	Regulations relating to disallowed expenditure such as business entertaining, bad debt write-offs and provisions, private expenditure and capital expenditure (Element 18.2)	3, 14
9	Basis of assessment of unincorporated businesses (Element 18.2)	16
10	Basic allocation of income between partners (Element 18.3)	15
11	Identification of business assets disposed of including part disposals (Element 18.3)	20, 21, 22
12	Calculation of gains and losses on disposals of business assets including indexation allowance (Element 18.3)	21, 22, 23
13	Capital gains exemptions and reliefs on business assets including rollover relief and taper relief but excluding retirement relief (Element 18.3)	22, 24

KAPLAN PUBLISHING

The organisation

Element 18.1   Prepare capital allowances computations

Performance criteria		**Chapter**
In order to perform this element successfully you need to:		
A	Classify expenditure on capital assets in accordance with the statutory distinction between capital and revenue expenditure	4
B	Ensure that entries and calculations relating to the computation of capital allowance for a company are correct	4, 5
C	Make adjustments for private use by business owners	14
D	Ensure that computations and submissions are made in accordance with current tax law and take account of current HMRC practice	4, 5, 26
E	Consult with HMRC in an open and constructive manner	25
F	Give timely and constructive advice to clients on the maintenance of accounts and the recording of information relevant to tax returns	25
G	Maintain client confidentiality at all times	25

Range statement

Performance in this element relates to the following contexts:

Business owners:

· Self-employed individuals

· Partnerships

Element 18.2   Compute assessable business income

Performance Criteria	**Chapter**
In order to perform this element successfully you need to:	

A	Adjust trading profits and losses for tax purposes	3, 14, 17
B	Make adjustments for private use by business owners	14
C	Divide profits and losses of partnerships amongst partners	15, 17
D	Apply the basis of assessment for unincorporated businesses in the opening and closing years	16, 17
E	Identify the due dates of payment of Income Tax by unincorporated businesses, including payments on account	18
F	Identify the National Insurance Contributions payable by self-employed individuals	19
G	Complete correctly the self-employed and partnership supplementary pages to the Tax Return for individuals, together with relevant claims and elections, and submit them within statutory time limits	14, 18
H	Consult with HMRC staff in an open and constructive manner	18, 25
I	Give timely and constructive advice to clients on the maintenance of accounts and the recording of information relevant to tax returns	25
J	Maintain client confidentiality at all times	25

Range statement

Performance in this element relates to the following contexts:

Clients:

- Sole traders
- Partnerships

Element 18.3   Prepare capital gains computations

	Performance Criteria In order to perform this element successfully you need to:	**Chapter**
A	Identify and value correctly any chargeable assets that have been disposed of	20, 21, 22
B	Identify shares disposed of by companies	23
C	Calculate chargeable gains and allowable losses	21, 22
D	Apply reliefs, deferrals and exemptions correctly	24
E	Ensure that computations and submissions are made in accordance with current tax law and take account of current HMRC practice	21, 22, 26
F	Consult with HMRC staff in an open and constructive manner	25
G	Give timely and constructive advice to clients on the maintenance of accounts and the recording of information relevant to tax returns	25
H	Maintain client confidentiality at all times	25

Range statement

Performance in this element relates to the following contexts:

Chargeable assets that have been:
- Sold
- Gifted
- Lost
- Destroyed

Reliefs:
- Rollover relief
- Relief for gifts

Element 18.4 Prepare Corporation Tax computations

	Performance Criteria In order to perform this element successfully you need to:	**Chapter**
A	Enter adjusted trading profits and losses, capital allowances, investment income and capital gains in the Corporation Tax computation	2, 3, 4, 5, 6, 8, 9
B	Set-off and deduct loss reliefs and charges correctly	9
C	Calculate Corporation Tax due, taking account of marginal relief	7, 8
D	Identify and set-off Income Tax deductions and credits	10
E	Identify the National Insurance Contributions payable by employers	12
F	Identify the amount of Corporation Tax payable and the due dates of payment, including payments on account	11
G	Complete Corporation Tax returns correctly and submit them, together with relevant claims and elections, within statutory time limits	4, 5, 6, 7, 8, 11
H	Consult with HMRC staff in an open and constructive manner	11, 25
I	Give timely and constructive advice to clients on the maintenance of accounts and the recording of information relevant to tax returns	11, 25
J	Maintain client confidentiality at all times	25

Range statement

Performance in this element relates to the following contexts:

Loss reliefs relating to:

· Trade losses
· Non-trade losses

TAX RATES AND ALLOWANCES

Note: Tax rates and allowances that you need in the simulation will be given to you. These allowances are provided for use in this Study Pack.

1 Corporation tax

	Financial year 2003	Financial year 2004	Financial year 2005	Financial year 2006
Ordinary rate	30%	30%	30%	30%
Small companies' rate	19%	19%	19%	19%
Fraction for marginal relief	11/400	11/400	11/400	11/400
Lower profits limit for small companies' rate	£300,000	£300,000	£300,000	£300,000
Upper profits limit for small companies' rate	£1,500,000	£1,500,000	£1,500,000	£1,500,000

For FY 2002 to FY 2005 there is a starting rate of Nil% if profits do not exceed £10,000. For profits between £10,000 and £50,000 the 19% rate applies but with marginal relief using the fraction 19/400.

2 Income tax

	2005/06				2006/07	
Rate	Bands of income		Cumulative	Rate	Bands of income	Cumulative
%		£	£	%		£	£
10	First	2,090	209	10	First	2,150	215
22	Next	30,310	6,877	22	Next	31,150	7,068
40	Over	32,400		40	Over	33,300	

3 Personal allowances and reliefs

	2005/06 £	2006/07 £
Personal allowance	4,895	5,035

4 Capital gains tax

	2005/06 £	2006/07 £
Exempt amount	8,500	8,800

5 Taper relief

Comlete years after 5 April 1998 for which asset held	Percentage of gains chargeable Gains on business assets %
0	100
1	150
2 or more	25

KAPLAN PUBLISHING

INTRODUCTION TO BUSINESS TAX

INTRODUCTION

This chapter presents an overview of business tax for the Unit 18 assessment.

CONTENTS

1 Contents of the Study Text
2 Types of business entity

1 Contents of the Study Text

1.1 Four categories

The Study Text can be split into four specific categories:

		Chapters
·	Companies	2 – 12
·	Unincorporated traders (sole traders and partnerships)	13 – 19
·	Chargeable gains	20 – 24
·	Business environment	25 – 26

The aim is to gradually consider each of the ways of taxing a business. This will depend on whether an individual has decided to set up his business as a:

- · company;
- · sole trader; or } unincorporated trades
- · partnership

2 Types of business entity

2.1 Company

A company is a legal entity, separate from its owners and managers.

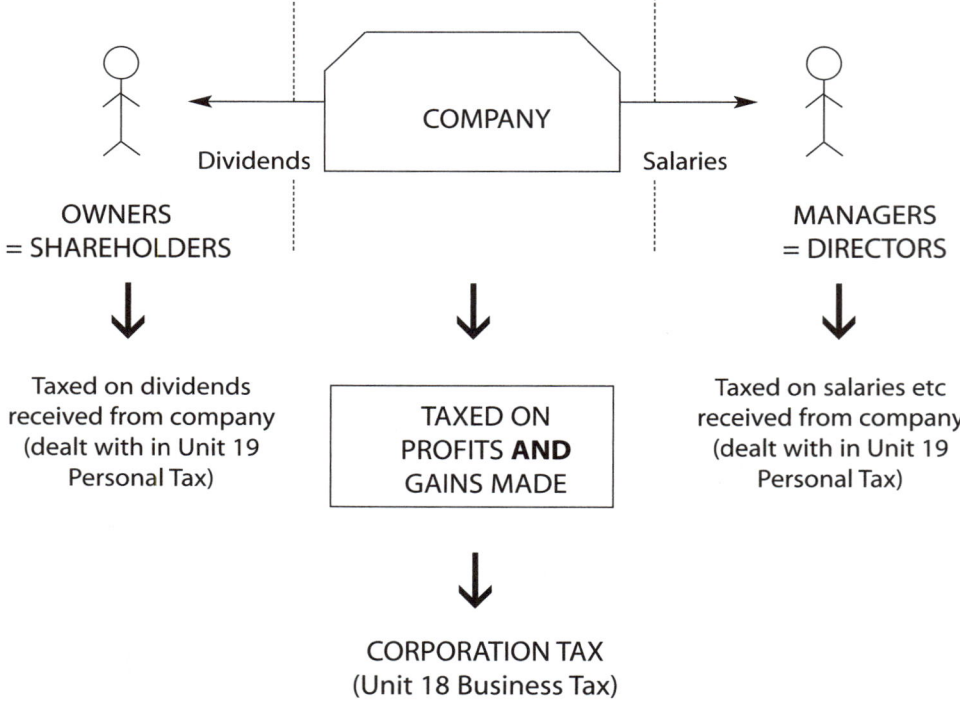

Note: In a lot of cases the shareholders and directors are the same people. However, this will have no effect on the Unit 18 assessment.

2.2 Sole trader

An individual setting up an unincorporated business (i.e. not a company) on his/her own is known as a sole trader.

A sole trader is not a separate legal entity.

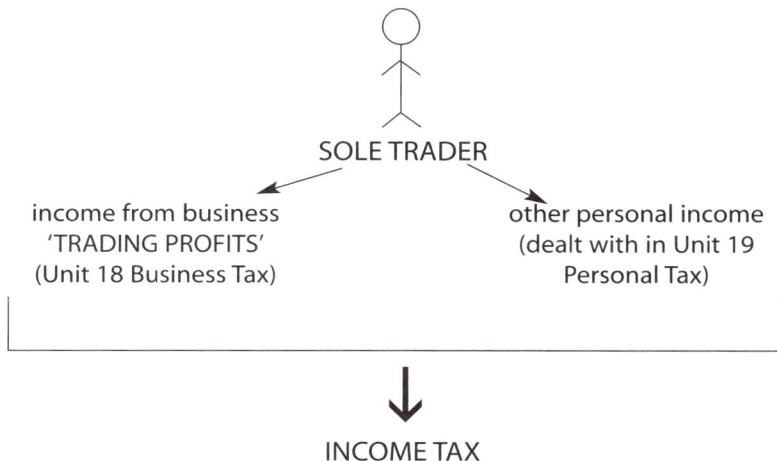

In the Unit 18 assessment, you are not required to complete a full income tax computation/ income tax return. You are only required to deal with the business aspects.

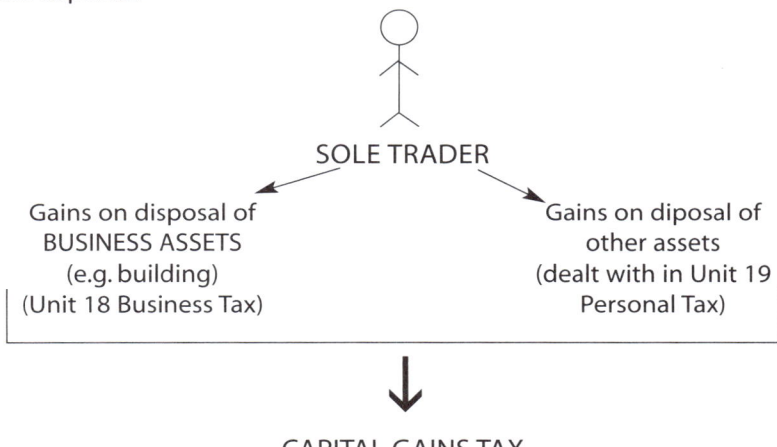

In the Unit 18 assessment, you may be required to complete a capital gains tax computation. However, the sole trader will only have disposed of business assets.

2.3 Partnership

A partnership is another form of unincorporated business, but it is not a separate legal entity.

A partnership is formed when a number of individuals carry on a business together with a view of profit, i.e. a partnership is effectively a collection of sole traders working together.

Each partner pays his own income tax and capital gains tax on his share of the partnership's profits and gains.

2.4 Business environment

Every person offering tax advice must be aware of his duties and responsibilities, and of how legislation applies. This is covered in chapters 25 and 26 of the manual.

3 Summary

There are three types of business entity to consider:
· Company
· Sole trader
· Partnership

Each has its own special rules for calculating profits, gains and tax.

KAPLAN PUBLISHING

PRINCIPLES OF CORPORATION TAX

INTRODUCTION

It is very likely that one of the 'tasks' in the assessment will include the preparation of a corporation tax computation. This chapter sets the scene.

CONTENTS

1   Introduction to corporation tax
2   The principle of chargeable accounting periods
3   Proforma corporation tax computation

PERFORMANCE CRITERIA

This chapter covers to the following performance criteria:

·   Enter adjusted trading profits and losses, capital allowances, investment income and capital gains in the corporation tax computation (18.4 A)

1 Introduction to corporation tax

1.1 Corporation tax

Corporation tax is paid by companies. A company can be recognised in the assessment because its name will end with:

· Ltd (which means limited); or
· plc (which means public limited company).

Sole traders and partnerships do not pay corporation tax.

> ○ **EXAMPLE**   ○ ○ ○ ○
>
> Which of the following businesses pay corporation tax?
>
> (a) Amy's Motor Dealers Ltd
> (b) Bert & Sons
> (c) Christopher Diamond plc
> (d) Eric & Co
>
> **Solution**
>
> Corporation tax is paid by companies:
>
> (a) Amy's Motor Dealers Ltd (name ends in Ltd); and
> (b) Christopher Diamond plc (name ends in plc).

1.2 Corporation tax computation

Companies pay corporation tax on the total of their income and gains received. Firstly, the period covered by the computation must be identified and then the income and gains calculated.

2 The principle of chargeable accounting periods

2.1 Chargeable accounting period

A company prepares a corporation tax computation for a 'chargeable accounting period' (CAP).

In a normal situation, a company prepares a 12 month set of accounts and has a matching CAP.

○ **EXAMPLE**   ○ ○ ○ ○

Fred Ltd has prepared accounts for the year ended 31 December 2006.

Gordon plc has prepared accounts for the year ended 31 March 2007.

For what period will the companies prepare their corporation tax computations?

Solution

Fred Ltd – computation for year ended 31 December 2006.

Gordon plc – computation for year ended 31 March 2007.

2.2 Accounts of less than 12 months

A CAP can be any length up to 12 months. Where a company prepares a set of accounts of less than 12 months, there is a short CAP.

○ **EXAMPLE**   ○ ○ ○ ○

Harry Ltd has previously prepared accounts to 31 December, until 31 December 2005. The company has now changed to preparing accounts to 30 September.

What is its first chargeable accounting period using the new date?

Solution

Harry Ltd has a CAP of 9 months ended 30 September 2006.

2.3 Accounts of more than 12 months

A CAP can never exceed 12 months. Therefore, when a company prepares accounts for a period of more than 12 months, there must be two CAPs.

The two CAPs are:

·   CAP for the first 12 months; and
·   a separate CAP for the balance.

No other combination is acceptable.

A corporation tax computation is prepared for each CAP.

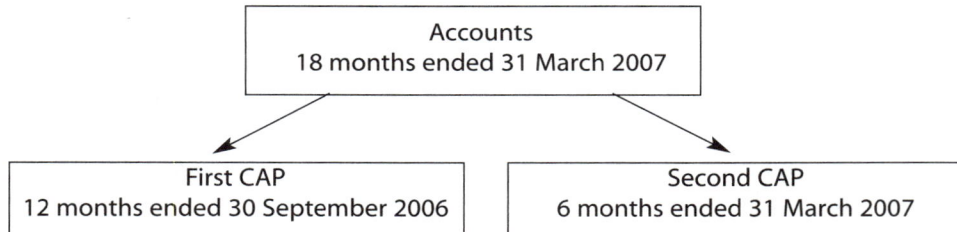

The method of allocating profits from the accounts between the two periods is covered in Chapter 8.

○ **EXAMPLE**   ○○○○

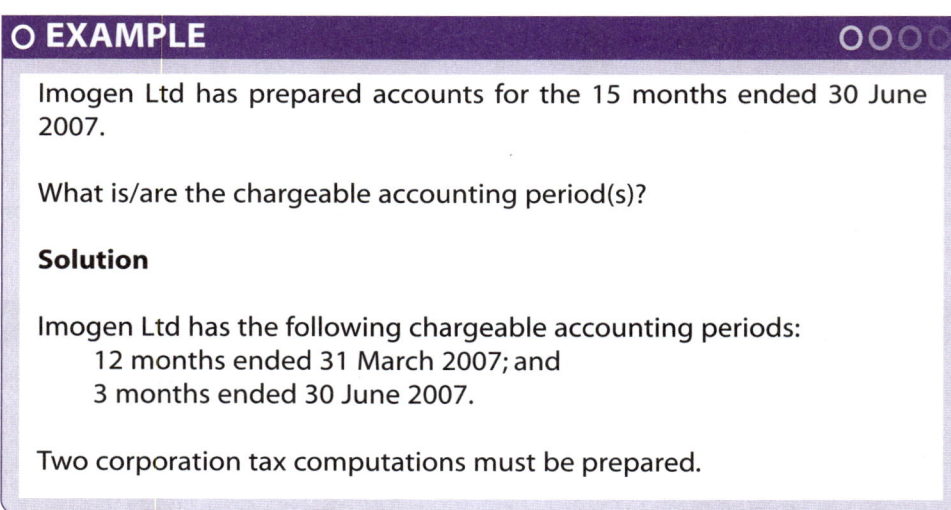

Imogen Ltd has prepared accounts for the 15 months ended 30 June 2007.

What is/are the chargeable accounting period(s)?

Solution

Imogen Ltd has the following chargeable accounting periods:
    12 months ended 31 March 2007; and
    3 months ended 30 June 2007.

Two corporation tax computations must be prepared.

3   Proforma corporation tax computation

3.1 The terminology

At first sight the terminology used in the computation can appear daunting. Over the next few chapters the proforma computation will be built up in detail and the terminology explained in full.

3.2 The proforma corporation tax computation

In the assessment you will be expected to prepare a corporation tax computation using the proforma set out below.

The proforma will become more familiar as you work through the chapters.

On the proforma is a reference to where in the textbook each entry is considered in detail.

Company name
Corporation Tax Computation for XX months ended ..... (the CAP)

	£	Chapter(s)
Schedule D Case I	X	3, 4, 5
Schedule D Case III	X	6
Schedule A	X	6
Chargeable gains	X	6
	⎯	
Total profits	X	
Less: Charges on income	(X)	6
	⎯	
Profits chargeable to corporation tax (PCTCT)	X	
	⎯	
Corporation tax liability (at relevant rate)	X	7

3.3 The schedular system

Historically, different types of income found in a corporation tax computation were given different schedule references, as follows:

Schedule D Case I	-	adjusted trading profits
Schedule D Case III	-	interest income
Schedule A	-	rental income

The examiner will expect the schedule references to be used in the assessment. These will be used throughout the remainder of this study material.

4 Test your knowledge ▷ ▷ ▷

1   What is the definition of a chargeable accounting period?

2   When a company prepares accounts for a period that exceeds 12 months, what will be the company's chargeable accounting periods?

[Answer on p. 10]

5   Summary

Identifying the correct chargeable accounting period(s) is an essential first step in correctly calculating corporation tax.

Answers to 'test your knowledge' questions

Test your knowledge

1   A chargeable accounting period is the period for which the corporation tax computation is prepared.

2   The company's chargeable accounting periods will be:
· the first 12 months, and
· the balance of the accounting period.

KAPLAN PUBLISHING

ADJUSTED TRADING PROFITS

INTRODUCTION

There will be several parts to the corporation tax task in the assessment. One of those parts will require a calculation of adjusted trading profits as discussed in this chapter.

CONTENTS

PERFORMANCE CRITERIA

This chapter covers the following performance criteria:
· Adjust trading profits and losses for tax purposes (18.2 A)
· Enter adjusted trading profits and losses, capital allowances, investment income and capital gains in the corporation tax computation (18.4 A)

1 Introduction to adjusted trading profits

1.1 Schedule D Case I – adjusted trading profits

The first entry shown on the proforma corporation tax computation is the adjusted trading profits of the company taxed under Schedule D Case I.

The starting point in determining the amount of profit taxable under Schedule D Case I is the net profit as shown in the accounts. However, the accounts may, for example, contain expenditure items which are not allowable for tax.

The net profit shown in the accounts of the company must be adjusted for tax purposes to give Schedule D Case I profit.

2 Adjustment of profits calculation

2.1 Proforma adjustment of profits calculation

	£	Detail in:
Net profit as per accounts	X	
Add: (a) Disallowable expenditure	X	Section 3
	X	
Less: (b) Income included in the accounts but not taxable under Schedule D Case I	(X)	Section 4
Adjusted trading profit	X	
Less: (c) Plant and machinery capital allowances	(X)	Chapter 4
(d) Industrial building allowances	(X)	Chapter 5
Schedule D Case I profit	X	

The four categories of adjustment are considered in turn, in the following sections/chapters as indicated. In this chapter you will calculate the 'adjusted trading profit'.

An adjustment of profits will definitely be in the assessment. It is essential that you become familiar with this proforma and understand the entries made.

3 Disallowable expenditure

3.1 The principle of disallowable expenditure

Expenditure included in the accounts has the effect of reducing the profits of the company.

However, some items of expenditure are acceptable deductions for accounting purposes but are not acceptable for corporation tax purposes.

As a result, the reduction that was made in the accounts must be reversed for corporation tax purposes, i.e. the expenditure must be added back.

KAPLAN PUBLISHING

This is known as 'disallowable expenditure'.

The general principle to be applied in relation to any particular item of expenditure is that it will only be allowable in arriving at the taxable profits under Schedule D Case I if it has been incurred 'wholly and exclusively' for the purposes of the trade.

○ EXAMPLE ○○○○

Jack Limited has the following profit and loss account for its year ended 31 March 2007:

	£
Sales	100,000
Less: Cost of sales	(40,000)
Gross profit	60,000
Less: Expenditure (Note 1)	(35,000)
Net profit per accounts	25,000

Note 1: The expenditure can be analysed as follows:

	£
Wholly and exclusively for the purposes of the trade	33,000
Not wholly and exclusively for the purposes of the trade (i.e. disallowable expenditure)	2,000
	35,000

What are the adjusted trading profits of Jack Limited for the year ended 31 March 2007?

Solution

Jack Ltd – Adjusted trading profit - Year ended 31 March 2007

	£
Net profit per accounts	25,000
Add: Disallowable expenditure	2,000
Adjusted trading profits	27,000

3.2 Examples of disallowable expenditure

The general principle of expenditure being incurred 'wholly and exclusively' for the purposes of the trade can be used in the assessment if you are in doubt.

However, there are many common examples of disallowable expenditure that tend to appear regularly in assessments. The common examples are set out in the remainder of Section 3.

3.3 Fines

Fines on the business should be disallowed as the business is expected to operate within the law. Typical examples are penalties for late payment of VAT or for breaking health and safety regulations.

In practice, HM Revenue and Customs usually allow a deduction for parking fines incurred by employees while on company business. This does not, however, apply to directors' parking fines.

○ EXAMPLE   ○ ○ ○ ○

King plc is a chemical manufacturing company.

King plc – Profit and loss account - Year ended 31 March 2007

		£	£
Sales			700,000
Less: Cost of sales			(200,000)
Gross profit			500,000
Less: Expenditure			
Fine for polluting rivers		20,000	
Other allowable expenditure		200,000	
			(220,000)
Net profit per accounts			280,000

What are the adjusted trading profits for the year ended 31 March 2007?

Solution

King plc – Adjustment of profits - Year ended 31 March 2007

	£
Net profit per accounts	280,000
Add: Disallowable expenditure	
Fine for polluting rivers	20,000
Schedule D Case I – adjusted trading profit	300,000

3.4 Fraud

Fraud undertaken by directors is disallowed. This is because the loss does not relate to the company's trading activities. However, petty theft by non-senior employees which is not covered by insurance is generally allowable.

3.5 Donations

Donations to charity usually fail the *wholly and exclusively* test.

In practice, this means that there is no deduction for donations to national charities or political parties, unless there is some clear benefit to the trade. However, small donations to local charities are allowable as they can effectively be classed as advertising.

Donations under the Gift Aid scheme (including those made under deed of covenant) are classed as charges on income and are always disallowed (see Chapter 6).

3.6 Charges on income

Charges on income are payments such as donations under the Gift Aid scheme. Charges are not allowable under Schedule D Case I but are deducted in arriving at PCTCT. This is considered in detail at Chapter 6.

○ EXAMPLE ○○○○

Louise Ltd has net profit before tax of £123,000. In calculating this profit a deduction has been made for charitable donations as follows:

	£
To NSPCC – national charity	5,000
To local children's hospital	3,000
To charity under the Gift Aid scheme	2,000
	10,000

Calculate the adjusted trading profit assuming all other expenses are allowable.

Solution

Louise Ltd – Adjusted trading profit

	£
Net profit per accounts	123,000
Add: Donation to national charity	5,000
Donation under Gift Aid	2,000
Adjusted trading profit	130,000

Note: If the donation is under the Gift Aid scheme, it is automatically disallowable. It is irrelevant whether it is to a national or local charity.

3.7 Capital expenditure

As a rule, capital expenditure charged to the profit and loss account (e.g. depreciation) is not an allowable expense for tax purposes. For this reason, 'repairs' expenditure requires careful review, as it often contains items of a capital nature.

In general, repairs and redecoration are considered to be revenue expenditure and are therefore allowable. *Improvements*, however, are disallowable. In practice, the distinction between a repair and an improvement is not clear-cut. Repairs usually involve restoring an asset to its original condition or replacing part of an asset with a modern equivalent. Improvements usually involve enhancing the asset in some way.

For example, the replacement of a single glazed window with a double glazed window would be a repair, whilst installing a new window in a brick wall would be an improvement.

Secondhand assets

If an asset is purchased in a dilapidated state, and the purchase price reflects this, then initial 'repairs' expenditure to bring the asset to a fit state for use in the business will not be allowable. Two cases illustrate the difficulty of applying this rule in practice.

In *Law Shipping Co Ltd v CIR (1923)* the company purchased a ship which was not in a seaworthy condition. Expenditure on making the ship seaworthy was held to be capital and therefore disallowed.

In *Odeon Associated Theatres Ltd v Jones (1971)* the company purchased some cinemas which were in a run-down condition. Expenditure incurred in renovating the cinemas was held to be revenue and therefore allowable.

These two cases can be distinguished. In the *Law Shipping* case, the ship was not usable until the repairs were undertaken and the purchase price reflected the condition it was in. By contrast, in the Odeon case, the cinemas were capable of being used for the purpose of the trade prior to their renovation. In addition, the repairs were to remedy normal wear and tear.

You do not need to remember the names of the legal cases mentioned.

Legal expenses of a capital nature

The general rule to determine whether legal expenses are allowable is to look at what they relate to. If they relate to a capital item, such as the purchase of a building, then the expenses will be disallowed. If they relate to a revenue item, such as the collection of trade debts or employee issues such as drawing up contracts of employment, then they will be allowable.

There are some exceptions to the capital rule. The following expenses are allowable:

- the legal costs of *renewing* a short lease (50 years or less).
- the legal costs of defending title to a fixed asset (e.g. disputes over land boundaries).

KAPLAN PUBLISHING

Depreciation

Depreciation, together with any loss on the sale of fixed assets, is disallowed. Instead of depreciation, capital allowances may be given (see Chapters 4 & 5).

3.8 Dividends

Dividends are paid out of profits after they have been subjected to tax. They are not expenses incurred in earning those profits. They are therefore not allowable expenditure.

3.9 Bad debts

The write off of a trade debt is an allowable deduction against Schedule D Case I profits. Consequently the recovery of a trade debt previously written off is taxable.

The write off of a non-trade debt, e.g. a loan to a former employee, is not an allowable Schedule D Case I deduction.

A provision for bad debts, which is calculated in accordance with UK generally accepted accounting practice (UK GAAP), is allowable when computing Schedule D Case I profits. As a company's accounts are required to be drawn up using UK GAAP a bad debt provision in a company's accounts will be allowable for tax purposes.

This is also the case for other provisions in a company's accounts e.g. stock provisions. You will see in Chapter 14 that this is not the case for provisions in the accounts of unincorporated businesses.

An increase in a provision is an allowable deduction from profits and a decrease in a provision represents a taxable increase in profits.

Bad debts are also often referred to as irrecoverable or impaired debts.

○ **EXAMPLE**   ·   ○○○○

The bad debts account of Greenidge Ltd for the year ended 30 April 2007 appears as follows:

	£		£
Written off		Balance brought down	
Trade debts	274	Provision for	
Former employee	80	irrecoverable debts	445
Balance carried down		Recoveries – trade debts	23
Provision for		Profit and loss account	305
irrecoverable debts	419		
	773		773

Show the adjustment for Schedule D Case I purposes.

Solution

In this example, the information is presented in the form of a 'T' account. The first stage is to establish a breakdown of the profit and loss account charge of £305. Remember that this figure comprises amounts written off and recovered, and movements in provisions.

Profit and loss account charge	£	Allowable?
Decrease in provision for irrecoverable debts (£445 - £419)	(26)	✓
Amounts written off:		
Trade debt	274	✓
Former employee	80	✗
Recoveries – trade	(23)	✓
	305	

The write off of the debt owed by the former employee is disallowed. The recovery of the trade debts is not taxable. The *decrease* in the provision for irrecoverable debts is taxable Schedule D Case I income.

The adjustment for Schedule D Case I purposes is therefore as follows:

	£
Add: Former employee, debt written off	80

Write-offs of non-trading loans (such as here to the former employee) are not allowed for Schedule D Case I, however they are allowed as a Schedule D Case III expense – easy to overlook (see Chapter 6).

3.10 Interest payable

For the purpose of computing a company's Schedule D Case I profits you need to distinguish between trading and non-trading payments.

Interest payable on trading loans is an allowable expense for Schedule D Case I purposes. For example, interest payable on bank overdrafts or debentures used for trading purposes.

Interest payable on non-trading loans is not allowable for Schedule D Case I. For example, interest on a loan to buy an investment. However non-trading loan interest is allowable as a Schedule D Case III expense (see Chapter 6).

3.11 Other miscellaneous adjustments

Pre-trading expenditure

Expenditure incurred up to seven years before a trade commences is allowed as an expense of the first CAP of trading, provided it would have been allowable had the trade existed at the time the expenditure was incurred.

KAPLAN PUBLISHING

Entertaining

The cost of entertaining customers and suppliers is disallowed. However, the cost of entertaining staff is allowable.

Gifts

Gifts to employees are allowable.

Other gifts are only allowable if they fulfil the following three conditions:

·   They incorporate a conspicuous advertisement for the business.
·   The total cost per donee is not more than £50 per annum.
·   The gift is not food, drink (alcoholic or otherwise) or tobacco or a voucher for such items.

Note that if the cost exceeds the £50 limit, the whole amount is disallowed.

Therefore desk diaries or biros embossed with the company name usually qualify but a bottle of whisky carrying an advert for the company would not!

Trade samples

Trade samples which are not for resale are allowable.

Hire or lease charges (expensive cars)

If a car costing more than £12,000 is leased or hired, part of the rental cost is disallowed.

The disallowable amount is calculated using the following formula.

$$\text{Disallowed amount} = \frac{{}^1\!/_2(\text{Retail price when new} - \text{£12,000})}{\text{Retail price when new}} \times \text{Hire charge}$$

○ **EXAMPLE**   ○○○○

HNN Ltd incurs annual rental expenditure of £1,960 on leasing a car with a retail price of £14,200. The car was first leased on 1 January 2006. HNN Ltd prepares accounts to 31 December.

Show the amount disallowed for Schedule D Case I purposes in the year ended 31 December 2006.

Solution

The following amount is disallowed:

$$\frac{{}^1\!/_2(\text{£14,200} - \text{£12,000})}{\text{£14,200}} \times \text{£1,960} = \text{£152}$$

4 Income included in the accounts but not taxable under Schedule D Case I

4.1 Types of income

The following are examples of income which may be included in the profit and loss account, but which are not taxable as trading profits under Schedule D Case I.

· Income taxed in another way, for example rental income (Schedule A), interest receivable (Schedule D Case III).
· Dividends received.
· Profits on sales of fixed assets.

4.2 Effect

As these types of income are not taxable under Schedule D Case I, they must be deducted to arrive at the correct adjusted trading profits.

5 Detailed proforma adjustment of profits

5.1 Proforma for a company

	+ £	- £
Net profit per accounts	X	
Add: Disallowable expenditure:		
Depreciation	X	
Loss on sale of fixed assets	X	
Capital expenditure	X	
Legal expenses of capital nature	X	
Fines and penalties	X	
Donations	X	
Entertaining (other than staff)	X	
Gifts to customers	X	
Proportion of expensive car leasing costs	X	
Less: Income included in accounts but not taxable under Schedule D Case I:		
Rental income		X
Profit on sale of fixed assets		X
Interest receivable		X
Dividend income		X
	X	X
	(X)	
Adjusted trading profit before capital allowances	X	

○ EXAMPLE ○○○○

The profit and loss account of STD Ltd for the year ended 31 March 2007 showed a profit of £42,000 after accounting for the following items:

Note	Expenditure	£	Income	£
	Depreciation	9,500	Insurance recovery re	
	Debenture interest	8,000	flood damage to	
	Loss on sale of lorry	6,000	trading stock	6,500
	Bad debts:		Rents received	8,400
	Trade debts written off	4,000	Profit on sale of plant	7,400
	Increase in provision	1,000		
(1)	Entertainment expenses	2,600		
	Legal fees:			
	Re new lease	3,200		
	Re recovery of employee loan	1,200		
	Re employees' service contracts	600		
(2)	General expenses	4,000		
(3)	Repairs and renewals	6,400		

Notes:

(1) Entertainment consists of expenditure on:

	£
Entertaining customers	1,200
Staff dance (30 people)	900
Gifts to customers of food hampers	600

(2) General expenses comprises:

	£
Penalty for late VAT return	2,200
Parking fines on company cars (whilst on company business)	300
Fees for employees attending courses	1,500

(3) Included in the figure for repairs is an amount of £5,000 incurred in installing new windows in a recently-acquired secondhand warehouse. This building had suffered fire damage resulting in all of its windows being blown out shortly before being acquired by STD Ltd. Other repairs were of a routine nature.

Compute the adjusted trading figure for the above period.

Your answer should show clearly your reasons for your treatment of each of the above items including those items not adjusted for in your computation.

Solution

Step 1: Start your solution with the company's net profit:

	+ £	- £
Net profit	42,000	

Step 2: Add back any disallowable items of expenditure.

Go through each expense in turn and decide whether or not it needs to be added back. If it does require adding back, add the figure to the + column of your proforma. If you do not know how to treat a particular item, guess. You have a good chance of getting the right answer. You might find it helpful to tick off each item as you deal with it. This ensures you do not miss any items.

You also need to explain the reason for your chosen treatment. This is probably best done on a separate page.

Step 3: Deduct income in accounts which is not taxable under Schedule D Case I

Deal with any income in the order in which it appears in the accounts. For each item, ask yourself whether it relates to the company's trade. If it does, no action is required. If it does not, include the figure in the – column.

Step 4: Finish by totalling the proforma

Note that it is not essential for you to put headings such as 'disallowable expenditure' on your proforma. You could simply state 'add' and 'less'. You do, however, need to list each adjusted item in words as well as figures.

STD Ltd – Adjustment of profit for the year ended 31 March 2007

	+ £	- £
Net profit	42,000	
Depreciation	9,500	
Loss on sale of lorry	6,000	
Entertainment expenses	1,800	
Legal fees	4,400	
General expenses	2,200	
Repairs and renewals	5,000	
Rents received		(8,400)
Profit on sale of plant		(7,400)
	70,900	(15,800)
	(15,800)	
Adjusted trading profit	55,100	

Explanation

1   Depreciation (capital expenditure) is not an allowable deduction.

2   Debenture interest is allowable (assuming the debenture proceeds were used for trading purposes).

3   Losses on the sale of fixed assets are treated in the same way as depreciation – they are added back. Conversely, profits on the sale of fixed assets are deducted.

4   Write-offs of trade debts and provisions in a company's accounts are allowable.

5   Expenditure on entertaining customers is not allowable. Expenditure on entertaining staff is. The cost of the hampers is not allowable as they contain food.

6   The legal fees in respect of the new lease are a capital item, and are therefore not allowable.   Employee loans are not for trading purposes, therefore the legal costs are also not allowable. Legal fees in connection with the service contracts are wholly and exclusively for the trade, therefore are an allowable expense.

7   VAT penalties are not allowable.   Parking fines incurred by employees will generally be allowed. Course fees are also allowable, assuming the course relates to the company's trade.

8   The cost of new windows is not allowable. It is capital expenditure required to put a new asset into a usable stage (Law Shipping case).

9   The insurance recovery is in respect of trading stock. It is therefore taxable under Schedule D Case I, and no adjustment needs to be made.

10   Rents received are taxable under Schedule A, not Schedule D Case I, therefore deduct.

In an exam you should try to work methodically through the profit and loss account, making sure that if you break off to deal with a note you come back to the same point on the profit and loss account. Ticking off items as you use them should help.

▷ ACTIVITY 1 ▷ ▷ ▷ ▷

Brazil Ltd

The following is the profit and loss account of Brazil Ltd, an established company, for the year ended 30 April 2006:

	£	£
Sales		240,458
Less: Cost of sales		(183,942)
Gross profit		56,516
Other income		5,000
Salaries and wages	24,184	
Rent and rates	8,560	
Repairs to premises	3,263	
Travelling and entertaining expenses	1,964	
Motor expenses	2,345	
Legal and professional charges	3,436	
Bad debts	(630)	
General expenses	1,021	
Depreciation	3,047	
Net profit	14,326	
	61,516	61,516

The following further information is given:

(1) **Other income**

This comprises bank deposit interest for the year received on 30 April 2006.

(2) **Repairs to premises**

Included in this item is £1,450 incurred in fitting a new shop-front to a former office and £250 for the initial repainting of a new shop.

(3) **Travelling and entertaining expenses**

These include expenses of entertaining UK customers of £326 and gifts to customers of Christmas hampers costing £528 (cost £48 each).

(4) **Legal and professional charges**

This items includes the following:

	£
Legal fees in connection with new lease	325
Legal fees in connection with action by employee for unfair dismissal	830
Payment to employee for unfair dismissal	1,200
Accountancy charges	1,081

(5) **Bad debts**

The figure in the accounts is made up as follows:

	£
Trade bad debt recoveries	(232)
Decrease in bad debt provision	(398)
	(630)

(6) **General expenses**

These include a Gift Aid payment of £200 to the Friends of the Local Hospital, and a donation of £25 to Save the Children.

Required:

You are required to calculate the adjusted trading profit of the year for tax purposes.

[Answer on p.27]

6 Test your knowledge

What adjustment, if any, should you make for the following items included in a company's profit and loss account?

1   Dividends paid,

2   Managing director's salary (he owns 99% of the shares),

3   Overdraft interest,

4   Interest on a loan to purchase an investment property,

5   Gifts of diaries to customers, costing £5 each and embossed with the company's name,

6   Gifts of bottles of wine to customers, costing £5 each and embossed with the company's name.

[Answer on p. 27]

7   Summary

You should now be able to successfully attempt questions requiring you to calculate the adjusted trading profit for corporation tax purposes.

The starting point for computing adjusted trading profits is the net profit shown in the company's accounts. This must be adjusted in respect of the following items:

· Disallowable expenditure.

The main types of disallowable expenditure are:

- expenditure not wholly and exclusively for the purpose of the trade.
- capital expenditure.

· Income included in the accounts but not taxable under Schedule D Case I.

For example:

- rents and interest.
- profits on the sale of fixed assets.

It is advisable to use a '+' and '-' column and deal with each adjustment as you work methodically through the question. There is no need to arrange your answer into the two types of adjustment shown above.

KAPLAN PUBLISHING

Answers to chapter activities & 'test your knowledge' questions

△ ACTIVITY 1   △ △ △ △

Brazil Ltd

Adjusted trading profit for tax purposes for year ended 30 April 2006.

	£	£
Net profits as per accounts	14,326	
New shop–front	1,450	
Entertaining customers	326	
Gifts	528	
Legal fees re new lease	325	
Gift Aid payment	200	
National charity donation	25	
Depreciation	3,047	
Less: Bank deposit interest		(5,000)
	20,227	(5,000)
	(5,000)	
Adjusted trading profit	15,227	

Notes:

·   The £250 initial repainting costs in respect of the new shop are considered to be allowable, following the decision in *Odeon Associated Theatres Limited v Jones (1973)*.

·   Although the hampers cost less than £50 each, the cost is disallowed as the gift is of food.

·   Legal fees and payment in connection with unfair dismissal are allowable.

·   The donation of £200 to the local charity might have been allowable as a business expense (small and local) had it not been declared as a Gift Aid payment.

Test your knowledge △ △ △

1   Add back – not a trading expense.

2   No adjustment required – allowable expense.

3   No adjustment required – allowable expense.

4   Add back – not allowable for Schedule D Case I but is deductible under Schedule D Case III.

5   No adjustment required – allowable expense.

6   Add back – gift of alcohol.

CAPITAL ALLOWANCES
– PLANT AND MACHINERY

INTRODUCTION

In the assessment there will be a calculation of Schedule D Case I profits. It will involve a task to adjust profits (as per Chapter 3) and a task to calculate the plant and machinery capital allowances. This chapter considers plant and machinery capital allowances.

CONTENTS

1 Introduction to capital allowances
2 Qualifying expenditure
3 Calculating the allowances
4 Capital allowances treatment of cars
5 Classifying plant and machinery
6 Impact of the length of the accounting period
7 Business cessation

PERFORMANCE CRITERIA

This chapter covers the following performance criteria:

· Classify expenditure on capital assets in accordance with the statutory distinction between capital and revenue expenditure (18.1 A)
· Ensure that entries and calculations relating to the computation of capital allowances for a company are correct (18.1 B)
· Ensure that computations and submissions are made in accordance with current tax law and take account of current HM Revenue & Customs practice (18.1 D)
· Enter adjusted trading profits and losses, capital allowances, investment income and capital gains in the corporation tax computation (18.4 A)
· Complete corporation tax returns correctly and submit them, together with relevant claims and elections, within statutory time limits (18.4 G)

1 Introduction to capital allowances

1.1 Capital allowances

Capital allowances are a form of depreciation but for tax purposes. The allowances are only given on certain items of capital expenditure.

Capital allowances in this syllabus are:

- Plant and machinery capital allowances (this chapter).
- Industrial buildings allowances (Chapter 5).

1.2 Capital allowances v depreciation

Each business can decide its own rate of depreciation for accounting purposes. In theory, identical businesses with the same assets could have different amounts of depreciation. HM Revenue & Customs are unhappy with this and instead use a standard calculation of capital allowances. The capital allowances are deducted instead of depreciation, to arrive at the adjusted trading profit.

○ EXAMPLE ○○○○

Marcus Ltd and Nigel Ltd are two companies making the same products.

In the year ended 31 December 2006, both companies made profits before depreciation/capital allowances of £200,000. Both have only one piece of machinery that they bought in the year for £50,000.

The companies have different methods of calculating depreciation, giving the following amounts:

Marcus Ltd	£15,000
Nigel Ltd	£25,000

For tax purposes, both companies would have capital allowances of £20,000.

Compare the accounting profits and adjusted trading profits of both companies.

Solution

	Marcus Ltd £	Nigel Ltd £
Profit before depreciation	200,000	200,000
Depreciation	(15,000)	(25,000)
Accounting profits	185,000	175,000
Adjusted profit before capital allowances	200,000	200,000
Capital allowances	(20,000)	(20,000)
Adjusted trading profit	180,000	180,000

In reality there are likely to be many more adjustments that could give rise to different adjusted trading profits for tax purposes (as per Chapter 3).

However, this example illustrates that identical businesses could have different accounting profits, but have the same adjusted trading profits on which their tax is calculated.

2 Qualifying expenditure

2.1 What qualifies as plant and machinery

There is no automatic right to tax relief for capital expenditure. In order to qualify for capital allowances, expenditure must usually be in respect of plant or machinery.

There is no definition of the words *machinery* and *plant*. The identification of *machinery* causes few problems. However in deciding whether an item can be considered to be *plant*, case law has dictated that the following factors should be considered:

· The degree of *permanence* – there should be some degree of durability of the item.

· The *function* of the item – plant is an item *with which* the trade is carried on, as opposed to being part of the setting *in which* the taxpayer carries on his trade.

2.2 Case law

The Courts' interpretation of these factors has led to the following items being classed as **plant**.

· Movable partitions (but not fixed partitions).
· Items that create atmosphere (e.g. atmospheric lighting used in pubs and restaurants).
· Dry dock for repairing ships.
· Swimming and paddling pool at a caravan park.
· Specialist lighting for window displays (e.g. moveable spotlights).
· Moveable decorative screens (e.g. in window displays).
· Dockside concrete silos.

The following items have been held **not to be plant**.

· General lighting.
· False ceilings (part of the building instead).
· Canopy over a petrol station.
· Football stand.

2.3 Statutory regulations

Certain items have been deemed to be plant by *statute*.

· Thermal insulation in industrial buildings.
· Expenditure on compliance with fire safety requirements of the business premises.
· Expenditure necessary to obtain sports stadium safety certificates.
· Computer software even where acquired electronically or where the company merely acquires a licence to use software.

The majority of the above examples will not appear regularly in a computational task on an assessment.

2.4 Common types of capital expenditure

The most common types of capital expenditure found in a set of accounts that are treated as 'plant and machinery' for tax purposes are:

· Plant and machinery
· Fixtures and fittings
· Motor vehicles
· Computer equipment

3 Calculating the allowances

3.1 Main types of capital allowances

The following are the main types of capital allowances that may be available to a company on plant and machinery.

(a) Writing-down allowance (WDA)

-   given at 25% on a reducing balance basis.

(b) First year allowance (FYA) 40%/50%

-   a 40% FYA is available on most plant and machinery in the accounting period it is purchased. This is only available to businesses which are classed as small or medium sized.

-   For small businesses only, a 50% FYA is available for the periods:

    -   1 April 2004 to 31 March 2005
    -   1 April 2006 to 31 March 2007

O EXAMPLE   O O O O

Olivia Ltd purchased a machine costing £40,000 on 1 February 2005 in its year ended 31 October 2005. This is its only capital item.

Assuming Olivia Ltd is a small company, what are the capital allowances for the first three years of ownership?

Solution

Olivia Ltd - Capital allowances

	£	Allowances £
Year ended 31 October 2005		
Cost	40,000	
FYA @ 50%	(20,000)	20,000
	20,000	
Year ended 31 October 2006		
WDA (25% x 20,000)	(5,000)	5,000
	15,000	
Year ended 31 October 2007		
WDA (25% x 15,000)	(3,750)	3,750
	11,250	

If instead of purchasing the machine on 1 February 2005, it had been purchased on 1 June 2005, the FYA would have been 40%.

3.2 Other types of capital allowances on plant and machinery

Additionally, there are other FYAs available at 100% to encourage businesses to invest in certain types of assets.

(a) For expenditure on computers (including software) by a 'small' business between 1 April 2000 and 31 March 2004. This also applies to internet enabled mobile phones.

(b) For any business for expenditure on 'low emission cars', i.e. either electronically propelled or emitting not more than 120g of carbon dioxide per kilometre travelled.

Very few cars are low emission, therefore never assume in an assessment that a car is eligible for a 100% FYA.

Beware of the purchase date of computer equipment for small businesses. If purchased:

- on or before 31 March 2004, it gets a 100% FYA.
- between 1 April 2004 and 31 March 2005, it gets a 50% FYA.

· between 1 April 2005 and 31 March 2006, it gets a 40% FYA.
· between 1 April 2006 and 31 March 2007, it gets a 50% FYA.
· on or after 1 April 2007, it gets a 40% FYA.

3.3 Layout of general pool for capital allowances on plant and machinery

Instead of calculating capital allowances for each individual asset, most types of expenditure are pooled (in the 'general pool').

The proforma below shows the layout which you should ideally use to present your answer. The examiner will certainly expect to see the use of an orderly layout.

	General pool		Total allowances
	£	£	£
WDV brought forward		X	
Additions not qualifying for FYAs*		X	
Disposals – lower of			
cost/sale proceeds		(X)	
		X	
WDA at 25%		(X)	X
		X	
Additions qualifying for FYA	X		
FYA at 40%/50%/100%	(X)		X
		X	
WDV carried forward		X	X

*To be explained in the next section.

Note the following abbreviation:

WDV = tax written down value (the amount of expenditure not yet written off by means of capital allowances).

In the solution to the example in Olivia Ltd above, for the year ended 31 October 2006 there is a WDV brought forward of £20,000 and a WDV carried forward of £15,000.

Disposals will be considered later in the chapter.

Be sure not to confuse the order of the steps. For example, additions qualifying for FYA do not attract WDA in the same year so they are dealt with after calculating WDA.

4   Capital allowances treatment of cars

4.1 Motor vehicles v motor cars

In accounts we tend to group all motor vehicles together. For example, we include cars, vans, lorries, motor bikes, etc. together as motor vehicles.

For tax purposes, vans, lorries and motorbikes are treated like any other plant and machinery, i.e. they are put in the general pool and get:

· FYAs in the accounting period of purchase (depending on the size of the business); and
· WDAs for the remainder of the time.

Motor cars have a different treatment.

4.2 Capital allowances treatment of motor cars

Motor cars never get the 40%/50% FYA. Only low emission motor cars are eligible for a FYA. The rate of the FYA is 100% and it is only for cars registered after 16 April 2002.

Generally, when a motor car is purchased, it goes as an addition in the general pool directly after the WDV brought forward (see 3.3 above).

○ EXAMPLE ○○○○

Patrick Ltd, a small company, has a year ended 30 June 2006. Its general pool had a WDV brought forward of £30,000 at 1 July 2005.

In the year ended 30 June 2006, it has purchased two assets:

(a) a car costing £10,000; and
(b) a van costing £5,000 (on 1 February 2006).

There were no disposals in the year.

Calculate the capital allowances for the year, assuming the car is not a low emission car.

Solution

Patrick Ltd - Capital allowances - year ended 30 June 2006

		General pool £	Capital allowances £
WDV brought forward		30,000	
Additions not qualifying for FYAs		10,000	
Disposals		-	
		40,000	
WDA (40,000 x 25%)		(10,000)	10,000
		30,000	
Additions qualifying for FYA			
Van	5,000		
FYA @ 40%	(2,000)		2,000
		3,000	
WDV carried forward		33,000	
Total capital allowances			12,000

4.3 Expensive cars

An expensive car is one costing more than £12,000. It is not put in the general pool. Each expensive car is considered separately and has a special treatment. This is considered further in Section 5 below.

5   Classifying plant and machinery

5.1 Expenditure not pooled

As companies may have many assets, it would be extremely time-consuming to calculate allowances separately for each asset. Therefore, all qualifying expenditure is pooled, apart from:

· expensive cars (costing more than £12,000); and
· assets for which a short life asset election has been made.

Each of the above categories will now be considered in detail below.

5.2 General pool

Most items of plant and machinery go into the general pool. Once an asset enters the pool, it loses its identity. This means that the writing down allowance (WDA) is calculated on the balance of the pool, rather than on the individual assets.

Allowances are given for accounting periods. Allowances commence in the year in which the expenditure is incurred. A full WDA is given in the year of purchase (unless FYA is claimed) irrespective of the date of purchase.

5.2.1   First year allowances

Plant and machinery (excluding cars) bought by *small and medium sized* businesses qualify for a first year allowance (FYA) of 40% (or 50% for small businesses for certain specified periods, see 3.1).

For a business to qualify for first year allowances as a small or medium sized business, it must meet at least two of the following three conditions:

· Turnover not exceeding £22.8 million.
· Assets not exceeding £11.4 million in value.
· No more than 250 employees.

Small businesses that invest in information and communication technology equipment between 1 April 2000 and 31 March 2004 can claim a 100% FYA.

This FYA covers expenditure on:

· computers, including peripherals and cabling.
· software.

· WAP and third generation mobile phones.

A business is classed as small for the purpose of claiming the 100% FYA if it satisfies at least two out of the following conditions:

· Turnover not exceeding £5.6 million.
· Assets not exceeding £2.8 million in value.
· No more than 50 employees.

When reading a task on capital allowances, look for any indication of business size, i.e. 'small' or 'medium'. The examiner should tell you or it should be obvious from other details such as turnover.

Businesses of *any* size qualify for 100% first year allowance on cars registered on or after 17 April 2002 provided that either the carbon dioxide emissions are not more than 120 grams per kilometre travelled or the car is electrically propelled.

5.2.2   Disposal in the general pool

When a pool item is sold, the *sale proceeds* are deducted from the pool. This deduction cannot exceed the asset's original cost.

The following example illustrates the working of the general pool, including disposals.

○ EXAMPLE   ○○○○

Apple Ltd prepares accounts to 30 April each year.

On 1 May 2005 Apple Ltd incurred expenditure of £7,200 on the purchase of shop fittings and machinery. On 1 June 2005 the company sold some machinery for £600 (cost £400) and on 1 June 2006 purchased more plant for £1,000.

On 5 May 2006 the company sold equipment for £9,395 which had cost £11,200 in May 2002. The tax written down value of the pool at 1 May 2005 was £8,260.

Compute the capital allowances for the years ended 30 April 2006 and 30 April 2007, assuming that Apple Ltd is a small company.

Solution

Step 1:   Identify the balance brought forward at the beginning of the accounting period.

This is called the *tax written down value* (tax WDV or TWDV).

	Pool £
Year ended 30 April 2006	
Tax WDV brought forward	8,260

Step 2: **Identify the accounting periods in which the additions and disposals occur.**

In the year ended 30 April 2006, Apple Ltd acquired plant costing £7,200 and sold plant for £600. All other additions and disposals occur in the second accounting period.

Step 3: Identify any additions for which a FYA can be claimed.

For example, the plant acquired on 1 May 2005 qualifies for a 40% FYA. Deal with this addition *after* calculating the WDA for that year on the other items in the general pool.

Step 4: Prepare the capital allowances computation

Deal with one accounting period at a time.

	£	Pool £	Allowances £
Year ended 30 April 2006			
Tax WDV b/f		8,260	
Additions without FYA		-	
Disposals			
1 June 2005 (proceeds			
restricted to cost)		(400)	
		7,860	
WDA at 25%		(1,965)	1,965
Additions (FYA)			
1 May 2005	7,200		
FYA at 40%	(2,880)		2,880
Balance added to pool		4,320	
Tax WDV c/f		10,215	
Total allowances			4,845
Year ended 30 April 2007			
Additions (no FYA)		-	
Disposals			
5 May 2006		(9,395)	
		820	
WDA at 25%		(205)	205
Additions (FYA)			
1 June 2006	1,000		
FYA at 50%	(500)		500
Balance added to pool		500	
Tax WDV c/f		1,115	
Total allowances			705

5.3 Expensive cars

Each car costing more than £12,000 is given a separate column in the capital allowances working. A 25% WDA is calculated for each individual car, but the maximum allowance that can be claimed is £3,000 per annum per car.

The expensive car rules do not apply to low emission cars (i.e. under 120 gms of carbon dioxide per kilometre) or electric cars registered since 16 April 2002.

The examples below illustrate the working of capital allowances for both inexpensive and expensive cars.

○ EXAMPLE   ○○○○

Grin Ltd prepares accounts to 31 December each year. No capital expenditure had been incurred prior to January 2005. In the year to 31 December 2005 the following expenditure is incurred.

		Cost
		£
31 January 2005	Motor car	7,000
12 February 2005	Motor car	14,000
17 June 2005	Motor car	10,000

Calculate Grin Ltd's capital allowances for the years ended 31 December 2005 and 31 December 2006.

Solution

In this example, there is no tax WDV brought forward, so the first task is to decide which cars will be brought into the general pool, and which need their own separate columns.

A proforma can then be set up as below:

	General pool	Expensive car	Allowances
	£	£	£
Year ended 31 December 2005			

Now the additions can be put into the appropriate columns and the allowances calculated, remembering that the allowance for the expensive car must be restricted to £3,000 per annum.

Grin Ltd - Capital allowances

	General pool £	Expensive car £	Allowances £
Year ended 31 December 2005			
Additions			
31 January 2005	7,000		
12 February 2005		14,000	
17 June 2005	10,000		
	17,000		
WDA at 25% (restricted)	(4,250)	(3,000)	7,250
Tax WDV c/f	12,750	11,000	
Total allowances			7,250
Year ended 31 December 2006			
WDA at 25%	(3,188)	(2,750)	5,938
Tax WDV c/f	9,562	8,250	
Total allowances			5,938

Note that the 25% WDA allowance for the expensive car is not restricted for the year ended 31 December 2006, as it is less than £3,000. The separate column is, however, retained.

5.4 Disposals of expensive cars

As each expensive car has its own column, there will be a balancing adjustment on the disposal of the car. The balancing adjustment is not restricted to £3,000, but is the figure needed to take the column to a nil balance.

If, after deducting the sale proceeds:

· a positive balance is left then a   BALANCING ALLOWANCE is given to reduce the column to nil.

· a negative balance is left then a   BALANCING CHARGE is given to take the column to nil.

A balancing allowance is treated as an additional capital allowance.

A balancing charge is treated as a negative capital allowance.

○ **EXAMPLE** ○○○○

If in the previous example, Grin Ltd sells the car, bought in February 2005, in August 2007.

Calculate the balancing adjustment on the car on the alternative assumptions:

(a) that the car is sold for £7,000.
(b) that the car is sold for £9,200.

Solution

In this example, the expensive car is sold, so there will be a balancing adjustment.

First, the proceeds (restricted to original cost if necessary) are deducted from the written down value.

Then, if the remaining balance is positive, a balancing allowance will be given, but if the balance is negative a balancing charge will arise. This is like a negative allowance. Instead of being deducted from Schedule D Case I profits, it will be added back. In both cases, the tax WDV carried forward will be nil.

The solutions to the two different scenarios are as follows:

(a) **Proceeds £7,000**

	General pool £	Expensive car £	Allowances £
Year ended 31 December 2007			
Tax WDV b/f	9,562	8,250	
Disposal proceeds	⎯⎯⎯	(7,000)	
	9,562	1,250	
Balancing allowance		(1,250)	1,250
WDA at 25%	(2,391)	-	2,391
Tax WDV c/f	7,171	-	
Total allowances			3,641

(b) Proceeds £9,200

	General pool £	Expensive car £	Allowances £
Year ended 31 December 2007			
Tax WDV b/f	9,562	8,250	
Disposal proceeds		(9,200)	
	9,562	(950)	
Balancing charge		950	(950)
WDA at 25%	(2,391)	-	2,391
Tax WDV carried forward	7,171	-	
Total allowances			1,441

Note that a balancing allowance is usually pooled with WDA/FYA and a balancing charge is usually offset against WDA/FYA. It there is a net allowance it is deducted in calculating the Schedule D Case I profits but if there is a net charge it is added in the calculation.

The example below demonstrates the full capital allowances working.

○ EXAMPLE ○○○○

JNN Ltd, a small company, has been trading since 1 June 2004, preparing accounts to 31 May each year.

The following assets have recently been purchased.

Date of purchase	Asset	Cost £
1 May 2004	Plant and machinery	13,940
9 November 2004	Used car	1,472
10 February 2005	Used car	928
8 June 2005	New car	19,500
2 July 2005	Equipment	1,433
2 May 2006	Computer equipment	1,178
10 July 2006	Office drinks machine	700
20 October 2006	New car	18,071

The new car acquired on 20 October 2006 was electric powered.

Calculate the capital allowances due for the three years ending 31 May 2007.

Solution

The approach is as follows:

· Allocate additions and disposals to the relevant accounting periods. Any acquisitions made prior to the commencement of trading are treated as if made on the first day of trading.

· Identify which additions qualify for FYA and which rate of FYA applies.

JNN Ltd - Capital allowances computation

		Pool	Expensive car	Allowances
Year ending 31 May 2005	£	£	£	£
Additions (no FYA)				
9 November 2004		1,472		
10 February 2005		928		
		2,400		
WDA at 25%		(600)		600
Addition (with FYA)				
1 June 2004	13,940			
FYA (50%)	(6,970)	6,970		6,970
WDV c/fwd		8,770		
Total allowances				7,570
Year ending 31 May 2006				
Additions (no FYA)				
8 June 2005			19,500	
WDA 25%/restricted		(2,192)	(3,000)	5,192
Addition (with FYA)				
2 July 2005	1,433			
FYA (40%)	(573)			573
		860		
2 May 2006	1,178			
FYA (50%)	(589)			589
		589		
WDV c/fwd		8,027	16,500	
Total allowances				6,354
Year ending 31 May 2007				
WDA 25%/restricted		(2,007)	(3,000)	5,007
Additions (with FYA)				
20 October 2006	18,071			
FYA (100%)	(18,071)			18,071
10 July 2006	700			
FYA (50%)	(350)			350
		350		
WDV c/fwd		6,370	13,500	
Total allowances				23,428

> **ACTIVITY 1**   ▷ ▷ ▷ ▷

ENT Ltd

ENT Ltd prepares accounts to 31 December annually. On 1 January 2005 the tax written down value of plant and machinery brought forward was £24,000. The following transactions took place in the year to 31 December 2005.

15 April 2005	Purchased car for £12,600
30 April 2005	Sold plant for £3,200 (original cost £4,800)
16 July 2005	Purchased car for £9,200
17 August 2005	Purchased car for £9,400

In the following year to 31 December 2006, ENT Ltd sold for £7,900 the car originally purchased on 17 August 2005. The car originally purchased on 15 April 2005 was sold for £9,400 on 9 March 2006. There were no other transactions.

Required

Compute the capital allowances and balancing adjustments for the years ended 31 December 2005 and 31 December 2006.

[Answer on p. 51]

5.5 Short life assets (SLA)

Where an asset is expected to have a short life of approximately four years or less, and is expected to decrease in value substantially, it may be beneficial to remove it from the general pool and treat it as a *short life asset*.

In doing this, a balancing allowance can be claimed when the asset is disposed of. Disposals of short life assets have the same treatment as those of expensive cars (Section 5.4).

Each asset treated as a short life asset should have a separate column in the capital allowances computation.

The following conditions apply:

·   Short life asset treatment is not available for cars.

·   If a short life asset is not sold within four years of the end of the accounting period in which it was purchased, its tax WDV will be transferred back into the general pool.

·   A short life asset election must be made within two years of the end of the accounting period in which the expenditure was incurred.

The following illustration demonstrates how short life asset treatment accelerates the allowances claimed.

○ EXAMPLE ○○○○

Purchase (for £10,000) and sale (for £1,000) of a short life asset.

Without election	General pool £	*With election*	General pool £	SLA £
Year 1		*Year 1*		
WDV b/f, say	50,000	WDV b/f, say	50,000	
WDA	(12,500)	Purchase		10,000
Purchase	10,000		50,000	10,000
FYA (40%)	(4,000)	WDA/FYA	(12,500)	(4,000)
Year 2		*Year 2*		
WDV b/f	43,500	WDV b/f	37,500	6,000
Disposal	(1,000)	Disposal	-	(1,000)
	42,500		37,500	5,000
BA	-	BA		(5,000)
WDA	(10,625)	WDA	(9,375)	
WDV c/f	31,875	WDV c/f	28,125	-
Total allowances given (£12,500 + £4,000		Total allowances given (£12,500 + £4,000		
+ £10,625)	27,125	+ £9,375 + £5,000)		30,875
WDV c/f	31,875	WDV c/f		28,125

It is important to note that a short life asset election is not beneficial if the asset is to be sold for more than its tax written down value. This is because the disposal would result in a balancing charge.

The total allowances eventually claimed on the asset will be the same with or without the election. However, as seen above, the claim for allowances is accelerated if the short life asset treatment is adopted.

○ ILLUSTRATION ○○○○

Continuing with the above example, assume instead that the asset was sold for £8,000.

Without election	General pool £	*With election*	General pool £	SLA £
Year 2		*Year 2*		
WDV b/f	43,500	WDV b/f	37,500	6,000
Disposal	(8,000)	Disposal	-	(8,000)
	35,500		37,500	(2,000)
BC	-	BC		2,000
WDA	(8,875)	WDA	(9,375)	
WDV c/f	26,625	WDV c/f	28,125	-

> In this instance, by leaving the asset in the general pool and not adopting the short life asset treatment the balancing charge is avoided.
>
> Where the asset qualifies for 100% FYA (e.g. computer bought by a small business before 31 March 2004) an short life asset election should not be made as a balancing charge would arise on any eventual proceeds.

5.6 Proforma computation for capital allowances on plant and machinery

	£	General pool £	Expensive car 1 £	Expensive car 2 £	SLA £	Total allowances £
WDV b/f		X	X		X	
Additions not eligible for FYA		X		X		
Disposals (lower of cost and sale proceeds)		(X)	(X)			
		X	(X)/X	X	X	
Balancing charge/allowance			X/(X)			(X)/X
			Nil			
WDA @ 25% pa		(X)			(X)	X
WDA restricted				(X)*		X
		X				
Additions eligible for FYA	X					
FYA @ 40% or 50% or 100%	(X)					X
		X				
WDV c/f		X		X	X	

Total capital allowances for accounting period   X

*Restricted to maximum of £3,000 pa.

6 Impact of the length of the accounting period

6.1 Short chargeable accounting periods

Capital allowances are computed for accounting periods and deducted in calculating Schedule D Case I profits.

The writing down allowances calculated so far were all for 12 month accounting periods.

Where the accounting period is less than 12 months long, the WDA must be scaled down accordingly. You must perform this calculation to the nearest month.

If the period for which accounts are drawn up exceeds 12 months, the capital allowances are computed in two stages – the first 12 months, then the balance (see Chapter 2, Section 2.3).

Note that first year allowances are always given in full even if the length of the accounting period is less than 12 months. It is only the WDA which is scaled down.

○ EXAMPLE   ○○○○

KNN Ltd started to trade on 1 June 2005 and, on that day, purchased an asset costing £21,900. KNN Ltd does not qualify for FYAs. Calculate the writing down allowances due for the first period of account on the assumption that accounts are prepared to

(i)   31 May 2006
(ii)   31 March 2006
(iii) 31 December 2006

Solution

First period of account		(i) 31 May 2006 (12 months) £	(ii) 31 March 2006 (10 months) £	(iii) 31 December 2006 (17 months) £
Cost		21,900	21,900	21,900
WDA	25%	(5,475)		
	25% x $^{10}/_{12}$		(4,563)	
(First 12 m)	25%			(5,475)
				16,425
(Balance)	25% x $^{7}/_{12}$			(2,395)
WDV c/f		16,425	17,337	14,030

Note that, as already explained in Chapter 2, in example (iii) corporation tax is charged separately on an accounting period of 12 months ending on 31 May 2006 and on an accounting period of 7 months ending on 31 December 2006.

7   Business cessation

7.1 Final accounting period

In the accounting period of cessation no WDAs or FYAs will be given.

Any additions and disposals in the final period are allocated to the appropriate columns in the capital allowance working.

At the end of the period there will be no tax WDV carried forward, so there must be a balancing adjustment on *all* categories in the capital allowances working.

- If there is a positive balance remaining, a balancing allowance is given.

- If there is a negative balance remaining, a balancing charge arises.

○ EXAMPLE ○○○○

DRN Ltd, a medium-sized company, had been trading for many years, preparing accounts to 31 December when it decided to cease trading on 30 June 2006.

The tax written down value of the pool at 1 January 2005 was £12,600.

On 1 October 2005, DRN Ltd purchased some plant for £4,600.

All items of plant were sold on 30 June 2006 for £5,000 (no item was sold for more than cost).

Calculate the capital allowances due for the year ended 31 December 2005 and the six months ended 30 June 2006.

Solution

DRN Ltd - Capital allowances computation

	£	General pool £	Allowances £
Year ended 31 December 2005			
Tax WDV brought forward		12,600	
WDA at 25%		(3,150)	3,150
		9,450	
Addition qualifying for FYA			
1 October 2005	4,600		
FYA at 40%	(1,840)		1,840
		2,760	
Tax WDV carried forward		12,210	
Total allowances			4,990
6 months ended 30 June 2006			
Disposal		(5,000)	
		7,210	
Balancing allowance		(7,210)	7,210

Note: If plant is not sold until after the date of cessation, the proceeds eventually realised are used as the market value on cessation. In effect it is treated as if sold on cessation for market value.

▷ ACTIVITY 2   ▷ ▷ ▷ ▷

RBT Ltd

RBT Ltd commenced trading on 1 January 2005. The first accounts were prepared to 30 June 2005 and thereafter to 30 June annually.

The following purchases and sales of fixed assets occurred.

			£
Purchases			
	1 January 2005	Secondhand loom	10,000
	1 February 2005	Motor car (used)	5,750
	30 September 2005	Motor car (new)	12,200
	1 October 2005	Motor car (used)	6,210
	1 October 2005	Computer	8,478
	1 February 2007	Motor car (new)	18,000
	1 June 2007	Motor car (new)	16,130
Sale			
	1 June 2007	Loom originally purchased 1 January 2005, a cheque for £4,000 being received as proceeds.	

The car purchased on 1 June 2007 had a carbon dioxide emission rating of 118 grams per kilometre (i.e. low emissions).

Required

Compute the capital allowances for the first three periods of account taking advantage of any beneficial elections available. Assume that RBT Ltd is a medium-sized business.

[Answer on p. 52]

Approach to the question

Note the following points:

· Watch the length of the first accounting period. Remember that WDAs must be scaled down if the accounting period is less than 12 months long. However, FYAs are never scaled down in such circumstances.

· Consider how best to treat the loom as it has been sold at a loss within a couple of years of its purchase.

8 Test your knowledge

1   ABC Ltd buys a car costing £15,000 in its chargeable accounting period of 9 months to 31 December 2006. What capital allowances are available?

2   DEF Ltd, a small company, buys a machine costing £10,000 in March 2006. It intends to sell the machine for £5,000 in two years' time. Should a short life election be made?

3   GHI plc, a large company, buys a machine costing £10,000 in March 2006. It intends to sell the machine for £4,000 in two years' time. Should a short life election be made?

4   JKL Ltd ceased trading on 31 March 2007. The tax written down value of the pool at 1 April 2006 was £1,000. What capital allowances are due assuming:

·   the plant was scrapped for no proceeds; or
·   the plant was sold for £1,200?

[Answer on p. 53]

9   Summary

Capital allowances are granted to give tax relief over the life of an asset, instead of depreciation.

A tabular layout is essential for computing capital allowances on plant and machinery. The table should have separate columns for each of the following:

·   General pool.
·   Each 'expensive' car.
·   Each short life asset.

When an asset is expected to have a short life and to decrease in value substantially, it may be beneficial to exclude it from the general pool and treat it as a short life asset.

When an accounting period is less than 12 months long, writing down allowances must be scaled down accordingly. First year allowances are never scaled down.

Answers to chapter activities & 'test your knowledge' questions

△ ACTIVITY 1   △ △ △ △

ENT Ltd

Capital allowances computation

	General pool £	Expensive car £	Allowances £
Year ending 31 December 2005			
Tax WDV b/f	24,000		
Additions (no FYA)			
15 April 2005		12,600	
16 July 2005	9,200		
17 August 2005	9,400		
Disposals			
30 April 2005	(3,200)		
	39,400	12,600	
WDA restricted		(3,000)	3,000
WDA 25%	(9,850)		9,850
WDV c/f	29,550	9,600	
Total allowances			12,850
Year ending 31 December 2006			
Disposals	(7,900)	(9,400)	
	21,650	200	
Balancing allowance		(200)	200
WDA 25%	(5,413)		5,413
Tax WDV c/f	16,237	-	
Total allowances			5,613

△ ACTIVITY 2   △ △ △ △

RBT Ltd

Capital allowances computation

	General pool £	Expensive car 1 £	Expensive car 2 £	Short life asset £	Allowances £
Six months to 30 June 2005					
Addition (no FYA)					
1 February 2005	5,750				
WDA (25% x ⁶/₁₂)	(719)				719
Addition (FYA)					
1 January 2005				10,000	
FYA (40%)				(4,000)	4,000
WDV c/f	5,031			6,000	
Total allowances					4,719
Year ending 30 June 2006					
Additions (no FYA)					
30 September 2005		12,200			
1 October 2005	6,210				
	11,241	12,200		6,000	
WDA (restricted)		(3,000)			3,000
WDA (25%)	(2,810)			(1,500)	4,310
Addition (FYA)					
1 October 2005	8,478				
FYA (40%)	(3,391)				3,391
WDV c/f	13,518	9,200		4,500	
Total allowances					10,701
Year ending 30 June 2007					
Addition (no FYA)					
1 February 2007			18,000		
Disposal					
1 June 2007				(4,000)	
	13,518	9,200	18,000	500	
Balancing allowance				(500)	500
WDA restricted			(3,000)		3,000
WDA (25%)	(3,380)	(2,300)			5,680
Addition (FYA)					
1 June 2007	16,130				
FYA (100%)	(16,130)				16,130
WDV c/f	10,138	6,900	15,000	-	
Total allowances					25,310

KAPLAN PUBLISHING

Test your knowledge △ △ △

1   A WDA of £3,000 x 9/12 = £2,250 is due.

2   A short life election should not be made as the WDV prior to sale will be £4,500 (Year 1 – FYA 40%, Year 2 – WDA 25%) and a balancing charge would arise on the disposal.

3   A short life election should be made as the WDV prior to sale will be £5,625 (Year 1 – WDA 25%, Year 2 – WDA 25%) and a balancing allowance would arise. Remember that FYAs are not available to large companies.

4   The capital allowances due will be:
·   a balancing allowance of £1,000; or
·   a balancing charge of £1,200 – £1,000 = £200.

CAPITAL ALLOWANCES – INDUSTRIAL BUILDINGS

INTRODUCTION

The assessment will include a calculation of capital allowances. This may include the calculation of industrial buildings allowances as discussed in this chapter.

CONTENTS

1 Eligible expenditure for IBA purposes
2 Allowances available for the first user of a building
3 The disposal of an industrial building
4 Allowances for second hand purchasers

PERFORMANCE CRITERIA

This chapter covers the following performance criteria:
· Ensure that entries and calculations relating to the computation of capital allowances for a company are correct (18.1 B)
· Ensure that computations and submissions are made in accordance with current tax law and take account of current HM Revenue & Customs practice (18.1 D)
· Enter adjusted trading profits and losses, capital allowances, investment income and capital gains in the corporation tax computation (18.4 A)
· Complete corporation tax returns correctly and submit them together with relevant claims and elections, within statutory time limits (18.4 G)

1 Eligible expenditure for IBA purposes

1.1 Qualifying expenditure

In the assessment you may need to identify the correct *amount* of expenditure eligible for Industrial Buildings Allowances (IBAs). You may also need to state the *types* of buildings which qualify for IBA.

Buildings qualify for IBA if they are of an industrial nature and are used in an industrial trade. This includes the following:

· A mill, factory or any building used in a manufacturing trade.
· Warehouses for the storage of stock (i.e. raw materials, finished goods) provided they are used in or derived from a manufacturing trade.
· Buildings used for the repair or maintenance of goods or services.
· Sports pavilions used in any trade.
· Canteens and other welfare buildings provided for workers in a manufacturing business.
· Drawing offices in factories.
· Qualifying hotels.

The qualifying costs of constructing such buildings or acquiring a new building include the following:

· Professional fees (e.g. architects, legal fees).
· The costs of preparing land (e.g. levelling, tunnelling, drainage).
· Associated structural undertakings (e.g. a car park adjoining a factory).

1.2 Non-qualifying expenditure

There are also some important exclusions which do not qualify.
· Land (including any costs pertaining to the land itself, e.g. legal fees).
· General offices, shops, showrooms and dwelling houses.
· Retailers' warehouses, i.e. used for storing bought in finished goods.
· Items which qualify alternatively for plant and machinery allowances (e.g. central heating, fire and safety equipment, ventilation, thermal insulation).

Non-industrial parts

Any 'non-industrial' portion of an industrial building (e.g. general offices) is only excluded if its cost represents more than 25% of the total building costs.

○ EXAMPLE   ○○○○

The cost of a factory, incurred in September 2006, is shown below:

	£
Purchase price of land (including £1,700 legal costs)	17,000
Buildings (including drawing office £4,900, canteen £10,000, general office £30,000)	144,000
	161,000

(a) What amount is eligible for industrial buildings allowance?

(b) If the general office had accounted for £37,000 of the £144,000 cost of the building, what would the eligible expenditure be?

Solution

(a) There is no allowance for the purchase price of the land. The drawing office and the canteen both qualify for IBA in their own right.

The cost of the general offices will also qualify as it represents 20.8% (£30,000/£144,000) of the total building cost excluding land, i.e. not exceeding 25%.

IBA will therefore be based on £144,000.

(b) If the general offices had cost £37,000, this would amount to 25.7% (£37,000/£144,000) of the total cost. As this exceeds 25%, none of the £37,000 would be allowable.

IBA would therefore be based on £107,000 (£144,000 - £37,000).

2 Allowances available for the first user of a building

2.1 Introduction

Two areas of allowance need to be considered:

· Writing down allowances.
· Balancing adjustments on disposal (see Section 3).

2.2 Writing down allowances (WDA)

WDA is given on a *straight line basis* of 4% per annum.

This means that it takes 25 years to obtain full relief, and so industrial buildings are often described as having a 25 year tax life. This tax life commences from the date the building is first put into use, industrial or otherwise, and lasts for 25 years.

Note that the tax life does not necessarily start on the date the building is purchased.

A claimant is entitled to WDA provided the building is in industrial *use* at the *end* of the accounting period.

For the purpose of calculating allowances, each new building has its own 25 year tax life, and should therefore be kept as a separate item.

No WDA is given in the accounting period in which a building is sold.

O EXAMPLE   OOOO

Quentin Ltd purchased a building on 1 November 2006, in its year ended 31 December 2006, for £200,000.

It took several weeks to fit out the factory prior to being brought into industrial use. The directors had to decide whether to start using the factory on 20 December 2006 or 4 January 2007.

What is the tax effect of their decision?

Solution

Use from 20 December 2006
·   The building's tax life starts on 20 December 2006.
·   As it is in industrial use on 31 December 2006 (i.e. the end of the accounting period), a full 4% WDA is available for the year ended 31 December 2006. The WDA is £8,000.

Use from 4 January 2007
·   The building's tax life starts on 4 January 2007.
·   As it is not in industrial use on 31 December 2006, no WDA is available for the year ended 31 December 2006. A 4% WDA is available from year ended 31 December 2007.

Note: The purchase date has no effect on capital allowances.

▷ ACTIVITY 1   ▷ ▷ ▷ ▷

Required

Briefly explain whether industrial buildings allowance is due on the following buildings.

(i)   A warehouse purchased by a clothes manufacturer to store cloth which is to be made into suits.

(ii)   The works canteen of a shoe manufacturer.

(iii) An office block used to accommodate the sales office of a heavy engineering manufacturing company.

(iv)   A repair workshop used by a lawn mower manufacturer to repair and service lawn mowers.

[Answer on p. 65]

3 The disposal of an industrial building

3.1 Balancing adjustments

When a building is sold, this triggers a balancing adjustment. Where insufficient allowances have been claimed, a balancing allowance will be given. Otherwise, a balancing charge will occur. Remember that the total allowances given must equal the net cost of the building.

One way to identify the balancing allowance or charge is to compare the 'net cost' of the building with the allowances claimed, as follows:

	£
Eligible cost	X
Less: Sale proceeds	(X)
Net cost	X

'Sale proceeds' in this calculation cannot exceed the eligible cost.

The net cost is therefore the real capital cost (ignoring inflation) incurred by the business.

· Where the net cost is *greater than* the total allowances claimed, a balancing allowance for the difference arises.

· Where the net cost is *less than* the total allowances claimed, the difference is clawed back as a balancing charge.

· The net cost will be nil if the building is sold for more than its original eligible cost. A balancing charge will therefore arise, to claw back all of the allowances given.

No balancing adjustments are required if a building is sold after its tax life has expired. This is easy to overlook in the assessment.

Just as the cost of the building has to exclude the land element and the cost of ineligible offices etc., sale proceeds are also restricted to the qualifying portion. If the assessment just gives 'sale proceeds' you should assume the land etc elements are excluded.

An alternative way of calculating a balancing allowance or charge is to perform a similar calculation to that used for expensive cars or short life assets (Chapter 4).

	£
WDV brought forward	X
Disposal – at lower of cost and sale proceeds (Note 1)	(X)
	(X)/X
Balancing charge/allowance (Note 2)	X/(X)
	NIL

Note 1: Where buildings are being disposed of, cost is often the lower of the two figures as buildings usually appreciate in value.

Note 2: The balancing charge/allowance is the balancing figure to ensure the total comes to nil.

You do not need to be able to use both methods of calculation of the balancing adjustment. Use the method that you find easiest.

○ EXAMPLE   ○○○○

Gray Ltd prepares accounts to 31 March. On 1 August 2004 it began to use a newly constructed factory which cost £60,000, including £4,000 for the land and £2,500 for offices. On 1 February 2007 the factory was sold to Heath Ltd for £64,200, including £12,000 for the land.

Calculate the allowances for Gray Ltd. Also consider the effect if the sale proceeds were alternatively £53,000 and £71,340 (in each case including £12,000 for the land).

Solution

	£	£
Cost excluding land		
(offices allowed, as not over 25%)		56,000
Year ended 31 March 2005 WDA (4%)	2,240	
Year ended 31 March 2006 WDA (4%)	2,240	
		(4,480)
WDV carried forward		51,520

There is no WDA in the period of sale (the year to 31 March 2007).

Year ended 31 March 2007

	(a)	(b)	(c)
Net cost (cost - proceeds)			
(a) (£56,000 - £52,200)	3,800		
(b) (£56,000 - £41,000)		15,000	
(c) (£56,000 - £56,000)			Nil
Allowances given	(4,480)	(4,480)	(4,480)
Balancing charge	(680)		(4,480)
Balancing allowance		10,520	

Solution – alternative

Year ended 31 March 2007

	(a)	(b)	(c)
WDV brought forward	51,520	51,520	51,520
Disposal, lower of:			
(i) cost; and			(56,000)
(ii) sale proceeds	(52,200)	(41,000)	
Balancing charge	(680)		(4,480
Balancing allowance		10,520	

▷ ACTIVITY 2   ▷▷▷▷

Leaden

Leaden Ltd is a manufacturer of plumbing components preparing accounts to 31 March annually. In December 2006 the company sold one of its workshops, the details of which are as follows:

Cost	£115,000
Sale proceeds	£190,000
Industrial buildings allowances received to date	£55,200

The above figures exclude the value of the land.

Required

(a) Calculate the balancing adjustment that arises as a result of the sale.

(b) Recalculate the balancing adjustment on the assumption that the sale proceeds were alternatively:

    (i)   £100,000
    (ii) £50,000

[Answer on p. 65]

4   Allowances for secondhand purchasers

4.1   Revised WDAs

So far we have looked at the allowances available to the purchaser of a new industrial building. For the purchaser of a used industrial building, the normal 4% writing down allowance is not available.

Instead, the purchaser of a used industrial building receives a special writing down allowance which spreads relief for the remaining qualifying expenditure evenly over the remaining tax life of the building.

The WDA is therefore calculated as follows:

$$\frac{\text{Remaining qualifying expenditure}}{\text{Tax life remaining}}$$

The remaining qualifying expenditure (RQE) is computed as follows:

		£
Tax written down value before sale		X
Plus Any balancing charge, or		
Less Any balancing allowance	}	X/(X)
Remaining qualifying expenditure		X

However, a short cut of getting to the RQE is to take the lower of:

(i) original qualifying expenditure; and
(ii) sale proceeds.

The tax life remaining is computed to the nearest month.

○ EXAMPLE ○○○○

Using the details in the earlier example (Gray Ltd), calculate the allowances for Heath Ltd, the secondhand purchaser, under the three sale proceeds options.

Solution

	(a)	(b)	(c)
	£	£	£
WDV b/f	51,520	51,520	51,520
Add Balancing charge	680		4,480
Less Balancing allowance		(10,520)	
RQE	52,200	41,000	56,000

All that is happening here is that HMRC are sharing the qualifying expenditure between the buyer and the seller. Any amount 'clawed' back as a balancing charge from Gray Ltd (the seller) is instead given to Heath Ltd (the buyer). Any allowance already given to the seller (i.e. £10,520 in option (b)) is not available for the buyer.

Note: The RQE can also be identified as lower of:

		£	£	£
(i)	Original qualifying expenditure	56,000	56,000	56,000
(ii)	Sale proceeds (excluding land)	52,200	41,000	59,340
	RQE	52,200	41,000	56,000

Heath Ltd then spreads the RQE over the remaining tax life.

Tax life = from 1 August 2004 to 1 February 2007   = 2 years 6 months
Therefore, remaining life = 25 years – 2 years 6 months = 22 years 6 months

Heath Ltd's allowance per annum is therefore as follows:

	(a)	(b)	(c)
	£	£	£
RQE	52,200	41,000	56,000
Remaining life	22.5	22.5	22.5
WDA (p.a.)	2,320	1,822	2,489

▷ ACTIVITY 3   ▷ ▷ ▷ ▷

Brown

During the year ended 31 December 2005, Brown Ltd incurred the following capital expenditure on the construction of an industrial building.

		£
12 April 2005	Land	50,000
15 May 2005	Ground levelling	3,125

The architect's certificates included the following:

		£
25 June 2005	Construction of building	351,750
5 October 2005	Car park for employees	12,000
20 December 2005	Ventilation equipment	39,400
20 December 2005	Central heating system	41,500
30 December 2005	Road construction	16,250

Professional fees were as follows:

		£
12 October 2005	Quantity surveyor's fees	5,250
21 October 2005	Architect's fees	11,875

The surveyor's and architect's fees relate wholly to the construction of the building. The building was brought into use on 25 January 2006.

On 24 February 2007, owing to subsidence, the building was sold to Smith Ltd, a company also with a 31 December year end, for £250,000. The purchase price included £40,000 for the land and £30,000 for fittings.

Required

(a) Compute the industrial buildings allowances due to Brown Ltd and Smith Ltd for the years ended 31 December 2005 to 2007 inclusive.

(b) Discuss briefly the tax allowances available to Brown Ltd in respect of the expenditure on the ventilation equipment and central heating system.

Approach to the question

The first step is to identify the qualifying eligible expenditure.

In claiming WDA consider when the building goes into industrial use.

Go through the disposal procedure outlined earlier to ascertain the balancing adjustment. Remember there is no WDA in the year of disposal.

Remember that the secondhand purchaser does not get 4% straight line WDA. Instead, you need to work out the WDA using the remaining qualifying expenditure divided by the remaining tax life.

[Answer on p.66]

5   Test your knowledge

1   ABC Ltd built a warehouse to store goods to be sold in its retail shop. It buys the goods ready for resale. Will IBA be available?

2   DEF Ltd bought a secondhand factory for £100,000 from GHI Ltd in December 2006. GHI had built the factory in 1979 at a cost of £50,000 and had first used it in October 1981. What IBAs will be available to DEF Ltd in its CAP to 31 March 2007.

3   Would your answer differ if GHI Ltd had first used the factory in January 1982?

4   JKL Ltd purchased a newly built factory for £120,000. £20,000 of the cost was attributable to land, and £27,000 to general office. How much of the expenditure qualifies for IBA?

[Answers on p. 68]

6   Summary

This concludes the material on capital allowances, a core area for the assessment.

The key points concerning IBA are as follows:

·   Land never qualifies for IBA.

·   The non-industrial parts of an industrial building will qualify for IBA if they amount to less than 25% of the total cost.

·   The initial purchaser of an industrial building receives a 4% WDA, calculated using the straight line method, if the building is in industrial use at the end of the accounting period.

·   The purchaser of a secondhand industrial building receives a WDA based on the remaining qualifying cost divided by the remaining tax life.

Answers to chapter activities & 'test your knowledge' questions

△ ACTIVITY 1   △ △ △ △

(i) The warehouse will qualify for IBA as it is a building used to store goods or materials to be used in a manufacturing process.

(ii) The canteen will qualify for IBA as it is a building provided for the welfare of workers employed in a manufacturing business.

(iii) No IBA will be due on the office as it is separate from the manufacturing building.

(iv) IBA will be available as the building is used for the maintenance or repair of goods.

△ ACTIVITY 2   △ △ △ △

Leaden

(a) Balancing adjustment on sale of the workshop:

	£
Allowable cost	115,000
Proceeds are £190,000, but limited to cost	(115,000)
Net cost	Nil

Since the use of the building has not 'cost' the company anything, any allowances given will be clawed back by HMRC in the form of a balancing charge.

A £55,200 *balancing charge i*s made to take back all the IBAs given.

(b) Alternative sales proceeds

		£
(i)	Allowable cost	115,000
	Proceeds	(100,000)
	Net cost	15,000
	Compare net cost with IBAs given	
	Net cost	15,000
	IBAs given	(55,200)
	Excess IBAs given = balancing charge	(40,200)
		£
(ii)	Allowable cost	115,000
	Proceeds	(50,000)
	Net cost	65,000

Compare net cost with IBAs given

	£
Net cost	65,000
IBAs given	(55,200)
Shortfall of IBAs given = balancing allowance	9,800

The balancing adjustments are effective in the year ended 31 March 2007.

2 Leaden – other method of calculation

	£
Original cost	115,000
Less: Allowances to date	(55,200)
TWDV before sale	59,800

	Sale proceeds £190,000	Sale proceeds £100,000	Sale proceeds £50,000
	£	£	£
TWDV b/f	59,800	59,800	59,800
Less: Disposal Lower of cost and sale proceeds	(115,000)	(100,000)	(50,000)
	(55,200)	(40,200)	9,800
Balancing charge	55,200	40,200	
Balancing allowance			(9,800)
	Nil	Nil	Nil

△ ACTIVITY 3 △△△△

Brown

Step 1: Identify qualifying eligible expenditure.

	£
Ground levelling	3,125
Construction of building	351,750
Car park	12,000
Road construction	16,250
Quantity surveyor's fees	5,250
Architect's fees	11,875
	400,250

Notes:

(1)   Land does not qualify for IBAs.

(2)   Writing down allowance is only available in respect of a period if the building is in industrial use at the end of a period. So no WDA is available in the year ended 31 December 2005.

(3)   Although the ventilation equipment and central heating system are installed in the building, they are normally treated as plant and machinery for capital allowances purposes.

Provided that Brown Ltd is a small or medium sized business, it will be able to claim 40% first year allowances in the year in which the expenditure was incurred (i.e. the year to 31 December 2005) even though the building was not brought into use until the following period.

If Brown Ltd is a large company, it will only be able to claim 25% WDA, again starting in the period of expenditure.

Step 2: Claim writing down allowances (excluding year of disposal)

	£	*Allowances given* £
Year ended 31 December 2006		
Qualifying expenditure	400,250	
WDA (4%)	(16,010)	16,010
	————	————
WDV before sale	384,240	
	————	

Step 3: Calculate the balancing adjustment - y/e 31 December 2007

	£
Cost	400,250
Sale proceeds (note 1)	(180,000)
	————
Net cost	220,250
Compare with allowances claimed	(16,010)
	————
Balancing allowance	204,240
	————

Notes:

(1)   The sale proceeds to be considered must be those which relate to the eligible expenditure (i.e. matching like with like). The total sale proceeds of £250,000 included items like land and fixtures, which need to be deducted.

Eligible sale proceeds = £180,000 (£250,000 - £40,000 - £30,000).

(2) The IBAs for each accounting period for Brown Ltd are as follows:

Year ended 31 December 2006	£16,010
Year ended 31 December 2007	£204,240

These are then deducted from the adjusted trading profit to find the Schedule D Case I profits.

Step 4: Calculate allowances available to Smith Ltd - y/e 31 December 2007

RQE = (£384,240 - £204,240) = £180,000

Tax life used:	25 January 2006 to 24 February 2007 = 1 year 1 month
Remaining tax life:	25 years - 1 year 1 month = 287 months
Annual WDA	$= \dfrac{£180,000}{287}$ x 12 months = £7,526 p.a.

Test your knowledge

1   IBAs will not be available as the warehouse is not used for storage of goods that ABC Ltd has itself manufactured or processed.

2   No IBAs will be available as the tax life of the factory expired in October 2006.

3   As the tax life of the factory does not expire until January 2007, DEF Ltd will be entitled to IBAs to write off the residue of qualifying expenditure (£50,000) in its CAP to 31 March 2007.

4   £73,000 of the expenditure qualifies for IBA. Land never qualifies, and the cost of the general offices exceeds 25% of the remaining cost.

KAPLAN PUBLISHING

CALCULATION OF PROFITS CHARGEABLE TO CORPORATION TAX

INTRODUCTION

In the Chapters 2 – 5 we have been working towards calculating the Schedule D Case I profit of a company, the major source of income found on most corporation tax computations. In this chapter that knowledge is to be enhanced to enable a full computation of the profits chargeable to corporation tax.

CONTENTS

1 Proforma corporation tax computation
2 Profits chargeable to corporation tax (PCTCT)
3 Corporation tax return (Part 1)

PERFORMANCE CRITERIA

This chapter covers the following performance criteria:
· Enter adjusted trading profits and losses, capital allowances, investment income and capital gain in the corporation tax computation. (18.4 A)
· Complete corporation tax returns correctly and submit them, together with relevant claims and elections, within statutory time limits. (18.4 G)

1 Proforma corporation tax computation

1.1 Proforma

The first stage of a single company computation is to ascertain the PCTCT. This comprises income and gains, less charges on income. The proforma that was set out in Chapter 2 is set out again below. It will be referred to throughout this chapter.

Company name

Corporation tax computation for XX months ended .... (the CAP)

	£
Schedule D Case I	X
Schedule D Case III	X
Schedule A	X
Chargeable gains	X
Total profits	X
Less: Charges on income	(X)
Profits chargeable to corporation tax (PCTCT)	X
Corporation tax liability at relevant rate (to be considered in Chapter 7)	X

2 Profits chargeable to corporation tax (PCTCT)

2.1 Schedule D Case I – adjusted trading profit

The adjusted trading profit and capital allowances have been covered in the previous chapters, so you can now compute the Schedule D Case I profit.

	Chapter	£
Adjusted trading profit	3	X
Less: *Capital allowances*		
Plant and machinery	4	(X)
Industrial building allowances	5	(X)
Schedule D Case I		X

Dividends paid by a company are not an allowable deduction in calculating Schedule D Case I profits being an appropriation of profit, not an expense of earning the profit. In any event, these should not have been deducted in arriving at the net accounting profit.

2.2 Interest (the loan relationship rules)

We consider the loan relationship rules at this point because of their relevance to Schedule D Case I and Schedule D Case III.

The loan relationship rules apply when a company pays or receives interest.

The legislation distinguishes between trading purposes and non-trading purposes, in relation to the interest.

For assessment purposes:

- if a company receives interest you can normally assume that it is for non-trading purposes.

  For example:
  - interest received on a building society account.
  - interest received on a bank deposit account.

- if a company pays interest you can normally assume that it is for trading purposes.

  For example:
  - interest paid on a bank overdraft.
  - interest paid on a loan to purchase new machinery.

You will, however, need to read the question carefully to make sure that these assumptions are not contradicted.

Net or gross?

Most interest is paid or received gross (with the exception of interest paid to individuals).

All amounts shown on corporation tax computations must be shown gross.

If interest is paid to an individual by a company it is paid net of 20% tax. Hence, the interest must be grossed up. The gross interest is calculated as follows:

Interest paid to individual x $\frac{100}{80}$

○ EXAMPLE   ○○○○

Rory Ltd pays and receives the following amounts of interest.

		£
(a)	Interest received on deposit account with Bat East Bank plc	5,000
(b)	Interest paid on overdrawn business bank account	(2,000)
(c)	Interest paid on loan made by Mr Smith	(2,000)

What are the gross figures to be used in the corporation tax computation?

Solution

Gross amounts to be included in PCTCT:

		£
(a)	Interest received	5,000
(b)	Interest paid on overdraft	(2,000)
(c)	Interest paid on loan by Mr Smith (2,000 x $\frac{100}{80}$)	(2,500)

Trading loans

Interest paid – all interest deducted in the profit and loss account will be an allowable deduction for Schedule D Case I purposes. This means you will not need to make any adjustments in converting the accounting profit into the Schedule D Case I profit.

Interest received – you are unlikely to see any interest received for trading purposes. However, if you do, such interest will be included in the trading profit and therefore needs no adjustment.

Non-trading loans

Interest paid – interest deducted in the profit and loss account on non-trading loans will be disallowed (i.e. add it back in the adjustment of profit computation). Instead, the interest will be deducted from the Schedule D Case III income. The main example of this type of interest will be interest paid on a loan to buy an investment property.

Interest received – interest received shown in the profit and loss account (e.g. interest on a deposit account) must be deducted from net profit, and instead treated as Schedule D Case III income.

Accruals basis

All interest in corporation tax computations must be dealt with on an accruals basis (not received and paid basis). The accruals basis means the amount due within the accounting period.

○ EXAMPLE   ○○○○

Sam Limited has received the following interest on its bank deposit account that was opened on 1 April 2006:

Date received	£
30 June 2006	1,000
31 December 2006	3,000
30 June 2007	4,000

Assuming interest accrues evenly between each date, what is the Schedule D Case III income to be shown in the corporation tax computation for year ended 31 March 2007?

Solution

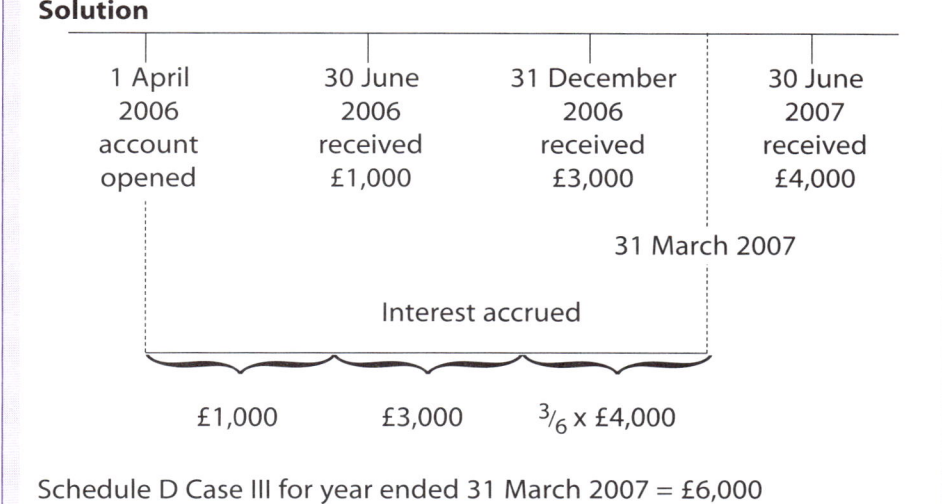

Schedule D Case III for year ended 31 March 2007 = £6,000
(1,000 + 3,000 + 2,000).

The figure shown in the accounts will normally be the accrued amount. You are therefore unlikely to have to calculate this.

2.3   Patent royalties

Patent royalties paid or received are dealt with for tax purposes on an accruals basis.

Royalties payable

Royalties are relieved as a trading expense against Schedule D Case I income on a normal accruals basis. So if they have been correctly charged through the accounts no adjustment should be needed.

Royalties receivable

Royalties receivable on patents are taxed under Schedule D Case I as trading income. Again, if the income has been correctly shown on an accruals basis no adjustment should be needed.

Royalties subject to income tax deductions

Patent royalties are usually received gross, except that patent royalties received from individuals are received net of basic rate tax (currently 22%). Similarly, all patent royalties are usually paid gross, except that patent royalties paid to individuals are paid net of basic rate tax.

All amounts shown in corporation tax computations must be shown gross. Therefore, patent royalties paid to/received from an individual must be grossed up. The gross patent royalties are calculated as follows:

Patent royalties x $\frac{100}{78}$

O EXAMPLE   O O O O

Tom Ltd receives the following patent royalties. What were the gross figures to be used in the corporation tax computation?

		£
(a)	Received from Rory Ltd	3,000
(b)	Received from Eric	3,900

Solution

Gross amounts to be used:

		£
(a)	From Rory Ltd	3,000
(b)	From Eric (3,900 x $\frac{100}{78}$)	5,000

2.4   Dividend income

Dividend income from UK resident companies is not chargeable to corporation tax. If it is included in the profit and loss account, it must be deducted for Schedule D Case I purposes.

This is because dividend income is paid out of after-tax profits of another company (i.e. the profits generating the dividend have already been subject to UK corporation tax).

2.5   Schedule A

Rental income is included under the heading Schedule A and comprises the following:

	£
Rental income (furnished or unfurnished)	X
Less: Expenses (excluding loan interest payable)	(X)
Schedule A	X

Rental income and expenses should be the accrued income and expenses for the accounting period. Expenses are allowed (disallowed) as if the letting business was a trade (i.e. under the rules in Chapter 3).

If the property is let furnished the landlord can claim a 'wear and tear' allowance equal to 10% of the rent received net of any council tax and water rates (if these are paid by the landlord).

○ **EXAMPLE** ○○○○

Ulysses Ltd has provided details of the following income and expenditure accrued in its year ended 30 June 2007, relating to a furnished property that it lets out.

	£	£
Rental income		10,000
Less: Expenses		
Insurance	1,000	
Repairs	500	
New kitchen	4,000	
Cleaning	500	
Advertising for tenants	200	
Council tax	800	
Water rates	500	
		(7,500)
Profit from letting		2,500

What is the Schedule A figure to be shown in the corporation tax computation?

Solution

	£
Profit from letting	2,500
Add: New kitchen (capital)	4,000
Less: Wear and tear allowance (furnished)	
10% x (10,000 – 800 – 500)	(870)
Schedule A	5,630

Schedule A losses are covered in Chapter 9.

2.8 Capital gains

A company's PCTCT includes capital gains as well as income.

The calculation of the capital gain or loss on individual transactions is covered in a later chapter. For the purpose of this chapter, all individual gains and losses are already computed. You will, however, need to be able to produce a summary of the position for PCTCT.

This is shown as follows:

	£
Gain (transaction 1)	X
Gain (transaction 2)	X
Loss (transaction 3)	(X)
	X
Less: Capital losses brought forward	(X)
Net chargeable gains	X

Current period gains and losses are netted off automatically.

Excess capital losses are covered in Chapter 9.

2.9   Charges on income

The final component in finding PCTCT is to deduct from the total profits (income and gains) any allowable payments known as *charges on income*.

The only form of charge an income you will meet in the assessment is the non-trade charge of Gift Aid payments to charities. These are paid gross by companies.

The gross amount deductible for a CAP is the amount *paid*. This may be different from the amount accrued in the accounts.

A Gift Aid donation is basically any donation by a company to a charity unless it already qualifies as a business expense. Only donations that are 'small' and 'local in effect' will normally be allowed as a Schedule D Case I expense.

▷ **ACTIVITY 1**   ▷ ▷ ▷ ▷

Laserjet Ltd (1)

Laserjet Ltd provided you with the following information for its year to 31 March 2007.

	£
Adjusted trading profit	500,600
Capital allowances	16,000
Rental income (net of expenses)	32,000
Bank loan interest payable on a loan to purchase rental property (accrued)	4,000
Building society interest receivable (accrued)	20,000
10% debenture interest receivable (accrued)	6,000
Gift Aid payment made	14,000

Compute the PCTCT for the year ended 31 March 2007.

Approach to the question

It is essential to develop a methodical approach from the outset in computing PCTCT, to enable you to tackle examination level questions later.

Step 1: Set up a skeleton CT computation proforma.

Keep this on a separate sheet of paper.

	£
Schedule D Case I (W1)	
Schedule D Case III (W2)	
Schedule A	
Less: Charges on income	_____
PCTCT	_____

The headings are not required to be in any particular order, but it is accepted best practice to put Schedule D Case I first.

Step 2: Set up a separate working sheet for any necessary workings

Work through the information methodically. Schedule D Case I often (though not in this example) requires more than one working for the component parts of:

·   adjusted profit.
·   capital allowances on plant and machinery, etc.

As you complete each working, slot the result into the proforma.

[Answer on p. 86]

3 Corporation tax return (part 1)

3.1 The short return

The corporation tax return, CT600, must be completed for the chargeable accounting period. The return can either be:

·   the short form (4 pages); or
·   the long form (8 pages).

In an assessment you would only be required to complete the short form. A copy of the form is reproduced on the following pages.

The first page includes details of the company and the chargeable accounting period, and whether any supplementary pages are required (these are outside the scope of your studies).

The last page requires details of the company's bank account if a repayment is due, and contains a declaration that the return is complete and correct.

The computation of profits chargeable to corporation tax and the corporation tax payable is required on pages 2 and 3. Page 3 also requires details of capital allowances and losses.

3.2   The return – up to the calculation of PCTCT

In this chapter we will consider the calculation of profits chargeable to corporation tax on the top of page 2 of the return.

We have not dealt with entries to go in all boxes. However, the main ones considered are:

	Boxes
Schedule D Case I	3
Schedule D Case III	6
Schedule A	11
Chargeable gains	16 – 18
Charges on income	35

There are gaps in the numbering of the boxes so that the numbers correspond with those used on the long form, which includes additional boxes.

The remainder of the short form (i.e. calculation of the tax) will be dealt with in Chapter 7.

Company – short tax return form

CT600 (Short) (2006) Version 2

for accounting periods ending on or after 1 July 1999

Your company tax return

If we send the company a *Notice* to deliver a company tax return (form *CT603*) it has to complete and send us a company tax return, at the latest by filing date, or the company may face a penalty. A company tax return includes a company tax return form, any Supplementary Pages, accounts, computations and any relevant information.

Is this the right form for the company? Read the advice on pages 3 to 6 of the Company tax return guide (2006) (the *Guide*) before you start.

The forms in the CT600 series set out the information we need and provide a standard format for calculations. Use the Guide to help you complete the return form. It contains general information you may need and box by box advice.

Company information

Company name

Company registration number   **Tax Reference as shown on the CT603**   **Type of company**

Registered office address

Postcode

About this return

This is the above company's return for the period

from (dd/mm/yyyy)   to (dd/mm/yyyy)

Put an 'X' in the appropriate box(es) below

A repayment is due for this return period

A repayment is due for an earlier period

Making more than one return for this period

This return contains estimated figures

Disclosure of tax avoidance schemes

Notice of disclosable avoidance schemes

Transfer pricing

Compensating adjustment claimed

Company qualifies for SME exemption

Accounts

I attach accounts and computations for the period to which this return relates

For a different period

If you are not attaching accounts and computations, say why not

Supplementary pages

If you are enclosing any Supplementary Pages put an 'X' in the appropriate box(es)

Loans to participators by close companies, form *CT600A*

Charities and Community Amateur Sports Clubs (CASCs), form *CT600E*

Disclosure of tax avoidance schemes, form *CT600J*

Page 2

Company Tax Calculation

Turnover

1	Total turnover from trade or profession	**1** £	

Income

3	Trading and professional profits	**3** £	
4	Trading losses brought forward claimed against profits	**4** £	
			box 3 minus box 4
5	Net trading and professional profits		**5** £
6	Bank, building society or other interest, and profits and gains from non-trading loan relationships		**6** £
11	Income from UK land and buildings		**11** £
14	Annual profits and gains not falling under any other heading		**14** £

Chargeable gains

16	Gross chargeable gains	**16** £	
17	Allowable losses including losses brought forward	**17** £	
			box 16 minus box 17
18	Net chargeable gains		**18** £
			sum of boxes 5, 6, 11 14 & 18
21	**Profits before other deductions and reliefs**		**21** £

Deductions and Reliefs

24	Management expenses under S75 ICTA 1988	**24** £
30	Trading losses of this or a later accounting period under S393A ICTA 1988	**30** £
31	*Put an 'X' in box 31 if amounts carried back from later Accounting periods are included in box 30*	**31**
32	Non-trade capital allowances	**32** £
35	Charges paid	**35** £

			box 21 minus boxes 24, 30, 32 and 35
37	**Profits chargeable to corporation tax**		**37** £

Tax calculation

38	Franked investment income	**38** £
39	Number of associated companies in this period or	**39**
40	Associated companies in the first financial year	**40**
41	Associated companies in the second financial year	**41**
42	*Put an 'X' in box 42 if the company claims to be charged at the starting rate or the Small companies' rate on any part of its profits, or is claiming marginal rate relief*	**42**

Enter how much profit has to be charged at and what rate of tax

Financial year *(yyyy)*	Amount of profit	Rate of tax	Tax
43	**44** £	**45**	**46** £ p
53	**54** £	**55**	**56** £ p

			Total of boxes 46 and 56
63	Corporation tax		**63** £ p
64	Marginal rate relief	**64** £ p	
65	Corporation tax net of marginal rate relief	**65** £ p	
66	Underlying rate of corporation tax	**66** . %	
67	Profits matched with non-corporate distributions	**67**	
68	Tax at non-corporate distributions rate	**68** £ p	
69	Tax at underlying rate on remaining profits	**69** £ p	*Enter value of box 643 or 65 or the total of boxes 68 and 69 if greater*
70	**Corporation tax chargeable**		**70** £ p

79	Tax payable under S419 ICTA 1988	79 £	p
80	*Put an 'X' in box 80 if you completed box A11 in the Supplementary Pages CT600A*	80	
84	Income tax deducted from gross income included in profits	84 £	p
85	Income tax repayable to the company	85 £	p
86	**Tax payable – this is your self-assessment of tax payable**	*total of boxes 70 and 79 minus box 84* 86 £	p

91	Tax already paid (an not already repaid)	91 £	p
92	Tax outstanding	*box 86 minus box 91* 92 £	p
93	Tax overpaid	*box 91 minus box 86* 93 £	p

Information about capital allowances and balancing charges

Charges and allowances included in calculation of trading profits or losses

		Capital allowances	Balancing charges
105 – 106	Machinery and plant – long-life assets	105 £	106 £
107 – 108	Machinery and plant – other (general pool)	107 £	108 £
109 – 110	Cars outside general pool	109 £	110 £
111 – 112	Industrial buildings and structures	111 £	112 £
113 – 114	Other charges and allowances	113 £	114 £

Charges and allowances not included in calculation of trading profits or losses

		Capital allowances	Balancing charges
115 – 116		115 £	116 £
117	*Put an 'X' in box 117 if box 115 includes flat conversion allowances*	117	

Expenditure

118	Expenditure on machinery and plant on which first year allowance is claimed	118 £
119	*Put an 'X' in box 119 if claim includes enhanced capital allowances for energy-saving investments*	119
120	Qualifying expenditure on machinery and plant on long-life assets	120 £
121	Qualifying expenditure on machinery and plant on other assets	121 £

Losses, deficits and excess amounts

122	Trading loss Case 1	*calculated under S393 ICTA 1988* 122 £	124	Trading losses Case V	*calculated under S393 ICTA 1988* 124 £
125	Non-trade deficits on loan relationships and derivative contracts	*calculated under S82 FA 1996* 122 £	127	Schedule A losses	*calculated under S392A ICTA1988* 127 £
129	Overseas property business losses Case V	*calculated under S392B ICTA 1988* 129 £	130	Losses Case VI	*calculated under S396 ICTA 1988* 130 £
131	Capital losses	*calculated under S16 TCGA 1992* 131 £	136	Excess management expenses	*calculated under S75(3) ICTA 1988* 136 £

Overpayments and repayments

Small repayments

If you do not want us to make small repayments please either put an 'X' in box 139 or complete box 140 below. 'Repayments' here include tax, interest, and late-filing penalties or any combination of them.

Do not repay £20 or less	139		Do not repay sums of	140	£		Or less. *Enter whole figure only*

Bank details (for person to whom the repayment is to be made)

Repayment is made quickly and safety by direct credit to a bank or building society account.
Please complete the following details:

Name of bank or building society

149

Branch sort code

150

Account number

151

Name of account

152

Building society reference

153

Payments to a person other than the company

Complete the authority below if you want the repayment to be made to a person other than the company.

I, as *(enter status – company secretary, treasurer, liquidator or authorised agent, etc.)*

154

of *(enter name of company)*

155

authorise *(enter name)*

156

(enter address)

157

Postcode

Nominee reference

158

To receive payment on the company'

Signature

159

Name *(in capitals)*

160

Declaration

Warning – Giving false information in the return, or concealing any part of the company's profits or tax payable, can lead to both the company and yourself being prosecuted.

Declaration

The information I have given in this company tax return is correct and complete to the best of my knowledge and belief.

Signature

Name *(in capitals)*

Date *(dd/mm/yyyy)*

Status

○ EXAMPLE ○○○○

Victor Ltd has the following results for its year ended 31 March 2007.

Complete computation of profits chargeable to corporation tax on the short form CT600 as indicated.

	£	£	CT 600 box
Schedule D Case I		100,000	3
Schedule D Case III		20,000	6
Schedule A		5,000	11
Chargeable gains	8,000		16
Less: Capital losses	(3,000)		17
		5,000	18
		130,000	
Less: Charges on income			
Gift Aid		(8,000)	35
PCTCT		122,000	

Don't forget to include sub-totals and totals in an exam question (i.e. boxes 5, 21, and 37).

Solution

Company Tax Calculation

Turnover

1	Total turnover from trade or profession		1	£	

Income

3	Trading and professional profits	3	£	100,000		
4	Trading losses brought forward claimed against profits	4	£			
5	Net trading and professional profits			box 3 minus box 4	5	£ 100,000
6	Bank, building society or other interest, and profits and gains from non-trading loan relationships				6	£ 20,000
11	Income from UK land and buildings				11	£ 5,000
14	Annual profits and gains not falling under any other heading				14	£

Chargeable gains

16	Gross chargeable gains	16	£	8,000		
17	Allowable losses including losses brought forward	17	£	3,000		
18	Net chargeable gains			box 16 minus box 17	18	£ 5,000
21	**Profits before other deductions and reliefs**			sum of boxes 5, 6, 11 14 & 18	21	£ 130,000

Deductions and Reliefs

24	Management expenses under S75 ICTA 1988	24	£			
30	Trading losses of this or a later accounting period under S393A ICTA 1988	30	£			
31	*Put an 'X' in box 31 if amounts carried back from later Accounting periods are included in box 30*	31				
32	Non-trade capital allowances	32	£			
35	Charges paid	35	£	8,000		
37	**Profits chargeable to corporation tax**			box 21 minus boxes 24, 30, 32 and 35	37	£ 122,000

▷ **ACTIVITY 2**   ▷ ▷ ▷ ▷

Laserjet Ltd (2)

Complete the extract (see below) of the short form CT600 for Laserjet Ltd in Activity 1

Company Tax Calculation

Turnover			
1	Total turnover from trade or profession		1 £

Income			
3	Trading and professional profits	3 £	
4	Trading losses brought forward claimed against profits	4 £	
5	Net trading and professional profits		box 3 minus box 4 5 £
6	Bank, building society or other interest, and profits and gains from non-trading loan relationships		6 £
11	Income from UK land and buildings		11 £
14	Annual profits and gains not falling under any other heading		14 £

Chargeable gains			
16	Gross chargeable gains	16 £	
17	Allowable losses including losses brought forward	17 £	
18	Net chargeable gains		box 16 minus box 17 18 £
21	**Profits before other deductions and reliefs**		sum of boxes 5, 6, 11 14 & 18 21 £

Deductions and Reliefs			
24	Management expenses under S75 ICTA 1988	24 £	
30	Trading losses of this or a later accounting period under S393A ICTA 1988	30 £	
31	*Put an 'X' in box 31 if amounts carried back from later Accounting periods are included in box 30*	31	
32	Non-trade capital allowances	32 £	
35	Charges paid	35 £	
37	**Profits chargeable to corporation tax**		box 21 minus boxes 24, 30, 32 and 35 37 £

[Answer on p. 87]

---

4 | **Test your knowledge** ▷ ▷ ▷

1   The profit and loss account of ABC Ltd includes interest received on an investment in Government securities. How should this be dealt with in the computation of the profits chargeable to corporation tax?

2   DEF Ltd received dividends from another UK company. How should this be dealt with in the computation of the profits chargeable to corporation tax?

3   GHI Ltd made a capital gain on the disposal of shares during 2006 of £60,000. It had capital losses brought forward of £25,000. How much should be included in profits chargeable to corporation tax?

4   How would your answer differ if capital losses brought forward had amounted to £75,000?

[Answers on p. 87]

5 Summary

Make sure you are very familiar with the proforma corporation tax computation.

Setting out your computations as shown in the proforma will help to ensure that your computations and submissions to HM Revenue and Customs (HMRC) are always made in accordance with the current law and take account of current HMRC practice.

The short return CT600 is set out in a similar manner to the proforma.

Answers to chapter activities & 'test your knowledge' questions

△ **ACTIVITY 1**   △ △ △ △

Laserjet Ltd (1)

Corporation tax computation - year ended 31 March 2007

	£
Schedule D Case I (W1)	484,600
Schedule D Case III (W2)	22,000
Schedule A	32,000
	538,600
Less: Charges on income – Gift Aid	(14,000)
PCTCT	524,600

Marks may be awarded for presentation and a clear structured answer creates a good impression with a marker!

Workings

(W1) Schedule D Case I

	£
Adjusted trading profit	500,600
Less: Capital allowances	(16,000)
Schedule D Case 1	484,600

In exam questions take great care not to adjust a profit which has already been adjusted for.

(W2) Schedule D Case III

	£
Building society interest	20,000
Debenture interest	6,000
	26,000
Less: Loan interest payable – rental property (note)	(4,000)
Schedule D Case III	22,000

Note: This is not a Schedule A deduction but has to be dealt with as a 'non-trading' loan.

△ ACTIVITY 2   △ △ △ △

2   Laserjet Ltd (2)

Turnover

1	Total turnover from trade or profession	**1**	£

Income

3	Trading and professional profits	**3**	£ 484,600
4	Trading losses brought forward claimed against profits	**4**	£
5	Net trading and professional profits	**5**	£ 484,600 *box 3 minus box 4*
6	Bank, building society or other interest, and profits and gains from non-trading loan relationships	**6**	£ 22,000
11	Income from UK land and buildings	**11**	£ 32,000
14	Annual profits and gains not falling under any other heading	**14**	£

Chargeable gains

16	Gross chargeable gains	**16**	£
17	Allowable losses including losses brought forward	**17**	£
18	Net chargeable gains	**18**	£ *box 16 minus box 17*

21	**Profits before other deductions and reliefs**	**21**	£ 538,600 *sum of boxes 5, 6, 11 14 & 18*

Deductions and Reliefs

24	Management expenses under S75 ICTA 1988	**24**	£
30	Trading losses of this or a later accounting period under S393A ICTA 1988	**30**	£
31	*Put an 'X' in box 31 if amounts carried back from later Accounting periods are included in box 30*	**31**	
32	Non-trade capital allowances	**32**	£
35	Charges paid	**35**	£ 14,000

37	**Profits chargeable to corporation tax**	**37**	£ 524,600 *box 21 minus boxes 24, 30, 32 and 35*

Test your knowledge △ △ △

1   The interest received will be included in the net profit per the accounts. It therefore needs to be deducted in the adjusted profit computation. It is instead included as Schedule D Case III income.

2   Dividends from another UK company are not included in the computation of the profits chargeable to corporation tax.

3   GHI Ltd would include chargeable gains of £60,000 - £25,000 = £35,000 in profits chargeable to corporation tax.

4   No chargeable gains would be included in profits chargeable to corporation tax as the losses exceed gains by £75,000 - £60,000 = £15,000.

CALCULATION OF CORPORATION TAX LIABILITY

INTRODUCTION

This follows on from the previous chapter. Once the calculation of profits chargeable to corporation tax has been completed, the task will lead on to a calculation of the corporation tax liability.

PERFORMANCE CRITERIA

This chapter covers the following performance criteria:

·   Calculate corporation tax due, taking account of marginal relief (18.4 C)
·   Complete corporation tax returns correctly and submit them, together with relevant claims and elections, within statutory time limits (18.4 G)

1 The corporation tax liability

1.1 Calculating the corporation tax liability

Once you have computed a company's PCTCT, the next stage of the computation is to calculate the corporation tax liability. This is essentially divided into two steps.

· Determining 'profits' (P), a term which is used to determine the tax rates that will apply.

· Applying relevant tax rates to calculate the liability.

Step 1: Determing 'profits'

	£	
PCTCT	X	'I'
Add: Current FII	X	
Profits	X	
		'P'

FII is franked investment income. Current FII is the term used to describe UK dividends received in the current period, grossed up by the tax credit of 100/90.

If you recall from Chapter 6, dividends received by a company are not taxed under corporation tax. However, they are used to determine the tax rate to apply to its other profits. (We still completely ignore dividends paid.)

PCTCT (sometimes labelled 'I' for short) is the profit which is charged to tax, but 'P' is used to determine the rate of tax.

Step 2: Apply the relevant tax rates

The tax calculation is based on two main factors:

· 'Profits' P (from Step 1).
· The Financial Year (FY) which matches the CAP.

A Financial Year (FY) runs from 1 April to the following 31 March.

FY 2006 is the period from 1 April 2006 to 31 March 2007 (note it tells you in which year the period **starts**).

For each FY the following information may be provided:

	FY 2005	FY 2006
Starting rate (SR)	0%	n.a.
Small company rate (SCR)	19%	19%
Ordinary rate (OR)	30%	30%

	FY 2005	FY 2006
	£	£
Starting rate		
- Lower limit	10,000	n.a.
- Upper limit	50,000	n.a.
- Fraction	$^{19}/_{400}$	n.a.
Small company rate		
- Lower limit	300,000	300,000
- Upper limit	1,500,000	1,500,000
- Fraction	$^{11}/_{400}$	$^{11}/_{400}$

Each of the rates will be considered in turn, so that we can eventually see where all of these numbers are used.

2 Rates of corporation tax

2.1 The main rates

As noted above, in FY 2006 the rates of corporation tax are based on the level of profits.

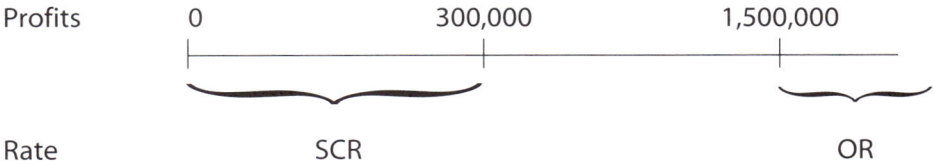

Profits	0	300,000	1,500,000
Rate	SCR		OR

2.2 Small company rate

If a company has profits (P) of up to £300,000 in FY 2006 then 'I' is taxed at 19%.

◦ EXAMPLE ◦ ◦ ◦ ◦

Zachary Ltd has profits chargeable to corporation tax of £148,000 in its year ended 31 March 2007, and dividends received of £4,500.

What is the corporation tax liability?

Solution

	£
PCTCT (I)	148,000
FII (4,500 x $^{100}/_{90}$)	5,000
Profits (P)	153,000

As 'P' is less than £300,000, then 'I' is taxed at 19%.

Corporation tax liability (£148,000 x 19%) = £28,120.

2.3 Ordinary rate

If a company has 'P' of at least £1,500,000 in FY 2006 then 'I' is taxed at 30%.

> ## ○ EXAMPLE ○○○○
>
> Argo Ltd has profits chargeable to corporation tax of £1,450,000 in its year ended 31 March 2007, and dividends received of £72,000.
>
> What is the corporation tax liability?
>
> **Solution**
>
> | | £ |
> |---|---:|
> | PCTCT (I) | 1,450,000 |
> | FII (72,000 x $^{100}/_{90}$) | 80,000 |
> | Profit (P) | 1,530,000 |
>
> As 'P' is at least £1,500,000, then 'I' is taxed at 30%.
>
> Corporation tax liability (1,450,000 x 30%) = £435,000.
>
> 'I' is below the limit of £1,500,000 but this is irrelevant. 'P' determines the tax rate.

2.4 Starting rate

In FY 2000 to FY 2005 a starting rate of tax applied where a company had profits of £10,000 or less. In FY 2005 the starting rate was 0%.

The starting rate does not apply in FY 2006 so that company's with profits of £300,000 or less are taxed at the small company rate of 19%.

Where a company's accounting period falls partly into FY 2005 and partly into FY 2006 (e.g. year ended 31 August 2006) the starting rate of tax may apply. This will be covered in more detail in chapter 8.

> ## ○ EXAMPLE ○○○○
>
> Yolanda Ltd has profits chargeable to corporation tax of £5,000 in its year ended 31 March 2006.
>
> What is the corporation tax liability assuming:
>
> (i) there are no dividends received.
> (ii) dividends received are £900.

Solution

(i) **No dividends received**

The year ended 31 March 2006 falls entirely within FY 2005.

	£
Profits chargeable to CT ('I')	5,000
FII (grossed up dividends received)	Nil
Profit ('P')	5,000

As 'P' is no more than £10,000, 'I' is taxed at 0%.

Corporation tax liability (5,000 x 0%)	£0

(ii) **Dividends received**

	£
Profits chargeable to CT ('I')	5,000
FII (900 x $^{100}/_{90}$)	1,000
Profit ('P')	6,000

As 'P' (£6,000) is no more than £10,000, 'I' is taxed at 0%.

Corporation tax liability (5,000 x 0%)	£0

Note the liability is **not** calculated using 'P' profit.
'P' is only used to determine the tax **rate**.

3 Marginal relief

3.1 The marginal band

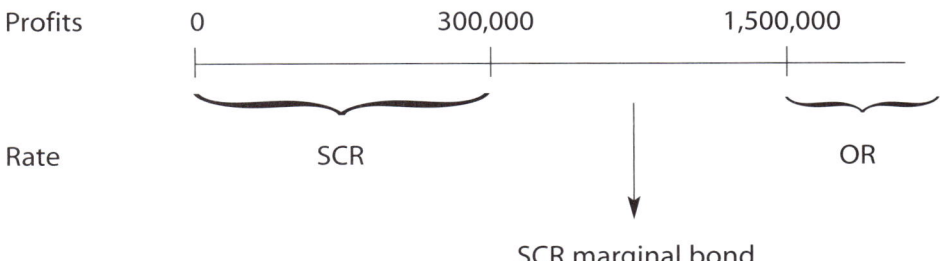

3.2 SCR marginal band

Where a company's profits exceed £300,000, corporation tax is paid at 30%.

Where profits however are between £300,000 and £1,500,000, marginal relief is given, which reduces the actual rate of tax paid to a rate between the small company rate of 19% and the ordinary rate of 30%.

The calculation is made using the next tax rate up (OR), and then making a deduction, as set out below.

	£
PCTCT at ordinary rate (30% in FY 2006)	X
Less: Marginal relief	(X)
Corporation tax liability	X

Marginal relief is found by using the formula:

$$\text{Fraction} \times (M - \text{'P'}) \times \frac{I}{P}$$

where I = PCTCT, M = upper limit, P = profit

As noted in 1.1 above, for the SCR marginal band, the fraction is $^{11}/_{400}$ and M is £1,500,000.

The following examples illustrate the calculation of the corporation tax liability.

○ EXAMPLE ○○○○

Small Ltd has the following PCTCT for the year ended 31 March 2007.

	£
Schedule D Case I	260,000
Schedule A	40,000
	300,000
Less: Gift Aid paid	(10,000)
PCTCT	290,000

What is the corporation tax liability if:

(a) no dividends are received from UK companies?
(b) £9,000 of dividends are received from UK companies?
(c) £45,000 of dividends are received from UK companies?

Solution

(a) **No dividends received**

	£
PCTCT (I)	290,000
FII	Nil
Profits (P)	290,000

Identify the financial year(s) which applies and determine the tax rate.

FY 2006 applies to the year ended 31 March 2007, and therefore to the whole of the accounting period.

'P' is below the lower limit therefore 'I' is taxed at 19%

Corporation tax liability (£290,000 x 19%)	£55,100

(b) **£9,000 dividends received**

	£
PCTCT (I)	290,000
FII (£9,000 x $\frac{100}{90}$)	10,000
Profits (P)	300,000

FY 2006 applies and 'P' is equal to the lower limit therefore 'I' is taxed at 19%.

Corporation tax liability (£290,000 x 19%)	£55,100

The 'profits' level has not altered the decision, the corporation tax liability is as before.

(c) **£45,000 dividends received**

	£
PCTCT (I)	290,000
FII (£45000 x $\frac{100}{90}$)	50,000
Profits (P)	340,000

'P' is above £300,000 but below £1,500,000; marginal relief applies.

	£
£290,000 x 30%	87,000
Less: Marginal relief	
$^{11}/_{400}$ x (£1,500,000 - £340,000) x $\frac{290,000}{340,000}$	(27,209)
Corporation tax liability	59,791

3.3 Starting rate marginal band

Remember that in FY 2005 there was a starting rate of tax, as well as small companies and ordinary rates of tax. In FY 2005 there was also marginal relief where a company's profits were more than £10,000 but no more than £50,000.

In FY 2006 neither the starting rate nor starting rate marginal relief apply.

The calculation for the starting rate (SR) marginal band is similar to that for the small companies rate (SCR) marginal band as follows:

	£
PCTCT at SCR (19% in FY 2005)	X
Less: Marginal relief	(X)
Corporation tax liability	X

The only difference to note here is that PCTCT is first taxed at the small companies rate (SCR) not the ordinary rate (OR).

The calculation of marginal relief is the same as for SCR marginal relief, except that the fraction is $^{19}/_{400}$ and M is £50,000.

○ EXAMPLE ○○○○

Tiny Ltd has PCTCT of £9,000 for the year ended 31 March 2006.

Calculate Tiny Ltd's corporation tax liability assuming that:

(a)   it received no dividends.
(b)   it received dividends of £1,800.

Solution

The year ended 31 March 2006 falls entirely within FY 2005.

(a) **No dividends received**

Tiny Ltd's profits will be subjected to tax at the starting rate of Nil% as they are below £10,000.

The corporation tax liability will therefore be Nil.

(b) **Dividends received**

Tiny Ltd's profits are as follows:

	£
PCTCT (I)	9,000
FII (£1,800 x $^{100}/_{90}$)	2,000
Profits (P)	11,000

As Tiny Ltd's profits fall between £10,000 and £50,000, 'I' will be subjected to corporation tax at the rate of 19%. However, its liability will be reduced by marginal relief.

	£
£9,000 x 19%	1,710
Less: Marginal relief	
$^{19}/_{400}$ x (£50,000 - £11,000) x $\dfrac{9,000}{11,000}$	(1,516)
Corporation tax liability	194

▷ ACTIVITY 1 ▷ ▷ ▷ ▷

Walton Ltd (1)

Walton Ltd's profit and loss account for the year ended 31 March 2007 was as follows:

	£	£
Sales		486,280
Bank interest receivable		2,900
UK dividends received (net of tax credit)		13,365
Profit on the sale of an investment		3,054
		505,599
Allowable trading expenses	109,756	
Disallowable trading expenses	6,344	
Overdraft interest payable	6,000	
		122,100
Net profit		383,499

Capital allowances have been calculated at £4,800. All dividends were received in July 2006. The capital gain on the sale of the investment has been calculated at £1,538.

Required

Calculate Walton Ltd's corporation tax liability for the year ended 31 March 2007.

[Answer on p. 102]

4 Corporation tax return (part 2)

4.1 The return – the calculation of the tax liability

In the previous chapter there was a copy of the short form CT600. We can now complete the tax calculation on the bottom of page 2 and the top of page 3.

The boxes likely to be completed in an assessment are as follows:

Box	Detail
38	Franked investment income – gross amount of dividends received.
39	Number of associated companies in this period – likely to be NIL (see Chapter 8).
40 and 41	See Chapter 8.
42	Check box to indicate if the SR, SCR or marginal relief apply.

Box	Detail
43 – 46	Shows the Financial Year and the level of profits, therefore identifying the relevant rate of tax. Leading to a calculation at 0/19/30%.
53 – 56	See Chapter 8.
64 – 65	Shows the result of the marginal relief calculation.
66 – 69	Will not be used in the assessment.
70	Shows the corporation tax payable. This will be the figure from box 63 or 65.

The only other boxes that will require completion relate to income tax deducted from income received (see Chapter 10) (box 84), payments of corporation tax already made and sub-totals and totals (boxes 86 and 92 or 93).

○ EXAMPLE ○○○○

Small Ltd in the previous example (part (c)) has the following results:

Year ended 31 March 2007	£	Box
PCTCT	290,000	
FII	50,000	38
Profits	340,000	
It has no associated companies		39
PCTCT x 30%	87,000	46
Less Marginal relief		
$^{11}/_{400}$ x (1,500,000 – 340,000) x $\dfrac{290,000}{340,000}$	(27,209)	64
Corporation tax liability	59,791	65, 70 etc

Complete the tax calculation on Form CT600.

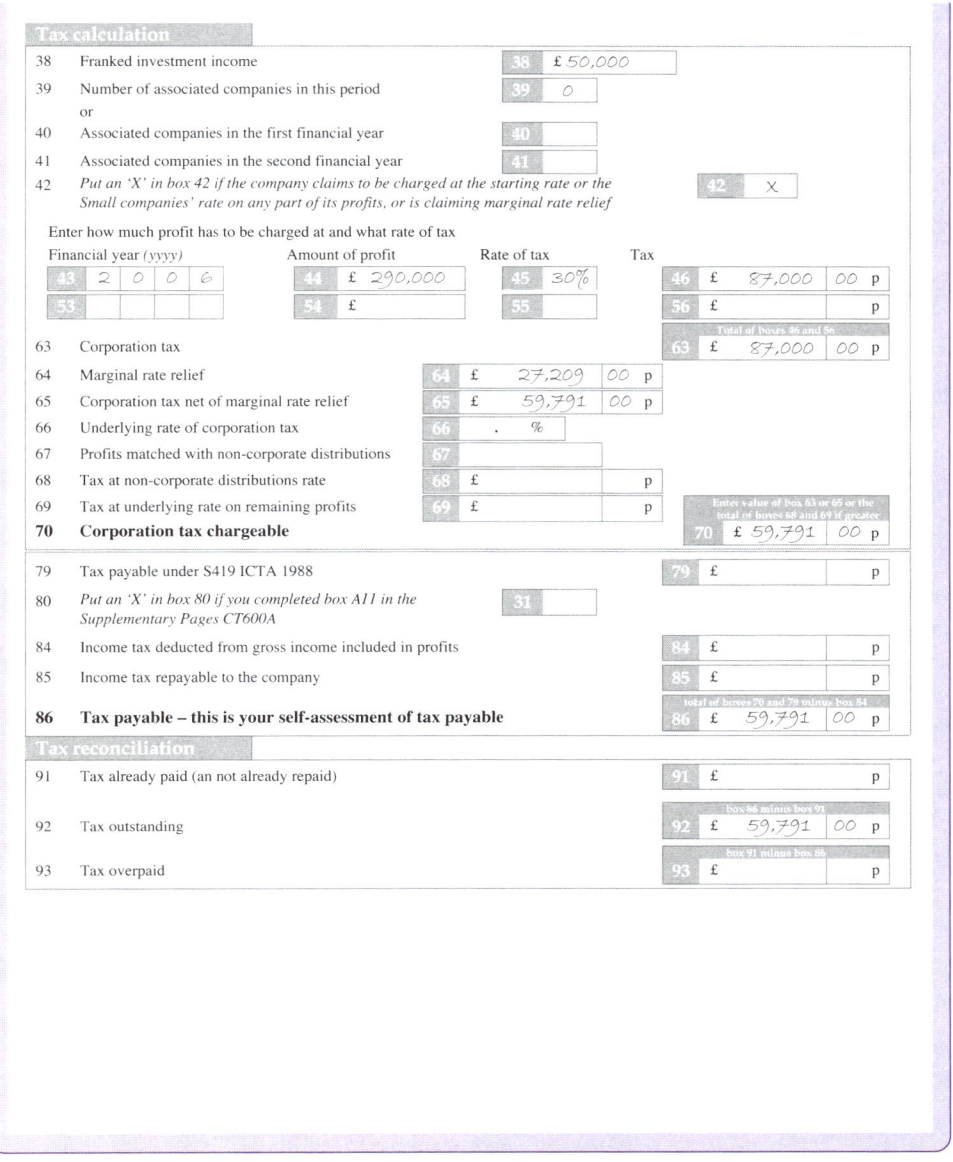

Tax calculation

38	Franked investment income	38 £ 50,000
39	Number of associated companies in this period	39 0
	or	
40	Associated companies in the first financial year	40
41	Associated companies in the second financial year	41
42	*Put an 'X' in box 42 if the company claims to be charged at the starting rate or the Small companies' rate on any part of its profits, or is claiming marginal rate relief*	42 X

Enter how much profit has to be charged at and what rate of tax

Financial year *(yyyy)*	Amount of profit	Rate of tax	Tax
43 2 0 0 6	44 £ 290,000	45 30%	46 £ 87,000 00 p
53	54 £	55	56 £ p

		Total of boxes 46 and 56
63	Corporation tax	63 £ 87,000 00 p
64	Marginal rate relief	64 £ 27,209 00 p
65	Corporation tax net of marginal rate relief	65 £ 59,791 00 p
66	Underlying rate of corporation tax	66 . %
67	Profits matched with non-corporate distributions	67
68	Tax at non-corporate distributions rate	68 £ p
69	Tax at underlying rate on remaining profits	69 £ p
70	**Corporation tax chargeable**	Enter value of box 63 or 65 or the total of boxes 68 and 69 if greater 70 £ 59,791 00 p

79	Tax payable under S419 ICTA 1988	79 £ p
80	*Put an 'X' in box 80 if you completed box A11 in the Supplementary Pages CT600A*	31
84	Income tax deducted from gross income included in profits	84 £ p
85	Income tax repayable to the company	85 £ p
86	**Tax payable – this is your self-assessment of tax payable**	total of boxes 70 and 79 minus box 84 86 £ 59,791 00 p

Tax reconciliation

91	Tax already paid (an not already repaid)	91 £ p
92	Tax outstanding	box 86 minus box 91 92 £ 59,791 00 p
93	Tax overpaid	box 91 minus box 86 93 £ p

▷ ACTIVITY 2   ▷ ▷ ▷ ▷

Walton Ltd (2)

Complete the tax calculation on the short Form CT600 (see below) for Activity 1.

Tax calculation

38	Franked investment income	38 £	
39	Number of associated companies in this period	39	
	or		
40	Associated companies in the first financial year	40	
41	Associated companies in the second financial year	41	
42	*Put an 'X' in box 42 if the company claims to be charged at the starting rate or the Small companies' rate on any part of its profits, or is claiming marginal rate relief*	42	

Enter how much profit has to be charged at and what rate of tax

Financial year *(yyyy)*	Amount of profit	Rate of tax	Tax
43	44 £	45	46 £ ___ p
53	54 £	55	56 £ ___ p

Total of boxes 46 and 56

63	Corporation tax	63 £ ___ p	
64	Marginal rate relief	64 £ ___ p	
65	Corporation tax net of marginal rate relief	65 £ ___ p	
66	Underlying rate of corporation tax	66 . %	
67	Profits matched with non-corporate distributions	67	
68	Tax at non-corporate distributions rate	68 £ ___ p	
69	Tax at underlying rate on remaining profits	69 £ ___ p	
70	**Corporation tax chargeable**	Enter value of box 63 or 65 or the total of boxes 68 and 69 if greater 70 £ ___ p	

79	Tax payable under S419 ICTA 1988	79 £ ___ p	
80	*Put an 'X' in box 80 if you completed box A11 in the Supplementary Pages CT600A*	31	
84	Income tax deducted from gross income included in profits	84 £ ___ p	
85	Income tax repayable to the company	85 £ ___ p	
86	**Tax payable – this is your self-assessment of tax payable**	total of boxes 70 and 79 minus box 84 86 £ ___ p	

Tax reconciliation

91	Tax already paid (an not already repaid)	91 £ ___ p	
92	Tax outstanding	box 86 minus box 91 92 £ ___ p	
93	Tax overpaid	box 91 minus box 86 93 £ ___ p	

5   Test your knowledge ▷ ▷ ▷

1   What is the ordinary rate of corporation tax?

2   When will a company be entitled to small companies marginal relief?

3   What is the formula for calculating small companies marginal relief?

[Answers on p. 104]

6 Summary

There are two main rates of corporation tax in FY 2006:

· Small company's rate 19%
· Ordinary rate 30%

In FY 2005 a starting rate of 0% also applied.

Between these rates there are marginal bands to gradually move between the rates.

The rate applying in a Financial Year is determined by:
· Profits

but the rate is applied to:
· PCTCT

Answers to chapter activities & 'test your knowledge' questions

△ ACTIVITY 1   △ △ △ △

Walton Ltd (1)

Corporation tax computation - year ended 31 March 2007

	£
Schedule D Case I (W1 and W2)	365,724
Schedule D Case III	2,900
Chargeable gains	1,538
PCTCT	370,162
Corporation tax liability (W3)	81,569

Workings

(W1) Schedule D Case I

	£
Adjusted profit (W2)	370,524
Less: Capital allowances	(4,800)
Schedule D Case I	365,724

(W2) Adjustment of profit

	£
Net profit	383,499
Add: Disallowable expenses	6,344
Less: Bank interest receivable	(2,900)
UK dividends (net)	(13,365)
Profit on sale of investment	(3,054)
Adjusted profit	370,524

(W3) Corporation tax liability

	£
PCTCT (I)	370,162
FII (£13,365 x $^{100}/_{90}$)	14,850
Profits (P)	385,012

- FY 2006 applies to the year ended 31 March 2007.
- 'P' is above the lower limit of £300,000; marginal relief applies.

	£
£370,162 x 30%	111,049
Less: Marginal relief	
$^{11}/_{400}$ x (£1,500,000 - £385,012) x $\dfrac{370,162}{385,012}$	(29,480)
Corporation tax liability	81,569

△ ACTIVITY 2

Walton Ltd (2)

Tax calculation

38	Franked investment income	**38** £ 14,850	
39	Number of associated companies in this period	**39** 0	
	or		
40	Associated companies in the first financial year	**40**	
41	Associated companies in the second financial year	**41**	
42	Put an 'X' in box 42 if the company claims to be charged at the starting rate or the Small companies' rate on any part of its profits, or is claiming marginal rate relief		**42** X

Enter how much profit has to be charged at and what rate of tax

Financial year (yyyy)	Amount of profit	Rate of tax	Tax	
43 2 0 0 6	**44** £ 370,162	**45** 30%	**46** £ 111,049	00 p
53	**54** £	**55**	**56** £	p
			Total of boxes 46 and 56	
63 Corporation tax			**63** £ 111,049	00 p

64	Marginal rate relief	**64** £ 29,480 00 p		
65	Corporation tax net of marginal rate relief	**65** £ 81,569 00 p		
66	Underlying rate of corporation tax	**66** % .		
67	Profits matched with non-corporate distributions	**67**		
68	Tax at non-corporate distributions rate	**68** £ p		
69	Tax at underlying rate on remaining profits	**69** £ p	Enter value of box 63 or 65 or the total of boxes 68 and 69 if greater	
70	**Corporation tax chargeable**		**70** £ 81,569	00 p

79	Tax payable under S419 ICTA 1988	**79** £ p	
80	Put an 'X' in box 80 if you completed box A11 in the Supplementary Pages CT600A	**80**	
84	Income tax deducted from gross income included in profits	**84** £ p	
85	Income tax repayable to the company	**85** £ p	
		total of boxes 70 and 79 minus box 84	
86	**Tax payable – this is your self-assessment of tax payable**	**86** £ 81,569	00 p

Tax reconciliation

91	Tax already paid (an not already repaid)	**91** £ p	
		box 86 minus box 91	
92	Tax outstanding	**92** £ 81,569	00 p
		box 91 minus box 86	
93	Tax overpaid	**93** £ p	

Test your knowledge

1   The ordinary rate of corporation tax is 30%

2   A company is entitled to small companies marginal relief if its profits fall
    between the lower and upper limits of £300,000 and £1,500,000.

3   The formula for calculating small companies marginal relief is:

Fraction x $(M - 'P') \times \dfrac{I}{P}$

where I = PCTCT, M = upper limit, P = profit

The fraction is $^{11}/_{400}$ and M is £1,500,000.

KAPLAN PUBLISHING

CORPORATION TAX
– SPECIAL SCENARIOS

INTRODUCTION

There are a number of different issues that could make the calculation of corporation tax slightly more complex. These include short and long accounting periods and accounting periods which straddle 31 March, as well as the effect of associated companies. These issues are considered in this chapter.

CONTENTS

1 Associated companies
2 Short accounting periods
3 Non 31 March year ends
4 Long periods of account

PERFORMANCE CRITERIA

This chapter covers the following performance criteria:
· Enter adjusted trading profits and losses, capital allowances, investment income and capital gains in the corporation tax computation (18.4 A)
· Calculate corporation tax due, taking account of marginal relief (18.4 C)
· Complete corporation tax returns correctly and submit them, together with relevant claims and elections, within statutory time limits (18.4 G)

1   Associated companies

1.1   The principle of associated companies

Two companies are associated if:

· one controls the other; or

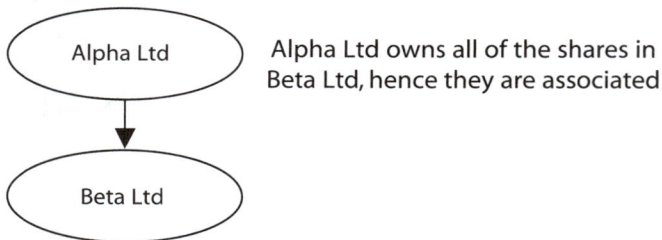

Alpha Ltd owns all of the shares in Beta Ltd, hence they are associated

· both are controlled by the same person(s):

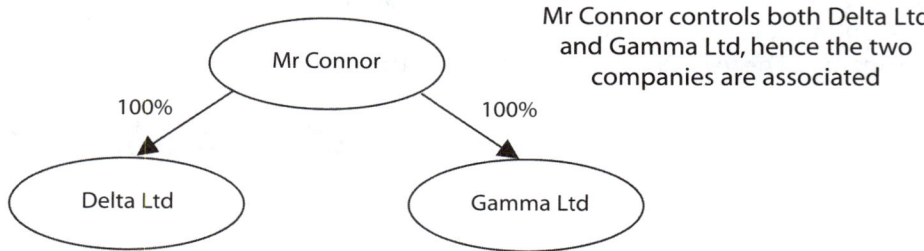

Mr Connor controls both Delta Ltd and Gamma Ltd, hence the two companies are associated

· combining both of these rules:

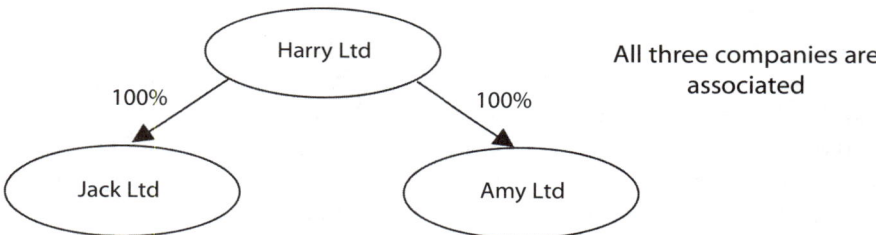

All three companies are associated

Essentially control means that more than 50% of the shares are owned by a 'person'.

1.2   The effect of being associated companies

The profit limits for corporation tax rates are divided by the total number of associated companies.

Hence, for the Harry Ltd group of companies shown in 1.1 above, each company will have profit limits of:

· £1,500,000 ÷ 3   =   £500,000
· £300,000 ÷ 3   =   £100,000

O **EXAMPLE**   O O O O

Andrew Ltd has one wholly owned subsidiary, Beckham Ltd (i.e. Andrew Ltd owns 100% of the shares in Beckham Ltd). Andrew Ltd has the following results for its year ended 31 March 2007:

	£
Adjusted trading profit	600,000
Schedule A – rental profits	100,000
Schedule D III – bank interest	30,000
Dividends received	27,000

Calculate the corporation tax liability of Andrew Ltd for its year ended 31 March 2007.

Solution

Step 1: Calculate PCTCT and profits.

Andrew Ltd
Corporation tax computation – year ended 31 March 2007

	£
Schedule D I	600,000
Schedule A	100,000
Schedule D III	30,000
PCTCT	730,000
PCTCT (I)	730,000
FII (27,000 x $^{100}/_{90}$)	30,000
Profits (P)	760,000

Step 2: Draw a diagram of the group. Identify the associated companies.

Andrews Ltd

100%   2 associated companies

Beckham Ltd

Step 3: Calculate the profit limits and identify the relevant tax rate for Andrew Ltd.

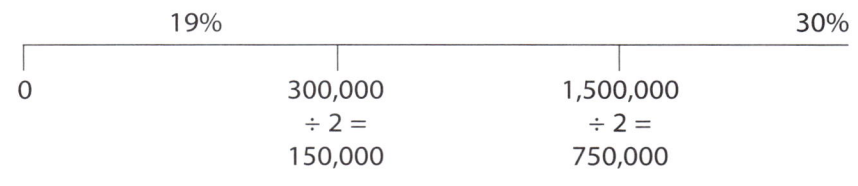

19%		30%
0	300,000	1,500,000
	÷ 2 =	÷ 2 =
	150,000	750,000

As profits are more than £750,000, PCTCT is taxed at the full rate of 30%.

Step 4:   Apply the tax rate to PCTCT (not 'profits').

PCTCT x 30%

Corporation tax liability (£730,000 x 30%) = £219,000

2   Short accounting periods

2.1   Changing the profit limits

Short accounting periods (i.e. those of less than 12 months) can have an impact on the calculation of the corporation tax liability. This is because the lower and upper limits are annual limits and have to be time apportioned to match the length of the accounting period.

○ **EXAMPLE**   ○○○○

June Ltd had a nine month accounting period to 31 March 2007. It received a dividend of £9,000 and its PCTCT was £290,000.

What is June Ltd's corporation tax liability for the period to 31 March 2007?

Solution

Step 1: Calculate profits and compare to limits

	£
PCTCT (I)	290,000
FII	10,000
Profits (P)	300,000

FY 2006 applies, but to a nine month period therefore:

Lower limit = $^9/_{12}$ x £300,000	225,000
Upper limit = $^9/_{12}$ x £1,500,000	1,125,000

'P' is *between* the limits therefore marginal relief applies.

Step 2: Calculate the tax liability

	£
£290,000 x 30%	87,000
Less: Marginal relief	
$^{11}/_{400}$ x (£1,125,000 - £300,000) x $\dfrac{290,000}{300,000}$	(21,931)
Corporation tax liability	65,069

Make sure you calculate tax on PCTCT not on 'P' – an easy mistake to make. Note that 'M' in the formula is the time apportioned upper limit.

---

3 Non 31 March year ends

3.1 The principle of different Financial Years and tax rates

Many companies do not have CAPs which fall neatly into a Financial Year.

A company with a year end of 31 December 2006 is affected as follows:

- three months of the year falls in FY 2005
- nine months of the year falls in FY 2006

The following rates apply:

	FY 2005 1 January 2006 – 31 March 2006	FY 2006 1 April 2006 – 31 December 2006
Starting rate	0%	n.a.
Small company rate	19%	19%
Ordinary rate	30%	30%
SR Fraction	$\dfrac{19}{400}$	n.a.
Lower limit	£10,000	n.a.
Upper limit	£50,000	n.a.
SCR fraction	$\dfrac{11}{400}$	$\dfrac{11}{400}$
Lower limit	£300,000	£300,000
Upper limit	£1,500,000	£1,500,000

As the corporation tax rates change from FY 2005 to FY 2006, it is necessary to time apportion the PCTCT and 'P' and compute the corporation tax for each Financial Year separately as follows:

Step 1

Determine 'P' as before, compare to the limits and decide the level of tax (i.e. starting rate, small, ordinary, marginal).

Step 2

Time apportion PCTCT between the Financial Years and proceed as before, taking the number of months into account.

If profits for the year to 31 December 2006 are below £10,000:

$PCTCT \times 0\% \times \dfrac{3}{12}$ FY 2005

$PCTCT \times 19\% \times \dfrac{9}{12}$ FY 2006

Note that where there is no change in the rates and limits between Financial Years there would be no need to time apportion.

For example, there is no change in the small company rates and limits between FY 2005 and FY 2006. Therefore for a company with a 31 December 2006 year end with profits in the small company's rate band, there would be no need to time apportion the profits between the Financial Years as the tax rates and limits are the same (i.e. 19%).

If that situation arises in an assessment task (i.e. Financial Years 'straddle' 31 March without a change of rates) you should explain briefly why you have not split up the calculation.

Although the corporation tax return form provides space to split the calculation over two Financial Years, it is acceptable not to split the calculation on the form if the rates have not changed over the two years. We will, however, show the split entries for completeness.

○ EXAMPLE ○ ○ ○ ○

Marginal Ltd had PCTCT of £295,000 for the year ended 30 September 2006 and received a dividend of £32,400 on 15 May 2006.

Calculate Marginal Ltd's corporation tax liability for inclusion on the corporation tax return form.

Solution

	Year ended 30 September 2006 £
PCTCT (I)	295,000
FII (32,400 x $^{100}/_{90}$)	36,000
Profits (P)	331,000

Therefore, marginal relief applies.

Calculate the tax for each Financial Year separately

	6m FY 2005 £	6m FY 2006 £	Total £
PCTCT	147,500	147,500	
Tax @ 30%	44,250	44,250	88,500
Marginal relief:			
FY 2005 $^{11}/_{400}$ x (1,500,000 - £331,000) x $\frac{295,000}{331,000}$ x $^{6}/_{12}$	(14,326)		
			(28,652)
FY 2006 $^{11}/_{400}$ x (1,500,000 - £331,000) x $\frac{295,000}{331,000}$ x $^{6}/_{12}$		(14,326)	
Corporation tax liability	29,924	29,924	59,848

4 Long periods of account

4.1 Impact on the corporation tax computation

In Chapter 2 you learned that, although a company can draw up financial accounts for a period of more than 12 months, a company's 'chargeable accounting period' (CAP) for corporation tax purposes can never exceed 12 months.

Therefore, if the financial accounts cover more than 12 months, two chargeable accounting periods are required; one for the first 12 months and one for the balance. This section tackles the allocation of income, chargeable gains and charges on income between the two periods in finding PCTCT.

Item	Method of allocation
Trading income before deducting capital allowances	Time apportioned
Capital allowances accounting period (see Chapters 4 and 5)	Separate computation for each CAP
Schedule A	Time apportioned
Schedule D Case III	Period for which accrued
Chargeable gains	Period of disposal
Charges (e.g. Gift Aid)	Period in which paid

Do not miscalculate the number of months in the second period – double check it – as it is crucial for time apportioning calculations and easy to get wrong.

> ## ○ EXAMPLE   ○○○○
>
> Printer Ltd has prepared accounts for the 17 months to 30 June 2006, with the following information.
>
> | | £ |
> |---|---|
> | *Adjusted trading profit before capital allowances* | 365,000 |
> | *Building society interest* | |
> | Received 30 April 2005 (of which £1,950 related to year ended 31 Jan 2005) | 2,450 |
> | Received 30 April 2006 | 2,675 |
> | Accrued on 30 June 2006 | 200 |
> | *Rents from property* | 26,010 |
> | *Chargeable gains* | |
> | Disposal on 31 January 2006 | 28,700 |
> | Disposal on 1 February 2006 | 49,760 |
> | *Dividend received from UK company (gross amount) on 1 December 2005* | 10,000 |
> | *Gift Aid paid* | |
> | Paid 31 July 2005 | 6,000 |
> | Paid 31 January 2006 | 6,000 |

Capital allowances for the two CAPs derived from the 17 month period of account are £20,000 and £6,250 respectively.

Show how the company's period of account will be divided into CAPs and compute the PCTCT for each CAP assuming, where relevant, that all income is deemed to accrue evenly.

Solution

The procedure to be followed is exactly the same as for a 12 month period, but incorporating the allocation rules.

	12 months to 31 January 2006 £	5 months to 30 June 2006 £
Schedule D Case I (W1)	237,647	101,103
Schedule D Case III (W2)	2,382	993
Schedule A (W3)	18,360	7,650
Chargeable gains	28,700	49,760
	287,089	159,506
Less: Charges on income (W4)	(12,000)	Nil
PCTCT	275,089	159,506

Note: The dividend received is not relevant for PCTCT. The chargeable gains are allocated according to the date of the transaction.

Workings

(W1)   Schedule D Case I

	Total £	12m £	5m £
Adjusted profit (see note)	365,000	257,647	107,353
Capital allowances		(20,000)	(6,250)
Schedule D Case I		237,647	101,103

Note: Trading profit is time apportioned.

(W2) Building society interest

The amount which would be included in the profit and loss account for the 17 month period on the accruals basis would be as follows:

		Total £	12m £	5m £
Received	30 April 2005	2,450		
	30 April 2006	2,675		
Add	Year end accrual	200		
Less	Opening accrual	(1,950)		
(See note)		3,375	2,382	993

Note: The total is then time apportioned as the accrual at 31 January 2006 is not supplied.

(W3) **Schedule A**

Rental income is assessable under Schedule A, which is assessed on an accrued basis for the 17 months and then time apportioned into the two CAPs.

	Total £	12m £	5m £
Schedule A	26,010	18,360	7,650

(W4) **Charges on income**

	£
31 July 2005	6,000
31 January 2006	6,000
	12,000 in year ended 31 January 2006

Nil in 5 months to 30 June 2006 as none paid.

The procedure for finding the corporation tax liability now follows the rules outlined earlier, except that you have *two* calculations.

The point to watch, however, is that as the second computation is the 'balance' of the accounts it will always be a *short* period. The limits of £300,000 and £1,500,000 therefore need to be reduced proportionately when considering the tax rate to apply.

○ EXAMPLE   ○ ○ ○ ○

Calculate the corporation tax liability for Printer Ltd for its two chargeable accounting periods.

Solution

Step 1: Calculation profits

	12 months to 31 January 2006 £	5 months to 30 June 2006 £
PCTCT (as above)	275,089	159,506
FII (received December 2005)	10,000	-
'Profits'	285,089	159,506

Step 2: Compare with the limits for the appropriate Financial Years

	FY 2004 2 months	FY2005 10 months	FY2005 2 months	FY2006 3 months
Lower limit (annual) £300,000: $(^5/_{12})$		£300,000 small rate		£125,000 marginal
Upper limit £1,500,000 x $(^5/_{12})$				£625,000
Rates to apply	19%	19%	30%	30%

Step 3: Calculate the corporate tax liability

12 months to 31 Jan 2006

	£
Corporation tax liability (£275,089 x 19%)	52,267

5 months to 30 June 2006

	£
(£159,506 x 30%)	47,852
Less: Marginal relief	
$^{11}/_{400}$ x (£625,000 - £159,506)	(12,801)
Corporation tax liability	35,051

As you can see, it is possible to have different tax rates applying even though the information is generated from the same set of accounts.

▷ ACTIVITY 1

Chinny

Chinny Ltd has for many years prepared accounts to 30 September, but changes its accounting date to 31 December by preparing accounts for the 15 months ended 31 December 2006. The accounts show a profit, as adjusted for tax purposes (but before deducting capital allowances), of £250,000.

Capital allowances for the two CAPs based on the 15 month period of account were £13,450 and £5,818 respectively.

The company also had income in the period as follows:

		£
Building society interest receivable	1 October 2005 – 30 September 2006	4,420
	1 October 2006 – 31 December 2006	780
Capital gains	Disposal 15 December 2006	55,000
Rents received	31 July 2006	8,000

The rents accrued at 30 September 2005 and 31 December 2006 were £3,000 and £5,000 respectively.

Required
Calculate the amounts of corporation tax payable for this 15 month period of account.

Approach to the question

The approach is exactly the same as developed previously, except that you are preparing two computations. You first need to check in any question whether the accounts provided exceed 12 months and determine the CAPs needed.

[Answer on p. 116]

5 Test your knowledge ▷ ▷ ▷

1   What are the small companies limits for a company with two associated companies?

2   How would your answer differ if the CAP were 9 months long?

3   If a company has an accounting period of longer than 15 months, the Schedule D Case I profits are time apportioned. True or False?

4   If a CAP straddles two financial years you should use the corporation tax rates for the year in which the company's CAP ends. True or False?

[Answers on p. 117]

6   Summary

If the CAP is less than 12 months long and/or there are associated companies, the small companies limits must be apportioned. If marginal relief applies, M in the formula is the adjusted upper limit.

If you are given more than a 12 month period of account, the first step is to split it into the two CAPs and compile the two separate PCTCT/profits figures using the apportioning rules.

Each CAP is then dealt with separately.

If a CAP straddles 31 March, PCTCT and FII are time apportioned into the two Financial Years for calculating the tax. There is, however, only one amount of CT payable – it is merely calculated in two parts.

Answers to chapter activities & 'test your knowledge' questions

△ ACTIVITY 1   △ △ △ △

Chinny

Corporation tax computations

	Year ended 30 September 2006 £	3 months to 31 December 2006 £
Schedule D Case I (W1)	186,550	44,182
Schedule D Case III	4,420	780
Schedule A (W2)	8,000	2,000
Chargeable gains	-	55,000
PCTCT	198,970	101,962
CT liability (W3)	37,804	23,080

Workings

(W1) Schedule D Case I

	Year ended 30 September 2006 £	3 months to 31 December 2006 £
Trading profits time apportioned (12:3)	200,000	50,000
Less:Capital allowances	(13,450)	(5,818)
Schedule D Case I	186,550	44,182

(W2) Schedule A

Rent receivable for 15 months: 8,000 – 3,000 + 5,000 = £10,000

	Year ended 30 September 2006 £	3 months to 31 December 2006 £
Time apportioned (12:3)	8,000	2,000

(W3) Corporation tax liabilities

		Year ended 30 September 2006 £	3 months to 31 December 2006 £
1	PCTCT and 'P' (as there are no dividends)	£198,970	£101,962

2	Financial years	FY 2005 6M	FY 2006 6M	FY 2006 6M
	Lower limit Annual		£300,000	
	Three months ($£300,000 \times {}^3/_{12}$)			£75,000

KAPLAN PUBLISHING

Upper limit	Annual	£1,500,000	
	Three months		
	($£1,500,000 \times {}^3/_{12}$)		£375,000
	Decision	Small rate	Marginal relief

3	Apply rates	FY 2005 and FY 2006	FY 2006
		19%	30%

4 Calculate liabilities

	Year ended 30 September 2006 £	3 months to 31 December 2006 £
PCTCT	198,970	101,962
(£198,970 x 19%)	37,804	
(£101,962 x 30%)		30,589
Less: Marginal relief		
$^{11}/_{400}$ x (£375,000 – £101,962)		(7,509)
Corporation tax liability		23,080

Test your knowledge △ △ △

1 As a company has two associated companies, there are three companies in the group. The limits must therefore be divided by three, and are:

Lower limit (£300,000 x 1/3) = £100,000
Upper limit (£1,500,000 x 1/3) = £500,000

2 The limits must be further scaled down for a short CAP and are:
Lower limit (£100,000 x 9/12) = £75,000
Upper limit (£500,000 x 9/12) = £375,000

3 False. The adjusted trading profits before capital allowances are time apportioned. But the capital allowances are computed separately for each period and deducted to give the Schedule D Case I profits.

4 False. The PCTCT and profits are apportioned between the underlying financial years and the relevant rate applied to each part separately.

RELIEF FOR COMPANY LOSSES

INTRODUCTION

This chapter covers the various reliefs available for losses within a company. This could form part of a written or computational task.

CONTENTS

1   Trading losses
2   Non-trading losses

PERFORMANCE CRITERIA

This chapter covers the following performance criteria:

·   Enter adjusted trading profits and losses, capital allowances, investment income and capital gains in the corporation tax computation (18.4 A)
·   Set off and deduct loss reliefs and charges correctly (18.4 B)

1 Trading losses

1.1 Adjusted trading losses

In Chapter 3 we considered how to calculate an adjusted trading profit. An adjusted trading loss is computed in the same way. However, when a company makes an adjusted trading loss, its Schedule D Case I assessment for the accounting period is nil.

○ EXAMPLE ○○○○

Carlos Ltd has had the following results for its year ended 31 March 2007:

	£	£
Gross profit		30,000
Less: Expenditure		
Depreciation	5,000	
Allowable costs	12,000	
		(17,000)
Net profit per accounts		13,000

The capital allowances for the year amount to £21,000.

Calculate the adjusted trading profit/(loss) for the year.

Solution

Step 1: Set up an adjustment of profits proforma as in Chapter 3.

Step 2: Calculate the adjusted trading profit/(loss)

Work through the profit and loss account line by line as previously to calculate the adjusted trading profit/(loss).

Carlos Ltd
Adjustment of profit/(loss) – year ended 31 March 2007

	£
Net profit per accounts	13,000
Add: Disallowable expenses	
Depreciation	5,000
	18,000
Less: Capital allowances	(21,000)
Adjusted trading loss	(3,000)
Schedule D Case I assessment	Nil

The Schedule D Case I to be entered onto the proforma corporation tax computation is nil.

The accounts may show a net **loss** to be adjusted. If this is the case, adding disallowable expenses will REDUCE the loss.

○ EXAMPLE ○○○○

If Carlos Ltd in the previous example had a net loss per accounts of, say, (£10,000), calculate the adjusted trading loss.

Solution

	£
Net loss per accounts	(10,000)
Add: Depreciation	5,000
	(5,000)
Less: Capital allowances	(21,000)
Adjusted trading loss	(26,000)

1.2   Summary of loss reliefs

There are three forms of relief available to a company which makes a trading loss:

· Current year relief
· Carry back relief
· Carry forward relief

1.3   Current year relief - S393A(1)(a) ICTA 1988

A trading loss can be relieved against total profits of the loss making accounting period. The set off is against profits before the deduction of charges on income.

A claim for current year (or carry back) relief must be made within two years of the end of the loss making accounting period.

The statutory reference for current year relief is S393A(1)(a) ICTA 1988. This is one of the few references that is worth learning and using as a label in your answers. It is not required in the assessment, but is a useful label to use.

○ EXAMPLE ○○○○

Sage Ltd had the following results for the year ended 31 March 2007.

	£
Adjusted trading loss	(40,000)
Schedule A	10,000
Chargeable gain	50,000
Gift Aid	10,000

Show how relief would be obtained for the loss under S393A(1)(a) in the current period.

Approach to the example

It is *essential* once a loss has been identified to set up a loss memorandum as a working and allocate the loss to it, so that the method of relief for the loss can be clearly illustrated.

Even where there is a Schedule D Case I loss, this does not alter the basic approach.

·   Present the CT computation in the standard proforma.
·   Support it with workings (one of which will be the loss memorandum).

Solution

Sage Ltd - Corporation tax computation - y/e 31 March 2007

	£
Schedule D Case I	Nil
Schedule A	10,000
Gains	50,000
Total profits (before charges)	60,000
S393A(1)(a) relief	(40,000)
	20,000
Less: Charges on income	(10,000)
PCTCT	10,000

Working

(W1) Loss memorandum

	£
Year ended 31 March 2007	
Current period loss	(40,000)
Relieved in current period	40,000
Loss c/f	Nil

Setting off the loss before the deduction of charges may result in the charges on income becoming unrelieved. Excess charges are lost.

○ **EXAMPLE**   ○○○○

What if Sage Ltd in the previous example made a loss of £60,000?

Solution

	£
Total profits before charges (as before)	60,000
S393A(1)(a) current relief	(60,000)
	Nil
Less Charges on income	(10,000)
PCTCT	Nil

The charges on income are unrelieved. They have become excess charges (i.e. not used) as there are insufficient profits to set them against.

It is an important principle in the use of most loss reliefs that, where there is an available loss, no restriction in set off is permitted. This means that it would *not* have been possible here to restrict the loss relief to (£50,000) so as to then relieve charges of (£10,000), and find an alternative use for the remaining (£10,000) loss.

Excess charges on income (i.e. Gift Aid donations) cannot be carried forward or back and are therefore wasted.

In exam answers you should highlight the fact that the charges are wasted even if not specifically asked to do so.

1.4   Carry back relief – S393A(1)(b) ICTA 1988

A Schedule D Case I loss may be carried back for relief, but only *after* the loss has first been relieved against any available current period profits.

The loss is set off against total profits *before* deducting Gift Aid. In other words, the order in which the loss is applied is as follows:

· First, against total profits of the current year (*before* Gift Aid).
· Second, against total profits of the previous 12 months (again, *before* the deduction of Gift Aid).

The correct statutory reference for the carry back relief is S393A(1)(b) ICTA 1988 and this is a useful label to show in your answer, although this is not required in the assessment.

Approach to losses questions

A question utilising company losses often involves several years and a methodical approach is therefore important.

· Lay out the years side by side in a table, leaving space to insert any loss reliefs.

· Keep a separate working for the trading loss – the memorandum.

· Firstly set the loss against the total profits (before Gift Aid) of the year of loss.

· Then carry the balance of the loss back against total profits (before Gift Aid) of the previous 12 months.

· State whether there is any unrelieved loss remaining.

· Keep a running tally in the loss memorandum working.

Here is a suitable proforma to use for layout, the loss being incurred in 2007.

Proforma corporation tax loss computation	*2006*	*2007*
	£	*£*
Schedule D Case I	X	Nil
Schedule D Case III	X	X
Schedule A	X	X
Chargeable gains	X	X
Total profits	X	X
Current period loss relief – S393A(1)(a)		(X)
Carry back loss relief – S393A(1)(b)	(X)	
	X	Nil
Charges on income	(X)	Wasted
PCTCT	X/Nil	Nil

Loss memorandum:

	£
Current year loss (2007)	X
Current year relief	(X)
Carry back relief	(X)
Loss still available	X

O **EXAMPLE**   O O O O

Marjoram Ltd has the following results for the three accounting periods to 31 March 2007.

Year ended 31 March	2005	2006	2007
	£	£	£
Trading profits/(loss)	11,000	9,000	(45,000)
Building society interest	500	500	500
Chargeable gains	-	-	4,000
Gift Aid payment (gross)	250	250	250

Required

Show the profits chargeable to corporation tax for all periods affected, assuming that loss relief is taken as soon as possible.

Solution

Marjoram Ltd
Corporation tax computations

Year ended 31 March	2006	2007
	£	£
Schedule D Case I	9,000	Nil
Schedule D Case III	500	500
Chargeable gain	Nil	4,000
Total profits	9,500	4,500
S393(A)(1)(a) current loss relief (W1)		(4,500)
S393A(1)(b) carry back relief (W1)	(9,500)	
	Nil	Nil
Gift Aid payment	Wasted	Wasted
PCTCT	Nil	Nil

Loss working

	£
Loss at year ended 31 March 2007	45,000
S393A(1)(a) current relief	(4,500)
	40,500
S393A(1)(b) carry back 12 months	(9,500)
Loss still available at 1 April 2007	31,000

Note: The year ended 31 March 2005 is not affected; the loss cannot be carried back that far.

▷ ACTIVITY 1 ▷▷▷▷

Alfred Ball Ltd

The following are the profits of Alfred Ball Ltd which commenced trading on 1 January 1991.

Year ended 31 December	2004	2005	2006
	£	£	£
Adjusted trading profit (loss)	42,000	19,000	(67,000)
Bank interest received	3,000	2,000	1,000
Chargeable gains	4,000	4,000	4,000
Gift Aid paid	10,000	10,000	-

Required

Calculate the profits chargeable to corporation tax for all of the accounting periods shown above, clearly indicating how you would deal with the trading loss to obtain relief as soon as possible.

Approach to the question

Ensure that you follow the procedure.
· Set up CT proformas in columnar format for each relevant period.
· Leave spaces at the appropriate points to slot in the loss reliefs.
· Set up a working sheet and open up a loss memorandum.
· Determine the reliefs available and update the proforma and memorandum accordingly.

[Answers on p. 132]

1.5   Carry forward relief - S393(1) ICTA 1988

Where any loss remains unrelieved after the current year and carry back claims have been made, the carry forward relief is available. This may also be used where no current year and carry back claims are made, as there is no compulsory requirement to use such reliefs.

The carry forward relief (S393(1) ICTA 1988) automatically allows trading losses to be set against future trading profits of the same trade as soon as they arise. They cannot be relieved against any other profits.

Such losses have to be used against the first available Schedule D Case I profits.

O EXAMPLE

Mint Limited has the following results:

Year ended 31 March	2005	2006	2007
	£	£	£
Adjusted trading profit/(loss)	15,000	(100,000)	40,000
Schedule D Case III	5,000	10,000	10,000
Chargeable gain	-	40,000	-

Show how the loss relief would be claimed as soon as possible.

Solution

Mint Ltd
Corporation tax computations

Year ended 31 March	2005	2006	2007
	£	£	£
Schedule D Case I	15,000	Nil	40,000
S393(1) carry forward relief			(30,000)
			10,000
Schedule D Case III	5,000	10,000	10,000
Chargeable gain	-	40,000	-
Total profits	20,000	50,000	20,000
S393A(1)(a) current year		(50,000)	-
S393A(1)(b) carry back	(20,000)		
PCTCT	Nil	Nil	20,000

Working: Loss memorandum

	£
Current year loss	100,000
Current year	(50,000)
	50,000
Carry back relief	
12 months year ended 31 March 2005	(20,000)
Loss c/f	30,000
Used in y/e 31 March 2007	(30,000)
Loss c/f	Nil

2 Non-trading losses

2.1 Types of loss

Both trading and non-trading losses regularly feature in questions. Often non-trading losses will occur in questions in isolation, but where a mixture of losses appear it is essential to distinguish the reliefs available.

Non-trading losses may comprise any of the following:

· Capital losses
· Schedule A losses

Each of these will be considered below.

2.2 Capital losses

The treatment of capital losses will be covered in detail in Chapter 21. However, in summary:

· A capital loss incurred in the current period is automatically relieved against current period gains. Any excess is then carried forward for relief against gains in future accounting periods.

· There is no carry back facility and a capital loss cannot be used against any other profit.

▷ **ACTIVITY 2** ▷ ▷ ▷ ▷

Coriander Ltd

Coriander Ltd has the following results:

Year ended 31 December:	Trading profit of (loss) £	Schedule D Case III £	Gift Aid paid £	Capital gains or (losses) £
2004	37,450	1,300	3,000	(6,000)
2005	(81,550)	1,400	3,000	
2006	20,000	1,600	3,000	12,000

Required
Show how the trading loss is relieved.

Approach to the question
· Set up CT proformas for all years leaving space to enter any loss reliefs.
· Set up a loss memorandum for the loss for year ended 31 December 2005.
· There is also a capital loss to deal with which has more restrictive use than a trading loss.

[Answers on p. 133]

2.3 Schedule A losses

Losses arising on property income are utilised as follows

·   By relief against total profits (including gains) of the current period *before* charges, and if any loss remains.

·   By carrying forward against *total* profits of future periods (i.e. before charges) provided there is still a Schedule A business source.

These reliefs are mandatory – i.e. they must be taken.

There is no carry back facility for Schedule A losses.

You may find yourself faced with Schedule A and trading loss reliefs available against total profits for a current period. Where total profits are not sufficient to utilise all available reliefs then losses must be used in the following order:

·   Schedule A loss
·   Trading loss

This order refers to losses incurred in the current period and should be sufficient for the assessment.

O EXAMPLE   O O O O

Comfy Ltd has the following results for the three years ending 31 December 2006.

	2004	2005	2006
	£	£	£
Adjusted trading profit or (loss)	12,450	(34,500)	4,000
Schedule A	2,000	1,800	(500)
Schedule D Case III	1,000	600	1,000
Gift Aid payments	(400)	(400)	(400)

Calculate PCTCT for all years, assuming all reliefs are claimed at the earliest opportunity.

Solution

Comfy Ltd
Corporation tax computations

Years ended 31 December	2003	2004	2005
	£	£	£
Schedule D Case I	12,450	Nil	4,000
S393(1) trading loss relief			(4,000)[3]
			Nil
Schedule A	2,000	1,800	Nil
Schedule D Case III	1,000	600	1,000
	15,450	2,400	1,000
Current year reliefs			
Schedule A (W2)			(500)
Schedule D Case I (W1)		(2,400)[1]	
Carry back relief S393A(1)(b)			
Schedule D Case I (W1)	(15,450)[2]		
	Nil	Nil	500
Gift Aid	Wasted	Wasted	(400)
PCTCT	Nil	Nil	100

(W1) Loss memorandum

	£
Trading loss in year ended 31 December 2005	34,500
Current year (S393A(1)(a))	(2,400)
Carry back (S393A(1)(b))	(15,450)
	16,650
Carry forward relief (S393(1))	(4,000)
Carry forward at 31 December 2006	12,650

(W2) Schedule A

	£
The loss in year ended 31 December 2006 will be relieved against total profits in that period	500
Year ended 31 December 2006 relief	(500)
Loss to carry forward	Nil

3 Test your knowledge

1 Trading losses can be relieved by carry back before being offset in the year of loss. True or false?

2 Capital losses can be offset against other income. True or false?

3 Trading losses are deducted from other income after deducting Gift Aid. True or false?

4 Trading losses carried forward need not be set off against trading income unless the company so elects. True or false?

[Answers on p. 134]

4 Summary

Losses often appear in assessments. You may have to give advice on how relief can be obtained.

The rules depend on the type of loss:

· Trading losses – current year and carry back relief against total profits before charges, carry forward against Schedule D Case I profits only.

· Schedule A losses – current year relief, carry forward against profits generally.

· Capital losses – current year against capital gains only, carry forward against capital gains only.

Answers to chapter activities & 'test your knowledge' questions

△ **ACTIVITY 1** △ △ △ △

Alfred Ball Ltd

Step 1: Set up CT proformas

Year ended 31 December	2004	2005	2006
	£	£	£
Schedule D Case I	42,000	19,000	Nil
Schedule D Case III	3,000	2,000	1,000
Chargeable gains	4,000	4,000	4,000
	49,000	25,000	5,000
S393A(1)(a) current year relief			(5,000)
	49,000	25,000	Nil
S393A(1)(b) carry back relief		(25,000)	
	49,000	Nil	Nil
Gift Aid	(10,000)	Wasted	-
PCTCT	39,000	Nil	Nil

The Gift Aid of £10,000 paid in the year ended 31 December 2005 is wasted.

Step 2: Prepare the Loss memorandum

	£
Year ended 31 December 2006	67,000
Current year relief	(5,000)
Carry back relief	
- 12 months to year ended 31 December 2005	(25,000)
Loss still available at 31 December 2006	37,000

△ ACTIVITY 2   △△△△

Coriander Ltd

Corporation tax computations

Year ended 31 December	2004 £	2005 £	2006 £
Schedule D Case I	37,450	Nil	20,000
S393(1) carry forward relief			(20,000)[3]
			Nil
Schedule D Case III	1,300	1,400	1,600
Chargeable gains			
(£12,000 - £6,000 brought forward)	Nil		6,000
	38,750	1,400	7,600
Current year relief – S393A(1)(a)		(1,400)[1]	
Carry back relief – S393A(1)(b)	(38,750)[2]		
	Nil	Nil	7,600
Gift Aid	Wasted	Wasted	(3,000)
PCTCT	Nil	Nil	4,600
Gift Aid wasted	3,000	3,000	

Loss memorandum

	£
Trading loss in year ended 31 December 2005	81,550
(1) Current period relief	(1,400)
(2) Carry back relief - year ended 31 December 2004	(38,750)
	41,400
(3) Carry forward against Schedule D Case I	
– year ended 31 December 2006	(20,000)
Loss to carry forward at 31 December 2006	21,400

Test your knowledge △ △ △

1   False. Trading losses can be only relieved by carry back after a claim for current year relief has been made.

2   False. Capital losses cannot be offset against other income. They can only be set against capital gains.

3   False. Trading losses are deducted from other income before deducting Gift Aid. Any excess charges remaining unrelieved are wasted.

4   False. Trading losses carried forward must be set off against the first available future trading income as soon as it arises.

ACCOUNTING FOR INCOME TAX

INTRODUCTION

In a few limited situations companies pay and receive amounts net of income tax. A mechanism is required for companies to deal with income tax.

CONTENTS

1 Introduction
2 Income tax deducted on payments
3 Income tax suffered on amounts received
4 Accounting for income tax

PERFORMANCE CRITERIA

This chapter covers the following performance criteria:
· Identify and set off income tax deductions and credits (18.4 D)

1 Introduction

1.1 Income tax

Companies pay amounts of interest and patent royalties to other companies gross. However, when these are paid to individuals they are paid net, i.e. after the deduction of income tax.

Companies receive patent royalties from individuals net, although patent royalties are received gross from other companies.

Gross amounts are used in the corporation tax computation. A system is required to deal with the income tax deducted.

2 Income tax deducted on payments

2.1 Types of payment

A company makes payments of:

· interest to individuals net of 20% tax.
· patent royalties to individuals net of 22% tax.

The gross amounts of these payments are used in calculating PCTCT. They will be Schedule D Case I allowable expenses if they are for trading purposes.

2.2 Dealing with the income tax

The amount of income tax deducted must be paid over to HM Revenue and Customs (HMRC).

A company must account to HMRC every three months, for each calendar quarter (i.e. quarters ended 31 March, 30 June, 30 September and 31 December) if a payment of this type has been made.

The return must be submitted and any income tax paid within 14 days of the end of the quarterly return period.

3 Income tax suffered on amounts received

3.1 Types of receipt

A company receives patent royalties from individuals net of 22%. This is the only type of income received net that would feature in an assessment.

3.2 Dealing with the income tax

The amount of income tax withheld can be reclaimed from HMRC. The income tax is reclaimed by deducting from any quarterly income tax payments due as explained above, if there are any. If not, it is reclaimed by deducted from the year end corporation tax liability.

○ EXAMPLE ○○○○

David Ltd has PCTCT of £100,000 for its year ended 31 March 2007.

Included within the PCTCT are patent royalties received from an individual on 31 March 2007 of £7,800. These were grossed up to £10,000 to be included in the computation (£7,800 x $\frac{100}{78}$).

There are no dividends received and the company did not make any interest or royalty payments to individuals during the year.

What is the corporation tax payable for the year?

Solution

Profits are £100,000, therefore David Ltd pays corporation tax at the small companies rate.

	£
PCTCT @ 19%	19,000
Less: Income tax suffered (22% x £10,000)	(2,200)
Corporation tax payable	16,800

---

4 Accounting for income tax

4.1 Receipts and payments net of income tax

Occasionally a company will have both:

· receipts net of income tax; and
· payments net of income tax.

This requires the quarterly returns mentioned in Section 2.2 to be considered.

4.2 Accounting for income tax

At the end of each return period the company compares the income tax it has suffered with the income tax it has deducted at source on payments made to individuals. If the amount deducted exceeds the amount suffered then the **excess is paid over** to HMRC.

If at the end of a particular return period the amount suffered exceeds the amount deducted then a **repayment** is due from HMRC. However, the company can only receive back income tax up to the amount that has been paid in the year to date.

If, at the end of the accounting year, the company has suffered more income tax than it has deducted the **excess amount suffered** is deducted from the **corporation tax liability**. Thus the company must wait until the end of the accounting year to obtain relief for excess income tax suffered.

However, if at the end of the accounting year the income tax deducted exceeds the tax suffered, the income tax suferred must have already been recovered by offset against amounts to be paid at the end of the relevant return period. Thus, at the end of the year, no adjustment needs to be made to the corporation tax liability.

The quarterly returns for income tax are completed in terms of the **tax suffered or deducted**. This is because different types of income and payment incur **different rates of income tax**.

· Tax is deducted from interest at the lower rate of 20%.
· Tax is deducted from patent royalties at the basic rate of 22%.

○ **EXAMPLE**   ○○○○

Jo Soap Limited had the following net payments and receipts of income for the two years to 31 March 2007:

		£	£
12.4.05	Patent royalties received from individuals		7,800
13.5.05	Patent royalties received from individuals		3,900
18.7.05	Patent royalties received from individuals		1,170
20.7.05	Patent royalty paid to individuals	19,500	
10.12.05	Patent royalties received from individuals		9,360
13.4.06	Interest paid to Jo Soap Limited's debenture holders (all individuals)	16,000	

Set out the quarterly returns for the above two accounting periods.

Solution

Step 1: Work out the gross, tax and net amounts on all payments and receipts and determine which year and which quarter they relate to

Year ended 31 March 2006

Date	Net payment	Rate	Tax	Gross payment	Net receipt	Rate	Tax suffered	Gross receipt	Return period ended
	£	%	£	£	£	%	£	£	
12.4.05					7,800	22	2,200	10,000	30.6.05
13.5.05					3,900	22	1,100	5,000	30.6.05
18.7.05					1,170	22	330	1,500	30.9.05
20.7.05	19,500	22	5,500	25,000					30.9.05
10.12.05					9,360	22	2,640	12,000	31.12.05
				25,000				28,500	

Year ended 31 March 2007

Date	Net payment	Rate	Tax	Gross payment
	£	%	£	£
13.4.06	16,000	20	4,000	20,000

Step 2: Prepare the quarterly accounts

Year ended 31 March 2006

Return period ended	Tax deducted on payments	Tax suffered on income received	Cumulative net	Income tax paid/ (repaid)
	£	£	£	£
30.6.05 (£2,200 + £1,100)(Note 1)	-	(3,300)	(3,300)	-
30.9.05	5,500	(330)	5,170	1,870
			1,870	
31.12.05 (Note 2)	-	(2,640)	(2,640)	(1,870)
			(770)	
31.3.06	-	-	-	-
At end of year (Note 3)			(770)	Nil

Notes:

(1) Income tax has been suffered but can not be repaid under the quarterly system unless some income tax has been paid in the CAP. Jo Soap Ltd will have to wait to recover the income tax suffered by offset against amounts to be paid later in the year.

(2)   The income tax repaid in this quarter cannot exceed the income tax previously paid in the accounting period.

(3)   At the end of the year there is income tax suffered, not recovered through quarterly accounting system of £770. This will be set against Jo Soap Ltd's corporation tax liability for the year ended 31 March 2006.

Year ended 31 March 2007

Return period ended	Tax deducted on payments £	Tax suffered on income received £	Cumulative net £	Income tax paid/(repaid) £
30.6.06	4,000	-	4,000	4,000
30.9.06	-	-	-	-
31.12.06	-	-	-	-
31.3.07	-	-	-	-
At the end of the year			4,000	4,000

Note:
No income tax has been suffered in this CAP, therefore there is no effect on Jo Soap Ltd's comparation tax liability computation.

5   Summary

·   Companies account to HMRC for income tax on a quarterly basis for each of the quarters ended 31 March, 30 June, 30 September and 31 December.

·   If, at the end of the accounting year, the company has suffered more income tax than it has deducted, the excess is deducted from the corporation tax liability.

·   If, at the end of the accounting year, the company has deducted more income tax than it has suffered, no adjustment is necessary.

This area has become less important over recent years as fewer items are paid and received net by companies.

PAYMENT AND ADMINISTRATION

INTRODUCTION

In each assessment there are some written tasks. The written task often considers the payment and administration of tax.

This chapter looks at those aspects for corporation tax (see Chapter 18 for sole traders and partnerships).

CONTENTS

1 Corporation tax self assessment (CTSA)
2 HM Revenue and Customs' (HMRC) powers of enquiry
3 Record keeping requirements
4 Payment of corporation tax

PERFORMANCE CRITERIA

This chapter covers the following performance criteria:

· Identify the amount of corporation tax payable and the due dates of payment, including payments on account (18.4 F)
· Complete corporation tax returns correctly and submit them, together with relevant claims and elections, within statutory time limits (18.4 G)
· Consult with HM Revenue & Customs staff in an open and constructive manner (18.4 H)
· Give timely and constructive advice to clients on the maintenance of accounts and the recording of information relevant to tax returns (18.4 I)

1 Corporation tax self assessment (CTSA)

1.1 Scope

Corporation tax self assessment (CTSA) requires companies to submit a tax return and a self assessment of any tax payable.

1.2 Filing the return

A company is required to file a return (form CT600) when it receives a notice requiring it to do so.

A company which is chargeable to tax, but which does not receive a notice requesting a return, must notify HM Revenue and Customs within 12 months of the end of the accounting period. If it fails to do so, it is liable to a penalty of up to the amount of tax unpaid 12 months after the end of the accounting period.

A notice to file a return may also require other information, such as the annual accounts.

The return must include a calculation (self assessment) of the corporation tax payable for the accounting period covered by the return.

The return must be made within 12 months of the end of the period of account or, if later, three months from the date of the notice requiring the return.

Note: the return date is based on the period of account (which may be more than 12 months long). For a set of accounts of more than 12 months long, there will be two corporation tax computations and therefore two returns to file.

However, both returns will have the same filing date.

○ EXAMPLE ○ ○ ○ ○

Edgar Ltd has prepared a set of accounts for the 15 months ended 31 March 2007.

Identify the period(s) for which return(s) must be completed and the filing date(s).

Solution

Periods for returns	Filing date
(i) First 12 months – 12 months ended 31 December 2006	31 March 2008
(ii) Balance – 3 months ended 31 March 2007	31 March 2008

Penalties for late filing

· There is a £100 penalty for failure to submit a return on time. This rises to £200 if the delay exceeds three months.

· There is an additional tax geared penalty if the return is more than six months late. This is 10% of the tax unpaid six months after the return was due. This rises to 20% if the return is over 12 months late.

· A penalty of up to the amount of tax that would have been lost can be imposed for a fraudulent or negligent return.

1.3 Amending the return

A company can amend a return within 12 months of the filing date.

HMRC can amend a return to correct errors within nine months of the date it was filed or within nine months of the filing of an amendment.

If the company disagrees with HMRC's amendment it may reject it. This rejection should be made within the normal time limit for amendments or, if this time limit has expired, within three months of the date of correction.

1.4 Errors

A company may make an error or mistake claim within six years of the end of an accounting period. An appeal against HMRC's decision on such a claim must be made within 30 days.

A company is not allowed to make an error claim if its return was made in accordance with a generally accepted accounting practice which prevailed at the time.

1.5 Interest on late payments of corporation tax

Interest is charged automatically on late paid corporation tax from the due date to the date of payment.

Where there is an amendment to the self assessment or a 'discovery assessment' (see below) interest runs from the date the tax would have been payable had it been correctly self assessed in the first place.

Interest paid on late payments of corporation tax is allowable as a Schedule D Case III expense.

1.6 Interest on overpaid corporation tax

If corporation tax is overpaid HMRC will pay interest from the later of the normal due date (see below) and the date of overpayment to the date it is refunded.

Interest received on overpaid corparation tax is assessable as Schedule D Case III income.

2   HM Revenue and Customs' powers of enquiry

2.1   Basic rules

HMRC may enquire into a return, provided they first give written notice.

Notice must normally be given:

· within a year of the filing date or, if later
· within a year of the 31 January, 30 April, 31 July or 31 October following the actual date of delivery of the return.

If notice of an enquiry has been given, HMRC may demand that the company produce documents for inspection. If the company fails to do so, a penalty of £50, plus £30 a day, may be imposed.

An enquiry ends when HMRC give notice that it has been completed and notify what amendments they believe to be necessary. The company has 30 days from the end of an enquiry to amend its return.

If HMRC are not satisfied with the company's amendments, they have a further 30 days to amend the return. The company then has a further 30 days in which to appeal against this latest HMRC amendment.

○ EXAMPLE   ○○○○

CTS Ltd has produced accounts for the year ended 30 June 2006. The company filed its return on 1 April 2007. What is the latest date by which HMRC must give notice of an enquiry?

How would your answer differ if CTS Ltd had filed its return on 1 September 2007?

Solution

HMRC must give notice within a year of the filing date. The filing date is 30 June 2007, therefore notice must be given by 30 June 2008.

If the company had filed its return on 1 September 2007, HMRC would need to give notice by 31 October 2008 (i.e. 12 months after 31 October following the actual date of delivery of the return).

2.2   Determinations

If a company fails to deliver a return by the filing date, HMRC may issue a determination of the tax payable within five years from the filing date.

There is no appeal against a determination. However, it is replaced if the company makes a self assessment within:

- five years of the filing date or, if later
- 12 months from the determination.

2.3 Discovery assessments

A discovery assessment may be issued if HMRC believe that insufficient tax has been collected. The time limit for a discovery assessment is six years from the end of the accounting period. This is extended to 21 years if there has been negligent or fraudulent conduct by the company.

3 Record keeping requirements

Companies must keep records until the latest of:

- six years from the end of the accounting period.
- the date any enquiries are completed.
- the date after which enquiries may not be commenced.

Failure to keep records can lead to a penalty of up to £3,000 for each accounting period affected.

The company must keep original records of:

- distributions (i.e. dividends) and tax credits.
- payments and any tax deducted.
- certificates of payments to sub-contractors.
- details of foreign tax paid.

It is acceptable to keep copies of other records. The record keeping requirements will normally be satisfied by the same records that satisfy Companies Act requirements.

4 Payment of corporation tax

4.1 Payment date

All companies (except large companies – see 4.2 below) pay their corporation tax within 9 months and one day of the end of the chargeable accounting period (CAP).

Hence, Edgar Ltd (in the previous example) which had a long period of account would have two payment dates. Edgar Ltd would pay corporation tax for:

- CAP 1 = 2 months ended 31 December 2006, by 1 October 2007.
- CAP 2 = 3 months ended 31 March 2007, by 1 January 2008.

From this we can see that a company with a long period of account can have:

· two separate payment dates; but
· one common filing date.

Note that the payment dates are earlier than the filing date.

4.2   Payment by instalments

Large companies are required to make quarterly payments on account of their Corporation tax liability.

A large company is a company which pays corporation tax at the ordinary rate of 30%. Note that this normally where profits exceed £1,500,000. However remember that the upper limit is divided between associated companies and time apportioned for short accounting periods. Therefore, a company with two other associates will pay tax at 30% and will be required to pay its corporation tax in instalments if its profits exceed £500,000 (£1,500,000/3).

A company is not required to make quarterly instalment payments in the year in which it becomes large, unless its profits exceed £10 million. This £10 million limit is also shared between associated companies. In addition, a company does not have to make quarterly instalment payments if its liability does not exceed £10,000.

The quarterly payments are based on the actual corporation tax liability for the current year.

The first payment is made on the 14th day of the seventh month of the accounting period. The other quarterly payments are due on the 14th day of months 10, 13 and 16. Therefore estimates of the corporation tax liability for the year need to be made at each payment date.

Note that the payments begin during the accounting period itself, not afterwards. So you must begin counting months from the start of the accounting period.

O EXAMPLE   OOOO

What are the payment dates for a company with an accounting period ending on 28 February 2007?

Solution

The payments on account are due on:
· 14 September 2006
· 14 December 2006
· 14 March 2007
· 14 June 2007

Each payment due is a quarter of the corporation tax liability for the year which, for at least the first three and for probably all four instalments, would have to be estimated.

The first instalment payment would be a quarter of the best estimate at that date. The second payment would require a revised estimate and add or deduct any difference in respect of the first instalment and so on.

HMRC may expect to see some proof that the estimates were made with care.

4.3 Interest

Companies should revise the estimate of their corporation tax liability every quarter. It is a good idea to keep records showing how the estimate has been calculated. This will help to justify the size of a payment if HMRC should dispute the amount paid.

Interest runs from the due date on any underpayments or overpayments. Interest paid by the company is a deductible expense. Interest received by the company is taxable income. Both are dealt with under Schedule D Case III.

Penalties may be charged if a company deliberately fails to pay instalments of a sufficient size.

▷ ACTIVITY 1   ▷ ▷ ▷ ▷

Space plc

Space plc, which has profits chargeable to corporation tax of £2 million annually, is preparing its budget for the year ending 31 March 2007. It does not have any dividend income.

Required

(a) Prepare a plan of projected corporation tax payments based on its results for the year, stating the amounts due and the due dates.

(b) Advise of any other administrative requirements for corporation tax purposes.

Approach to the question

Step 1: Calculate the corporation tax liability.

Step 2: Consider the impact of the instalment system on this large company.

Step 3: Consider the *returns* required, and the impact of late payments.

 [Answer on p. 149]

---

5 Test your knowledge

1 Companies must file their corporation tax returns before they pay their corporation tax. True or false?

2 ABC Ltd has four associated companies. In the year to 31 March 2006 its profits were £200,000. In the year to 31 March 2007 it sold its factory and had profits of £3million. When is the corporation tax for the year to 31 March 2007 due?

3 What is the filing date for a company which prepares accounts for the 11 months to 28 February 2007?

4 DEF Ltd filed its corporation tax return for the year ended 31 March 2006 on 19 May 2007. What is the latest date that it can amend the return?

[Answer on p. 150]

6 Summary

There are numerous deadlines and penalties under CTSA.

The key points are summarised as follows:

· A company must file a return within 12 months of the end of its period of account or, if later, three months from the date of the notice from HMRC.

· Failure to submit a return on time results in a penalty of £100.

· The company can amend a return within 12 months of the filing date.

· HMRC can enquire into a return provided they give written notice within a year of the filing date.

· Companies must keep records for six years from the end of the accounting period. Failure to do so can result in a penalty of up to £3,000.

· The due date for corporation tax is nine months and one day after the end of the accounting period.

· Companies liable at the ordinary rate of CT (30%) must pay their liability in quarterly instalments, commencing on the 14th day of the seventh month of the accounting period.

Answers to chapter activities & 'test your knowledge' questions

△ **ACTIVITY 1**   △ △ △ △

1   Space plc

(a) Projected corporation tax payments

	Year ended 31 March 2007 £
PCTCT & 'Profits'	2,000,000
Rate	30%
Corporation tax liability	600,000

The accounting period will be subject to self assessment and to the quarterly system of instalments as the company is large and was large in the previous year.

The liability for the year ended 31 March 2007 should be settled by four equal instalments of £150,000 (£600,000 ÷ 4).

		£
Instalment 1	14 October 2006	150,000
Instalment 2	14 January 2007	150,000
Instalment 3	14 April 2007	150,000
Instalment 4	14 July 2007	150,000
		600,000

(b) Administrative requirements

(1) A return, including statutory accounts and computations, must be submitted within 12 months of the accounting period end otherwise penalties will be exacted, i.e. by 31 March 2008

(2) Late payments of tax will give rise to interest charges, which will be deductible under Schedule D Case III.

Test your knowledge

1   False. The due date for the payment of the corporation tax falls before the due filing date. Companies may need to estimate the payment of corporation tax that is due.

2   ABC Ltd is a large company in the year to 31 March 2007 and its profits exceed £2 million (i.e. £10 million x 1/5) (four associated companies).

    It must pay its corporation tax in instalments even though it was not a large company in the year to 31 March 2006.

    The tax is due on 14 October 2006, 14 January 2007, 14 April 2007 and 14 July 2007.

3   The filing date is 12 months from the end of the accounting period, 28 February 2008.

4   The latest date that DEF Ltd can amend its return is 31 March 2008, 12 months after the due filing date not the actual filing date.

KAPLAN PUBLISHING

NATIONAL INSURANCE CONTRIBUTIONS

INTRODUCTION

As an employer, a company may be required to pay National Insurance contributions in respect of its employees.

PERFORMANCE CRITERIA

This chapter covers the following performance criteria:
·   Identify the National Insurance contributions payable by employers (18.4 E)

1 Principle of contributions payable by employers

1.1 Employers contribution

Employers have two main types of contribution to pay regarding their employees' pay.

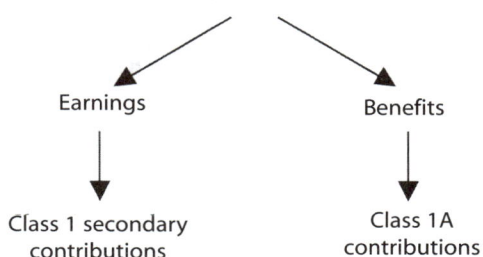

Employment income

Earnings

Benefits

Class 1 secondary contributions

Class 1A contributions

2 Class 1 contributions

2.1 Class 1 secondary contributions

Class 1 secondary contributions at the rate of 12.8% are due from employers.

They are paid for all employees who are over 16 and are based on earnings in excess of £5,035 per annum (£97 per week or £420 per month). They are an allowable deduction from the employer's trading profit.

'Earnings' for Class 1 purposes includes cash payments (salary, bonuses, commissions, etc), vouchers exchangeable for cash or goods (except for childcare vouchers), and payments which are as good as cash. This latter category would include paying bills which the employee had incurred (e.g. school fees).

'Earnings' does not include the reimbursement of business expenses, nor most benefits (such as the use of a company car).

> ### ○ EXAMPLE   ○ ○ ○ ○
>
> Peter earns £130 a week. Using the annual limits calculate the Class 1 contributions payable by his employer for 2006/07.
>
> **Solution**
>
> Earnings = £130 x 52 weeks = £6,760
> Class 1 Secondary NICs = (£6,760 - £5,035) x 12.8% = £221

2.2 Class 1 primary contributions

Class 1 primary contributions are payable by employees.

The employer is responsible for calculating the amount due and deducting these from the employee's wages or salary. However, they do not represent a cost to the business as they are ultimately paid by the employee.

3   Class 1A contributions

3.1   Payment of Class 1A contributions

Class 1A contributions are payable by employers only on most taxable benefits provided to employees. These contributions are only payable by employees.

The contributions are calculated at the full rate of 12.8% on the value of the benefits as calculated under the income tax rules. Note that benefits provided to employees earning less than £8,500 per annum are exempt from Class 1A NIC. The value of the taxable benefits will be given in the assessment.

Note that, if an item, such as a voucher, is charged to Class 1, it is not also chargeable to Class 1A.

Class I NICs for employees and employers is paid to HM Revenue and Customs with PAYE tax. Class 1A NICs on taxable benefits, payable by the employer only, is paid annually by 19 July following the tax year.

○ EXAMPLE   ○○○○

Jill earns £22,000 a year and a new car is made available to her with petrol provided. The value of the car and fuel benefits are £9,269 in total.

What is the Class 1A liability?

Solution

Only the employer has a Class 1A liability. There is no additional employee NIC for Jill.

Class 1A is (12.8% x the value of the benefit for income tax) which is:

Class 1A liability = £9,269 x 12.8% = £1,186.

---

4   Test your knowledge

1   At the end of the month ABC Ltd pays an employee salary of £1,000 and reimbursed business expenses of £150. How much of this is liable to NICs?

2   ABC Ltd provided benefits with a taxable value of £500 to two employees, Sue whose weekly pay is £120, and Sarah whose weekly pay is £220. What Class 1A NICs are payable in respect of the benefits?

[Answers on p. 155]

5   Summary

There are two types of National Insurance contributions suffered by companies as employers.

- Class 1 secondary on cash earnings of employees.
- Class 1A on benefits provided to employees.

Answers to 'test your knowledge' questions

Test your knowledge △ △ △

1   Reimbursed business expenses are not liable to Class 1 NICs, so secondary contributions will only be due on the salary of £1,000.

2   Sue is paid less than £8,500 per annum, so her benefits will not be liable to Class 1A NICs. Sarah is paid more than £8,500 per annum, so her benefits will be liable to Class 1A NICs of £64 (£500 x 12.8%).

SOLE TRADERS AND PARTNERSHIPS – PRINCIPLES OF TAXATION

INTRODUCTION

In Chapters 2 – 12 we have considered how we tax the profits and gains of one type of business entity – a company. In the next few chapters we look at how we tax those of sole traders and partnerships (unincorporated businesses).

This chapter is an introduction to the main differences in the method of dealing with the tax affairs of these business entities.

CONTENTS

1 Sole trader
2 Partnerships
3 Terminology

1 Sole trader

1.1 No separate legal entity

A sole trader is an individual who has set up his/her own business. The business is not a separate legal entity.

1.2 Types of tax payable

The individual who sets up as a sole trader pays:

- income tax, on income including adjusted trading profits; and
- capital gains tax, on chargeable gains.

○ EXAMPLE   ○ ○ ○ ○

Which of the following business entities is a sole trader?

(a) Fred Flint, haulage contractors.
(b) Fred Flint Ltd, haulage contractors.

Solution

(a) Fred Flint is a sole trader. Fred pays income tax on his adjusted trading profit and capital gains tax on his gains.

(b) Fred Flint Ltd is a company (a separate legal entity). The company pays corporation tax on income and gains.

2 Partnerships

2.1 No separate legal entity

A partnership is a group of individuals carrying on in business together. The business is not a separate legal entity.

2.2 Types of tax payable

Each partner individually pays:

- income tax, on his share of the partnership's adjusted trading profit together with his own personal income.

- capital gains tax on his share of gains on partnership assets, together with his own personal gains.

A partnership is effectively a collection of sole traders working together, each responsible for his own tax liability.

The allocation of partnership profits is considered further in Chapter 15.

3 Terminology

When dealing with companies, we saw that the profits from a trade were labelled 'Schedule D Case I' income.

The tax legislation is in the course of being rewritten in plainer English under the Tax Law Rewrite Project. Currently the income tax rules are being redrafted, whereas the corporation tax rules have not yet been redrafted.

As a result the term 'Schedule D Case I' is not used for income tax. Instead we simply refer to taxable trading profits.

4 Summary

Sole traders and partnerships:

· DO NOT pay corporation tax.
· DO pay income tax and capital gains tax.
· ARE NOT separate legal entities.

TAXABLE TRADE PROFITS FOR UNINCORPORATED BUSINESSES

INTRODUCTION

The assessment will have a task that looks at the taxable trading profits of a sole trader or partner (unincorporated businesses).

There are some differences in the computation of adjusted trading profits and capital allowances for unincorporated businesses compared to companies.

CONTENTS

1 Adjusted trading profits for individuals
2 Adjustment of trading profits
3 Capital allowances for individuals
4 Income tax return – self employment

PERFORMANCE CRITERIA

This chapter covers the following performance criteria:
· Make adjustments for private use by business owners (18.1 C)
· Adjust trading profits and losses for tax purposes (18.2 A)
· Make adjustments for private use by business owners (18.2 B)
· Complete correctly the self employed and partnership supplementary pages to the tax return for individuals, together with relevant claims and elections, and submit them within statutory time limits (18.2 G)

1 Adjusted trading profits for individuals

1.1 Badges of trade

We are concerned with taxing the profits of a trade. Status law defines a 'trade' as including every trade, manufacture, adventure or concern in the nature of trade. This is not particularly helpful and it has been necessary for the Courts to decide whether an activity is or is not a trade.

In 1954 a Royal Commission summarised the existing case law relevant to 'trade' by identifying six attributes or 'badges' of trade:

·   *Subject matter.* Assets are generally acquired either for personal use, or as an investment, or as stock in trade or as a fixed asset for use in a trade. An investment may be income generating (e.g. shares) or for pleasure (e.g. a painting). If an asset is clearly neither acquired as an investment or for the use of the owner or his family or friends, the inference of trading arises.

·   *Length of ownership.* A brief period of ownership is indicative of a trade.

·   *Frequency of similar transactions.* The more frequent a transaction the more likely a trade is being conducted.

·   *Supplementary work.* An asset bought and enhanced in some way before sale is more likely to be a trading asset than a similar asset simply bought and sold without improvement.

·   *Circumstances of realisation.* It can be argued that the forced sale of an asset to relieve a cash flow crisis is less likely to be a disposal in the course of a trade.

·   *Motive.* The presence of a profit motive is indicative of a trade.

In borderline cases it is necessary to look at all the 'badges' together and not give undue weight to any particular test.

This could be a written part of a task in the assessment.

○ EXAMPLE   ○ ○ ○ ○

James Aslett renovates classic cars as a 'hobby' in his spare time and exhibits them at classic car events. He has accepted the occasional offer to sell and usually makes a profit if the time he has spent is ignored.

Will James be treated as trading in cars by HMRC?

Solution

The situation has to be measured against the 'badges of trade'.

A car could be a trading asset or an investment or for personal use so the first test is inconclusive.

If James owns the cars for only a brief period and is constantly buying, renovating and selling, perhaps even advertising, there comes a point where the hobby becomes a trade.

1.2 Professions and vocations

The profits made by a self employed person from a profession or vocation are taxed in the same way as the profits of a trade.

2 Adjustment of trading profits

2.1 Comparison between individuals and companies

The starting point in determining the amount of taxable trading profits is the net profit as shown in the accounts, but this must be adjusted for tax purposes in a similar way to companies.

We have already seen in Chapter 3 in the context of a company how to adjust the accounting profits to find the adjusted trading profits. The first part of this Chapter will concentrate on approaching the topic from an individual trader's perspective.

Taxable trading profits for an individual comprises adjusted trading profits (Chapter 3) less capital allowances (Chapter 4), less industrial buildings allowances (Chapter 5) for an accounting period in much the same way as it does for a company. This Chapter covers the minor adjustments needed to the rules seen earlier in the context of companies.

The net profit shown in the accounts of a business must be adjusted to comply with the rules of taxable income and allowable expenditure for trades. The profit as adjusted for income tax is referred to as the *adjusted* trading profit.

Outline proforma for adjustment of profits computation

			Section	£	£
Net profit per accounts					X
Add:	(a)	Disallowable expenditure	2.2	X	
	(b)	Income not included in the accounts but taxable as trading income	2.3	X	
					X
					X
Less:	(c)	Income included in the accounts but not taxable as trading income	2.8	X	
	(d)	Expenditure not in the accounts but allowable as a trading deduction	2.9	X	
					(X)
Adjusted trading profit					X

The same profit adjustment rules for companies apply for individual (or 'sole') traders but with minor adjustments explained as follows.

2.2 Disallowable expenditure differences

Adjustments for private expenditure

Any private expenditure of the owner of the business deducted in the accounts should be disallowed.

There will sometimes be an estimated proportion of business use, for example with motor expenses or telephone expenses. If this is the case, only the private element should be disallowed and therefore added back.

Under self assessment the trader has to be prepared to justify his estimate of the private element if HM Revenue and Customs enquire into his self assessment return.

Salary to proprietor

The salary or drawings paid to the owner is the equivalent of a dividend paid by a company. It is an appropriation of profit, not a business expense, and must therefore be added back to profit.

O EXAMPLE

Gordon has his own business as a motor dealer. His accounts for the year ended 31 December 2006 show the following results:

	£	£
Gross profit		80,000
Less: Expenses		
Salaries (including Gordon's 'salary' of £20,000)	30,000	
Motor expenses	3,000	
Allowable expenses	22,000	
		(55,000)
Net profit per accounts		25,000

Included in motor expenses is £1,000 relating to the cost of running Gordon's car which is used 60% for business purposes.

What is Gordon's adjusted trading profit?

Solution

	£
Net profit per accounts	25,000
Add: Disallowable expenses	
Gordon's 'salary'/drawings	20,000
Private motor expenses (£1,000 X 40%)	400
Adjusted trading profit	45,400

Note: Do not add back salaries or private motor expenses of **employees**. These are allowable expenses for the business (just as they are in a company's computation).

Bad debts

We saw in Chapter 3 that as companies are required to produce their accounts in accordance with UK generally accepted accounting practice, any bad debt provisions included within the accounts are allowable for tax purposes.

The accounts of an unincorporated business however are not bound by the Companies Act requirements and therefore may contain *general* provisions which are not allowable for tax purposes.

Movements in general provisions, for example the *general* bad debt provision, are not allowable. An increase in a general provision must be added back, and a decrease in a general provision must be deducted, to arrive at adjusted trading profits.

Movements in *specific* provisions are allowable and do not need adjusting for in calculating the adjusted trading profits.

Note that movements in any other *general* provisions charged to the profit and loss account should also be disallowed e.g. stock provisions.

○ EXAMPLE ○○○○

The bad debts account of Greg, an interior designer, for the year ended 30 June 2007 appears as follows:

	£		£
Written off		Balance brought down	
Trade	274	Specific provision	185
Former employee	80	General provision	260
Balance carried down		Recoveries – trade	23
Specific provision	194	Profit and loss account	305
General provision	225		
	773		773

Show the adjustment required in computing the adjusted trading profit.

Solution

The first stage is to establish a breakdown of the profit and loss account charge of £305. Remember that this figure comprises amounts written off and recovered, and movements in provisions.

Profit and loss account charge	£	Allowable?
Increase in specific provision (£194 - £185)	9	✓
Decrease in general provision (£225 - £260)	(35)	✗
Trade debt written off	274	✓
Former employee loan written off	80	✗
Recoveries – trade	(23)	✓
	305	

The movement in the general provision and the amount owed by the former employee are both disallowed. In this case, the movement in the general provision is a *decrease*, so the adjustment made is to *deduct* it from the profit per the accounts.

The adjustments required to compute the adjusted trading profit are therefore as follows:

		£
Add:	Former employee, debt written off	80
Less:	Decrease in general provision	(35)

2.3   Income not included in the accounts but taxable as trading income

This category does not exist for the adjustment of profits for a company.

The most common example is goods taken by the owner for his own use. The proprietor must be taxed on the profit he would have made if the goods had been sold at market value (i.e. at retail or wholesale price as appropriate).

If closing stock in the profit and loss account has been reduced for the goods taken for own use but no other adjustments made, then the amount to be added back to arrive at the adjusted profit will be the *selling price*.

If closing stock has not been reduced for the goods taken for own use, or an adjustment has been made for the cost of the goods taken, then the amount added back will be the *profit*.

○ EXAMPLE   ○○○○

Sammy operates a toy store and has taken goods for his own use costing £500 during the year ended 31 December 2006. An adjustment has already been made to reflect the cost of the goods taken.

What is the increase to net profit required if:

(a) Sammy operates a mark-up basis of pricing of 40%; or alternatively
(b) Sammy operates on a gross profit margin of 40%?

Read the requirement carefully in the assessment. These will give different results.

Solution

(a) Mark-up means that the cost of the goods represents 100% and that sales value is therefore 140%.

	%
Sales	140
Cost	100
∴ Profit	40

The profit is therefore 40% of £500 = £200.

(b) Where a gross profit margin is supplied, sales represents 100% of the value.

If the profit is 40% of sales then the cost of goods is 60%.

	%
Sales	100
∴ Cost	60
Profit	40

Therefore the profit element is £500 x $^{40}/_{60}$ = £333.

○ EXAMPLE ○○○○

Mr Bean has taken £500 of goods from stock. The cost of this has been reflected in the accounts. An extract from the profit and loss account shows the following:

	£	£
Sales		450,000
Opening stock	160,000	
Purchases	210,000	
Closing stock	(120,000)	
Cost of sales		(250,000)
Gross profit		200,000

What adjustments are needed if the net profit shown in the accounts is £90,000?

Solution

The increase to net profit for the profit element of goods for own use must be calculated by reference to the correct relationship between cost and gross profit.

If cost of goods used is £500 and £250,000 of costs generates £200,000 of profit then:

Profit element = £500 $\times \frac{200}{250}$ = £400

Therefore net profit adjustments are as follows:

	£
Net profit	90,000
Add: Increase in profit for goods for own use	400
Adjusted profit	90,400

2.4   Income included in the accounts but not taxable as trading income

The following are examples of amounts which may be included in the profit and loss account, but which are not taxable as trading income. Hence they should be deducted.

· Income taxed in another way, e.g. rent, interest receivable.
· Income exempt from income tax, e.g. interest on delayed tax repayments.
· Profits on sales of fixed assets.

These adjustments are essentially the same as those for companies.

2.5 Expenditure not in the accounts but allowable

This category of adjustment does not arise for companies.

Any business expense not charged in the profit and loss account but paid for or borne privately by the proprietor can be deducted as a business expense.

For example, where a home telephone is used for business calls, the cost of the business calls can be deducted (although it is more common for the whole amount to be charged to the profit and loss account, in which case the private portion should be disallowed).

▷ ACTIVITY 1 ▷▷▷▷

Capone (1)

Capone is in business as a wine merchant preparing accounts to 30 June annually. His profit and loss account for the period ended 30 June 2006 was as follows:

	£	£
Gross profit		64,279
Bank deposit interest		160
Dividends (net)		140
		64,579
Rent and business rates	9,740	
Light and heat	120	
Office salaries	19,660	
Repairs to premises	2,620	
Motor expenses	740	
Depreciation		
Motor vans	3,400	
Equipment	750	
Loss on sale of equipment	40	
Bad and doubtful debts	6,030	
Professional charges	375	
Interest on bank overdraft	240	
Sundry expenses	770	
Salary		
Capone	14,000	
Wife, as secretary	1,450	
		59,935
Net profit		4,644

The following information is given:

	£
Repairs to premises	
Alterations to flooring in order to install new bottling machine	1,460
Decorations	475
Replastering walls damaged by damp	685
	2,620

Bad and doubtful debts account

	£		£
Trade debts written off	1,300	Provision brought forward	
Loan to ex-employee		General	1,850
written off	400	Specific	580
Provisions carried forward		Profit and loss account	6,030
General	5,200		
Specific	1,560		
	——		——
	8,460		8,460
	——		——

Professional charges	£
Accountancy	200
Court action for failing to observe Customs regulations	130
Debt collection	45
	——
	375
	——

Interest on bank overdraft
The overdraft was obtained in order to finance the purchase of stock.

Sundry expenses	£
Fine re breach of Customs bonding regulations	250
Subscription to Wine Retail Trade Association	50
Donation to Police Welfare Fund	20
Entertaining customers	300
Calendars bearing firm's name sent to 60 customers	120
Miscellaneous allowable expenses	30
	——
	770
	——

During the year Capone had withdrawn goods from stock for his own consumption. The cost of this stock was £455. The business makes a uniform gross profit of 35% on selling price. No entry had been made in the books in respect of the goods taken, other than the resulting reduction in closing stock.

Most mornings Capone telephoned his importing agent from home; the cost of these calls, extracted from his private British Telecom bills, was £290. No entry has been made in the accounts.

Required
Compute Capone's adjusted trading profit for tax purposes for the period ended 30 June 2006, giving reasons for the adjustments made.

Note: Reasons for the adjustments do not have to be shown unless specified as a requirement in the assessment.

[Answer on p. 182]

3 Capital allowances for individuals

3.1 The general rules

The capital allowance rules for plant and machinery (Chapter 4) and industrial buildings (Chapter 5) have already been explained in detail for companies. The modifications needed to apply these rules for sole traders are explained below.

3.2 Private use assets

Any asset used partly *by the proprietor* for private purposes must be given a separate column in the capital allowances working. Such assets cannot be covered by a short life asset election.

The allowances deducted from the written down value will be the usual 25% WDA (restricted to £3,000 if the asset is an expensive car) or FYA @ 40%, 50% or 100%. However, the allowance actually *claimed* will be reduced for private use. Only the proportion relating to business use can be claimed.

On disposal, a balancing adjustment will be calculated. However, the balancing adjustment will be similarly reduced for private use. Only the business proportion can be claimed.

The following example demonstrates this.

> ## ○ EXAMPLE   ○○○○
>
> Gerard is a trader preparing accounts for calendar years. In 2005 he bought a motor car for £7,200. He sold the car in February 2007 for £4,500 replacing it with a car costing £18,800.
>
> Gerard uses his cars for both business and private purposes and estimates an 80% business use proportion.
>
> Show the capital allowances and balancing adjustments on the cars for the years ended 31 December 2005, 2006 and 2007.
>
> **Solution**
>
> This example involves two private use cars, one of which an inexpensive car (less than £12,000), the other an expensive car.
>
> Each car will have a separate column, as a private use asset.
>
> The first stage is to calculate the allowances as usual at 25% (restricted to £3,000 for the expensive car). Then multiply these allowances by 80%, the business use proportion, to find the allowances that can be claimed.
>
> On disposal, the balancing allowance or charge will be calculated as usual, and again multiplied by 80% to find the actual amount to be deducted or added back to adjusted trading profits.

The answer is therefore as follows:

Gerard - Capital allowances

	Private use Car 1 £	Private use Car 2 £	Allowances £
Year ended 31 December 2005			
Additions	7,200		
WDA at 25%	(1,800) x 80%		1,440
Tax WDV carried forward	5,400		
Year ended 31 December 2006			
WDA at 25%	(1,350) x 80%		1,080
Tax WDV carried forward	4,050		
Year ended 31 December 2007			
Additions		18,800	
Disposal proceeds	(4,500)		
	(450)		
Balancing charge	450 x 80%		(360)
WDA at 25% (restricted)		(3,000) x 80%	2,400
Tax WDV carried forward		15,800	
Total allowances			2,040

▷ ACTIVITY 2 ▷ ▷ ▷ ▷

Ernest

Ernest prepares accounts to 31 December annually. On 1 January 2005 he had a qualifying pool balance of plant and machinery brought forward of £24,000. The following transactions took place in the year to 31 December 2005.

15 April 2005	Purchased car for £12,600
30 April 2005	Sold plant for £3,200 (original cost £4,800)
16 July 2005	Purchased car for £9,200 (wholly business usage)
17 August 2005	Purchased car for £9,400 (30% private usage by Ernest)

In the following year to 31 December 2006, Ernest sold for £7,900 the car originally purchased on 17 August 2005. The car originally purchased on 15 April 2005 was sold for £9,400 on 9 March 2006. There were no other transactions.

Required

Compute the capital allowances and balancing adjustments for the years ended 31 December 2005 and 31 December 2006.

[Answer on p. 184]

KAPLAN PUBLISHING

3.3 The impact of the length of the accounting period (sole traders)

As we have seen, capital allowances are computed for accounting periods and deducted in calculating taxable trading profits.

The writing down allowances calculated so far were all for 12 month accounting periods.

Where the accounting period is more or less than 12 months' long, the WDA must be scaled up or down accordingly. You must perform this calculation to the nearest month.

Note the important difference between companies and sole traders. A company cannot have an accounting period greater than 12 months but a sole trader can.

Note that first year allowances are given in full regardless of the length of the accounting period. They are never scaled up or down according to the length of the accounting period.

○ **EXAMPLE** ○○○○

Ken started to trade on 1 June 2005, and on that day he purchased three cars for the use of his employees for £21,900.

Calculate the writing down allowances due for his first two accounting periods on the assumption that he makes up his first accounts to:

(i)   31 May 2006
(ii) 31 March 2006
(iii) 31 August 2006

and annually on those dates thereafter.

Solution

First accounting period		_(i)_ _31 May 2006_ _(12 months)_ £	_(ii)_ _31 March 2006_ _(10 months)_ £	_(iii)_ _31 August 2006_ _(15 months)_ £
Cost	21,900	21,900	21,900	
WDA 25%		(5,475)		
25% x $^{10}/_{12}$			(4,563)	
25% x $^{15}/_{12}$				(6,844)
WDV carried forward		16,425	17,337	15,056
Second accounting period				
WDA 25%		(4,106)	(4,334)	(3,764)
WDV carried forward		12,319	13,003	11,292

4 Income tax return – self employment

4.1 Self employment supplementary pages

An individual may be required to complete a tax return. There is a main return (SA100) and several supplementary pages to be completed as appropriate. One of the sets of supplementary pages consists of four pages on self employment (SA103).

The first two pages of the SA103 may appear in the assessment. These are set out on the following pages.

4.2 Page SE1

The first part of this page is used to gather details of the business, including the date of the accounting period (this is looked at in detail in Chapter 16).

The second part of the page analyses the results of the capital allowances calculations.

The left hand column is used to gather both writing down allowances, first year allowances **and** balancing allowances. The right hand column is only for balancing charges.

The final section of the page is only used for businesses with annual turnover (sales) of below £15,000. For larger businesses, use page 2.

If using the final section:

· box 3.24 is for sales plus balancing charges (from box 3.23).

· box 3.25 is for allowable expenses plus capital allowances (from box 3.22).

· box 3.26 is the net result of the previous two boxes.

4.3 Page SE2

This page is for traders with a turnover of at least £15,000. The detailed section on expenses must be completed, as must the section at the end for final tax adjustments to arrive at adjusted trading profits.

The top section of the page has three columns:

· The middle column includes all expenses shown in the accounts (analysed as appropriate).

· The left hand column shows the disallowable expenditure included within the middle column.

It is possible that boxes in both columns could include the same figure; for example, if depreciation in the accounts is £3,000 then:

· box 3.44 will show £3,000; and
· box 3.62 will show £3,000.

Usually the boxes will show different figures; for example, if employee costs of £50,000 included the owner's drawings of £20,000 then:

· box 3.33 will show £20,000; and
· box 3.51 will show £50,000.

The right hand column includes the following items:

Box 3.29   total sales.

Box 3.49   will be box 3.29 less box 3.46 cost of sales (we will not use 3.47 and 3.48 in the assessment).

Box 3.50   will include other income received by the business (e.g. bank interest), but this must then be deducted at box 3.71 to arrive at trading profit.

Box 3.64   is the total of the middle column.

Box 3.65   is the net profit as shown in the accounts.

The final section of this page is the equivalent of the adjustment of profits proforma shown earlier in this chapter, with further adjustments for capital allowances and balancing charges.

Outline proforma for adjustment of profits computation

			Box	£	£
Net profit per accounts					X
Add:	(a)	Disallowable expenditure	3.66	X	
	(b)	Income not included in the accounts but taxable as trading income	3.67	X	
				—	X
					X
Less:	(c)	Income included in the accounts but not taxable as trading income	3.71	X	
	(d)	Expenditure not in the accounts but allowable as a trade deduction	3.71	X	
				—	(X)
Adjusted trading profit before capital allowances					X

Income for the year ended 5 April 2007

Inland Revenue

SELF-EMPLOYMENT

Fill in these boxes first

Name

Tax reference

If you want help, look up the box numbers in the Notes

Business details

Name of business

3.1

Description of business

3.2

Address of business

3.3

Postcode

Accounting period - read the Notes, page SEN2 before filling in these boxes

Start

3.4 / /

End

3.5 / /

- Tick box 3.6 if details in boxes 3.1 or 3.3 have changed since your last Tax return **3.6**

- Date of commencement if after 5 April 2004 **3.7** / /

- Date of cessation if before 6 April 2007 **3.8** / /

- Tick box 3.9 if the special arrangements for certain trades apply - read the Notes, pages SEN11 and SEN12 **3.9**

- Tick box 3.10 if you entered details for all relevant accounting periods on last year's Tax Return and boxes 3.14 to 3.73 and 3.99 to 3.115 will be blank (read Step 3 on page SEN2) **3.10**

- Tick box 3.11 if your accounts do not cover the period from the last accounting date (explain why in the 'Additional information' box, box 3.116) **3.11**

- Tick box 3.12 if your accounting date has changed (only if this is a permanent change and you want it to count for tax) **3.12**

- Tick box 3.13 if this is the second or further change (explain in box 3.116 on Page SE4 why you have not used the same date as last year) **3.13**

Capital allowances - summary

	Capital allowances	Balancing charge
- Car costing more than £12,000 (excluding cars with low CO$_2$ emissions). (A separate calculation must be made for each car.)	**3.14** £	**3.15** £
- Other business plant and machinery (including cars with low CO$_2$ emissions and cars costing less than £12,000) read the Notes, page SEN4	**3.16** £	**3.17** £
- Agricultural or Industrial Buildings Allowance (A separate calculation must be made for each block of expenditure.)	**3.18** £	**3.19** £
- Other capital allowances claimed (Separate calculations must be made.)	**3.20** £	**3.21** £
	total of column above	total of column above
Total capital allowances/balancing charges	**3.22** £	**3.23** £

- Tick box 3.22A if box 3.22 includes enhanced capital allowances for environmentally friendly expenditure. **3.22A**

Income and expenses - annual turnover below £15,000

If your annual turnover is £15,000 or more, ignore boxes 3.24 to 3.26. Instead fill in Page SE2

If your annual turnover is below £15,000, **fill in boxes 3.24 to 3.26 instead of Page SE2.** Read the Notes, page SEN4.

- Turnover including other business receipts and goods etc. taken for personal use (and balancing charges from box 3.23) **3.24** £

- Expenses allowable for tax (including capital allowances from box 3.22) **3.12** £

	box 3.24 minus box 3.25
Net profit (put figure in brackets if a loss)	**3.13** £

SA103

Now fill in Page SE3

Income for the year ended 5 April 2007

Inland Revenue

SELF-EMPLOYMENT

Fill in these boxes first

Name	Tax reference

If you want help, look up the box numbers in the Notes

Business details

Name of business

3.1

Description of business

3.2

Address of business

3.3

Postcode

Accounting period - read the Notes, page SEN2 before filling in these boxes

Start

3.4 / /

End

3.5 / /

- Tick box 3.6 if details in boxes 3.1 or 3.3 have changed since your last Tax return **3.6**

- Date of commencement if after 5 April 2004 **3.7** / /

- Date of cessation if before 6 April 2007 **3.8** / /

- Tick box 3.9 if the special arrangements for certain trades apply - read the Notes, pages SEN11 and SEN12 **3.9**

- Tick box 3.10 if you entered details for all relevant accounting periods on last year's Tax Return and boxes 3.14 to 3.73 and 3.99 to 3.115 will be blank (read Step 3 on page SEN2) **3.10**

- Tick box 3.11 if your accounts do not cover the period from the last accounting date (explain why in the 'Additional information' box, box 3.116) **3.11**

- Tick box 3.12 if your accounting date has changed (only if this is a permanent change and you want it to count for tax) **3.12**

- Tick box 3.13 if this is the second or further change (explain in box 3.116 on Page SE4 why you have not used the same date as last year) **3.13**

Capital allowances - summary

	Capital allowances	Balancing charge
Car costing more than £12,000 (excluding cars with low CO₂ emissions). (A separate calculation must be made for each car.)	**3.14** £	**3.15** £
Other business plant and machinery (including cars with low CO₂ emissions and cars costing less than £12,000) read the Notes, page SEN4	**3.16** £	**3.17** £
Agricultural or Industrial Buildings Allowance (A separate calculation must be made for each block of expenditure.)	**3.18** £	**3.19** £
Other capital allowances claimed (Separate calculations must be made.)	**3.20** £	**3.21** £
	total of column above	total of column above
Total capital allowances/balancing charges	**3.22** £	**3.23** £

- Tick box 3.22A if box 3.22 includes enhanced capital allowances for environmentally friendly expenditure. **3.22A**

Income and expenses - annual turnover below £15,000

If your annual turnover is £15,000 or more, ignore boxes 3.24 to 3.26. Instead fill in Page SE2

If your annual turnover is below £15,000, **fill in boxes 3.24 to 3.26 instead of Page SE2.** Read the Notes, page SEN4.

- Turnover including other business receipts and goods etc. taken for personal use (and balancing charges from box 3.23) **3.24** £

- Expenses allowable for tax (including capital allowances from box 3.22) **3.12** £

	box 3.24 minus box 3.25
Net profit (put figure in brackets if a loss)	**3.13** £

SA103   TAX RETURN ■ SELF-EMPLOYMENT: PAGE SE1   *Now fill in Page SE3*

> ▷ **ACTIVITY 3**   ▷ ▷ ▷ ▷

Capone (2)

Required

Complete the first two pages of the self employment supplementary pages (see below) for Capone in Activity 1.

[Answer on p. 185]

Income for the year ended 5 April 2007

Inland Revenue

SELF-EMPLOYMENT

Fill in these boxes first

Name	Tax reference

If you want help, look up the box numbers in the Notes

Business details

Name of business
3.1

Description of business
3.2

Address of business
3.3

Postcode

Accounting period - read the Notes, page SEN2 before filling in these boxes

Start
3.4 / /

End
3.5 / /

- Tick box 3.6 if details in boxes 3.1 or 3.3 have changed since your last Tax return **3.6**

- Date of commencement if after 5 April 2004 **3.7** / /

- Date of cessation if before 6 April 2007 **3.8** / /

- Tick box 3.9 if the special arrangements for certain trades apply - read the Notes, pages SEN11 and SEN12 **3.9**

- Tick box 3.10 if you entered details for all relevant accounting periods on last year's Tax Return and boxes 3.14 to 3.73 and 3.99 to 3.115 will be blank (read Step 3 on page SEN2) **3.10**

- Tick box 3.11 if your accounts do not cover the period from the last accounting date (explain why in the 'Additional information' box, box 3.116) **3.11**

- Tick box 3.12 if your accounting date has changed (only if this is a permanent change and you want it to count for tax) **3.12**

- Tick box 3.13 if this is the second or further change (explain in box 3.116 on Page SE4 why you have not used the same date as last year) **3.13**

Capital allowances - summary

	Capital allowances	Balancing charge
Car costing more than £12,000 (excluding cars with low CO2 emissions). (A separate calculation must be made for each car.)	**3.14** £	**3.15** £
Other business plant and machinery (including cars with low CO2 emissions and cars costing less than £12,000) read the Notes, page SEN4	**3.16** £	**3.17** £
Agricultural or Industrial Buildings Allowance (A separate calculation must be made for each block of expenditure.)	**3.18** £	**3.19** £
Other capital allowances claimed (Separate calculations must be made.)	**3.20** £	**3.21** £
	total of column above	total of column above
Total capital allowances/balancing charges	**3.22** £	**3.23** £

- Tick box 3.22A if box 3.22 includes enhanced capital allowances for environmentally friendly expenditure. **3.22A**

Income and expenses - annual turnover below £15,000

If your annual turnover is £15,000 or more, ignore boxes 3.24 to 3.26. Instead fill in Page SE2

If your annual turnover is below £15,000, **fill in boxes 3.24 to 3.26 instead of Page SE2.** Read the Notes, page SEN4.

- Turnover including other business receipts and goods etc. taken for personal use (and balancing charges from box 3.23) **3.24** £

- Expenses allowable for tax (including capital allowances from box 3.22) **3.12** £

	box 3.24 minus box 3.25
Net profit (put figure in brackets if a loss)	**3.13** £

SA103   TAX RETURN ■ SELF-EMPLOYMENT: PAGE SE1   *Now fill in Page SE3*

Income and expenses - annual turnover £15,000 or more

You must fill in this Page if your annual turnover is £15,000 or more - read the Notes, page SEN2

If you were registered for VAT, do the figures in boxes 3.29 to 3.64, include VAT? **3.27** ☐ or exclude VAT? **3.28** ☐

Sales/business income (turnover)

3.29 £ ☐

Disallowable expenses included in boxes 3.33 to 3.50   **Total expenses**

	Disallowable	Total expenses	
Cost of sales	**3.30** £	**3.46** £	
Construction industry subcontractor costs	**3.31** £	**3.47** £	
Other direct costs	**3.32** £	**3.48** £	box 3.29 *minus* boxes 3.46 + 3.47 + 3.48
		Gross profit/(loss)	**3.49** £
		Other income/profits	**3.50** £
Employee costs	**3.33** £	**3.51** £	
Premises costs	**3.34** £	**3.52** £	
Repairs	**3.35** £	**3.53** £	
General administrative expenses	**3.36** £	**3.54** £	
Motor expenses	**3.37** £	**3.55** £	
Travel and subsistence	**3.38** £	**3.56** £	
Advertising, promotion and entertainment	**3.39** £	**3.57** £	
Legal and professional costs	**3.40** £	**3.58** £	
Bad debts	**3.41** £	**3.59** £	
Interest	**3.42** £	**3.60** £	
Other finance charges	**3.43** £	**3.61** £	
Depreciation and loss/(profit) on sale	**3.44** £	**3.62** £	
Other expenses	**3.45** £	**3.63** £	

Put the total of boxes 3.30 to 3.45 in **box 3.66 below**

Total expenses total of boxes 3.51 to 3.63 **3.64** £

boxes 3.49 + 3.50 *minus* 3.64

Net profit/(loss) **3.65** £

Tax adjustments to net profit or loss

		total of boxes 3.30 to 3.45
Disallowable expenses		**3.66** £
Adjustments (apart from disallowable expenses) that increase profits. Examples are goods taken for personal use and amounts brought forward from an earlier year because of a claim under ESC B11 about compulsory slaughter of farm animals	**3.67** £	
Balancing charges	**3.68** £	
Total additions to net profit (deduct from net loss)		boxes 3.66 + 3.67 + 3.68 **3.69** £
Capital allowances	**3.70** £	
Deductions from net profit (add to net loss)	**3.71** £	boxes 3.70 + 3.71 **3.72** £
Net business profit for tax purposes (put figure in brackets if a loss)		boxes 3.65 + 3.69 *minus* 3.72 **3.73** £

Now fill in Page SE3 ➤

5 Test your knowledge ▷ ▷ ▷

1 Adam's business accounts for the year to 31 March 2007 include the following items. What, if any, adjustments are required?

- Motor expenses for a car used by an employee, private use estimated at 20%.
- Motor expenses for a car used by Adam, private use estimated at 30%.
- Overdraft interest on the business bank account.
- Bank interest on the business deposit account.
- Goods taken by Adam which he paid for at cost.

2 The tax WDV of Adam's car at 1 April 2006 was £16,000. What capital allowances will be given for the year to 31 March 2007 and what will be the tax WDV carried forward at 31 March 2007?

[Answers on p. 188]

6 Summary

Sole traders must adjust their accounting profits in the same way as companies:

- add back disallowable expenditure
- deduct allowable expenditure which is not shown in the accounts
- deduct income shown in the accounts not taxable as trading income
- add income taxable as trading income which is not shown in the accounts.

The main adjustments applying to individuals but not companies are the disallowance of the proprietor's salary and private expenses, and the adjustment of goods taken for the proprietor's own use.

Capital allowances are then deducted from the adjusted trading profits to give the taxable trading profits. The capital allowances must be restricted for the proprietor's own use of business assets.

Answers to chapter activities & 'test your knowledge' questions

△ **ACTIVITY 1**   △ △ △ △

Capone (1)

Adjusted trading profit for 12 months ended 30 June 2006

Expenditure charged but not allowable

Most of the required adjustments will be under this heading. Start at the top of the profit and loss account and work down considering the admissibility of each item in turn and reading any relevant notes. Do not flit from item to item at random since this is a sure way to overlook something. If you do not know for certain whether any particular item is allowable or not, do not waste time by inconclusive pondering – take an informed guess; more often that not you will guess right. Tick off each item as you deal with it.

Remember the main rule of admissibility – the expenditure must be 'incurred wholly and exclusively for the purposes of the trade', in this case the trade of a wine merchant.

The adjustments under this heading are as follows:

	+ £	*Reason*
Net profit per accounts	4,644	
Repairs to premises – floor alterations	1,460	Capital cost
Depreciation – vans and equipment	4,150	Capital cost
Loss on sale of equipment	40	Capital cost
Bad and doubtful debts		
General provision increase	3,350	An appropriation
Loan to employee written off	400	Not wholly and exclusively
Professional charges		
Costs of court action	130	Not wholly and exclusively
Sundry expenses		
Fine	250	Not wholly and exclusively
Donation	20	Not wholly and exclusively
Entertaining	300	Statutory disallowance
Salary – Capone	14,000	Appropriation

Notes:

(1) A company could treat the employee loan write-off as a Schedule D Case III expense under the loan relationship rules. No such relief is available for a sole trader incurring a similar loss.
(2) It is assumed that Capone's wife's salary can be justified as a business expense.

Income credited but not taxable as trading income

It is fairly certain that all credit items will either be assessed under a different heading or will be capital items or will not be taxable.

The adjustments under this heading are as follows:

	- £	*Reason*
Bank deposit interest	160	Taxed under a different heading
Dividends (net)	140	Taxed under a different heading

Expenditure not charged but allowable

Where the home is used for business purposes, part of the running expenses can be allocated to the business, e.g. the business use of the private telephone.

Show £290 as adjustment on the minus side of the computation.

Income not credited but assessable

An adjustment under this heading will normally arise because goods have been taken for the proprietor's own use. Legal precedent has established that this 'sale' is to be brought to account for tax purposes at full market price, i.e. (£455 x $^{100}/_{65}$) = £700.

The £700 will be an adjustment on the plus side of the computation.

Capone
Adjustment of profits for 12 months ended 30 June 2006

	+	-
	£	£
Net profit per accounts	4,644	
Repairs – alterations to flooring	1,460	
Depreciation of vans and equipment	4,150	
Loss on sale of equipment	40	
Bad and doubtful debts		
General provision increase	3,350	
Loan to employee written off	400	
Professional charges		
Costs re court action	130	
Sundry expenses		
Fine	250	
Donation	20	
Entertaining customers	300	
Salary – Capone	14,000	
Bank deposit interest		160
Dividends		140
Business calls from home telephone		290
Goods withdrawn by Capone (£455 x $\frac{100}{65}$)	700	
	29,444	590
	(590)	
Adjusted trading profit (before capital allowances)	28,854	

△ ACTIVITY 2   △ △ △ △

Ernest

Capital allowances computation – plant and machinery

	General pool £	Expensive car £	Private use asset £	Allowances £
Year ended 31 December 2005				
WDV b/f at 1 January 2005	24,000			
Additions				
15 April 2005		12,600		
16 July 2005	9,200			
17 August 2005			9,400	
Disposals				
30 April 2005	(3,200)			
	30,000			
WDA (25%)	(7,500)	(3,000) [1]	(2,350) [2]	12,145
WDV c/f	22,500	9,600	7,050	
Total allowances				12,145
Year ended 31 December 2006				
Disposals				
Car proceeds		(9,400)	(7,900)	
Balancing charge			(850) [3]	(595)
Balancing allowance		200		200
WDA 25%	(5,625)			5,625
WDV at 31 December 2006	16,875			
Total allowances				5,230

Notes:

(1)   Restricted to maximum £3,000

(2)   Business use for allowances column = (2,350 x 70%) = 1,645.

(3)   Business portion of charge = (850 x 70%) = 595.

△ ACTIVITY 3   △△△△

Income for the year ended 5 April 2007

Inland Revenue

SELF-EMPLOYMENT

	Name	Tax reference
Fill in these boxes first		

If you want help, look up the box numbers in the Notes

Business details

Name of business

3.1 Manuel Costa

Description of business

3.2 Wholesale clothing distributor

Address of business

3.3

Accounting period - read the Notes, page SEN2 before filling in these boxes

Start	End
3.4 01 / 07 / 05	**3.5** 30 / 06 / 06

Postcode

- Tick box 3.6 if details in boxes 3.1 or 3.3 have changed since your last Tax return **3.6**

- Date of commencement if after 5 April 2004 **3.7** / /

- Date of cessation if before 6 April 2007 **3.8** / /

- Tick box 3.9 if the special arrangements for certain trades apply - read the Notes, pages SEN11 and SEN12 **3.9**

- Tick box 3.10 if you entered details for all relevant accounting periods on last year's Tax Return and boxes 3.14 to 3.73 and 3.99 to 3.115 will be blank (read Step 3 on page SEN2) **3.10**

- Tick box 3.11 if your accounts do not cover the period from the last accounting date (explain why in the 'Additional information' box, box 3.116) **3.11**

- Tick box 3.12 if your accounting date has changed (only if this is a permanent change and you want it to count for tax) **3.12**

- Tick box 3.13 if this is the second or further change (explain in box 3.116 on Page SE4 why you have not used the same date as last year) **3.13**

Capital allowances - summary

	Capital allowances	Balancing charge
• Car costing more than £12,000 (excluding cars with low CO$_2$ emissions). (A separate calculation must be made for each car.)	**3.14** £	**3.15** £
• Other business plant and machinery (including cars with low CO$_2$ emissions and cars costing less than £12,000) read the Notes, page SEN4	**3.16** £ 2,480	**3.17** £
• Agricultural or Industrial Buildings Allowance (A separate calculation must be made for each block of expenditure.)	**3.18** £	**3.19** £
• Other capital allowances claimed (Separate calculations must be made.)	**3.20** £	**3.21** £
	total of column above	total of column above
Total capital allowances/balancing charges	**3.22** £ 2,480	**3.23** £

- Tick box 3.22A if box 3.22 includes enhanced capital allowances for environmentally friendly expenditure. **3.22A**

Income and expenses - annual turnover below £15,000

If your annual turnover is £15,000 or more, ignore boxes 3.24 to 3.26. Instead fill in Page SE2 ➤

If your annual turnover is below £15,000, **fill in boxes 3.24 to 3.26 instead of Page SE2**. Read the Notes, page SEN4.

- Turnover including other business receipts and goods etc. taken for personal use (and balancing charges from box 3.23) **3.24** £

- Expenses allowable for tax (including capital allowances from box 3.22) **3.12** £

	box 3.24 minus box 3.25
Net profit (put figure in brackets if a loss)	**3.13** £

SA103   TAX RETURN ■ SELF-EMPLOYMENT: PAGE SE1   *Now fill in Page SE3* ➤

Income and expenses - annual turnover £15,000 or more

You must fill in this Page if your annual turnover is £15,000 or more - read the Notes, page SEN2

If you were registered for VAT, do the figures in boxes 3.29 to 3.64, include VAT? 3.27 ☐ or exclude VAT? 3.28 ☐

Sales/business income (turnover)
3.29 £ 400,000

	Disallowable expenses included in boxes 3.33 to 3.50	Total expenses
● Cost of sales	3.30 £	3.46 £ 232,000
● Construction industry subcontractor costs	3.31 £	3.47 £
● Other direct costs	3.32 £	3.48 £

box 3.29 minus boxes 3.46 + 3.47 + 3.48
Gross profit/(loss) 3.49 £ 168,000

Other income/profits 3.50 £

● Employee costs	3.33 £ 15,709	3.51 £ 84,655
● Premises costs	3.34 £	3.52 £ 35,310
● Repairs	3.35 £	3.53 £ 3,490
● General administrative expenses	3.36 £	3.54 £
● Motor expenses	3.37 £ 710	3.55 £ 2,000
● Travel and subsistence	3.38 £	3.56 £
● Advertising, promotion and entertainment	3.39 £	3.57 £
● Legal and professional costs	3.40 £ 640	3.58 £ 1,060
● Bad debts	3.41 £	3.59 £
● Interest	3.42 £	3.60 £
● Other finance charges	3.43 £	3.61 £
● Depreciation and loss/(profit) on sale	3.44 £ 3,510	3.62 £ 3,510
● Other expenses	3.45 £	3.63 £ 5,770

Put the total of boxes 3.30 to 3.45 in box 3.66 below

total of boxes 3.51 to 3.63
Total expenses 3.64 £ 135,795

boxes 3.49 + 3.50 *minus* 3.64
Net profit/(loss) 3.65 £ 32,205

Tax adjustments to net profit or loss

	total of boxes 3.30 to 3.45
● Disallowable expenses	3.66 £ 20,569
● Adjustments (apart from disallowable expenses) that increase profits. Examples are goods taken for personal use and amounts brought forward from an earlier year because of a claim under ESC B11about compulsory slaughter of farm animals	3.67 £
● Balancing charges	3.68 £

Total additions to net profit (deduct from net loss)

boxes 3.66 + 3.67 + 3.68
3.69 £ 20,569

● Capital allowances	3.70 £ 2,480
● Deductions from net profit (add to net loss)	3.71 £

boxes 3.70 + 3.71
3.72 £ 2,480

Net business profit for tax purposes (put figure in brackets if a loss)

boxes 3.65 + 3.69 *minus* 3.72
3.73 £ 50,294

TAX RETURN ■ SELF-EMPLOYMENT: PAGE SE2

Now fill in Page SE3

Test your knowledge △ △ △

1   The adjustments required are:

· None. The employee may have a taxable benefit.

· 30% of the motor expenses should be added back.

· None. Allowable trade expense.

· Deduct. Taxed under a different heading

· Add the profit that would have been made had Adam paid the full selling price.

2   Capital allowances £3,000 (restricted) x 70% = £2,100.

Tax WDV carried forward at 31 March 2007 = £16,000 - £3,000 = £13,000

PARTNERSHIP PROFIT ALLOCATION

INTRODUCTION

One of the tasks in the assessment will relate to either a sole trader or a partnership (i.e. an unincorporated business).

Both are given the same tax treatment with one extra step for partnerships, which is covered in this chapter.

CONTENTS

1 Allocation of profits
2 Change in profit sharing arrangements
3 Partnership changes

PERFORMANCE CRITERIA

This chapter covers the following performance criteria:
· Divide profits and losses of partnerships amongst partners (18.2 C)

1 Allocation of profits

1.1 Computation of taxable trade profits

There is no difference between a sole trader and a partnership when applying the rules for computing the adjustment of the profits of a partnership. A partnership is merely treated for tax purposes as a collection of sole traders.

Each partner is assessed on his share of partnership profits as if he were a sole trader earning those profits.

1.2 Division of profits between partners

Profits are allocated according to the profit sharing arrangements during the *accounting period* in which profits are earned.

○ EXAMPLE   ○○○○

Andrew and Bernard have been in business for many years, drawing up their accounts to 31 December each year, and sharing profits in the ratio of 2:1.

The partnership's taxable trade profits for the year ended 31 December 2006 were £37,500.

Show how these profits are allocated to partners.

Solution

	Andrew	Bernard	Total
1 January 2006 – 31 December 2006	£25,000	£12,500	£37,500

○ EXAMPLE   ○○○○

Vivienne, Caroline and Marie started business on 1 January 2006. They shared profits as follows:

Interest on fixed capital	10%
Salaries	
Vivienne	£3,000 per annum
Caroline	£4,000 per annum
Marie	£3,000 per annum
Share of balance	
Vivienne	60%
Caroline	20%
Marie	20%

Capital account balances were as follows:

Vivienne	£10,000
Caroline	£5,000
Marie	£5,000

The taxable trade profits of the partnership for the year ended 31 December 2006 were £80,000.

Show how these profits are allocated to the partners.

Solution

Profits are allocated as follows:

	Total £	Vivienne £	Caroline £	Marie £
Interest on capital (10% x capital)	2,000	1,000	500	500
Salaries	10,000	3,000	4,000	3,000
Balance 60:20:20	68,000	40,800	13,600	13,600
Total adjusted trading profits	80,000	44,800	18,100	17,100

It is important to realise that the whole profit of £80,000 is classed as taxable trade profits.

Even though there is reference to salaries and interest, this is merely a means of allocation. For example, Vivienne is now treated as having taxable trade profits of £44,800, *not* employment income.

2 Change in profit sharing arrangements

2.1 Principle of allocating profits

Where there is a change in the profit sharing arrangements during the accounting period, the period must be split into two or more parts (depending on the number of changes), with a separate division among the partners for each part.

○ EXAMPLE

Rosie, Fran and Gilly have been in business for many years.

During the year ended 31 December 2006, their taxable trade profits were £94,000. Profits were shared as follows:

	Rosie £	Fran £	Gilly £
To 30 June 2006			
Salary (per annum)	10,000	6,100	-
Balance	1	1	1
To 31 December 2006			
Salary (per annum)	-	-	-
Balance	2	1	1

Beware, the salaries are quoted per annum. However, if a change occurs during an accounting period the salary must be pro rated.

Show how the profits would be allocated between the partners.

Solution

Year ended 31 December 2006

	Total £	Rosie £	Fran £	Gilly £
Period 1 January 2006				
- 30 June 2006 ($^6/_{12}$)				
Salary	8,050	5,000	3,050	
Balance (1:1:1)	38,950	12,983	12,983	12,984
	———			
(£94,000 x $^6/_{12}$)	47,000			
	———			
Period 1 July 2006				
- 31 December 2006 ($^6/_{12}$)				
Balance (2:1:1)	47,000	23,500	11,750	11,750
	———	———	———	———
Total	94,000	41,483	27,783	24,734
	———	———	———	———

The profits are deemed to accrue evenly over time. Each partner now has their own taxable trade profits for the accounting period.

3 Partnership changes

3.1 Principle of allocating profits

Where there is a change in the partnership during the accounting period, the period must be split into two or more parts (depending on the number of changes), exactly as for a change in the profit share arrangement.

○ EXAMPLE ○○○○

Charles and David began to trade in partnership with effect from 1 July 2003, preparing accounts to 30 June each year and sharing profits equally.

On 1 January 2005, Edward joined the partnership. Profits were then split in the ratio 2:2:1 until 31 October 2006 when David died. Profits and losses were then split in the ratio 3:2.

The tax adjusted trading profits of the partnership were as follows:

	£
Year ended 30 June 2004	70,000
Year ended 30 June 2005	73,200
Year ended 30 June 2006	74,000
Year ended 30 June 2007	75,600

Show the profit allocation for each partner for each accounting period.

Solution

Allocate accounting period profits to partners according to profit share, splitting the accounting period where appropriate.

	C £	D £	E £	Total £
Year ended 30 June 2004 (1:1)	35,000	35,000	–	70,000
Year ended 30 June 2005				
1 July 2004 – 31 Dec 2004 (1:1) $(^6/_{12})$	18,300	18,300	–	36,600
1 Jan 2005 – 30 June 2005 (2:2:1)$(^6/_{12})$	14,640	14,640	7,320	36,600
	32,940	32,940	7,320	73,200
Year ended 30 June 2006 (2:2:1)	29,600	29,600	14,800	74,000
Year ended 30 June 2007				
1 July 2006 – 31 Oct 2006 (2:2:1) $(^4/_{12})$	10,080	10,080	5,040	25,200
1 Nov 2006 – 30 June 2007 (3:2) $(^8/_{12})$	30,240	–	20,160	50,400
	40,320	10,080	25,200	75,600

▷ ACTIVITY 1

John, Michael, Nick and Liz

John, Michael and Nick commenced business on 1 October 2003, making up accounts to 30 September each year and sharing profits equally.

On 1 January 2005, Liz was admitted to the partnership and profits continued to be shared equally.

On 1 July 2006, Michael retired and on 31 December 2007 the partnership was dissolved.

The adjusted profits of the partnership, after deducting capital allowances, were as follows:

	£
Year ended 30 September 2004	30,000
Year ended 30 September 2005	36,000
Year ended 30 September 2006	42,500
Year ended 30 September 2007	40,000
Three months to 31 December 2007	17,500

Required

Show the allocation of profits to each partner for all accounting periods.

[Answer on p. 195]

4   Test your knowledge

1   Brian and Mary trade in partnership sharing profits equally and preparing accounts to 31 December. If they want to change their profit shares to 1/3:2/3 on 1 July 2006 they need to prepare accounts to 30 June 2006. True or false?

2   Partners' salaries and interest on capital are deductible in computing adjusted trading profit. True or false?

[Answers on p.195]

5   Summary

The taxable trade profits of a partnership are apportioned amongst the partners in accordance with the profit sharing arrangements during the accounting period.

Where there are salaries and interest on capital these should be dealt with first, and then any balance shared out using the profit sharing ratio.

Answers to chapter activities & 'test your knowledge' questions

△ ACTIVITY 1   △△△△

John, Michael, Nick and Liz

	Total £	John £	Michael £	Nick £	Liz £
Year ending 30 September 2004	30,000	10,000	10,000	10,000	-
Year ending 30 September 2005					
1 October 2004 – 31 December 2004	9,000	3,000	3,000	3,000	
1 January 2005 – 30 September 2005	27,000	6,750	6,750	6,750	6,750
	36,000	9,750	9,750	9,750	6,750
Year ending 30 September 2006					
1 October 2005 – 30 June 2006	31,875	7,969	7,969	7,969	7,968
1 July 2006 – 30 September 2006	10,625	3,541	-	3,542	3,542
	42,500	11,510	7,969	11,511	11,510
Year ending 30 September 2007	40,000	13,334		13,333	13,333
Period ending 31 December 2007	17,500	5,833		5,833	5,834

Test your knowledge △ △ △

1   False. The profits are time apportioned to the period before and after 30 June, and then allocated using the profit sharing ratio in each period.

2   False. Salaries and interest must be added back in calculating adjusted trading profit. They are then taken into account in apportioning the profit between the partners.

BASIS PERIODS

INTRODUCTION

Sole traders and partners must complete a tax return each year.

There are rules to determine which profits go onto which tax return, with special rules for the opening and closing years of a business.

CONTENTS

1 Fiscal years
2 Current year basis
3 Opening year rules
4 Closing year rules
5 Partnerships

PERFORMANCE CRITERIA

This chapter covers the following performance criteria:
·   Apply the basis of assessment for unincorporated businesses in the opening and closing years (18.2 D)

1   Fiscal years

1.1   Fiscal year

An individual in business will need to complete a tax return for a fiscal year (also known as a tax year or year of assessment).

A fiscal year runs from 6 April to the following 5 April.

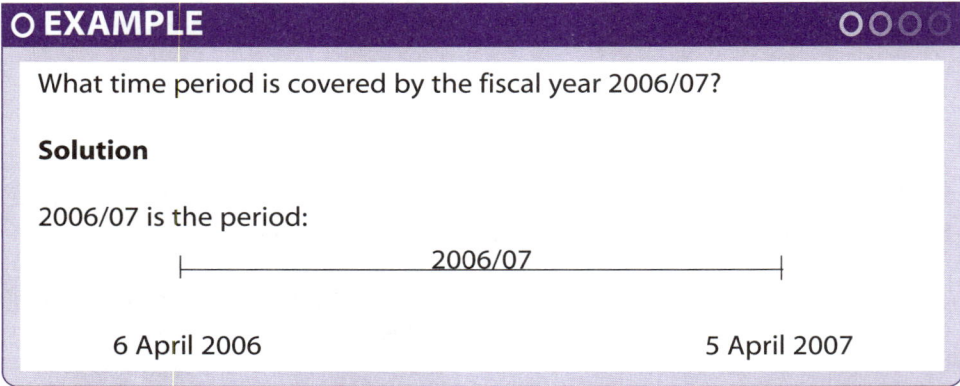

○ **EXAMPLE**   ○○○○

What time period is covered by the fiscal year 2006/07?

Solution

2006/07 is the period:

2006/07

6 April 2006   5 April 2007

We need to determine which taxable trade profits are to be dealt with in which fiscal year.

2   Current year basis

2.1   Ongoing business

The basic rule is that the taxable trade profits for any fiscal year will be based on the profit for the 12 month period of account ending in that year. This is known as the current year basis.

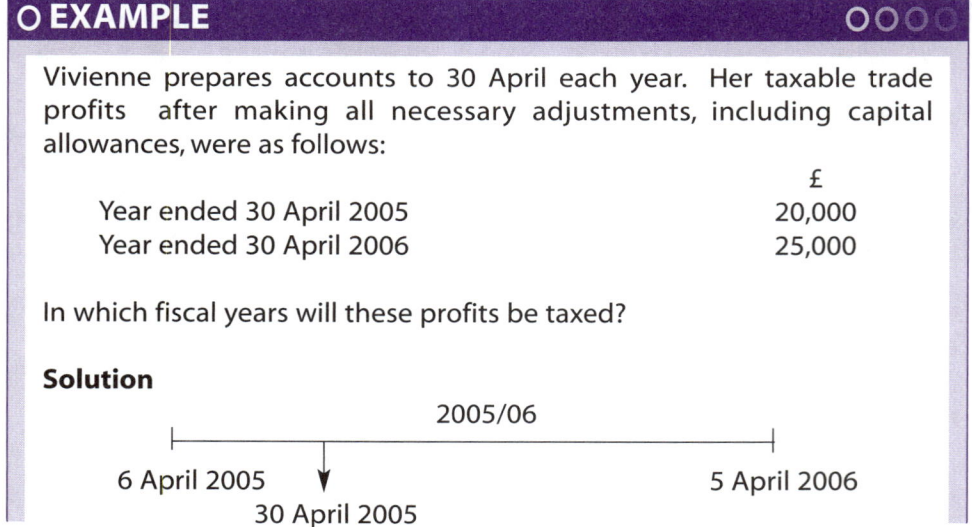

○ **EXAMPLE**   ○○○○

Vivienne prepares accounts to 30 April each year. Her taxable trade profits after making all necessary adjustments, including capital allowances, were as follows:

	£
Year ended 30 April 2005	20,000
Year ended 30 April 2006	25,000

In which fiscal years will these profits be taxed?

Solution

2005/06

6 April 2005   5 April 2006

30 April 2005

Year ended 30 April 2005 ends in 2005/06 and will therefore be taxed fully in 2005/06.

Likewise, year ended 30 April 2006 ends in 2006/07 and will therefore be taxed fully in 2006/07.

An individual can choose whichever accounting period it wants for its business, but care must be taken to tax the profits in the correct accounting period.

O EXAMPLE OOOO

In which tax years will the following profits be taxed?

Profits for year ending: 30 April 2007
31 March 2007
30 June 2007
31 January 2007
31 December 2006

Solution

Profits for year ending:	*Tax year of assessment*
30 April 2007	2007/08
31 March 2007	2006/07
30 June 2007	2007/08
31 January 2007	2006/07
31 December 2006	2006/07

It often helps to draw a diagram showing the beginning and end of the fiscal year and mark on the accounting period end to ensure you select the correct fiscal year.

3 Opening year rules

3.1 Special rules

It is a fundamental concept of the current year basis that, over the life of a business, profits should be taxed once and once only.

Suppose a business starts trading on 1 July 2006 and prepares accounts up to 30 June 2007.

Although the business starts in 2006/07 there is no accounting period ending in 2006/07, so if the normal current year basis applied, there would be no assessment in 2006/07.

To make sure that there is an assessment in every year the business trades, there are special opening year rules. These are explained below.

(a) **First tax year**

The first tax year is the year in which the business started. The basis of assessment is the period from the commencement date to the following 5 April. This is known as the actual basis of assessment.

(b) **Second tax year**

(i) If accounts are prepared to a date in the second tax year which is 12 months or more after the business started, the assessment is based on the profits of the 12 months to the end of that period.

(ii) If accounts are prepared to a date in the second tax year which is less than 12 months after the business started, the assessment is the profits of the first 12 months trading.

(iii) If no accounts are prepared to a date in the second tax year, the assessment is the actual profits of the second tax year (6 April to 5 April).

(c) **Third year**

The third tax year the assessment is the 12 months to the accounting date, this is usually the current year basis.

Note:

(i) HM Revenue and Customs aim to tax something in the first year of trading, and the amount will depend on when trading started.

(ii) In the second year of trading, 12 months of profits will be taxed. Which 12 months this is depends on the accounting date selected by the individual.

For the purposes of your assessment, any apportionments of profit are made on a monthly basis (not daily).

The following examples will illustrate the three possibilities for the second tax year.

○ EXAMPLE   ○○○○

Lara started in business on 1 November 2004, preparing accounts on 31 October each year.

Her adjusted profits were as follows:

	£
Year ended 31 October 2005	18,000
Year ended 31 October 2006	37,500
Year ended 31 October 2007	44,000

What are the taxable trade profits for the first four fiscal years of trading?

Solution

Her taxable trade profits are therefore as follows:

Year of assessment	Basis period	Assessment £
2004/05	1 November 2004 – 5 April 2005 £18,000x $^5/_{12}$	7,500
2005/06	1 November 2004 – 31 October 2005	18,000
2006/07	1 November 2005 – 31 October 2006	37,500
2007/08	1 November 2006 – 31 October 2007	44,000

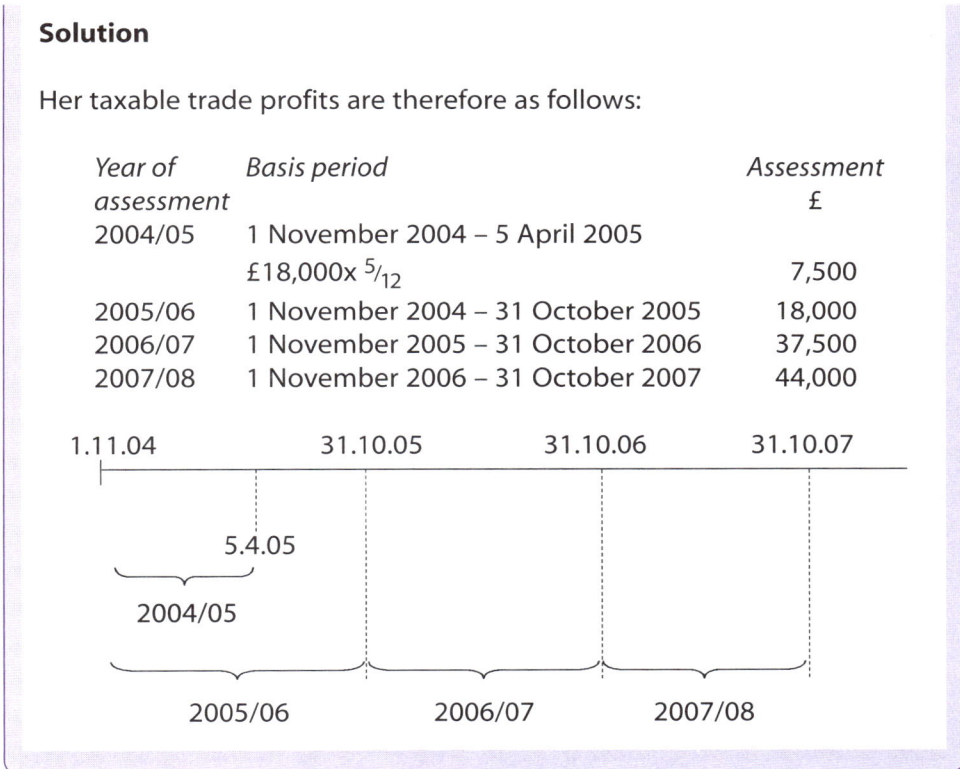

3.2 Overlap profits

When an individual starts to trade, some profits are often taxed twice. Profits assessed in more than one year are called overlap profits.

In the previous example, the following profits are assessed in both 2004/05 and 2005/06.

1 November 2004 to 5 April 2005 = £18,000 x $^5/_{12}$ = £7,500

One of the fundamental features of the current year basis is that a trader will, over the life of the business, be taxed on profits only once.

Overlap profits are relieved by being deducted from the final assessment when an individual ceases to trade. This will be considered later in the chapter.

○ EXAMPLE ○○○○

Edrich started in business on 1 July 2004. He prepared his first set of accounts for the six months ended 31 December 2004 and then for calendar years thereafter.

His adjusted profits were as follows:

	£
Six months ended 31 December 2004	3,100
Year ended 31 December 2005	7,600
Year ended 31 December 2006	8,200
Year ended 31 December 2007	6,400

Show the taxable trade profits for the tax years 2004/05 to 2007/08 inclusive, and calculate the amount of any overlap profits.

Solution

His taxable trade profits are therefore as follows:

Year of assessment	Basis period	Assessment £
2004/05	1 July 2004 – 5 April 2005	
	£3,100 + (£7,600 x $^3/_{12}$)	5,000
2005/06	1 January 2005 – 31 December 2005	7,600
2006/07	1 January 2006 – 31 December 2006	8,200
2007/08	1 January 2007 – 31 December 2007	6,400

There are overlap profits of £1,900 (£7,600 x $^3/_{12}$) for the period from 1 January 2005 to 5 April 2005.

O EXAMPLE   O O O O

Hammond started in business on 1 January 2005. He made up his first set of accounts for the seven months ended 31 July 2005 and annually to 31 July thereafter.

His adjusted profits were as follows:

	£
Seven months ended 31 July 2005	10,500
Year ended 31 July 2006	33,600
Year ended 31 July 2007	19,800

Show the taxable trade profits for the tax years 2004/05 to 2007/08 inclusive, and calculate the amount of any overlap profits.

Solution

The business commenced on 1 January 2005, which is in 2004/05.

The second tax year is 2005/06 and the accounts ending in that period are those for the seven months to 31 July 2005. This date is less than 12 months after the business started. Therefore the second year assess the first 12 months trading.

Remember we must tax 12 months of profits in the second year.

His taxable trade profits are therefore as follows:

Year of assessment	Basis period	Assessment £
2004/5	1 January 2005 – 5 April 2005	
	£10,500 x $^3/_7$	4,500
2005/06	1 January 2005 – 31 December 2005	
	£10,500 + (£33,600 x $^5/_{12}$)	24,500
2006/07	1 August 2005 – 31 July 2006	33,600
2007/08	1 August 2006 – 31 July 2007	19,800

There are overlap profits of £18,500 (£4,500 + (£33,600 x $^5/_{12}$)).

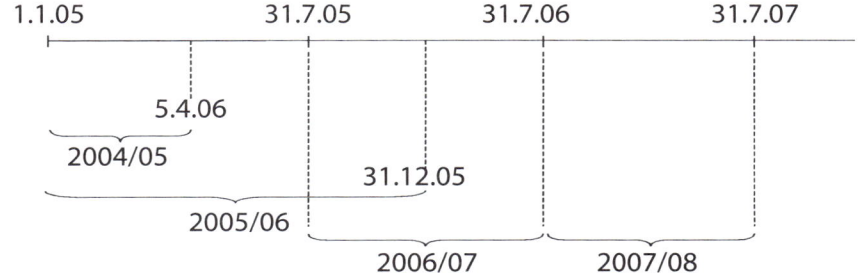

○ EXAMPLE ○○○○

Yallop started in business on 1 February 2005. He prepared his first set of accounts for the 18 months to 31 July 2006 and annually to 31 July thereafter.

His adjusted profits were as follows:

	£
18 months ended 31 July 2006	9,000
Year ended 31 July 2007	2,680

Show the taxable trade profits for the tax years 2004/05 to 2007/08 inclusive, and calculate the amount of any overlap profits.

Solution

The taxable trade profits are as follows:

Year of assessment	Basis period	Assessment £
2004/05	1 February 2005 – 5 April 2005	
	£9,000 x $^2/_{18}$	1,000
2005/06	6 April 2005 – 5 April 2006	
	£9,000 x $^{12}/_{18}$	6,000
2006/07	1 August 2005 – 31 July 2006	
	£9,000 x $^{12}/_{18}$	6,000
2007/08	1 August 2006 – 31 July 2007	2,680

There are overlap profits of £4,000 (£9,000 x $^8/_{18}$).

These cover the period 1 August 2005 to 5 April 2006.

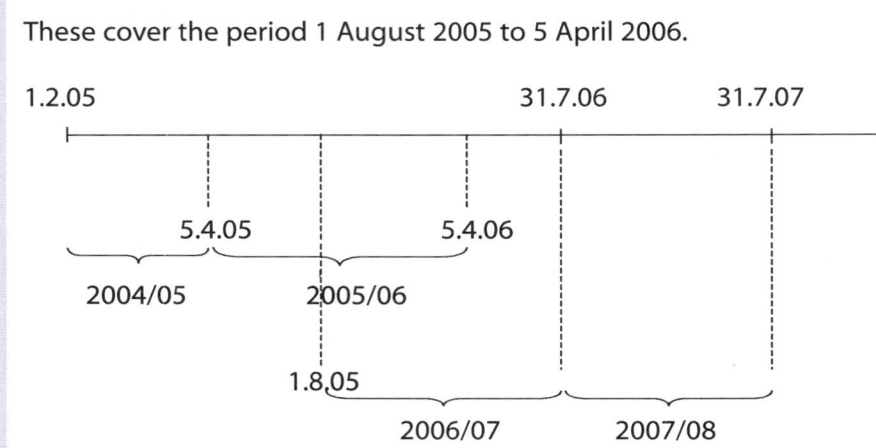

Note: In this example there is only an 18 month period ending in 2006/07. However, as we must only assess 12 months of profits, so we take the last 12 months ending on the accounting date (i.e. 12 m/e 31 July 2006).

4 Closing year rules

4.1 Method of assessment

When an individual trader ceases to trade, any profits not yet assessed will be taxed in the tax year in which trading ceases.

Therefore, for the last few accounting periods, identify in which fiscal year they end. Assess the profits in these fiscal years.

This could result in more than one account period's profits being assessed in the final fiscal year.

○ EXAMPLE ○○○○

Hutton has been in business for many years, preparing his accounts to 30 June each year. Owing to ill-health, he stopped trading on 31 January 2007.

His adjusted profits were as follows:

	£
Year ended 30 June 2005	12,000
Year ended 30 June 2006	10,000
Seven months ended 31 January 2007	3,640

Show the taxable trade profits for the last two fiscal years of assessment.

Solution

Step 1: Identify in which fiscal year the last few accounting periods end.

Accounting period	Ends in
Year ended 30 June 2005	2005/06
Year ended 30 June 2006	2006/07
Seven months ended 31 January 2007	2006/07

Step 2: Assess the profits in the fiscal years shown on the right hand side.

His taxable trade profits are therefore as follows:

Year of assessment	Basis period	Assessment £
2005/06	1 July 2004 – 30 June 2005	12,000
2006/07	1 July 2005 – 31 January 2007	
	(£10,000 + £3,640)	13,640

4.2   Overlap profits

As previously stated, one of the fundamental features of the current year basis is that a trader will, over the life of the business, be taxed on profits only once.

Overlap profits are relieved by being deducted from the assessment of the final fiscal year.

○ EXAMPLE   ○○○○

Barrington started in business on 1 August 2003, making up accounts to 31 July each year. He ceased to trade on 31 July 2007, on which date his business was acquired by another firm.

His adjusted profits were as follows:

	£
Year ended 31 July 2004	15,000
Year ended 31 July 2005	23,000
Year ended 31 July 2006	27,000
Year ended 31 July 2007	35,600
	———
Total adjusted profits	100,600
	———

Show the taxable trade profits for the tax years 2003/04 to 2007/08 inclusive and calculate the amount of any overlap profits.

Solution

Step 1: Identify the fiscal year in which trade commences.

In this year profits from the date of commencement to 5 April will be assessed (1 August 2003 is in 2003/04).

Step 2: Deal with the second fiscal year.

After this you should be able to identify the amount of the overlap profits (second fiscal year has a 12 month period ending in it).

Step 3: Work out assessments for all years up to year of cessation

All other years will be taxed on the current year basis until the year of cessation.

Step 4: Work out the final year assessment

In the tax year of cessation all profits not yet assessed are assessed. In this example it is straightforward as all periods are 12 months long. (Note in which fiscal years the last few accounting periods end – e.g. year ended 31 July 2007 ends in 2007/08.)

Step 5: Deduct overlap profits

Finally, deduct from the final assessment the overlap profits.

The taxable trade profits are as follows:

Year of assessment	Basis period	Assessment £
2003/04	1 August 2003 – 5 April 2004 £15,000 x $^8/_{12}$	10,000
2004/05	1 August 2003 – 31 July 2004	15,000
2005/06	1 August 2004 – 31 July 2005	23,000
2006/07	1 August 2005 – 31 July 2006	27,000
2007/08	1 August 2006 – 31 July 2007 (£35,600 - £10,000)	25,600
Total assessments		100,600

The overlap profits amount to £10,000. This sum is deducted from the assessment for the final tax year (2007/08) which thus becomes £35,600 - £10,000 = £25,600.

Barrington's aggregate profits over his four years of trading total £100,600 and his aggregate taxable trade profits for the five tax years involved come to exactly the same figure.

> ## ▷ ACTIVITY 1   ▷ ▷ ▷ ▷
> **Robert and Jack**
>
> (a) Robert started in business on 1 May 2004. His first set of accounts was
>   prepared to 30 September 2004 and he then retained 30 September as
>   his year end.
>
>   Adjusted results in the early years were as follows:
>
> | | £ |
> |------------------------------------|--------|
> | 1 May 2004 – 30 September 2004 | 20,250 |
> | Year ended 30 September 2005 | 29,700 |
> | Year ended 30 September 2006 | 36,450 |
> | Year ended 30 September 2007 | 28,350 |
>
> (b) Jack started in business on 1 January 2004 and prepared his first set of
>   accounts to 30 April 2005. He then continued to make up his accounts
>   to 30 April and adjusted results in the early years were as follows:
>
> | | £ |
> |---------------------------------|--------|
> | 1 January 2004 – 30 April 2005 | 37,800 |
> | Year ended 30 April 2006 | 26,325 |
> | Year ended 30 April 2007 | 28,350 |
>
> **Required:**
>
> Show the amounts assessable for all fiscal years affected by these results and
> compute any overlap profits.
>
> [Answer on p. 210]

5   Partnerships

5.1   Separate traders

A partnership is treated as a collection of individual traders.

Therefore, if some individuals have been trading in partnership for many years,
each will be assessed on his own share of the profits on a current year basis.

5.2   Partners joining

Where an individual joins the partnership, he alone will be assessed using the
opening year rules on his share of the partnership profits. The remaining
partners will use the current year basis.

5.3   Partners leaving

Where an individual leaves the partnership, he alone will be assessed using the
closing year rules on his share of the partnership profits. The remaining
partners will use the current year basis.

5.4 Procedure for partnerships

The correct procedure to follow for partnerships is:

Step 1: Adjust profits of the accounting period (including calculating capital allowances) for the partnership as a whole.

Step 2: Allocate the profits of the accounting period to the partners using the profit share arrangement.

Step 3: Take each partner in turn to determine whether to apply current year basis, opening year rules or closing year rules.

O EXAMPLE   OOOO

Using the results of the Charles and David example in Chapter 15 as set out below, calculate the taxable trade profits for each partner in 2003/04 to 2007/08.

	C £	D £	E £	Total £
Year ended 30 June 2004 (1:1)	35,000	35,000	-	70,000
Year ended 30 June 2005				
1 July 2004 – 31 Dec 2004 (1:1) ($^6/_{12}$)	18,300	18,300	-	36,600
1 Jan 2005 – 30 June 2005 (2:2:1) ($^6/_{12}$)	14,640	14,640	7,320	36,600
	32,940	32,940	7,320	73,200
Year ended 30 June 2006 (2:2:1)	29,600	29,600	14,800	74,000
Year ended 30 June 2007				
1 July 2006 – 31 Oct 2006 (2:2:1) ($^4/_{12}$)	10,080	10,080	5,040	25,200
1 Nov 2006 – 30 June 2007 (3:2) ($^8/_{12}$)	30,240	-	20,160	50,400
	40,320	10,080	25,200	75,600

Solution

Steps 1 and 2 of the procedure have already been completed.

Step 3: Determine the basis of assessment for each partner.

· Charles commenced in partnership on 1 July 2003, hence apply the opening year rules:

Year of assessment	Basis period	Assessment £
2003/04	1 July 2003 – 5 April 2004	
	£35,000 x $^9/_{12}$	26,250
2004/05	Year ended 30 June 2004	35,000
	(Overlap profits = £26,250)	
2005/06	Year ended 30 June 2005	32,940
2006/07	Year ended 30 June 2006	29,600
2007/08	Year ended 30 June 2007	40,320

·   David commenced in partnership on 1 July 2003 and ceased on 31 October 2006, hence apply both opening and closing year rules:

Year of assessment	Basis period	Assessment £
2003/04	1 July 2003 – 5 April 2004	
	£35,000 x $^9/_{12}$	26,250
2004/05	Year ended 30 June 2004	35,000
	(Overlap profits = £26,250)	
2005/06	Year ended 30 June 2005	32,940
2006/07	1 July 2004 – 31 October 2006	
	(29,600 + 10,080 – 26,250)	13,430

·   Edward commenced on 1 January 2005 (i.e. his first accounts are for the 6 months ended 30 June 2005), hence apply opening year rules:

Year of assessment	Basis period	Assessment £
2004/05	1 January 2005 – 5 April 2005	
	$^3/_6$ x £7,320	3,660
2005/06	1 January 2005 – 31 December 2005	
	£7,320 + ($^6/_{12}$ x £14,800)	14,720
	Overlap profits (£3,660 + 7,400)	11,060
2006/07	Year ended 30 June 2006	14,800
2007/08	Year ended 30 June 2007	25,200

In the assessment you will probably only need to perform Step 3 for one of the partners.

6   Test your knowledge

1   The basis of assessment is always the 12 months to the accounting date ending in the tax year. True or false?

2   If Paul started trading on 1 August 2005 and prepares account to 5 April each year, he will have no overlap profits. True or false?

3   If a new partner joins, he is straight away taxed on his share of the profits of the accounting period ending in the tax year. True or false.

[Answers on p.209]

7   Summary

As the final step in assessing profits of an individual, we must consider whether to apply:

·   current year basis.
·   opening year rules (and calculate overlap profits).
·   closing year rules (and deduct overlap profits).

Answers to chapter activities & 'test your knowledge' questions

△ ACTIVITY 1   △ △ △ △

1   Robert and Jack

(a)   Robert

Year of assessment	Basis period	Assessment £
2004/05	1 May 2004 – 5 April 2005	
	$20{,}250 + (£29{,}700 \times {}^6/_{12})$	35,100
2005/06	Year ending 30 September 2005	29,700
2006/07	Year ending 30 September 2006	36,450
2007/08	Year ending 30 September 2007	28,350

There are overlap profits of £14,850 ($£29{,}700 \times {}^6/_{12}$).

(b)   Jack

Year of assessment	Basis period	Assessment £
2003/04	1 January 2004 – 5 April 2004 ($£37{,}800 \times {}^3/_{16}$)	7,087
2004/05	Year ending 5 April 2005 ($£37{,}800 \times {}^{12}/_{16}$)	28,350
2005/06	Year ending 30 April 2005 ($£37{,}800 \times {}^{12}/_{16}$)	28,350
2006/07	Year ending 30 April 2006	26,325
2007/08	Year ending 30 April 2007	28,350

There are overlap profits of £25,987 ($£37{,}800 \times {}^{11}/_{16}$).

These cover the period 1 May 2004 to 5 April 2005.

Test your knowledge △ △ △

1   False. This is not true in the opening and closing years.

2   True. The taxable trade profits of 2005/06 will be those of the period to 5 April 2006, and for 2006/07 will be those of the year to 5 April 2007, and so on. There are no overlap periods.

3   False. The opening year rules apply to individuals joining a partnership as if they had commenced a new trade.

TRADING LOSSES FOR INDIVIDUALS

INTRODUCTION

As for companies, individuals can also make trading losses. This chapter discusses how a loss is calculated and how it can be relieved. This could form a written or computational part of a task.

PERFORMANCE CRITERIA

This chapter covers the following performance criteria:

· Adjust trading profits and losses for tax purposes (18.2 A)
· Divide profits and losses of partnerships amongst partners (18.2 C)
· Apply the basis of assessment for unincorporated businesses in the opening and closing years (18.2 D)

1 Identification of a trading loss

A trading loss is identified in exactly the same way as a trading profit.

In other words, the accounting profit (or loss) is adjusted for tax purposes, and capital allowances are taken into account. The adjusted loss is then identified with the tax year in which it arose. This is shown in the examples below.

○ EXAMPLE

A trader has a net accounting profit of £10,000 for the year ended 31 December 2006 which includes £2,000 of disallowable expenses. Capital allowances of £14,000 are available.

What are the taxable trade profits for 2006/07?

Solution

	£
Year ended 31 December 2006	
Net profit	10,000
Add back Disallowable expenses	2,000
	12,000
Less: Capital allowances	(14,000)
Adjusted loss	(2,000)

In this situation when a loss is identified, the 2006/07 assessment is determined as nil and there is a (£2,000) trading loss available for relief.

○ EXAMPLE

A trader has a net accounting loss of £10,000 for the year ended 31 December 2006 which includes £2,000 of disallowable expenses. Capital allowances of £14,000 are available.

What are the taxable trade profits for 2006/07 and the trading loss available for relief?

Solution

	£
Accounting loss	(10,000)
Add back disallowables	2,000
	(8,000)
Less: Capital allowances	(14,000)
Adjusted loss	(22,000)

The assessment for 2006/07 is nil. The loss available is £22,000.

It is easy to identify the wrong amount of loss available by not paying sufficient attention to the arithmetic. Capital allowances, which normally reduce a profit, will increase a loss.

2 Ongoing businesses

2.1 Options available

There are two ways of relieving a trading loss in an ongoing business.

· S380 relief against total income of the current and/or preceding year.
· S385 relief against future trading profits only.

You are not required to know the section numbers referred to above but they are useful identification labels.

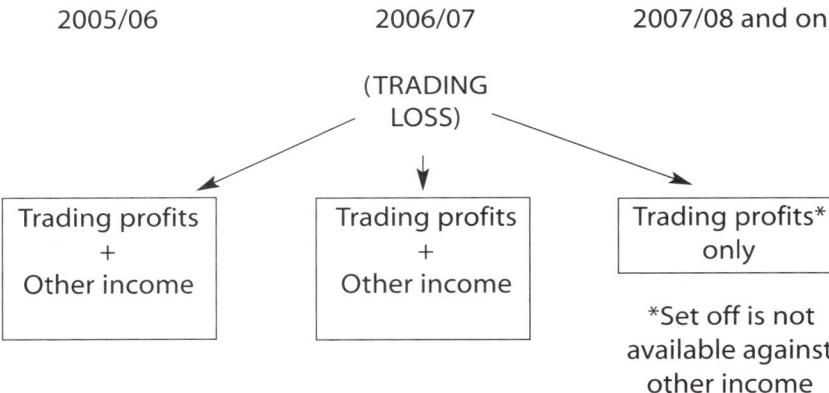

2005/06	2006/07	2007/08 and on

(TRADING LOSS)

Trading profits + Other income	Trading profits + Other income	Trading profits* only

*Set off is not available against other income

2.2 S380 ICTA 1988 - Set off of trading loss against total income

S380 relief allows the trading loss to be set against total income for the tax year of the loss and/or the preceding tax year, in any order.

A claim can be made to obtain relief in either year in isolation, or in both years, in any order.

When applying the loss relief it cannot be restricted to preserve the personal allowance.

Any excess loss over and above total income is available for relief by carrying forward.

○ **EXAMPLE**　　　　　　　　　　　　　　　　○○○○

Beryl has a trading loss in her accounting year ended 30 September 2006 of £18,000.

Her other income is as follows:

	2005/06	2006/07
	£	£
Taxable trade profits	14,000	Nil
Other income	2,000	6,000

What alternative claims could she make to obtain loss relief under S380 ICTA 1988?

Solution

The loss for the year ended 30 September 2006 is identified with the tax year 2006/07 as the year ends in the fiscal year 2006/2007. As a result the taxable trade profits for that year are nil.

Under S380, the loss could be used either in that year and/or the previous tax year 2005/06 as follows:

· Set off £6,000 in 2006/07 and relieve the balance of £12,000 in 2005/06, or
· Set off £6,000 in 2006/07 and make no claim for 2005/06, or
· Set off £16,000 in 2005/06 and relieve the balance of £2,000 in 2006/07, or
· Set off £16,000 in 2005/06 and make no claim for 2006/07.

It is important to identify all the options available (this is a frequent question requirement) before deciding the course of action you will take.

2.3　S385 ICTA 1988 - Future relief for trading losses

As we have seen, S380 relief (against total income) can only be used in the same tax year as the loss and/or the previous year. This may mean that there is still an amount of trading loss unrelieved after considering this option.

However, the individual taxpayer does not *have* to claim relief for the loss under S380 at all, so all of the loss is unrelieved. Whatever the reason, any trading loss *not* relieved in the same or previous tax year is carried forward.

The trading loss carried forward must then be relieved against the first available taxable trading profits from the same trade. This is known as S385 relief.

The loss will reduce any future taxable trade profits to nil as long as the loss is available; the set off cannot be restricted.

O EXAMPLE ○○○○

Derek has been trading for some time preparing accounts to 31 July.

His recent adjusted trading results are as follows:

		£
Year ended 31 July 2004	Profit	18,000
Year ended 31 July 2005	Loss	43,200
Year ended 31 July 2006	Profit	13,000
Year ended 31 July 2007	Profit	15,000

Derek's other income each year is £12,000 (gross).

Show Derek's total income for all fiscal years affected by the above results assuming:

(a) no claim is to be made against total income for a relevant year under S380 for the trading loss.

(b) full S380 claims are to be made to obtain relief in respect of as early a year as possible.

Solution

(a) **If no claim is made under S380**

The trading loss of 2005/06 is carried forward against future trading profits.

	2004/05	2005/06	2006/07	2007/08
	£	£	£	£
Taxable trade profits	18,000	Nil	13,000	15,000
S385 relief carry forward			(13,000)	(15,000)
	18,000	Nil	Nil	Nil
Other income	12,000	12,000	12,000	12,000
Total income	30,000	12,000	12,000	12,000

Loss memorandum

	£
Year ended 31 July 2005	43,200
S385 2006/07	(13,000)
2007/08	(15,000)
Carry forward to 2007/08	15,200

(b) **Full S380 claims made**

S380 can only be made for 2004/05 and 2005/06 and any balance is carried forward for relief against future trading profits.

	2004/05 £	2005/06 £	2006/07 £	2007/08 £
Taxable trade profits	18,000	Nil	13,000	15,000
S385 relief			(1,200)	-
			11,800	15,000
Other income	12,000	12,000	12,000	12,000
STI	30,000	12,000	23,800	27,000
S380 relief	(30,000)	(12,000)		
Revised total income	Nil	Nil	23,800	27,000

Loss memorandum

	£
Year ended 31 July 2005	43,200
S380 2004/05	(30,000)
2005/06	(12,000)
	1,200
S385 carry forward 2006/07	(1,200)
Loss left to carry forward	Nil

▷ ACTIVITY 1

Caroline

Caroline, a single woman, has been in business as a gourmet caterer since 1 July 2003.

She made up accounts for calendar years and her adjusted trading results before capital allowances were as follows:

	£
Six months ended 31 December 2003	4,900
Year ended 31 December 2004	10,500
Year ended 31 December 2005	(25,000)
Year ended 31 December 2006	350

Caroline also receives a salary of £2,000 per annum from part-time secretarial work. On 1 January 2004 she opened a bank deposit account; interest was credited to her account in June and December each year as follows (gross amounts are given).

	£
June 2004	100
December 2004	120
June 2005	110
December 2005	105
June 2006	98
December 2006	102

In each of 2005/06 and 2006/07 Caroline received building society interest of £8,500 (gross).

Required

Calculate Caroline's total income for the years 2004/05 to 2006/07 inclusive, assuming reliefs for losses are claimed as early as possible.

[Answer on p. 224]

3 New businesses

3.1 Interaction of losses with rules on basis periods

When an individual sets up a new business, trading losses are often incurred in the early years until the business is established. The loss reliefs available to an ongoing business (i.e. S380 relief and S385 relief) are all available and, in addition, there is a special relief available known as S381 relief.

As well as considering any loss reliefs available, it is important in a new business to take account of the interaction of those losses with the opening year basis periods rules.

Whereas the assessment of taxable trade profits can give rise to 'overlap' profits, which are relieved either on a subsequent cessation or change of accounting date, a trade loss can only be used once. Remember that all calculations where an apportionment is required must be done on a 'monthly' basis for exam purposes.

○ EXAMPLE ○○○○

Darwin starts to trade on 1 January 2005.

Adjusted trading results are as follows:

	£
6 months to 30 June 2005	(10,000)
Year ended 30 June 2006	8,000

Show the opening assessments, and compute the loss available for relief.

Solution

		Available loss	Assessment
	£	£	£
2004/05 (opening year rule 1 Jan 2005 – 5 Apr 2005) (£10,000) x $^3/_6$		(5,000)	Nil
2005/06 (year 2 – first 12 months rule applies as no 12 month period ended in tax year) *6 months ended 30 June 2005* *Less* Allocated to 2004/05	(10,000) 5,000		
	(5,000)		
Plus 6 months of year ended 30 June 2006 £8,000 x $^6/_{12}$	4,000		
	(1,000)	(1,000)	Nil
2006/07 Year ended 30 June 2006		_____	8,000
		(6,000)	

There is only (£6,000) loss available for use under the loss relief rules as £4,000 has been used to extinguish a profit in 2005/06 automatically under the basis of assessment rules.

3.2 S381 ICTA 1988 - Special relief available to new businesses

In addition to the loss reliefs covered so far, a trading loss arising in any of the first four tax years of assessment of a new business may be carried back against total income of the three tax years immediately preceding the loss making year.

This is done on a 'first in first out' basis (FIFO). The figure below illustrates how this works.

S381 relief

2001/02	2002/03	2003/04	2004/05 Year 1	2005/06 Year 2	2006/07 Year 3	2007/08 Year 4
			Business commences			
			Profit	Loss	Profit	Profit
	(1)	(2)	(3)			
	total income	total income	total income			

○ **EXAMPLE**   ○○○○

In which years could the loss of 2007/08 be relieved using S381 relief?

Solution

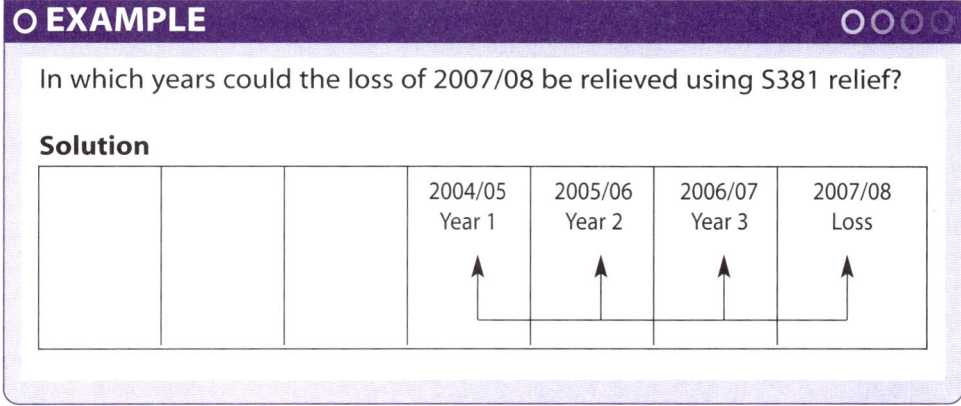

			2004/05 Year 1	2005/06 Year 2	2006/07 Year 3	2007/08 Loss

As with S380, the set off is against total income.

The claim is a single claim for all three years. It cannot be made separately for any of the years.

S381 and S380 claims can be made in any order the taxpayer chooses.

○ **EXAMPLE**   ○○○○

Livingstone commenced a new business on 1 January 2005. The adjusted trading profits or losses were as follows:

		£
Year to 31 December 2005	Loss	(13,400)
Year to 31 December 2006	Profit	1,800

There are no capital allowances. Previously Livingstone had been employed and his earnings for recent years were as follows:

	£
2004/05	6,000
2003/04	14,000
2002/03	13,000
2001/02	11,000

He had no other sources of income.

Show the possible claims for loss relief under:

(a)   S380; and
(b)   S381.

Approach to the example

·   First identify the available trading losses and profits for trading income assessment purposes.
·   Outline the various ways any losses available could be relieved under S380.

- Show the alternative situation under S381.
- In carrying out these steps deal with losses in chronological date order.

Step 1: Available losses and trading income assessments

- Opening year is 2004/05.

- Opening accounting period 1 January 2005 – 31 December 2005.

Year of assessment	Basis period	£	Loss £	Assessment £
2004/05	1 January 2005 – 5 April 2005			
	(£13,400 x $^3/_{12}$)		(3,350)	Nil
2005/06	Year ended 31 December 2005			
	Loss	(13,400)		
	Less Allocated to 2004/05	3,350		
			(10,050)	Nil
	Loss available for loss reliefs		(13,400)	
2006/07	Year ended 31 December 2006			1,800

Steps 2 and 4: Consider S380 relief

S380 relief allows a trading loss to be used against total income in the year of loss and/or the preceding year.

- 2004/05 loss (£3,350) could be used against total income £6,000 in 2004/05, or could be used against total income £14,000 in 2003/04.

  There is insufficient loss to consider both, but the loss would be fully utilised.

- 2005/06 loss (£10,050) could be partly used against total income £6,000 in 2004/05.

  It could not be used in 2005/06 as there is no total income so the balance (£10,050 - £6,000) = £4,050 would have to be carried forward for relief against future trading profits. Note that this assumes that the 2004/05 loss is relieved against 2003/04 in priority to 2004/05.

Step 3: Consider S381 relief

S381 allows any loss in the first four tax years to be carried back. The losses in 2004/05 and 2005/06 therefore qualify and would be relieved as follows:

		£	Notes
2004/05	Loss	3,350	Relieve against total income of £11,000 for 2001/02, therefore fully utilised.
2005/06	Loss	10,050	Relieve against total income of £13,000 for 2002/03, therefore fully utilised.

> **ACTIVITY 2**

Knight

Knight, a bachelor, started a business on 1 May 2004. His taxable trade profits are as follows:

		£
Year ended 30 April 2005	Profit	6,120
Year ended 30 April 2006	Loss	(28,480)
Year ended 30 April 2007	Profit	7,630

Prior to commencing in business Knight had been in salaried employment.

His employment earnings for 2002/03 and 2003/04 were £9,400 and £13,660 respectively. In addition he enjoys savings income amounting to £1,700 (gross) each year.

Required

Show how Knight will obtain relief for the loss if he makes a claim under S381, the special loss relief available to a new business.

Approach to the question

First identify the opening year basis periods and calculate the taxable trade profits or losses available.

Then calculate total income for all relevant years.

Set up a loss memorandum working and enter the loss(es) available.

Allocate the loss relief by carry back under S381.

[Answer on p. 224]

4 Cessation of a business

4.1 Calculating the terminal loss

The following loss reliefs need to be considered when a business ceases.

· S380 relief against total income.
· A special relief known as 'terminal loss' relief under S388 ICTA 1988.

If the business is ceasing, then any trading losses not relieved will be lost. There can be no carry forward under S385 against future trading profits, as it is a requirement that such losses are used against profits *of the same trade*.

Under S388 ICTA 1988, the terminal loss is available for relief against:

· the taxable trade profits for the final tax year (if any); and

· the taxable trade profits of the *three* preceding tax years on a last in first out basis.

The terminal loss is the loss of the last 12 months of trading. This will include relief for overlap profits brought forward.

5 Partnership losses

5.1 Reliefs available to partners

Partners are allocated losses in the same way as profits. Each partner is then entitled to decide independently on how to use his individual share of loss.

An ongoing partner could use his loss under S380 or S385.

A partner newly arrived can add S381 to his list of possible claims.

A partner ceasing could claim S380 or S388.

6 Test your knowledge

1   Kate has been trading for many years. How can a trading loss of the year to 31 December 2006 be relieved?

2   A trader who ceases trading can carry any unrelieved trading losses forward against future income. True or false?

3   If a partnership makes a loss, all partners must claim loss relief in the same way. True or false?

4   Fred started trading on 1 May 2006. If he makes a trading loss in the 11 month accounting period to 5 April 2007, how can it be relieved?

[Answers on p. 225]

7 Summary

The loss reliefs available are summarised below.

Commencement

· Consider S381 – losses in first four years carry back.
· Use S380 relief against total income – year of loss and/or preceding year.
· Then use S385 to relieve against future trading profits.

Ongoing business

·   S380
·   S385

Cessation

·   S380
·   S388 – terminal loss relief

Answers to chapter activities & 'test your knowledge' questions

△ ACTIVITY 1 △ △ △ △

Caroline

Income tax computations

	2004/05 £	2005/06 £	2006/07 £
Taxable trade profits	10,500	Nil	350
S385	-	-	(350) [3]
	10,500	Nil	Nil
Employment income	2,000	2,000	2,000
Bank deposit interest (actual)	220	215	200
Building society interest	-	8,500	8,500
	12,720	10,715	10,700
S380	(12,720) [1]	(10,715) [2]	-
Total income	Nil	Nil	10,700

Loss memorandum

		£
Loss in 2005/06 – year ended 31 December 2005		25,000
Less: S380 claim 2004/05 (preceding year)	(1)	(12,720)
		12,280
Less: S380 claim 2005/06 (year of loss)	(2)	(10,715)
		1,565
Less: S385 claim 2006/07 (carry forward)	(3)	(350)
Loss carried forward		1,215

△ ACTIVITY 2 △ △ △ △

Knight

(a) First identify the basis periods and hence taxable trade profits or losses available arising in each fiscal year.

		Loss available £	Taxable trade profits £
2004/05	(1 May 2004 – 5 April 2005) £6,120 x $^{11}/_{12}$		5,610
2005/06	(Year ended 30 April 2005)		6,120
2006/07	(Year ended 30 April 2006)	28,480	Nil
2007/08	(Year ended 30 April 2007)		7,630

2006/07 is the year of the loss.

(b) The loss of £28,480 sustained in 2006/07 will be set off under S381 as follows:

	2003/04 £	2004/05 £	2005/06 £
Employment income	13,660	-	-
Taxable trade profits	-	5,610	6,120
Savings income	1,700	1,700	1,700
	15,360	7,310	7,820
Less: S381 claim	(15,360)	(7,310)	(5,810)
Revised total income	Nil	Nil	2,010

(c) **Loss memorandum**

	£
S381 loss	28,480
Less: S381 claim 2003/04	(15,360)
	13,120
Less: S381 claim 2004/05	(7,310)
	5,810
Less: S381 claim 2005/06	(5,810)
	Nil

Test your knowledge △ △ △

1   Under S380 by set off against other income of 2005/06 and/or 2006/07 (in any order). Any balance unrelieved can be carried forward and set against future trading profits of the same trade.

2   False. Losses carried forward can only be set against future trading income from the same trade. If the trade ceases, the losses cannot be carried forward.

3   False. Each partner can choose independently what loss relief to claim.

4   Under S380 by set off against other income of 2005/06 and/or 2006/07 (in any order). Under S381 against other income of 2003/04, 2004/05 and 2005/06, in that order.   Any balance unrelieved can be carried forward and set against future trading income.

PAYMENT AND ADMINISTRATION

INTRODUCTION

In the assessment, a client may ask for written advice on when to submit tax returns, or pay tax, for example. This could be in the form of an e-mail, letter or a memorandum. This chapter covers tax returns and amendments, the payment of tax and enquiries.

CONTENTS

1 Introduction to the self assessment return
2 Payment of income tax and capital gains tax
3 Interest and penalties on payments of tax
4 HM Revenue and Customs' enquiries

PERFORMANCE CRITERIA

This chapter covers the following performance criteria:

- Identify the due dates of payment of income tax by unincorporated businesses, including payments on account (18.2 E)
- Complete correctly the self-employed and partnership supplementary pages to the tax return for individuals, together with relevant claims and elections, and submit them within statutory time limit (18.2 G)
- Consult with HM Revenue & Custom's staff in an open and constructive manner (18.2 H)

1 Introduction to the self assessment return

1.1 The self assessment return

Certain individuals are required to complete a return for every fiscal year. Amongst other things this covers trading income and capital gains and, in some cases, a calculation of the tax payable.

The key details to grasp concerning the return are the *dates*.

The completed and signed return must normally be filed by:

- *30 September* following the fiscal year if you would prefer HM Revenue and Customs (HMRC) to compute the tax payable, or

- *31 January* following the fiscal year with a computation ('self assessment') of the tax payable.

The relevant dates for a 2006/07 return are therefore 30 September 2007 and 31 January 2008.

When a return is not issued until after *31 October* following a tax year, then filing is required within three months after the date of issue.

The return consists of a ten page summary form with supplementary pages. Some individuals with simpler affairs may receive a short four page return.

In the assessment you will only be required to complete the first two of the self employment supplementary pages.

Where a tax return is not issued, an individual is required to notify HMRC by *5 October* following the fiscal year where there is chargeable income (i.e. new sources of income) or gains arising. Notification is not required where there are no assessable gains or where the income is either covered by allowances or the full tax liability has been deducted at source.

The taxpayer is permitted to correct or 'repair' his self assessment return within 12 months of the filing date. HMRC can correct 'obvious errors' in the period of nine months from actual filing.

1.2 Records

An individual must retain certain records to support the completed tax return.

Self employed people must keep records for five years after the filing date (i.e. until 31 January 2013 for 2006/07 information).

Examples of records to be kept include the following:

- Accounts.
- Documentation, receipts, invoices.
- Dividend vouchers.

1.3 Penalties for late filing

Failure to submit a return by 31 January *following a fiscal year* will result in a flat rate penalty. The system operates as follows:

Short delay (i.e. between 31 January and 31 July)	£100
Delay of more than six months (i.e. 31 July – up to 12 months late)	a further £100
Delay of more than 12 months	Tax geared penalty

In certain cases, HMRC may apply to the General or Special Commissioners (independent Tribunals) for a penalty of up to £60 per day. This will be used where HMRC are of the opinion that fixed penalties alone will not result in the submission of the return.

However, the penalties cannot exceed any tax liability due (i.e. if the tax liability is only £90, the fixed penalty will be so restricted).

2 Payment of income tax and capital gains tax

2.1 The instalment system

The return of tax information, and the penalties relating thereto, should not be confused with the fact that certain individuals will also need to make payments of tax.

Self employed individuals are subject to an instalment system based upon total liability.

The instalment system operates as follows:

· 31 January *in* the fiscal year: first payment on account (POA).
· 31 July *following* the fiscal year: second payment on account (POA).
· 31 January *following* the fiscal year: final payment

For example in 2006/07 the following dates are relevant:

The payments on account are estimated, in that they are based on the previous year's tax payable.

○ EXAMPLE　○○○○

Roderic, who is 47 and single, is self employed. His only source of income is from his trade. The income tax payable for 2005/06 was £5,100.

His taxable trade profits for the year ended 31 July 2006 are £38,000, giving total tax payable of £6,994.

Ignoring NICs, state Roderic's payments in respect of his 2006/07 income tax liability.

Solution

Step 1: Determine the relevant dates.

31 January 2007	-	first payment on account
31 July 2007	-	second payment on account
31 January 2008	-	final payment

Step 2: Determine the amounts due.

· The amounts due for the 'payments on account' are based on an equal division of the previous year's tax payable, hence £2,550 (£5,100 ÷ 2).

· The final payment on account will be based on the final liability for 2006/07 less the payments on account already made.

	£
2006/07 IT liability	6,994
Payments on account	(5,100)
Final payment	1,894

Step 3: Prepare a final summary.

	£
31 January 2007	2,550
31 July 2007	2,550
31 January 2008	1,894

The amount due on 31 January following the end of the fiscal year is not only the final payment on account for the year just ended, but is also the first payment on account for the new fiscal year.

In Roderic's case this means that on 31 January 2008 he will start the instalment option all over again, by making the first payment on account of his 2007/08 liability based on 2006/07 tax payable.

Hence his 31 January 2008 payment is £5,391 ((£6,994 x ½) + £1,894).

The Class 4 National Insurance contributions payable by a self employed person are also paid by the instalment system (see Chapter 19).

2.2 No requirement for payments on account

Payments on account are not required in the following circumstances:

·   The income tax payable for the previous year by self assessment is less than £500.

·   More than 80% of the income tax liability for the previous year was met through tax deducted at source.

2.3 Capital gains tax

The capital gains tax due for a fiscal year (see Chapter 22) is payable on 31 January following the end of the fiscal year, together with the final payment of income tax.

CGT is therefore paid in one instalment on 31 January following the tax year regardless of whether there was a CGT liability for the previous year.

The CGT liability is not taken into account when determining the payments on account for income tax.

Payments on account of capital gains tax are never required.

▷ **ACTIVITY 1**   ▷ ▷ ▷ ▷

Required

(a)   State the latest date by which the taxpayer should submit the tax return if:
(i)   he wishes HMRC to calculate his income tax liability; and
(ii)   he wishes to calculate his own liability.

(b)   State:
(i)   the normal dates of payment of income tax and Class 4 NIC for a sole trader in respect of the fiscal year 2006/07; and
(ii)   how the amounts of these payments are arrived at.

(c)   State:
(i)   the fixed penalties for late submission of tax returns and when they apply;
(ii)   the circumstances under which the penalties will be reduced; and
(iii) the further penalties which may be imposed where HMRC believe that the fixed penalties will not result in the submission of the return.

[Answer on p. 236]

Approach to the question

When answering a *written* question you should:
·   state your points briefly but in complete sentences or phrases.
·   make each new technical point on a new line to aid clarity.

3 Interest and penalties on payments of tax

3.1 Interest and surcharges

Failure to make payments, whether payments on account or final payments, by the due date will attract interest. Interest is not perceived as being a penalty but merely as commercial restitution for late payment. There is also a penalty system known as *surcharges*.

Interest strictly is calculated on a daily rate, however calculations are required to the nearest month in the assessment.

○ EXAMPLE ○○○○

Rodney was due to make the following payments of tax for 2006/07.

		Actual date of payment
31 January 2007	£2,100	28 February 2007
31 July 2007	£2,100	31 August 2007
31 January 2008	£1,000	31 March 2008

For what periods will interest be charged?

Solution

On first POA	31 January 2007 – 28 February 2007	1 month
On second POA	31 July 2007 – 31 August 2007	1 month
On final payment	31 January 2008 – 31 March 2008	2 months

3.2 Surcharge

In addition to interest, the taxpayer may incur a surcharge on unpaid tax. This only applies to the final payment of income tax and CGT.

The surcharge system operates as follows:

· More than 28 days late   =   5%
· More than six months late   =   Further 5%

A surcharge may be mitigated where the taxpayer can provide a reasonable excuse. Insufficiency of funds or lack of knowledge on self assessment are not reasonable excuses.

4 HM Revenue and Customs' enquiries

4.1 Introduction

HM Revenue and Customs have the statutory power to enquire into an individual's tax return (similar to the enquiry system on corporation tax returns).

They have to issue a written notice to initiate an enquiry and cannot issue a notice more than 12 months after the 31 January filing date or 12 months after the quarter day following the date the return was actually filed if later. The quarter days are 31 January, 30 April, 31 July and 31 October.

The deadline for commencing an enquiry normally allows a taxpayer to assume his return is accepted as final once the anniversary of the filing date is passed.

HMRC may choose a return for enquiry if they suspect that it is incomplete or inaccurate in some respect or it may be selected at random. Their own internal instructions forbid an Officer from giving any reason for the enquiry.

An enquiry may be a full investigation or only concern a part of the return – 'an aspect enquiry'. Once the enquiry is complete it should be closed. As a closed enquiry cannot be re-opened, the Officer might be reluctant to issue a closing notice in case further points arise.

The taxpayer can apply to the General or Special Commissioners for them to set a date for closing the enquiry if the Officer has no grounds for keeping it open.

4.2 Enquiry procedure

Once the enquiry notice is given, an Officer can request relevant documents and written particulars. This means he is entitled to full answers to any specific questions.

There is normally a minimum of 30 days to respond to his requests. An Officer may ask for information not directly relevant to the return such as private bank statements. Opinions differ on whether such requests should be resisted.

At the end of the enquiry a completion notice is issued stating the outcome of the enquiry (e.g. no amendment made or business profits increased by £10,000!).

If HMRC issue an amended assessment on completion, the taxpayer has 30 days from completion to appeal to the General or Special Commissioners against HMRC's amendment.

4.3 Discovery assessments

Although HMRC usually only have 12 months from the filing date to open an enquiry, they can replace a self assessment at a later date by making a discovery assessment.

A discovery assessment can be made where tax has been lost (i.e. under self assessed) even though there has been no fraud or negligence on the part of the taxpayer or his agent.

This usually means that there was insufficient information in the tax return or contentious items in the tax return had not been brought to HMRC's attention for them to choose to open an enquiry within the time limit.

HMRC has five years from the filing date to make a discovery assessment. Where tax is lost through fraud or negligence the time limit is extended to 20 years from the filing date.

The taxpayer can appeal to the Commissioners against a discovery assessment.

4.4 The Appeal Commissioners

The Appeal Commissioners are the Tribunal of first resort to determine disputes between the taxpayer and HMRC. There are two equivalent bodies of Commissioners:

(1) **The General Commissioners**
These are usually local businessmen appointed for their ability to establish the facts. They are supported by a clerk, a solicitor with a knowledge of tax law.

(2) **The Special Commissioners**
These are experienced barristers or solicitors who will normally hear more complicated cases involving interpretation of law.

Both Tribunals are under the Lord Chancellor's Office and are independent of HMRC.

Appeals on points of law (but not on a point of fact) may be taken higher to the High Court, the Court of Appeal and eventually the House of Lords.

The main advantages of using a Tribunal to start (and usually finish) the resolution of a dispute with HMRC is that both parties normally bear their own costs and the procedures are fairly informal.

5   Test your knowledge

1   James commenced his own business in February 2007. If he does not receive a tax return to complete for 2006/07, by what date should he notify HMRC that he is chargeable to tax for 2006/07?

2   Isabel made her second payment on account of tax for 2006/07 on 15 September 2007. What are the consequences?

3   Mike filed his 2006/07 tax return on 19 February 2008. What is the latest date for HMRC to open an enquiry?

[Answers on p. 236]

6   Summary

This chapter covers a core topic – self assessment.

Traders have to self assess because they receive trading income gross.

Pay days

31 January	-	Balancing IT due for fiscal year to previous 5 April.
	-	CGT due for disposals in fiscal year to previous 5 April.
	-	First POA for current fiscal year (based on previous year's liability).
31 July	-	Second POA for current fiscal year.

Main surcharges/penalties

Miss the filing date (normally 31 January)	-	£100 penalty
Tax (not POA) unpaid by 28 February	-	5% surcharge

If no enquiry notice issued by anniversary of the filing date, taxpayer can assume it is 'final'.

However, if HMRC are able to show they had insufficient information supplied in the tax return they have up to five years to make a 'discovery'

Answers to chapter activities & 'test your knowledge' questions

△ ACTIVITY 1   △ △ △ △
Self assessment

(a) (i)   30 September following the tax year to which the return relates (i.e. 30 September 2007 for 2006/07).

   (ii)   31 January following the tax year to which the return relates (i.e. 31 January 2008 for 2006/07).

(b) (i)   (1)   31 January in the tax year (i.e. 31 January 2007).
          (2)   31 July following the tax year (i.e. 31 July 2007).
          (3)   31 January following the tax year (i.e. 31 January 2008).

   (ii)   Payments one and two are equal amounts each amounting to half the income tax payable in respect of the preceding income tax year. Payment three is the balancing figure, i.e. it is the amount of the final tax liability for the year, less payments one and two and any tax deducted at source in 2006/07.

(c) (i)   (1)   £100 if the return is outstanding after 31 January following the tax year.
          (2)   A further £100 if the return is still outstanding 6 months later.

   (ii)   Where a fixed penalty has been imposed for late submission of a return, i.e. £100, but the amount of the income tax liability is less than the penalty (i.e. say £90), the penalty will be reduced to the amount of the liability.

   (iii) Where HM Revenue and Customs consider that the imposition of fixed penalties will not result in the return being submitted, they may ask the General or Special Commissioners to apply further penalties of up to £60 a day until the return is submitted.

Test your knowledge △ △ △

1   James must notify HMRC by 5 October 2007.

2   Isabel will be charged interest from the due date of 31 July 2007 until payment on 15 September 2007. No surcharge is levied on late payments on account.

3   The latest date for opening an enquiry is 30 April 2009, as Mike's return was filed after the due date of 31 January 2008.

NATIONAL INSURANCE CONTRIBUTIONS PAYABLE BY SELF-EMPLOYED INDIVIDUALS

INTRODUCTION

A self employed individual has his/her own National Insurance contributions to pay, but may also have to pay contributions as an employer.

PERFORMANCE CRITERIA

This chapter covers the following performance criteria:

· Identify the National Insurance contributions payable by self employed individuals (18.2 F)

1 Contributions as an employer

1.1 Class 1 secondary and Class 1A contributions

In exactly the same way as a company can be an employer, so can a sole trader or partnership.

The Class 1 secondary and Class 1A contributions payable are calculated in the same way as shown in Chapter 12.

2 Contributions as a sole trader

2.1 Class 4 NICs

A self employed person, whether operating as a sole trader or as a partner, pays two types of National Insurance contributions: Class 2 and Class 4.

Class 4 NICs are calculated by applying a fixed percentage (currently 8%) to the amount by which the taxpayer's 'profits' (or share of 'profits', where the taxpayer is a member of a partnership) exceed a lower limit (£5,035 for 2006/07).

○ EXAMPLE ○○○○

If Nicholas has 'profits' of £10,630 for 2006/07, he will be liable to pay Class 4 NICs calculated as follows:

	£
'Profits'	10,630
Less lower limit	(5,035)
Excess	5,595
Class 4 NICs (8% x £5,595)	448

The 8% rate only applies up to an upper limit of profits (£33,540 for 2006/07).

Where a taxpayer's 'profits' exceed the upper limit, the excess profit is liable to Class 4 NICs at 1%.

For example, if a taxpayer has taxable trading profits of £50,000 for 2006/07 he is liable to Class 4 NICs of £2,445 calculated as follows:

	£
(£33,540 - £5,035) x 8%	2,280
(£50,000 - £33,540) x 1%	165
	2,445

Note that where a taxpayer's 'profits' do not exceed the lower limit (i.e. £5,035 for 2006/07), there is no liability to Class 4 NICs.

2.2   Profits

The 'profits' to be used in the calculation of the taxpayer's liability to Class 4 NICs are the taxable trade profits for the year less trading losses brought forward.

2.3   Payments of Class 4 NICs

Class 4 NICs are payable at the same time as the related income tax liability.

Interest will be charged on late payments.

A taxpayer does not have to pay Class 4 NICs if:

·   aged 65 (or 60, if a woman) or over at the beginning of the fiscal year.
·   aged under 16 at the beginning of the fiscal year.

2.4   Class 2 NICs

In addition to Class 4 NICs, a trader is also liable for Class 2 NICs. This is payable at a fixed rate of £2.10 per week. There is no liability if the 'profits' are below the small earnings limit of £4,465.

'Profits' for Class 2 NICs purposes are the accounts profits (i.e. not tax adjusted) falling in the fiscal year.

3   Effect of partnerships

3.1   Each partner is treated as a separate sole trader

Each have to pay:

·   his own Class 2 contributions; and
·   his own Class 4 contributions.

The Class 4 contributions are based on his own share of profits, as assessed for the fiscal year.

4 Test your knowledge

1 Anne has taxable trading profits for 2006/07 of £4,500. Her accounts show a net profit of £4,600 for the year to 31 March 2007.

· What Class 4 NICs are due?
· What Class 2 NICs are due?

2 Tom trades in partnership. How will his Class 2 and Class 4 NICs be calculated?

3 Graham is a sole trader. He has one employee, James. Must Graham pay any NICs in respect of James?

[Answers on p.241]

5 Summary

Sole traders and partnerships may have to pay the following contributions:

· As employers:
  - Class 1 secondary
  - Class 1A

· As traders:
  - Class 2
  - Class 4

Answers to 'test your knowledge' questions

Test your knowledge △ △ △

1 Anne's NICs for 2006/07 are:

   · Class 4 – Nil, taxable profits less than £5,035;
   · Class 2 - £2.10 per week, accounts profits exceed £4,465.

2 Tom must pay weekly Class 2 NICs, and Class 4 NICs based on his share of profits. 8% on profits in excess of £5,035 up to £33,540. 1% on profits above £33,540.

3 As the employer, Graham is liable to pay secondary Class 1 NICs and will also have to pay Class 1A NICs if any taxable benefits are provided to James.

INTRODUCTION TO CHARGEABLE GAINS

INTRODUCTION

Both individuals and companies pay tax on chargeable gains. We need to identify when chargeable gains arise.

CONTENTS

1   Principle of a chargeable gain
2   Chargeable disposal
3   Chargeable person
4   Chargeable asset

PERFORMANCE CRITERIA

This chapter covers the following performance criteria:
·   Identify and value correctly any chargeable assets that have been disposed of (18.3 A)

1 Principle of a chargeable gain

1.1 The three essential elements

In order for a chargeable gain to be calculated there are three essential requirements.

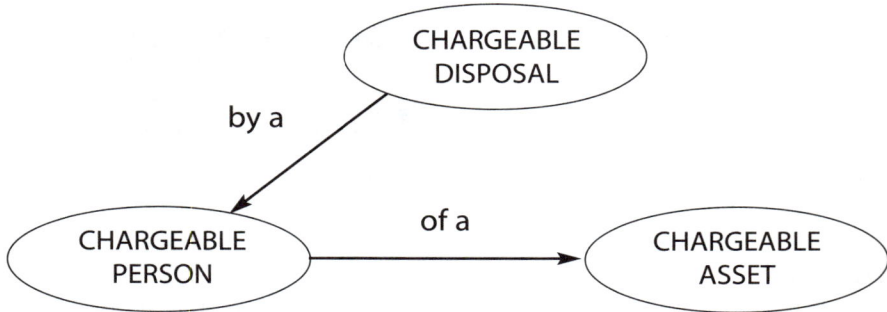

2 Chargeable disposal

2.1 Main types of disposal

A chargeable disposal will include:

· a sale of an asset (whole or part of an asset),
· a gift of an aset, or
· an exchange of an asset.

2.2 Exempt disposals

No gain will be calculated if:

· the sale is a trading disposal (badges of trade – Chapter 14).
· on death of an individual.
· the gift is to a charity.

In the assessment it will be obvious whether the disposal is of:

· stock, therefore dealt with as trading income; or
· a capital item (for example land), therefore calculate a gain.

3 Chargeable person

3.1 Types of person

Chargeable gains will be calculated on disposals by:

· Individuals
· Partners in partnership } - pay capital gains tax
· Companies   - pay corporation tax (see Chapter 6 proforma)

4 Chargeable asset

4.1 Exempt assets

All assets are chargeable unless in the specific list of exempt assets set out below. The list includes those likely to be found in an assessment.

Exempt assets in the list below need to be learned so that you can identify them in a question.

· Motor vehicles.

· Sterling currency, i.e. legal tender in the UK, notably gold sovereigns minted after 1837.

· Any form of loan stock.

· Wasting chattels:
    - a chattel is property that is tangible and moveable.
    - 'wasting' means that it has a life of less than or equal to 50 years.
  The most common examples of wasting chattels are racehorses, greyhounds, boats and caravans.

· Non-wasting chattels, that have both sale proceeds and cost of £6,000 or less.
  The most common examples are works of art and antiques.

· An individual's principal private residence (main house).

5 Test your knowledge ▷ ▷ ▷

1 Bill gave away his trading premises to his daughter Beatrice. Is this a chargeable disposal?

2 ABC Ltd is a building company. It built a small development of 5 houses and sold them. Are these sales chargeable disposals?

3 DEF Ltd sold a racehorse for £10,000. Is this a chargeable disposal?

4 DEF Ltd also sold a portrait for £10,000 which had been hanging in the boardroom. Is this a chargeable disposal?

[Answers on p. 247]

6   Summary

The requirements for a chargeable gain to be calculated are:

· a chargeable disposal; by
· a chargeable person; of
· a chargeable asset.

Answers to 'test your knowledge' questions

Test your knowledge △ △ △

1 Yes, even though Bill receives no actual payment for the property.

2 No. As ABC Ltd is a building company, the proceeds will be dealt with as trading income.

3 No. A racehorse is a wasting chattel and therefore exempt.

4 Yes. The painting is a chattel which was sold for more than £6,000, but is not a wasting chattel.

GAINS AND LOSSES FOR COMPANIES

INTRODUCTION

A company pays corporation tax on its chargeable gains. A calculation of gains may be required as part of a task to compute profits chargeable to corporation tax. This chapter sets out the pro forma for calculating the gain, and explains the separate entries required in the computation.

CONTENTS

1 Proforma computation
2 The capital gains computation
3 Special rules

PERFORMANCE CRITERIA

This chapter covers the following performance criteria:
·   Identify and value correctly any chargeable assets that have been disposed of (18.3 A)
·   Calculate chargeable gains and allowable losses (18.3 C)
·   Ensure that computations and submissions are made in accordance with current tax law and take account of current HM Revenue & Custom's practice (18.3 E)

1 Proforma computation

1.1 The proforma computation (for corporation tax)

Gains and losses are calculated for chargeable accounting periods. Once you have calculated all the individual gains and losses for an accounting period, summarise them as follows:

	£
Gain (1)	X
Gain (2)	X
Loss (3)	(X)
Net gains/(losses) for the current year	X
Capital losses brought forward	(X)
Chargeable gains	X

The chargeable gains are then put into the PCTCT computation and the tax liability is calculated in the normal way. If there is an overall capital loss, it is carried forward and set against future gains. It cannot be relieved against other income.

○ EXAMPLE   ○○○○

Alpha Ltd made three disposals in its year ended 31 March 2007, giving the following results:

Asset	Gain/(loss)
	£
1	20,000
2	5,000
3	(8,000)

What are the net chargeable gains shown on the corporation tax computation?

Solution

Included within PCTCT will be net chargeable gains of £17,000 (20,000 + 5,000 – 8,000).

If the loss on asset 3 had been £(28,000), the corporation tax computation would show net chargeable gains of **nil**. A net loss of £(3,000) (20,000 + 5,000 – 28,000) would be carried forward to offset against the next available net chargeable gains.

The remainder of this chapter considers how to calculate the gains and losses on individual disposals.

2 The capital gains computation

2.1 The standard proforma

	Notes	£
Gross sale proceeds	1	X
Less: Selling costs	2	(X)
Net sale proceeds		NSP
Less: Allowable cost	3	(Cost)
Unindexed gain	4	X
Less: Indexation allowance = Cost x 0.XXX	5	(IA)
Indexed/chargeable gain		Gain

Notes to the proforma

(1) Sale proceeds are usually obvious. However, where a disposal is not at arm's length (e.g. a gift) then *market value* will be substituted.

(2) The selling costs incurred on the disposal of an asset are an allowable deduction. Examples of such costs include valuation fees, advertising costs, legal fees, auctioneer's fees.

(3) The purchase price of an asset is the main allowable cost, but this will also include any additional purchase expenses including legal fees, stamp duty, etc.

(4) The gain after deducting the costs above is known as an unindexed gain.

(5) An indexation allowance may then be available to reduce that gain. This indexation allowance is based upon the retail prices index (RPI) and is intended to give relief for inflation. (RPI = Retail Price Index.)

2.2 The indexation allowance

The indexation allowance runs from the date of the purchase (i.e. when the cost was incurred) to the date of disposal. It is computed by multiplying the acquisition cost by an indexation factor.

The indexation factor, or even the amount of the indexation allowance, may be provided in the assessment. The indexation allowance represents the amount of inflation since the asset was purchased.

The formula for the indexation factor is:

$$\frac{\text{RPI for month of disposal - RPI for month of acquisition}}{\text{RPI for month of acquisition}}$$

This produces a decimal figure which must be rounded to three decimal places.

○ **EXAMPLE** ○○○○

JNN Ltd purchased an asset in August 1984 (RPI = 89.94) and sold it in August 2006 (RPI = 197.6).

What is the indexation factor to be applied to the allowable cost?

Solution

$$\text{Indexation factor} = \frac{\text{RPI August 2006 - RPI August 1984}}{\text{RPI August 1984}}$$

$$= \frac{197.6 - 89.94}{89.94} = 1.1970202\ldots\ldots$$

but rounded to three decimal places = 1.197.

This indicates that for each £1 originally spent in August 1984 there has been £1.197 of inflation to August 2006.

○ **EXAMPLE** ○○○○

ELI Ltd sells a chargeable asset on 31 March 2007 for £24,600 after deducting auctioneer's fees of £400. The asset was acquired on 1 May 1990 for £10,000. What is the chargeable gain?

Assume that the indexation factor for May 1990 to March 2007 is 0.639.

Solution

	£
Gross sales proceeds (March 2007)	25,000
Less: Incidental costs	(400)
Net sale proceeds	24,600
Allowable cost (May 1990)	(10,000)
Unindexed gain	14,600
Indexation allowance (£10,000 x 0.639)	(6,390)
Indexed gain	8,210

Note: Ensure you index the allowable expenditure and not the unindexed gain.

In the assessment you are likely to be given the indexation factor (0.639) or even the indexation allowance amount (£6,390) to make life easier! We use a similar approach for the examples in this text.

Indexation allowance cannot be used to turn a gain into a loss, nor is it available where there is an unindexed loss.

○ **EXAMPLE**　　　　　　　　　　　　　○○○○

JNN Ltd is considering selling a field at auction in August 2006. It acquired the field in August 1984 for £10,000 and the sale proceeds are likely to be one of three results.

(a)　£25,000
(b)　£12,000
(c)　 £8,000

What is the capital gain or loss under each of these alternatives?

The indexation factor from August 1984 to August 2006 is 1.197.

Solution

	(a)	(b)	(c)
	£	£	£
Sale proceeds	25,000	12,000	8,000
Cost	(10,000)	(10,000)	(10,000)
Unindexed gain or (loss)	15,000	2,000	(2,000)
Indexation allowance			
1.197 x £10,000 = £11,530	(11,970)	(2,000)*	Nil**
Indexed gain or allowable loss	3,030	Nil	(2,000)

Notes:
* Restricted, because indexation cannot create a loss.
** No indexation because indexation cannot increase a loss.

▷ **ACTIVITY 1**　　　　　　　　　　　　　▷▷▷▷

JHN Ltd

JHN Ltd made the following disposals in the year ended 31 March 2007.

(1)　On 9 June 2006 it sold some plant for £15,000. The plant was bought in October 1989 for £8,000.

(2)　On 5 September 2006 it sold a building which had been purchased for £27,500 in November 1990. Sale proceeds were £26,500.

(3)　On 1 March 2007 it sold a car, a Trabant, which was bought in February 1984 for £3,000. By the time of the sale, it had become a collector's item and JHN Ltd managed to obtain proceeds of £9,000, out of which it paid £450 in auctioneer's fees.

(4) On 3 March 2007 it sold a collection of military memorabilia for £19,000. It had cost £7,000 in March 1984.

(5) Also on 3 March 2007, it sold some land which was purchased in April 1983 for £15,000. It was sold for £25,000.

Required

Calculate the chargeable gains on each of the above transactions in the year ended 31 March 2007. You should use the following indexation factors.

April 1983 – March 2007	-	1.326
Feb 1984 – March 2007	-	1.272
March 1984 – March 2007	-	1.268
Oct 1989 – June 2006	-	0.706
Nov 1990 – Sept 2006	-	0.581

Approach to the question

It is important that the gain or loss on each transaction is *separately* computed. Finally, prepare a summary adding gains and losses together to arrive at one overall figure.

[Answer on p. 259]

3 Special rules

3.1 Changes to the calculation of the gain

There are a number of special situations that will give rise to slight changes in the calculation of the gains. They are:

· Enhancement expenditure
· Part disposals
· Non-wasting chattels

3.2 Enhancement expenditure

The main allowable cost in computing an unindexed gain is the purchase cost (including incidental costs). Any additional capital expenditure on the asset is also an allowable cost. This normally takes the form of improvement (i.e. enhancement) expenditure.

As the additional expenditure is incurred later than the original expenditure, there will be an impact on the calculation of indexation allowance. Indexation can only be calculated from the actual date of expenditure; therefore, where there is cost plus enhancement expenditure, *two* indexation calculations will be required. It is easy to overlook this extra step.

○ EXAMPLE ○○○○

RMY Ltd bought a shop in November 1987 for £13,200. The company spent £3,800 on improvements in May 1990. The shop was sold for £49,000 in October 2006.

The indexed rise from November 1987 to October 2006 is 0.919 and from May 1990 to October 2006 is 0.572.

You are required to calculate the chargeable gain on the sale of the shop.

Solution

	£
Sale proceeds (October 2006)	49,000
Cost (November 1987)	(13,200)
Enhancement (May 1990)	(3,800)
	———
Unindexed gain	32,000
Indexation allowance	
(a) £13,200 x 0.919	(12,131)
(b) £3,800 x 0.572	(2,174)
	———
Chargeable gain	17,695

3.3   Part disposal

A disposal can be of all or part of an asset. It could for example apply to a disposal of part of a plot of land.

When only **part of an asset is sold**, we know how much the proceeds are, but we cannot immediately determine what the cost was of that part of the asset.

The allowable cost of the part disposed of is calculated using the following formula:

$$\text{Allowable cost of whole asset} \times \frac{A}{A+B}$$

where A =   gross sale proceeds of part disposed of
(i.e. before deducting selling costs).
   B =   market value of the remaining part (will be given in assessment).

○ EXAMPLE ○○○○

John Ltd bought a piece of land in January 1991 for £5,000.

In March 2007 the company sold part of the land for £4,500. At the same time the remaining part was valued at £20,500.

The indexation factor from January 1991 to March 2007 is 0.667.

Calculate the chargeable gain arising on the part disposal of land.

Solution

	£
Sale proceeds	4,500
Less: Allowable cost (£5,000) x $\dfrac{4,500}{4,500 + 20,500}$	(900)
Unindexed gain	3,600
Less: Indexation allowance (0.667 x £900)	(600)
Chargeable gain	3,000

3.4 Non-wasting chattels

In the previous chapter we noted that wasting chattels (i.e. expected life of no more than 50 years) are exempt (e.g. racehorses, greyhounds, boats, caravans).

Special rules apply to non-wasting chattels (e.g. furniture, works of art, antiques).

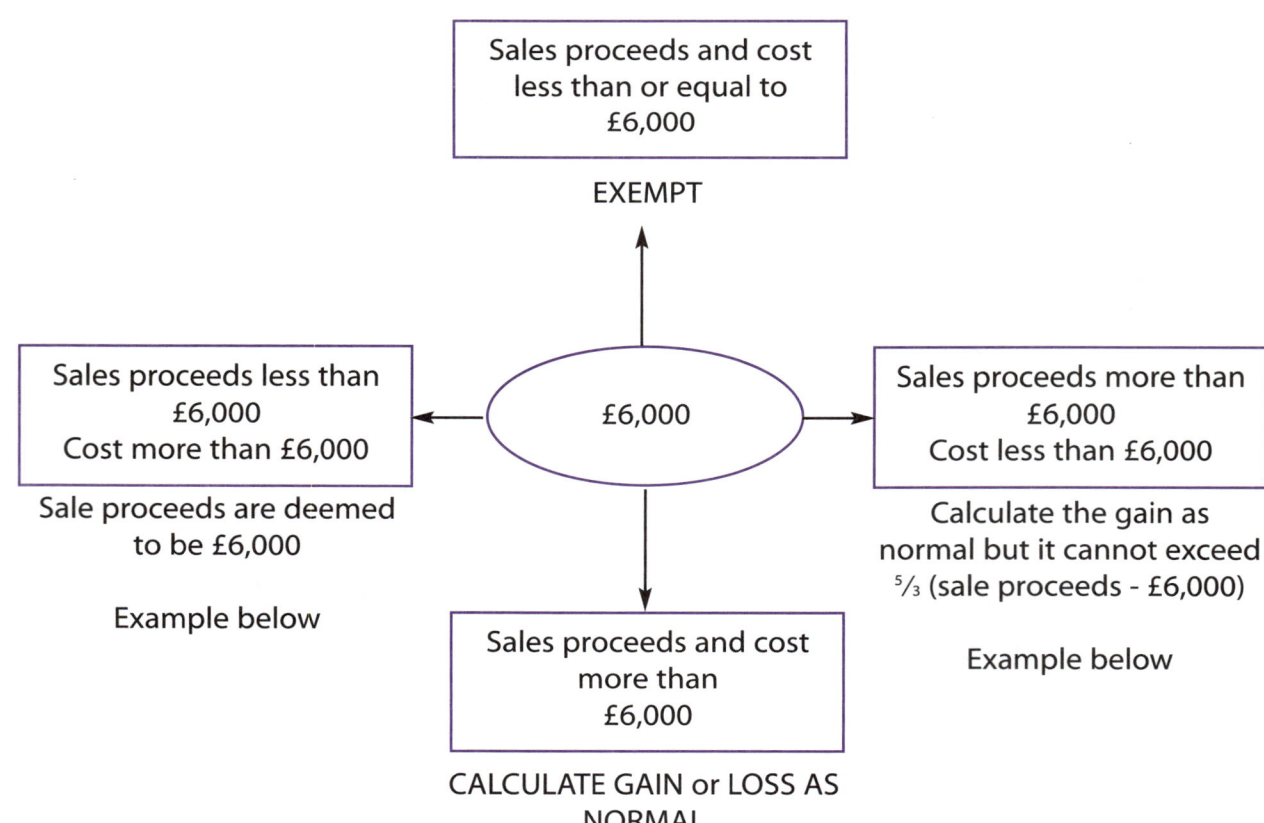

○ EXAMPLE   ○○○○

Harry Ltd sold some antique furniture for £5,000 in January 2007. It had originally purchased the furniture in August 1996 for £8,000.

Calculate the chargeable gain or allowable loss on disposal.

Solution

	£
Sale proceeds (deemed)	6,000
Less: Allowable cost	(8,000)
Unindexed loss	(2,000)
Less: Indexation allowance	Nil
(restricted as it cannot increase a loss)	
Indexed loss	(2,000)

○ EXAMPLE   ○○○○

Kevin Ltd has sold a painting for £6,600 that it originally purchased for £2,000. The indexation factor is 0.800.

Calculate the chargeable gain on disposal.

Solution

	£
Sale proceeds	6,600
Less: Allowable cost	(2,000)
Unindexed gain	4,600
Less: Indexation allowance (0.800 x £2,000)	(1,600)
Chargeable gain	3,000
Restricted to $5/3$ x (6,600 – 6,000)	1,000

4 Test your knowledge

1 If ABC Ltd sold a chattel for £6,500 realising an indexed gain of £2,000, what will be the chargeable gain?

2 DEF Ltd sold a chattel for £4,000. It had originally cost £7,500. How much of the loss is allowable?

3 GHI Ltd disposed of two assets during its accounting period to 31 March 2007, realising a chargeable gain of £13,000 and an allowable loss of £4,000. It had allowable losses brought forward of £2,000. How much will be included in profits chargeable to corporation tax for the year to 31 March 2007?

4 The indexation allowance can create or increase a loss. True or false?

[Answers on p. 260]

5   Summary

There is a proforma computation for calculation of individual gains and losses.

The gains and losses of the accounting period are netted off to give the net chargeable gains to include on the company's corporation tax computations.

Special rules exist for improvements, part disposals (using the formula A/A+B), and for chattels.

Answers to chapter activities & 'test your knowledge' questions

△ ACTIVITY 1   △△△△

JHN Ltd

Chargeable gains

	£
Plant (W1)	1,352
Building (W2)	(1,000)
Car – exempt	Nil
Memorabilia (W3)	3,124
Land (W4)	Nil
Total chargeable gains	3,476

Workings

(W1) Plant

	£
Proceeds	15,000
Cost	(8,000)
Unindexed gain	7,000
Indexation allowance (£8,000 x 0.706)	(5,648)
Chargeable gain	1,352

(W2) Building

	£
Proceeds	26,500
Cost	(27,500)
Allowable Loss	(1,000)

No indexation is available to increase the loss.

(W3) Memorabilia

	£
Proceeds	19,000
Cost	(7,000)
Unindexed gain	12,000
Indexation allowance (£7,000 x 1.268)	(8,876)
Chargeable gain	3,124

(W4) Land

	£
Proceeds	25,000
Cost	(15,000)
Unindexed gain	10,000
Indexation allowance (£15,000 x 1.326) (restricted)	(10,000)
	Nil

The IA is restricted because indexation cannot create an allowable loss.

Test your knowledge △ △ △

1 The gain will be restricted to 5/3 x (6,500 – 6,000) = £833.

2 The allowable loss will be restricted to (6,000 – 7,500) = £1,500.

3 The amount to include in profits chargeable to corporation tax will be (13,000 – 4,000 – 2,000 b/f) = £7,000.

4 False. The indexation allowance can reduce a gain to nil, but cannot create or increase a loss.

KAPLAN PUBLISHING

GAINS AND LOSSES FOR INDIVIDUALS

INTRODUCTION

An individual (including a sole trader or a partner) pays capital gains tax on his chargeable gains. This chapter compares and contrasts the rules for individuals with those for companies. In particular it focuses on business assets taper relief which is available to individuals but not to companies.

PERFORMANCE CRITERIA

This chapter covers the following performance criteria:

· Identify and value correctly any chargeable assets that have been disposed of (18.3 A)
· Calculate chargeable gains and allowable losses (18.3 C)
· Ensure that computations and submissions are made in accordance with current law and take account of current HM Revenue & Custom's practice (18.3 E)

1 Individual v company – similarities

1.1 Calculation of individual gains and losses

The standard proforma used to calculate a gain or loss on disposal of an asset is essentially the same.

	£
Gross sale proceeds	X
Less: Selling costs	(X)
Net sale proceeds	NSP
Less: Allowable cost	(X)
Unindexed gain	X
Less: Indexation allowance = 0.XXX x cost	(X)
Indexed gain	X

However, see in Section 2 further issues relating to indexation allowance and its replacement with taper relief.

1.2 Special rules

The special rules discussed in Chapter 21 also apply for individuals, namely:

· Enhancement expenditure
· Part disposals
· Non-wasting chattels

2 Individual v company – differences

2.1 Capital gains tax

Individuals pay capital gains tax on their taxable gains for the fiscal year (e.g. 2006/07).

Individuals are entitled to an annual exemption for each tax year (£8,800 in 2006/07). The annual exemption is deducted from the total net chargeable gains of the year to give the taxable gains.

	£
Chargeable gains	X
Less: Capital losses	(X)
Net chargeable gains	X
Less: Annual exemption	(8,800)
Taxable gains	X

Capital gains tax is then calculated on the taxable gains.

2.2 The annual exemption and brought forward losses

Brought forward capital losses are not allocated against gains where this would lead to a wastage of the annual exemption. This rule does *not apply* to current tax year capital losses, which must be set off against gains and can therefore result in a wastage of the annual exemption.

○ EXAMPLE   ○ ○ ○ ○

Mica has the following chargeable gains and losses for the two years ended 5 April 2007.

	2005/06 £	2006/07 £
Gains	12,000	11,000
Losses	(14,000)	(2,000)

What gains (if any) are chargeable after considering all reliefs and exemptions?

Solution

	2005/06 £	2006/07 £
Current gains	12,000	11,000
Current losses	(12,000)	(2,000)
Brought forward losses*		(200)
	Nil	8,800
Annual exemption	Wasted	(8,800)
	Nil	Nil
Loss carried forward		
(£14,000 - £12,000)	2,000	
(£2,000 - £200)		1,800

*Utilised to reduce gains to annual exemption.

2.3 Calculating the tax payable

The capital gains tax payable on any gains remaining after the annual exemption has been applied depends upon the level of taxable income of the individual.

An individual's tax liability is computed first on income then on gains. The gains are taxed as if they were income on top of taxable income.

Gains are taxed using the savings income rates. This means that gains are taxed at:

Tax band £	Rate
0 – 2,150	10%
2,151 – 33,300	20%
33,301 +	40%

○ EXAMPLE ○○○○

Megan has chargeable gains after losses, and the annual exemption of £13,000 in 2006/07. Her taxable income is £21,000. What is the CGT payable?

Solution

Step 1: Identify (from the tax tables) the available tax bands for the current tax year 2006/07.

	Tax band £	Rate	
Starting rate	0 – 2,150	10%	
Basic rate	2,151 – 33,300	22%	(but recall this is 20% for gains)
Higher rate	33,301	40%	

Step 2: Identify the bands used against taxable income

The bands are first allocated to taxable *income*. There is no need to calculate the income tax unless specifically requested.

Taxable income of £21,000 will utilise the 10% band in full (£2,150) plus £18,850 of the 22% band.

Step 3: Calculate the remaining basic rate band

	£
Basic rate band	33,300
Taxable income	(21,000)
Remaining basic rate band	12,300

Step 4: Calculate the CGT liability

This balance is then applied to the capital gains of £13,000.

£		£
12,300 x 20%		2,460
700 x 40%		280
13,000		2,740

2.4 Treatment of inflation

For companies, inflation is removed from a gain by the deduction of indexation allowance, running from the date of purchase until the date of disposal.

For individuals the method of removing inflation changed on 6 April 1998.

	6 April	
Indexation allowance	1998	Taper relief

2.5 Indexation allowance

Indexation allowance for individuals is the same as for companies in that:

·   the factor is rounded to three decimal places.
·   it cannot increase or create a loss.

However, in calculating the factor we use the formula:

$$\frac{\text{RPI for April 1998 - RPI for month of acquisition}}{\text{RPI for month of acquisition}}$$

Do not use the RPI for the month of disposal, if after April 1998.

○ EXAMPLE   ○○○○

John purchased an asset in August 1984 (RPI = 89.94) and sold it in August 2006 (RPI = 197.6). The RPI for April 1998 is 162.6.

What is the indexation factor to be applied to the allowable cost?

Solution

$$\text{Indexation factor} = \frac{\text{RPI April 1998 - RPI August 1984}}{\text{RPI August 1984}}$$

$$= \frac{162.6 - 89.94}{89.94} \quad = 0.8078719$$

but rounded to three decimal places = 0.808.

In the assessment you are likely to be given the indexation factor, or even the amount of the indexation allowance.

2.6 Taper relief

For disposals after 5 April 1998 only, chargeable gains may be reduced by taper relief. This relief provides a progressive reduction in the amount of a gain, according to how long the asset has been owned since 6 April 1998. It replaces the indexation allowance. It is, however, completely different in concept as it is also intended to reward longer term investment.

Taper relief operates as a percentage reduction on individual gains **after** indexation to 5 April 1998. The amount of the relief depends upon:

· whether the asset is a business or a non-business asset, and
· the number of complete years (after 5 April 1998) for which the asset has been owned.

For the unit 18 assessment we will consider only business assets (non-business assets are dealt with in unit 19).

The percentage amount of the gain chargeable (i.e. after giving the reduction for taper relief) is as follows:

Complete years of ownership after 5 April 1998	Gain on business asset chargeable %
0	100
1	50
2 or more	25

Note that for business assets the maximum taper relief which reduces gains to 25% of the indexed gain is achieved after two years of ownership. This means that the gain may be significantly reduced relatively quickly.

O EXAMPLE   O O O O

Scott bought two assets as follows:

(a) A business asset on 1 May 1986 for £12,000.
(b) A business asset on 1 May 2004 for £14,000.

Both assets were sold on 10 April 2006 for £30,000 each.

The indexation allowance from May 1986 to April 1998 for asset (a) is £7,944.

What is Scott's taxable gains for 2006/07?

Solution

Step 1: Calculate the gain on each transaction before considering taper relief.

	Asset (a)	Asset (b)
	£	£
Sale proceeds	30,000	30,000
Cost	(12,000)	(14,000)
Unindexed gain	18,000	16,000
Indexation allowance	(7,944)	-
Indexed gain	10,056	16,000

No indexation allowance is available on asset (b) as the asset was acquired after 5 April 1998.

Step 2: Consider taper relief.

Asset (a) is a business asset that has been held for at least two years since 6 April 1998, which means that only 25% of the gain is chargeable.

Chargeable gain = £10,056 x 25% = £2,514.

Asset (b) is a business asset. This asset was held for only one complete year: 1 May 2004 to 30 April 2005. The gain chargeable is therefore 50% chargeable.

Chargeable gain = £16,000 x 50% = £8,000.

Step3 - Calculate taxable gains

	£
Asset (a)	2,514
Asset (b)	8,000
Total chargeable gains	10,514
Less: Annual exemption	(8,800)
Taxable gain	1,714

The rate capital gains tax charged depends on the level of Scott's taxable income.

2.7   Definition of a business asset

Business assets are defined as:

· Those used for the purposes of a trade carried on by any sole trader or partner.

· Those used for the purposes of a trade carried on by a qualifying company of the individual concerned.

· Those held for the purposes of an office or employment.

· Shares in a qualifying company.

A qualifying company is a trading company or the holding company of a trading group which is either:

· unquoted (this includes companies quoted on the Alternative Investment Market); or

· quoted and the individual:
  - is an employee (full or part-time); or
  - has at least 5% of the shares.

Provided the shares are held by an employee with less than a material interest (i.e. not more than 10% of the shares) the company does not have to be a trading company for the business asset taper rate to apply.

In the assessment you will only be dealing with disposals of business assets.

2.8   Taper relief and capital losses

Taper relief is computed on the gains chargeable *after* the deduction of any current year losses and losses brought forward. The special rule that restricts the set off of brought forward losses to avoid wasting the annual exemption is applied *before* taper relief. This means that the taper relief is wasted.

To ensure that taper relief (where available) is maximised, capital losses can be allocated against chargeable gains on the most beneficial basis to the taxpayer. This means ranking the various assets, according to the complete years of ownership which qualify for taper relief before allocating the loss.

Always apply losses to the gain with the highest chargeable percentage first.

O EXAMPLE   OOOO

The total gains on three business assets are £30,000 before deducting available current period losses of £5,000.

		£	Years qualifying for taper relief
Asset	1	2,000	0
	2	10,000	1
	3	18,000	2

What is the most beneficial allocation of the losses available?

Solution

The loss should be allocated to:

		£
Asset	1	(2,000)
	2	(3,000)

This is to preserve all of the taper relief on asset 3. The gains remaining chargeable will then be as follows:

			£
Asset	2	£7,000 x 50%	3,500
	3	£18,000 x 25%	4,500
			————
			8,000
			————

Capital losses are *not* themselves subject to taper relief (i.e. the whole loss will always be available for relief). So you do not need to work out the complete years of ownership of an asset if it has made a loss.

2.9   Connected persons

Where a disposal is between connected persons:

(i)   sale proceeds are deemed to be market value (any real sale proceeds are ignored); and

(ii)   if a loss arises on a disposal to a connected person it can only be offset against a gain made on disposal to the **same** connected person.

Connected persons are mainly relatives and their spouses/civil partners or relatives of your spouse/civil partner.

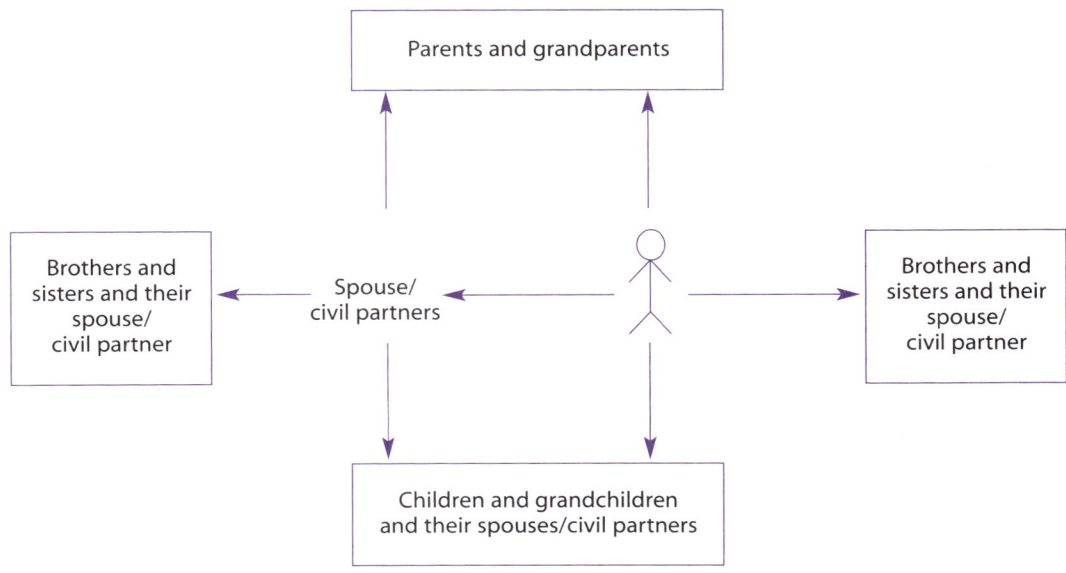

An individual is also connected with a company he controls and a partner is connected with his other business partners.

Whilst an individual is connected to their spouse, transactions between husband and wife are not made at market value but on the basis that no gain or loss arises. Transfers between civil partners also take place on a gain/no loss basis.

3 Test your knowledge

1 Ann buys a business asset in May 1999 and sells it in June 2006. Is she entitled to:
   · indexation allowance?
   · taper relief?

2 Bert made capital gains of £12,000 and capital losses of £4,000 in 2006/07. He had losses brought forward of £3,000. What losses will be carried forward to 2007/08?

3 Taper relief is given before losses are offset. True or false?

4 The annual exemption is deducted before taper relief. True or false?

[Answers on p. 272]

4 Summary

The main differences between calculating gains for individuals and those for companies is the method of dealing with inflation.

· In calculating an individual's gains, only index up to April 1998.

· Then to calculate the taxable gains use the following proforma:

	Indexed	Loss	Net gains	Chargeable	Chargeable gain
	£	£	£	%	£
Asset 1	X	(1)	X	100%	X
Asset 2	X	(2)	X	50%	X
Asset 3	X	(3)	X	25%	X
Total chargeable gains					X
Annual exemption					(X)
Taxable gains					X

Answers to 'test your knowledge' questions

Test your knowledge △ △ △

1   Ann is:
- not entitled to indexation allowance as this is only available up to April 1998 and the asset was acquired after that date.
- entitled to taper relief. Only 25% of the gain is chargeable as it is a business asset held for more than 2 years.

2   Bert's net gains for 2006/07 are £8,000. The capital losses brought forward of £3,000 will be carried forward to 2007/08 as the net gains for 2006/07 are below the amount of the annual exemption (£8,800).

3   False. Taper relief is given after losses have been offset.

4   False. The annual exemption is given against tapered gains.

SHARES AND SECURITIES – DISPOSALS BY COMPANIES

INTRODUCTION

A company may hold another company's shares as an investment. Special rules apply to share disposals.

CONTENTS

1 The matching rules
2 Bonus issues and rights issues

PERFORMANCE CRITERIA

This chapter covers the following performance criteria:
· Identify shares disposed of by companies (18.3 B)

1 The matching rules

1.1 Disposal of shares and securities

What distinguishes a share disposal from other asset disposals is the need for matching rules. Before considering what these matching rules are, it helps to understand why we need them.

1.2 Principle of matching rules

Suppose that a company makes the following purchases of shares in A plc:

1 July 1998	500 shares for	£1,000
3 February 1992	300 shares for	£1,000
1 September 1989	800 shares for	£2,000

On 1 November 2006, 400 of these shares are sold – but which 400?

- It could be the 300 acquired in 1992 and 100 acquired in 1989.
- It could be 400 out of the 500 acquired in 1998.
- It could be based on 400 out of the total 1,600 with costs being averaged.

We need matching rules so that we can establish *which* shares have been sold, and consequently what allowable costs and indexation allowances can be deducted from the sale proceeds.

The rules dictate the order in which the shares disposed of are matched with purchases.

1.3 The matching rules for companies

Shares of the same type (for example Lionel Ltd ordinary shares) are matched as follows:

(1) first, with shares bought on the **same day**; then

(2) second, with shares bought in the previous **nine days** (on a first in first out basis);

(3) third, with shares in the '**1985 pool**'.

The '1985 pool' is considered in detail below, but for companies shares are pooled together from 10 days after purchase.

It is possible that the matching rules could form part of a task. However, the majority of the time we will just be dealing with the 1985 pool.

(The matching rules for individuals are different but are not in this syllabus.)

Note that if matched with the first two rules there will be no indexation allowance available.

○ EXAMPLE   ○○○○

Minnie Ltd has sold 3,000 shares in Mickey plc for £15,000 on 2 February 2007. The shares in Mickey plc were purchased as follows:

Date	Number	Cost
		£
1 July 1989	1,000	2,000
1 September 1999	1,000	2,500
27 January 2007	500	1,200
2 February 2007	1,500	6,000

Which shares did Minnie Ltd sell?

Solution

Using the matching rules, the 3,000 shares sold are as follows:

		Number
2 February 2007 (same day purchase)		1,500
27 January 2007 (in previous 9 days)		500
		2,000

1985 pool:
All other shares were purchased more than
9 days ago, therefore must be in the pool.

1 July 1989	1,000	
1 September 1999	1,000	
Total number of shares in pool	2,000	
Out of the pool (1,000 out of 2,000)		1,000
Shares disposed of		3,000

Note: When dealing with the pool we do not identify which 1,000 shares are sold.

1.4   Calculation of gains on same day and previous 9 day purchases

As noted above, there is no indexation on either of these calculations. Hence, the gain is calculated as:

	£
Sale proceeds	X
Less: Allowable cost	(X)
Chargeable gain	X

○ **EXAMPLE** ○○○○

For Minnie Ltd in the previous example, calculate the gains on the shares purchased:

(1) on the same day; and
(2) in the previous 9 days.

Solution

Step 1: Calculate sale proceeds per share.

3,000 shares are sold for £15,000.
Hence: 1 share is sold for £5.00 (£15,000 ÷ 3,000).

In this case the share price works out at a round number. You may need to keep an unrounded number in your calculator for the next steps.

Step 2: Calculate the gain on the same day purchase (1,500 shares).

	£
Sale proceeds (£5.00 x 1,500)	7,500
Less: Allowable cost	(6,000)
Chargeable gain	1,500

Step 3: Calculate the gain on the previous 9 days purchase (500 shares).

	£
Sale proceeds (£5.00 x 500)	2,500
Less: Allowable cost	(1,200)
Chargeable gain	1,300

1.5 The operation of a 1985 pool

Any purchases from 1 April 1982 are 'pooled' in the '1985 pool'. Purchases before 1 April 1982 are not in the syllabus.

Indexation will apply to the pool from the date of acquisition to the date of disposal. To enable the correct indexation to be calculated, a separate working is needed to identify the amount available. The working is also used to find the average cost of a partial disposal.

The pool is initially set up with three columns as follows:

	Number	Cost £	Indexed cost £
Purchases (say) June 1986	1,000	2,000	2,000

Then every time there is an 'operative event' (an event involving cash – i.e. a sale or a purchase), two steps must be performed.

Step 1: An indexation update.

In the indexed cost column, add in indexation from the last operative event until this one. This is calculated by multiplying the balance in the indexed cost column by the increase in the RPI since the last operative event.

Step 2: Deal with the operative event:

-   for a purchase add in the new shares. The cost must be added in to both the cost and indexed cost columns.

-   for a sale eliminate some shares. The amounts to be deducted from the cost and indexed cost columns are calculated in proportion to the number of shares being removed from the pool.

The following working should be produced:

Proforma for 1985 pool

	Number	Cost £	Indexed cost £
Purchase	X	X	X
Index to next event*			X
Record next event			
e.g. Purchase	X	X	X
	X	X	X
Index to next event*			X
	X	X	X
Record next event			
e.g. Sale	(X)	(X) ^{W1}	(X) ^{W2}
Pool carried forward	X	X	X

*For the 'indexed rises' the indexation factor is **not** rounded. This is the only situation where a non-rounded factor is ever used. However, you are likely to be given a rounded indexation factor in the assessment.

The purpose of the working is to find:

·   the average pool cost of shares disposed of = working 1.
·   the average *indexation* of shares disposed of = working 2 – working 1.

The gain on the shares is then calculated as normal:

	£
Sale proceeds	X
Less: Cost (W1)	(X)
Unindexed gain	X
Less: Indexation allowance (W2 – W1)	(X)
Chargeable gain	X

The indexation factor is **always** applied to the total on the indexed cost column (**not** cost).

A partial disposal from a 1985 pool uses straight line apportionment of cost and indexation.

○ **EXAMPLE**   ○○○○

For Minnie Ltd in the previous example, calculate the gain on the disposal from the 1985 pool.

The indexation factors are as follows:
July 1989 – September 1999	0.439
September 1999 – February 2007	0.203

Solution

Step 1: Calculate cost and indexed cost from the 1985 pool.

	Number	Cost	Indexed cost
		£	£
July 1989 purchase	1,000	2,000	2,000
Index to next event			
(July 1989 to September 1999)			
Indexed cost x 0.439			
(2,000 x 0.439)			878
September 1999 purchase	1,000	2,500	2,500
	2,000	4,500	5,378
Index to next event			
(September 1999 to February 2007)			
(5,378 x 0.203)			1,092
	2,000	4,500	6,470
February 2007 sale (half)	(1,000)	(2,250)	(3,235)
Pool carried forward	1,000	2,250	3,235

Step 2: Calculate the gain on 1985 pool shares.

	£
Sale proceeds (£5.00 x 1,000)	5,000
Less: Allowable cost	(2,250)
	2,750
Less: Indexation allowance	
(3,235 – 2,250)	(985)
Chargeable gain	1,765

Step 3:   Calculate total chargeable gains on the disposal of all 3,000 shares

The total chargeable gains = £4,565 (1,500 + 1,300 + 1,765).

▷ ACTIVITY 1 ▷▷▷▷

FDC Ltd

FDC Ltd has purchased shares in DCC Ltd. The 1985 pool information of FDC Ltd is given below.

		Cost
		£
1 June 1985	4,000 shares for	8,000
30 July 1994	1,800 shares for	9,750

FDC Ltd disposed of 2,000 of its shares in DCC Ltd for £20,571 in March 2007.

The indexation factors to use are as follows:

June 1985 – July 1994	0.509
July 1994 – March 2007	0.392

What is the gain on the 1985 pool shares?

[Answer on p. 284]

2 Bonus issues and rights issues

2.1 Principle of bonus issues and rights issues

A bonus issue is the distribution of free shares to shareholders based on existing shareholdings.

A rights issue involves shareholders paying for new shares, usually at a rate below market price and in proportions based on existing shareholdings.

Matching

In both cases, therefore, the shareholder is making a new acquisition of shares. However, for *matching* purposes, such acquisitions arise out of the original holdings.

Bonus and rights issues therefore attach to the original shareholdings for the purposes of the identification rules.

○ EXAMPLE ○○○○

Alma Ltd acquired shares in S plc, a quoted company, as follows:

· 2,000 shares acquired June 1987 for £11,500.
· In October 1988 there was a 1 for 2 bonus issue.
· In December 1994 there was a 1 for 4 rights issue at £3 per share.

Alma Ltd sold 2,600 shares in December 2006 for £30,000.

You are required to calculate the number of shares in the 1985 pool.

Solution

Deal with each event in chronological order.

	Number
June 1987 purchase	2,000
October 1988 bonus issue (1 for 2)	
½ x 2,000	1,000
	3,000
December 1994 rights issue (1 for 4)	
¼ x 3,000	750
	3,750
December 2006 sale	(2,600)
Balance in pool - carry forward	1,150

2.2 Bonus issue

A bonus issue is the issue of free shares (i.e. no cost is involved). As there is no expenditure involved it is not an operative event and therefore no indexation to be calculated.

Simply add the bonus issue shares to the pool. When the next event occurs (e.g. next sale or purchase) index from the operative event before the bonus issue.

○ EXAMPLE ○○○○

For Alma Ltd in the previous example, set up the 1985 pool and deal with events up to and including the bonus issue.

Solution

1985 pool	Number	Cost	Indexed cost
		£	£
Purchase June 1987	2,000	11,500	11,500
Bonus issue October 1988			
(1 for 2) ¹/₂ x 2,000	1,000	Nil	Nil
	3,000	11,500	11,500

Note: we have NOT indexed up before recording the bonus issue (as no cost is involved). Therefore, next time there is an operative event we will index from June 1987 (the last operative event involving cost).

2.3   Rights issue

A rights issue involves a payment for new shares, therefore it is treated simply as a purchase of shares (usually at a price below the market rate).

Hence, it should be treated in the same way as a purchase in the 1985 pool:

·   index up to the rights issue; then
·   add in the new shares and cost.

○ EXAMPLE   ○○○○

For Alma Ltd in the previous example, you are required to calculate the gain on disposal.

Assume that the indexed rise from June 1987 to December 1994 is 0.433 and from December 1994 to December 2006 is 0.364.

Solution

1985 pool	Number	Cost	Indexed cost
		£	£
Purchase June 1987	2,000	11,500	11,500
Bonus issue October 1988 (1 for 2)	1,000	Nil	Nil
	3,000	11,500	11,500
Indexed rise to December 1994 (£11,500 x 0.43)			4,980
	3,000	11,500	16,480
Rights issue (1 for 4) at £3	750	2,250	2,250
	3,750	13,750	18,730
Indexed rise to December 2006 (£18,730 x 0.364)			6,818
	3,750	13,750	25,548
Disposal December 2006	(2,600)		
Allocate costs $\frac{2,600}{3,750}$ x £13,750/£25,548		(9,533) W1	(17,713) W2
Balance carry forward	1,150	4,217	7,835

Computation of gain – 1985 pool

	£
Proceeds	30,000
Cost (W1)	(9,533)
	———
Unindexed gain	20,467
Indexation (£17,713 - £9,533)	(8,180)
	———
Chargeable gain	12,287
	———

Note that the indexed cost is updated prior to the rights issue, because there is a purchase which involves additional cost.

Following the disposal there are 1,150 shares in the pool with a cost of £4,217 and an indexed cost of £7,835. This will be used as the starting point when dealing with the next operative event.

In the assessment you may be given details of brought forward amounts, rather than the complete history of the share pool.

▷ ACTIVITY 2

Scarlet

On 20 September 2006, Scarlet Ltd sold 1,500 ordinary shares in Red plc for £4,725. The company's previous transactions were as follows.

Balance on 1985 pool at 5 May 1996, 2,500 shares with a qualifying cost of £3,900 and an indexed cost of £4,385.

Transactions from 5 May 1996 were as follows:

4 April 1997	Took up 1 for 2 bonus issue
19 January 1998	Took up 1 for 3 rights issue at 140p per share

The indexed rise from May 1996 to January 1998 is 0.043 and from January 1998 to September 2006 is 0.241.

Required

Calculate Scarlet Ltd's chargeable gain on the disposal on 20 September 2006.

[Answer on p. 285]

3 Test your knowledge ▷ ▷ ▷

1 What are the identification rules for matching shares disposed of?

2 You must apply an indexed rise when there is a bonus issue. True or false?

3 Rights issue are treated as separate acquisitions. True or false?

[Answers on p. 285]

4 Summary

When disposing of shares we apply matching rules to identify which shares have been disposed of. These rules are needed so that we can deduct the appropriate acquisition costs from the disposal proceeds.

The matching rules for companies generally match disposals with shares held in the 1985 pool.

Bonus and rights issues attach themselves to the original shareholdings.

Answers to chapter activities & 'test your knowledge' questions

△ ACTIVITY 1   △ △ △ △

FDC Ltd

1985 pool working	Note	Number	Cost	Indexed cost
			£	£
Purchase 1 June 1985	1	4,000	8,000	8,000
Indexed rise to July 1994	2			
£8,000 x 0.509				4,072
Purchase – July 1994		1,800	9,750	9,750
		5,800	17,750	21,822
Indexed rise to March 2007				
£21,822 x 0.392				8,554
		5,800	17,750	30,376
Sale of 2,000 shares	3	(2,000)		
$\frac{2,000}{5,800}$ x £17,750/£30,776			(6,121) W1	(10,474) W2
Carried forward		3,800	11,629	19,902

Notes:

(1) Any entry in the cost column must also be made in the indexed cost column.

(2) Indexation must be added before the purchase in July 1994 is added to the pool.

(3) Use apportionment to allocate cost and indexed cost.

Gain on 1985 pool shares

	£
Sale proceeds	20,571
Cost (W1)	(6,121)
Unindexed gain	14,450
Indexation allowance (£10,474 - £6,121)	(4,353)
Chargeable gain	10,097

Note: In the assessment it is not acceptable just to deduct the indexed cost from the proceeds. This shortcut can only be used if the final result is a gain (not a loss). This is because the indexation allowance cannot increase a loss and has to be therefore separately identifiable.

△ ACTIVITY 2   △ △ △ △

Scarlet Ltd

1985 pool	Number	Cost	Indexed cost
		£	£
Balance at 5 May 1996	2,500	3,900	4,385
4 April 1997 Bonus issue 1 for 2	1,250	-	-
	3,750	3,900	4,385
Indexed rise to January 1998			
£4,385 x 0.043			189
			4,574
19 January 1998			
Rights issue 1 for 3 x140p	1,250	1,750	1,750
	5,000	5,650	6,324
Indexed rise to September 2006			
£6,324 x 0.241			1,524
	5,000	5,650	7,848
Cost of sale $\frac{1,500}{5,000}$ x £5,650/£7,848	(1,500)	(1,695)	(2,354)
Pool balance carried forward	3,500	3,955	5,494

Gain on the disposal of shares

Proceeds	4,725
Less: Cost	(1,695)
Unindexed gain	3,030
Less: Indexation allowance (£2,354 - £1,695)	(659)
Chargeable gain	2,371

Test your knowledge △ △ △

1   The identification rules are that you match disposals:
    · first with same day acquisitions; and
    · then with acquisitions within the previous nine days; and
    · finally with the 1985 pool.

2   False. You do not apply an indexed rise as you do not need to add or deduct anything to or from the cost column.

3   False. The rights shares relate to the underlying shares.

CHARGEABLE GAINS - RELIEFS

INTRODUCTION

The sale of a substantial asset within a business, or the sale of a business, could give rise to a large gain. If all of the gain was subject to tax it could make the sale prohibitive. Reliefs exist to reduce the gain in specific circumstances, such as when a replacement asset is acquired or if an asset is given away. These are likely to be the subject of a written part of a task.

CONTENTS

1. Rollover relief
2. Gift relief

PERFORMANCE CRITERIA

This chapter covers the following performance criteria:
· Apply reliefs, deferrals and exemptions correctly (18.3 D)

1 Rollover relief

1.1 Principle of rollover relief

Rollover relief allows a company to defer a chargeable gain, provided certain conditions are met. This relief is also available for unincorporated businesses (sole traders and partnerships).

In order to qualify for relief, the company (sole trader or partnership) must reinvest the proceeds from the sale of a qualifying business asset into another qualifying business asset. Any gain on the disposal of the first asset is then 'rolled over' against the capital gains cost of the new asset.

A typical situation can be depicted as follows.

A company sells its building, then buys a new bigger building.

		£
Building (1)	Sale proceeds	100,000
	Cost and indexation allowance	(40,000)
	Indexed gain	60,000
	Rollover relief	(60,000)
	Remaining gain	Nil
Building (2)	Purchase price	150,000
	'Rolled over gain'	(60,000)
	Revised base cost	90,000

The gain on building (1) has been deferred against the base cost of building (2). Provided that *at least* the same amount as the proceeds recieved are reinvested, then *full* deferral applies.

On the sale of the second building, a higher gain will result, as this represents both the gain on the second asset and the deferred gain from the first.

	If no rollover relief claimed on building (1)		*If rollover relief is claimed on building (1)*
	£		£
Sale of building (2)			
Sale proceeds, say	200,000	Sale proceeds	200,000
Original cost	(150,000)	Revised base cost	(90,000)
Unindexed gain	50,000	Unindexed gain	110,000

The benefit of rollover relief is that tax which would otherwise be payable now is deferred possibly for many years. There is a drawback however in that the indexation allowance on the second gain is calculated on a lower base cost if rollover relief is claimed.

1.2   Conditions for relief

Now that we have considered the mechanics, it is necessary to look at the other conditions which apply.

There must be a disposal of and reinvestment in:

· a qualifying business asset,
· within a qualifying time period.

Qualifying business assets
The assets must be used in a *trade*. Where they are only partly used in a trade then only the gain on the trade portion is eligible.

The main qualifying assets are as follows:
· Land and buildings (freehold and leasehold).
· Fixed plant and machinery.
· Goodwill (for unincorporated business only, see below).

Note that *shares* of a company are *never* qualifying assets for rollover relief purposes.

Qualifying time period.
The qualifying period for reinvestment in the replacement asset is up to 12 months before the sale to within 36 months after the sale.

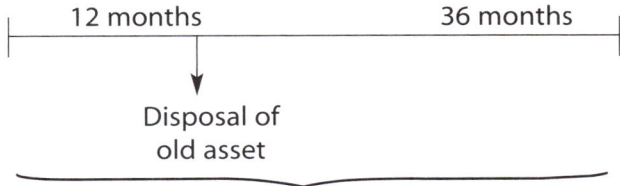

Goodwill
For a company, goodwill acquired on or after 1 April 2002 is no longer a chargeable asset so cannot be used as a qualifying replacement asset. Goodwill is still a qualifying asset for unincorporated businesses.

1.3   Partial reinvestment

Rollover relief may still be available even where only part of the proceeds is reinvested. However, it will be restricted, as there is some cash retained which is available to settle tax liabilities. This is logical as the main purpose of the relief is not to charge tax where cash has been reinvested in the business.

The amount which *cannot* be rolled over is the lower of:
· the proceeds not reinvested.
· the chargeable gain.

The following example will demonstrate where full relief is available, partial relief is available and no relief is available.

○ EXAMPLE   ○ ○ ○ ○

AB Ltd sold an office block for £500,000 in December 2006. It had been acquired for £200,000 and was used throughout AB Ltd's ownership for trade purposes. The indexation allowance on the disposal was £213,100. A replacement office block was acquired in February 2007.

Assuming rollover relief is claimed where possible, calculate the gain assessable on AB Ltd and the base cost of the replacement office block if it cost:

(a) £610,000
(b) £448,000
(c) £345,000

Solution

Gain on sale of old office block.

	£
Proceeds	500,000
Cost	(200,000)
Unindexed gain	300,000
Indexation allowance	(213,100)
Chargeable gain	86,900

(a) As all the proceeds have been reinvested, the full gain is rolled over and no gain is immediately chargeable.

	£
Indexed gain	86,900
Less: Rollover relief	(86,900)
Remaining gain	Nil

Base cost of new asset	£
Cost	610,000
Less: Gain rolled over	(86,900)
Base cost	523,100

(b) As not all of the proceeds have been reinvested, a gain arises when the old office block is sold as follows:

Gain chargeable now = lower of

(i) Proceeds not reinvested (£500,000 - £448,000)	£52,000
(ii) All chargeable gain	£86,900

	£
Chargeable gain	86,900
Less: Rollover relief (balance)	(34,900)
Remaining gain chargeable now	52,000

Base cost of new asset	£
Cost	448,000
Less: Gain rolled over	(34,900)
Base cost	413,100

(c) As not all of the proceeds have been reinvested, a gain arised immediately.

Gain chargeable now = lower of
(i) Proceeds not reinvested
     (£500,000 - £345,000)   £155,000

(ii) Full chargeable gain   £86,900

	£
Chargeable gain	86,900
Less: Rollover relief (balance)	(Nil)
Remaining gain chargeable now	86,900

As the proceeds not reinvested exceed the gain, the full gain of £86,900 is chargeable and no rollover relief is available.

Base cost of new asset   £345,000

1.4   Interaction with taper relief for unincorporated businesses

Taper relief only applies to gains remaining chargeable:

	£
Gain on asset	100,000
Less: Rollover relief (say)	(80,000)
Remaining gain chargeable immediately	20,000

Assuming 1 complete year of ownership, the gain is 50% chargeable

Chargeable gain (£20,000 x 50%)	10,000

Taper relief entitlement accrued on the rolled over gain of £80,000 is wasted.

Taper relief for the replacement asset runs from the date the replacement is acquired.

2 Gift relief

2.1 Principle of gift relief

When a gift is made by an individual, the capital gain rules require any gain to be calculated as if the disposal had been a sale at full market value.

The legislation allows a claim to defer the gain where the asset is a 'business asset' as defined for 'gift relief' purposes.

The broad purpose of gift relief is to encourage sole traders and shareholders of family companies to pass on their business or shares to the next generation. Note that this relief is not available for gifts by companies.

Gift relief works by 'deducting' the gain (often described as 'holding over' the gain) from the base cost to the donee (i.e. the person receiving the asset).

	Donor		*Donee*
	£		*£*
Market value	50,000	Deemed cost	50,000
Cost	(10,000)		
	40,000		
IA (say)	(5,000)		
Gain	35,000		
Less: Gift relief	(35,000)	Held over gain	(35,000)
Remaining gain	Nil	Revised CGT cost	15,000

In effect, the donee 'takes over' the responsibility for the donor's gain until such time as he makes a disposal of the asset.

2.2 Conditions for relief

There are various conditions which must be considered before applying gift relief. We discuss them under the following headings:

· Assets which qualify for the relief.
· Administration of the election.

Assets which qualify for the relief include the following:

· Assets used in a trade by the donor or by his personal trading company.

· Shares and securities in either the donor's personal trading company (quoted or unquoted), or in any unquoted trading company.

A 'personal company' is one in which the donor holds at least 5% of the voting rights.

Administration of the election.

Gift relief requires a *joint* election by donor and donee. This must be made within five years of 31 January following the end of the year of assessment in which the gift takes place. Therefore, for a gift in 2006/07, the election must be made by 31 January 2013.

It is not possible in a claim to specify the amount of the gain to holdover. All the gain qualifying is held over if a claim is made.

○ EXAMPLE ○○○○

Jones, aged 48, gave the factory that he used in his business to his son on 16 June 2006 when it was valued at £600,000. The factory cost him £150,000 on 16 October 1995. The indexation allowance due on the factory is £12,750.

You are required to compute the gain and to show the base cost for Jones' son, assuming gift relief is claimed.

Solution

Step 1: Calculate the gain on the gift using market value

	£
Proceeds (use market value)	600,000
Cost	(150,000)
Unindexed gain	450,000
Indexation allowance (given in question)	(12,750)
Indexed gain	437,250

Step 2: Consider whether the gift relief conditions are satisfied

·   Asset used in Jones' trade.
·   Factory is a qualifying asset.

Step 3: Hold over the gain against the base cost of the factory

	£
Gain (originally computed)	437,250
Less: Gift relief	(437,250)
Chargeable now	Nil

Base cost of factory for Jones' son.

	£
Market value of factory	600,000
Less: Gain held over	(437,250)
Base cost	162,750

2.3 Interaction of gift relief and taper relief

A claim for gift relief is optional.

Where gift relief is claimed there is no gain remaining chargeable at the time of the gift.

Where gift relief is not claimed, taper relief may be due based on the donor's length of ownership.

In future years, the *donee* will be able to claim taper relief on gains subsequently charged on a disposal. However, taper relief is calculated with reference to the donee's period of ownership only. Therefore, if gift relief is claimed, taper relief accrued by the donor is lost.

In the above example, Jones wastes 75% taper relief on the gain of £437,250 held over. The donee's taper relief on the factory in the future runs from 16 June 2006 when he acquires the factory, whether or not gift relief is claimed.

3 Test your knowledge ▷ ▷ ▷

1 What are the main assets on which rollover relief is available?

2 Can companies claim gift relief?

3 Celia bought a business asset costing £100,000 in 2000. She gave it to her son Dave in May 2006 when it was worth £150,000. Dave sold it in December 2006 for £160,000. What are Celia and Dave's chargeable gains after taper relief assuming gift relief is claimed?

4 What would the chargeable gains after taper relief be if gift relief had not been claimed?

[Answers on p. 295]

4 Summary

The reliefs available are as follows:

	For companies	For individuals
Rollover relief		
- defer the gain against cost of the new asset	✓	✓
Gift relief		
- defer the gain by reducing the donee's cost	✗	✓

Answers to 'test your knowledge' questions

Test your knowledge △ △ △

1 Land and buildings
  Fixed plant and machinery
  Goodwill (but not for a company)

2 No. A gift relief claim can only be made by an individual.

3 Celia's gain £(150,000 – 100,000) = £50,000 held over.

  Dave's gains £160,000 - £(150,000 – 50,000) = £60,000. No taper relief – held for less than 1 year.

4 Celia's gain £(150,000 – 100,000) = £50,000. Chargeable gain £50,000 x 25% = £12,500.

  Dave's gains £(160,000 - 150,000) = £10,000. No taper relief – held for less than 1 year.

DUTIES AND RESPONSIBILITIES OF A TAX ADVISER

INTRODUCTION

A tax adviser must ensure that he has the best interests of his clients in mind at all times, whilst ensuring that he complies with his legal duties.

CONTENTS

1   Duties and responsibilities
2   Confidentiality
3   Ethical issues
4   Tax advice and records

PERFORMANCE CRITERIA

This chapter covers the following performance criteria:

·   Consult with HM Revenue & Custom's staff in an open and constructive manner (18.1 E, 18.2 H, 18.3 F, 18.4 H)
·   Give timely and constructive advice to clients on the maintenance of accounts and the recording of information relevant to tax returns (18.1 F, 18.2 I, 18.3 G, 18.4 I)
·   Maintain client confidentiality at all times (18.1 G, 18.2 J, 18.3 H, 18.4 J)

1 Duties and responsibilities

1.1 AAT expectations

The AAT expects its members to:

· adopt an ethical approach to work, employers and clients.

· acknowledge your professional duty to society as a whole.

· maintain an objective outlook.

· provide professional, high standards of service, conduct and performance at all times.'

These expectations are discussed in greater depth in the 'Guidelines on Professional Ethics' that can be found on the AAT website – www.aat.co.uk.

A person advising either a company or an individual on taxation issues has duties and responsibilities towards both:

· their client; and
· HM Revenue and Customs.

2 Confidentiality

2.1 Dealings with third parties

A tax adviser has an overriding duty on confidentiality towards his client. Under normal circumstances a client's tax affairs should not be discussed with third parties.

The exceptions to this rule mentioned in the Guidelines are where:

· authority has been given by the client; or
· there is a legal, regulatory or professional duty to disclose, e.g. in the case of suspected money laundering.

This issue is a regular topic for the assessment.

2.2 Dealing with HM Revenue and Customs

The duty of confidentiality also relates to dealings with HMRC. However, the tax adviser must ensure that whilst acting in the client's best interests, he must consult with HMRC staff in an open and constructive manner (see below).

3 Ethical issues

3.1 Dealing with problems

In spite of guidelines being available there can be situations where the method of resolving an ethical issue is not straightforward.

In those situations additional advice should be sought from:
· a supervisor.
· a professional body.
· a legal adviser.

4 Tax advice and records

4.1 Providing tax advice

When providing tax advice and preparing tax returns, a person should act in the best interests of his client. However, he must ensure that his services are consistent with the law and are carried out competently.

At all times an adviser 'must not in any way impair integrity or objectivity'.

4.2 Providing information to HM Revenue and Customs/other authorities

The 'Guidelines on Professional Ethics' state that:

'A member should not be associated with any return or communication in which there is reason to believe that it:

· contains a false or misleading statement;

· contains statements or information furnished recklessly or without any real knowledge of whether they are true or false; or

· omits or obscures information required to be submitted and such omission or obscurity would mislead the tax authorities.'

4.3 Tax records

The client and the tax adviser must keep records to assist in dealings with and support evidence given to HMRC. This should include invoices, bank statements and working papers.

The records should be kept:

· **Sole traders and partnerships**
 – for 5 years from the normal filing date, i.e. for 2006/07, filing date is 31 January 2008, hence records kept until 31 January 2013.

· **Companies**

– for 6 years after the accounting period end, i.e. for year ended 31 March 2007, until 31 March 2013.

5 **Test your knowledge**

1 How long must a company keep its tax records for?

2 You act for a company, its managing director and its finance director. Can you discuss:

· the company's tax affairs with either director; or
· the finance director's tax affairs with the managing director; or
· the managing director's tax affairs with the finance director?

[Answers on p. 301]

6 Summary

Client confidentiality is an adviser's main duty towards the client.

However, his responsibilities include openness in dealing with HMRC.

Answers to chapter activities & 'test your knowledge' questions

Test your knowledge △ △ △

1 A company must keep its tax records for 6 years from the end of the accounting period.

2 · You can discuss the company's tax affairs with either director, since they are both responsible for the company's tax affairs.

· You cannot discuss the finance director's tax affairs with the managing director without express authority from the finance director.

· You cannot discuss the managing director's tax affairs with the finance director without express authority from the managing director.

LEGISLATIVE FRAMEWORK

INTRODUCTION

The previous chapters have all evolved from the development of tax legislation. This chapter sets the principles of tax law.

CONTENTS

1   Tax law

PERFORMANCE CRITERIA

This chapter covers the following performance criteria:

· Ensure that computations and submissions are made in accordance with current tax law and take account of current HM Revenue & Custom's practice (18.1 D)

1 Tax law

1.1 Principle of tax law

There are two aspects of tax law that govern what tax should be calculated on and how much is due. These are:

· statute law; and
· case law.

1.2 Statute law

Statute law is legislation that has been passed by Parliament.

One of the main pieces of legislation governing large parts of this manual is the Income and Corporation Taxes Act 1988 (ICTA 1988). However the income tax legislation is in the course of being rewritten in plainer English under the Tax Law Rewrite Project. Most of the rules for sole traders and partnerships are now enacted in the Income Tax (Trading and Other Income) Act 2005 (ITTOIA 2005).

The capital allowances legislation for both income tax and corporation tax purposes has also been rewritten by the Capital Allowances Act 2001 (CAA 2001).

However, each year following the budget, tax legislation is updated by the Finance Act. In general election years there may also be a second Finance Act. The tax rates and allowances that have been used throughout this manual, and will be used in the assessment, are those of Finance Act 2006 (Financial Year 2006 for corporation tax, and 2006/07 for sole traders and partnerships).

You do not need to refer to specific legislation in the assessment.

1.3 Case law

Statute law can be very complex and open to interpretation. At times there have been differences in interpretation by HM Revenue and Customs and the taxpayers.

Where the differences have not been readily resolved, the final interpretation has been made by the courts. This is case law.

Often case law can result in the updating of the statute law in the next Finance Act.

You are not required to quote case law in the assessment.

1.4   Extra Statutory Concessions

At times HMRC agree to relax the application of tax law. For example, they may extend time limits. This is often in response to practical problems that a strict application would present. The relaxation of the law is formalised by issuing Extra Statutory Concessions.

1.5   Other guidance

Other guidance offered by HM Revenue & Customs (HMRC) can be found on their website www.hmrc.gov.uk.

This includes:
· Statements of practice
    – announcing HMRC's interpretation of certain legislation.

· Guides and help sheets
    – to assist in completing forms.

2   Test your knowledge

1 What are the two aspects of tax legislation?

2 What is an Extra Statutory Concession?

[Answers on p. 306]

3   Summary

The legislative framework is a complex matter, of which you need a general understanding.

Answers to 'test your knowledge' questions

Test your knowledge

1   Statute law and case law.

2   A relaxation of the application of tax law where strict application could result in practical problems or inequities.

KEY TECHNIQUES
QUESTIONS

Chapter 3

▷ ACTIVITY 1   ▷ ▷ ▷ ▷

Tricks Ltd

Tricks Ltd's profit and loss account for the year ended 31 March 2007 was as follows:

	£	£
Sales		370,150
Debenture interest receivable		4,100
UK dividends received (net of tax credit)		12,000
Profit on the sale of an investment		2,750
		389,000
Allowable trading expenses	125,750	
Disallowable trading expenses	5,900	
Debenture interest payable (Note)	8,100	
		139,750
Net profit		249,250

Note: The funds raised by the issue of the debenture were used to purchase machinery for use in the business.

Required

Calculate Tricks Ltd's adjusted trading profits for the year ended 31 March 2007.

▷ ACTIVITY 2   ▷ ▷ ▷ ▷

Prairie Limited

Prairie Limited's profit and loss account for the year ended 31 March 2007 was as follows:

	£		£
Rent, rates, insurance	63,576	Sales	286,280
Wages, salaries	46,180	Debenture interest	
Gift Aid paid	1,000	receivable (gross)	2,900
Depreciation	6,344	UK dividends received	
		(net of tax credit)	11,876
		Profit on sale of	
Net profit	186,499	investments	2,543
	303,599		303,599

Required

Calculate Prairie Limited's adjusted trading profits for the year to 31 March 2007.

▷ ACTIVITY 3 ▷ ▷ ▷ ▷

Cricket Limited

Cricket Limited has the following results for the year ended 31 March 2007:

	£		£
Salaries, wages	20,041	Gross trading profit	802,350
Legal charges (Note 1)	2,436		
Impaired debts (Note 2)	480		
Depreciation – Factory	20,000		
– Plant	10,000		
Repairs (Note 3)	7,800		
Sundry expenses			
(allowable)	3,492		
Net profit	738,101		
	802,350		802,350

Notes

(1) **Legal charges**

	£
Debt collection	1,136
Staff service agreements	300
In connection with lease of new office premises	1,000
	2,436

(2) **Impaired debts**

	£
Loan to former employee written off	200
Increase in provision for impaired debts	280
	480

(3) **Repairs**

	£
Repainting	200
New office furniture (December 2006)	7,600
	7,800

Required

Show Cricket Limited's adjusted trading profits for the year ended 31 March 2007.

▷ ACTIVITY 4

Uranus Ltd

The following items are charged against profit in the accounts of Uranus Ltd for the year ended 31 March 2007:

1 Running expenses of the managing director's BMW totalling £10,000 (including depreciation of £6,000). His total mileage in the year was 12,000 of which 6,000 was private. The car was owned by Uranus Ltd.

2 Entertainment expenditure totalling £25,000 of which £10,000 was incurred on overseas customers, £11,000 on UK customers and £4,000 on the annual company dinner for 200 employees.

3 Lease rental of £6,000 on sales director's car costing £20,000.

Required

State how you would deal with each of the above items when preparing the company's computation of adjusted trading profits for the year ended 31 March

▷ ACTIVITY 5

Saturn Ltd

The following items are charged against profit in the accounts of Saturn Ltd for the year ended 31 March 2007:

1 A payment of £616 to the Royal National Lifeboat Institution under the Gift Aid rules.

2 The write off of £8,000 against a trade debt of the company, being 80% of the debt. The liquidator of the debtor company had advised Saturn Ltd of this figure but in the event £5,000 of the debt was paid in May 2007.

3 Permanent repairs to the roof of a warehouse which was purchased on 1 August 2006 for £25,000. The warehouse, which was used to store raw materials, had a leaking roof when purchased but pending the permanent repairs this was covered by plastic sheeting to enable it to be used from the date of purchase.

Required

State how you would deal with each of the above items when preparing the company's computation of adjusted trading profits for the year ended 31 March 2007.

▷ ACTIVITY 6 ▷▷▷▷

OP Ltd

OP Ltd imports kitchen appliances from Europe which it sells to wholesale distributors in the United Kingdom. The trading and profit and loss account for its first year of trading to 30 June 2006 is:

	£	£
Sales		267,400
Purchases	146,200	
Closing stock	(27,700)	
Cost of sales		(118,500)
Gross profit		148,900
Wages and salaries	66,900	
Rent and rates	13,100	
Lighting and heating	1,690	
Insurance	2,280	
Entertaining (Note 1)	1,200	
Impaired debts (Note 2)	8,750	
Depreciation	5,500	
Travelling (Note 3)	9,800	
Sundry expenses (note 4)	230	
Legal and professional charges (note 5)	1,040	
Interest on bank overdraft	2,400	
Van expenses	3,100	
Sales commission	2,500	
		(118,490)
Net profit		30,410

Notes:

(1) Entertaining expenses

	£
Staff Christmas party	200
Entertaining suppliers	750
Entertaining customers	250
	1,200

(2) Impaired debts

	£
Trading debts written off	3,250
Provision against impaired debts	1,800
Loan to supplier written off	3,700
	8,750

The loan was made to a supplier who was having cashflow problems.

(3) Travelling

Included in travelling expenses are the running costs of a car provided to John Openshaw, Director.

One quarter of his mileage was private.

(4) Sundry expenses are all allowable for tax purposes.

(5) Legal and professional charges

	£
Legal fees for staff contracts	100
Accountancy fees	270
Legal fees in connection with action by employee for unfair dismissal	220
Debt collection	450
	1,040

Required

Calculate the adjusted profits for OP Ltd for the year to 30 June 2006.

Chapter 4

▷ ACTIVITY 7   ▷ ▷ ▷ ▷

Deni Ltd

Deni Ltd is a manufacturing business preparing accounts to 30 September each year. It is a medium sized business.

At 1 October 2005, the written-down value of plant and machinery in the general pool was £8,822.

During the year ended 30 September 2006, the following transactions were undertaken:

Purchases		£
15 February 2006	Second-hand machinery	2,050
20 June 2006	Managing director's car (used 80% for business)	19,600
1 September 2006	Machinery	1,500

Sales		
30 July 2006	Machinery (cost £6,000)	1,750

Required

Compute Deni Ltd's capital allowances for the accounting period ended 30 September 2006.

▷ ACTIVITY 8

Zeus Ltd

Zeus Ltd runs a small manufacturing business preparing accounts to 30 September each year. At 1 October 2005, the written-down value of plant and machinery was:

	£
General pool	13,212
Managing director's car (used 15% privately)	18,500

During the year ended 30 September 2006, the following transactions were undertaken:

Purchases		£
11 February 2006	Machinery	3,000
10 September 2006	Managing director's car (replacing the previous one for which £15,000 was received in part exchange)	
	Amount paid in cash for new car	3,000

Sales		
1 June 2006	Machinery (cost £14,100)	2,500
1 September 2006	Machinery (cost £600)	200

Required

Compute Zeus Ltd's capital allowances for the accounting period ended 30 September 2006.

▷ ACTIVITY 9

TEN Ltd

TEN Ltd prepares accounts to 31 December annually. On 1 January 2005, the balance of plant and machinery brought forward was £16,000.

The following transactions took place in the year to 31 December 2005.

15 March 2005	Purchased car for £13,200
30 April 2005	Sold plant for £2,000 (original cost £1,600)
26 July 2005	Purchased two cars for £9,300 each

In the following year to 31 December 2006, TEN Ltd sold for £7,600 one of the cars originally purchased on 26 July 2005. The car originally purchased on 15 March 2005 was sold for £9,000 on 9 March 2006. There were no other transactions.

Required

Compute the capital allowances and balancing adjustments for the years ended 31 December 2005 and 31 December 2006.

▷ ACTIVITY 10   ▷ ▷ ▷ ▷

Booker Ltd

Booker Ltd, a small company, trades as a manufacturer in York and prepares accounts to 31 December each year.

The WDV for plant and machinery was £18,150 at 1 January 2006. In July 2006, the company sold for £4,900 a car bought in 2004 for £7,800 and purchased a second-hand car for £4,400. There was 10% private use of both cars by employees.

In November 2006, the company purchased plant and machinery for £6,000. This is likely to be scrapped within three years with no residual value.

Required

Calculate Booker Ltd's capital allowances for the year to 31 December 2006 and show the tax written-down values carried forward. Comment on any election which may be beneficial.

Chapter 5

▷ ACTIVITY 11   ▷ ▷ ▷ ▷

Palmer Ltd

Palmer Ltd, a small company, trades as a manufacturer in Chester and prepares accounts to 31 December each year.

During the year to 31 December 2006, the company had built for it a new factory at a cost of £55,000, made up as follows:

	£
Land	5,000
Canteen	2,500
Offices	16,000
Factory	31,500
	55,000

The company moved into the factory and brought it into use in December 2006.

Required

Calculate Palmer Ltd's industrial buildings allowance for the year to 31 December 2006.

▷ ACTIVITY 12

Brazen Ltd (1)

Brazen Ltd is a manufacturer of heating components preparing accounts to 31 March annually. On 1 December 2006, the company sold one of its workshops, the details of which are as follows:

	£
Cost (excluding land)	150,000
Sale proceeds (excluding land)	210,000
Industrial buildings allowances received to date	24,000

The workshop had first been used on 1 June 2002.

Required

Calculate the balancing adjustment that arises as a result of the sale and the annual writing-down allowance for the purchaser.

▷ ACTIVITY 13

Brazen Ltd (2)

Using the facts from the previous question, recalculate the balancing adjustment and annual writing-down allowance for the purchaser on the assumption that the sale proceeds were £135,000.

▷ ACTIVITY 14

Brazen Ltd (3)

Using the facts from the previous question, recalculate the balancing adjustment and annual writing-down allowance for the purchaser on the assumption that the sale proceeds were £105,000.

Chapter 6

▷ ACTIVITY 15

Mount Ltd

Mound Ltd has the following results for the year ended 31 March 2007:

	£
Adjusted trading profits (before capital allowances)	176,524
Capital allowances	(4,800)
Debenture interest receivable (gross)	2,900
UK dividends received (net of tax credit)	11,876
Capital gain on sale of investments	1,376
Gift Aid paid	(1,000)

Required

Calculate Mound Ltd's profits chargeable to corporation tax for the year to 31 March 2007.

▷ ACTIVITY 16 ▷▷▷

Pitch Ltd (1)

Pitch Ltd has the following results for the year ended 31 March 2007:

	£
Adjusted trading profits (before capital allowances)	766,801
Capital allowances	(24,688)
Rents receivable	3,500
Bank deposit interest receivable	2,400
Dividends received from UK companies (including tax credit)	4,800
Gift Aid paid	(1,000)

Required

Show Pitch Ltd's profits chargeable to corporation tax for the year ended 31 March 2007.

▷ ACTIVITY 17 ▷▷▷

Pitch Ltd (2)

You are required to complete the following extract of the short form for Pitch Ltd for the year to 31 March 2007 (see below).

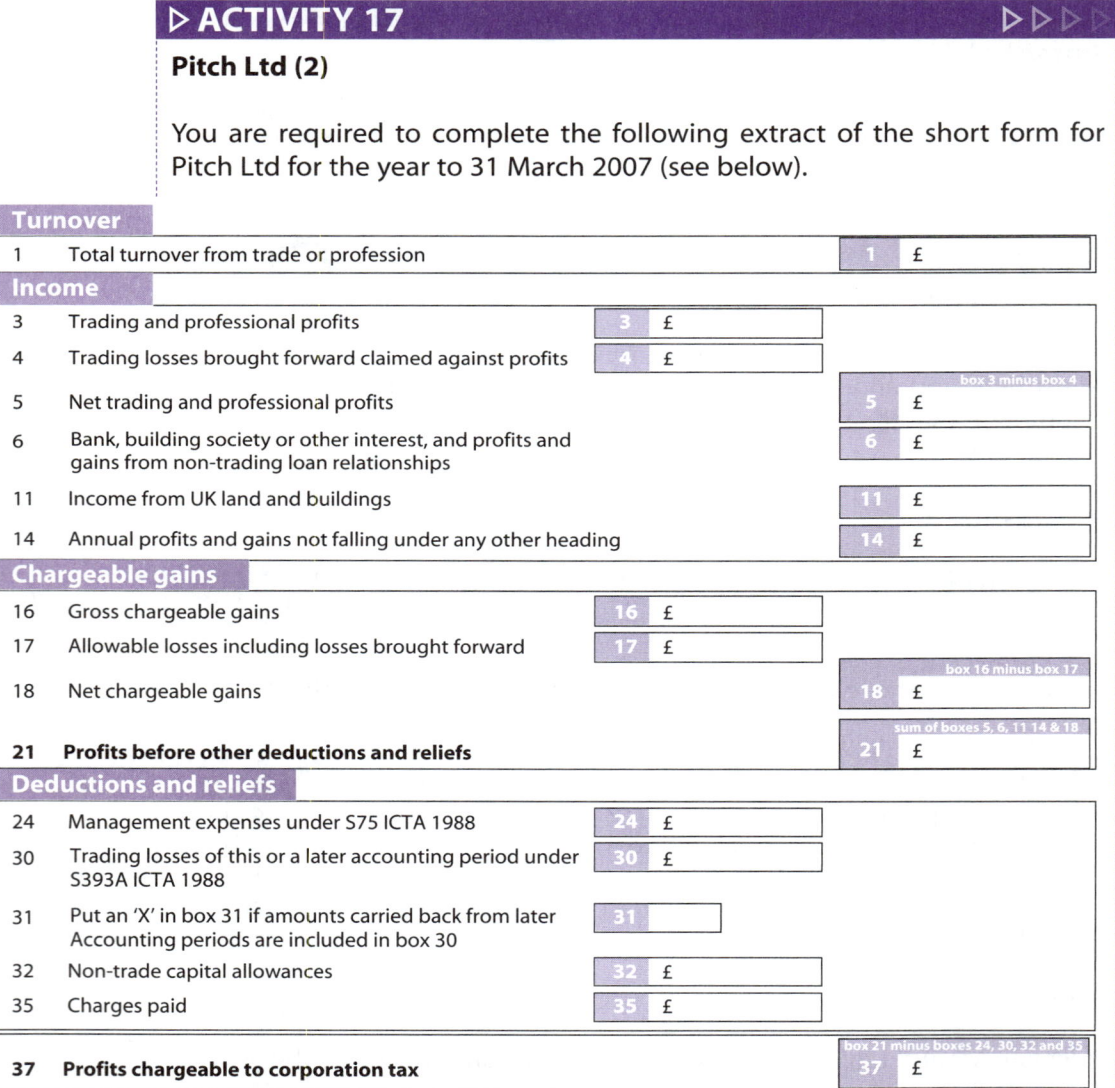

Turnover

1 Total turnover from trade or profession   **1** £

Income

3 Trading and professional profits   **3** £

4 Trading losses brought forward claimed against profits   **4** £

5 Net trading and professional profits   *box 3 minus box 4* **5** £

6 Bank, building society or other interest, and profits and gains from non-trading loan relationships   **6** £

11 Income from UK land and buildings   **11** £

14 Annual profits and gains not falling under any other heading   **14** £

Chargeable gains

16 Gross chargeable gains   **16** £

17 Allowable losses including losses brought forward   **17** £

18 Net chargeable gains   *box 16 minus box 17* **18** £

21 **Profits before other deductions and reliefs**   *sum of boxes 5, 6, 11 14 & 18* **21** £

Deductions and reliefs

24 Management expenses under S75 ICTA 1988   **24** £

30 Trading losses of this or a later accounting period under S393A ICTA 1988   **30** £

31 Put an 'X' in box 31 if amounts carried back from later Accounting periods are included in box 30   **31**

32 Non-trade capital allowances   **32** £

35 Charges paid   **35** £

37 **Profits chargeable to corporation tax**   *box 21 minus boxes 24, 30, 32 and 35* **37** £

Chapter 7

▷ ACTIVITY 18

Osmond Ltd

Osmond Ltd had the following results for the year ended 31 March 2007:

	£
Schedule D Case I	510,000
Debenture interest receivable	8,000
UK dividends received (net of tax credit)	18,000
Capital gain on the sale of an investment	7,500

Required

Calculate Osmond Ltd's corporation tax liability for the year ended 31 March 2007.

▷ ACTIVITY 19

Unpretentious Undercurrents Ltd

Unpretentious Undercurrents Ltd is a United Kingdom resident trading company which manufactures swimwear. It has no associated companies.

The company's results for the year ended 31 March 2007 are summarised as follows:

	£
Trading profits (as adjusted for taxation)	636,250
Dividends received from UK companies	67,500
Bank interest receivable	1,700
Building society interest receivable	2,700

Required

Calculate the corporation tax payable for the year ended 31 March 2007.

▷ ACTIVITY 20

Pitch Ltd (3)

The PCTCT for Pitch Ltd (Question 16) for the year to 31 March 2007 was £747,013. Dividends received amounted to £4,800.

Required

(a) Calculate the corporation tax liability for the year to 31 March 2007.

(b) Complete the tax short calculation on the extract of form CT600 (see below).

Tax calculation

38	Franked investment income	38	
39	Number of associated companies in this investment or	39	
40	Associated companies in the first financial year	40	
41	Associated companies in the second financial year	41	
42	*Put an 'X' in box 42 if the company claims to be charged at the starting rate or the Small companies 'rate on any part of it's profits, or is claimimg marginal rate relief*	42	

Enter how much profit has to be charged at what rate of tax

Finacial year (*yyyy*)	Amount of profit	Rate of tax	Tax
43	44	45	46 £
53	54	55	63 £

total of boxes 46 and 56

63	Corporation tax		63 £
64	Marginal relief rate	64 £	
65	Corporation tax net of marginal rate relief	65 £	
66	Underlying rate of corporation tax	66 £ . %	
67	Profits matched with non-corporate distrubutions	67	
68	Tax at non-corporate disatribution rate	68 £ p	
69	Tax at underlying rate on remaining profits	69 £ p	enter value of box 64 or 65 or the total of boxes 68 and 69 if greater
70	**Corporation tax chargeable**		70 £

79	Tax payable under S419 ICTA 1988		79 £ p
80	*Put an 'X' in box 80 if you completed boxA11 in the Supplementry Pages CT600A*	80	
84	Income tax deducted from gross income included in profits		84 £ p
85	Income tax payable to the company		85 £ p

total of boxes 70 and 79 minus 84

86	**Tax payable - this is your self-assessment of tax payable**		86 £

Tax reconciliation

91	Tax already paid (and not already repaid)		91 £ p
92	Tax outstanding	box 986 minus 93	86 £
93	Tax overpaid	box 986 minus 93	93 £ p

Chapter 8

▷ ACTIVITY 21 ▷ ▷ ▷ ▷

Wolf Ltd

Wolf Ltd has for many years prepared accounts to 30 September, but changes its accounting date to 31 December by preparing accounts for the 15 months ended 31 December 2006.

The accounts show a profit, as adjusted for tax purposes (but before deducting capital allowances) of £300,000.

Capital allowances for the two CAPs based on the 15 month period of account were £17,000 and £8,000 respectively.

The company also had income in the period as follows:

Capital gains (disposal 15 December 2006)	£25,000
Rents receivable	£20,000

Required

Calculate the amounts of corporation tax payable for this 15 month period of account.

▷ ACTIVITY 22 ▷ ▷ ▷ ▷

Unbelievable Upshots Ltd

Unbelievable Upshots Ltd is a UK resident company which manufactures industrial springs. It has one associated company. For many years it had prepared accounts to 31 May, but it decided to change its accounting date to 28 February.

The company's results for the 9 months ended 28 February 2007 are summarised below:

	£
Adjusted trading profit before capital allowances	270,000
Dividends received from UK companies	45,000
Interest receivable	13,000
Chargeable gains	50,000

On 1 June 2006 the tax written-down values of plant and machinery were:

	£
Pool	102,000
Expensive car	7,000
Short life asset (spring end grinding machine)	17,500

The short-life asset was purchased in August 2004 and sold on 19 November 2006 for £5,000.

On 1 January 2007 the expensive car was traded in for £6,000 against a new car costing £14,000.

There were capital losses brought forward at 1 June 2006 of £20,000.

Required

(a) Calculate the capital allowances for the 9 months to 28 February 2007.

(b) Calculate the profits chargeable to corporation tax for the 9 months to 28 February 2007.

(c) Calculate the corporation tax payable for the 9 months ended 28 February 2007.

▷ ACTIVITY 23

Upbeat Ukuleles Ltd

Upbeat Ukuleles Ltd is a United Kingdom resident company which has been manufacturing musical instruments for many years. It has no associated companies. The company has previously made up accounts to 31 March but has now changed its accounting date to 30 June.

The company's results for the 15 month period to 30 June 2007 are as follows:

	£
Trading profits (as adjusted for taxation but before capital allowances)	1,250,000
Bank interest receivable	37,500
Chargeable gain (Note 2)	10,000
Gift Aid payment (Note 3)	5,000
Dividends received from UK companies (Note 4)	33,750

Notes

(1) **Capital allowances**

On 1 April 2006 the tax written-down value of plant and machinery in the capital allowances pool was £100,000.

There were no additions or sales in the period of account to 30 June 2007.

(2) **Chargeable gain**

The chargeable gain of £10,000 is in respect of shares disposed of on 30 September 2006.

(3) **Gift Aid**

£5,000 was paid to a charity on 28 February 2007.

(4) **Dividends received**

	£
25 March 2007	20,250
29 June 2007	13,500
	33,750

Required

(a) Calculate the capital allowances for the accounting periods to 31 March 2007 and 30 June 2007.

(b) Calculate the Schedule D Case I profits for the accounting periods ending 31 March 2007 and 30 June 2007.

(c) Calculate the corporation tax liability for the accounting periods ended 31 March 2007 and 30 June 2007.

Assume the FY 2006 rates continue to apply in the future.

▷ ACTIVITY 24

Unpredictably Uptown Limited

Unpredictably Uptown Limited (UUL) is a United Kingdom resident company which makes fashionable ladies clothing. It has no associated companies. The company has previously prepared accounts to 31 March but has now changed its accounting date to 30 September.

In the 18 months period to 30 September 2007 the company had the following results:

	£
Adjusted trading profits (Note 1)	990,000
Gift Aid to charity (Note 2)	(20,000)
Bank interest receivable (Note 3)	12,500
Dividend received (net) (Note 4)	17,500

Note 1: Adjusted trading profits

No capital allowances are due.

Note 2: Gift Aid

On 31 December 2006 the company made a payment of £20,000 to a national charity.

Note 3: Bank interest

	£
30.09.06 received	5,000
31.03.07 received	4,000
30.09.07 received	3,500
	12,500

The interest is non-trading interest. The amounts received were the amounts accrued to date.

Note 4: Dividend received

On 28 February 2007, UUL received a dividend from another UK company of £17,500. The £17,500 represents the actual amount received without any adjustment for tax credit.

Required

You are required to calculate the corporation tax liability of Unpredictably Uptown Limited for the period ended 30 September 2007.

Assume the FY 2006 rates continue to apply in the future.

Chapter 9

▷ ACTIVITY 25 ▷▷▷▷

Eldorado (Birmingham) Limited

Eldorado (Birmingham) Limited prepares accounts annually to 31 August in each year. The results for the last few years were as follows:

	2005 £	2006 £	2007 £
Trading profits/(loss)	18,000	(81,000)	(6,000)
Capital gain	3,000		
Schedule A	22,000	22,000	22,000

Required

Show how relief is obtained for the trading losses, assuming that relief is claimed as soon as possible.

▷ ACTIVITY 26 ▷▷▷▷

Potter Limited

The following is the income of Potter Limited which commenced to trade on 1 October 2005.

Year end 30 September	2006	2007
	£	£
Adjusted trading profit (loss)	(35,000)	94,000
Bank interest receivable	11,400	8,400
Rents receivable (after deducting expenses)	21,300	21,400
Gift Aid paid 30 September – gross amount	500	500

Required

Calculate the profits chargeable to corporation tax for the years ending 30 September 2006 and 2007, indicating how you would obtain relief as soon as possible for the loss.

▷ ACTIVITY 27 ▷▷▷▷

Brian Phillips Ltd

The following are the profits of Brian Phillips Ltd which has been trading for many years.

	Year ended		
	31.10.04	31.10.05	31.10.06
	£	£	£
Adjusted trading profit (loss)	25,000	(50,000)	12,000
Bank interest received	6,000	2,000	1,000
Chargeable gains	4,000	5,000	7,000
Gift Aid paid	5,000	5,000	5,000

Required

Calculate the profits chargeable to corporation tax for all of the accounting periods shown above, clearly indicating how you would deal with the trading loss to obtain relief as soon as possible.

▷ ACTIVITY 28   ▷ ▷ ▷ ▷

Unseen Ultrasonics Ltd

Unseen Ultrasonics Ltd is a United Kingdom resident company which manufactures accessories for telecommunication systems. It has no associated companies.

The company's results for the year ended 31 December 2006 were as follows:

	£
Trading profits (as adjusted for taxation)	2,174,100
Dividends received from UK companies (see below)	60,000
Bank interest receivable	1,500
Chargeable gains	25,000
Debenture interest receivable	80,000
Gift Aid payment to a national charity	5,000

The company had received a dividend on 28 February 2006 for £60,000.

On 1 January 2006 the company had capital losses brought forward of £30,000.

On 1 January 2006 the company had trading losses brought forward of £567,750.

Required

Calculate the corporation tax liability for the year ended 31 December 2006. You should also state how any unrelieved amounts are to be dealt with.

▷ ACTIVITY 29 ▷ ▷ ▷ ▷

Uncut Undergrowth Ltd

Uncut Undergrowth Ltd is a United Kingdom resident company which has been manufacturing garden machinery since 1990. The company's results are summarised as follows:

	Year ended 30.6.05 £	6 months to 31.12.05 £	Year ended 31.12.06 £
Schedule D I profit/(loss)	35,000	25,000	(350,000)
Non-trade loan interest receivable	-	15,000	22,000
Schedule A	25,000	-	-
Chargeable gains	-	-	30,000
Gift Aid to charity	1,000	1,000	1,000

On 1 July 2004 there were no trading losses brought forward but £40,000 of capital losses were available.

Required

Calculate the profits chargeable to corporation tax for all years in the question after giving maximum relief at the earliest time for the trading losses sustained and any other reliefs. Also show any balances carried forward.

Chapter 10

▷ ACTIVITY 30 ▷ ▷ ▷ ▷

Chappell Limited

Chappell Limited has an accounting period ended 31 March 2007. The following is a summary of payments and receipts of patent royalties from and to individuals:

	Patent royalties paid (gross) £	Patent royalties received (gross) £
30.5.06	-	2,000
30.6.06	1,300	-
28.7.06	2,700	-
30.8.06	-	3,000
29.9.06	2,000	-
1.10.06	5,000	-
21.2.07	2,000	-

Required

Calculate the amount of income tax payable to, or recoverable from, HMRC for the quarters to 30 June 2006, 30 September 2006, 31 December 2006 and 31 March 2007.

▷ ACTIVITY 31

P Ltd

P Ltd is a company in receipt of periodic payments in respect of patent royalties from individuals and it pays debenture interest twice in each accounting period to private individual debenture holders.

The following is a list, in date order, of the various transaction of the above type during the year ended 31 March 2007 showing the actual net amount paid or received.

		£
10 May 2006	Patent royalties received	29,782
12 July 2006	Debenture interest paid	36,000
30 August 2006	Patent royalties received	17,018
24 November 2006	Debenture interest paid	45,600
30 November 2006	Gift Aid payment	9,642
15 January 2007	Patent royalties received	21,982

The directors wish to have information on the cash inflows and outflows arising from the taxation associated with each transaction.

Required

Calculate the amounts of income tax which became payable and/or recoverable in each case, stating the due date.

▷ ACTIVITY 32

Pack Ltd

Pack Ltd, a company which has no associates, carries on a manufacturing business.

It paid debenture interest to individuals of £4,000 (net) on each of 1 April 2006 and 1 October 2006. On 1 August 2006 it received patent royalties (net) of £15,600 from individuals.

The profits chargeable to corporation tax for the year to 31 March 2007 were £97,000 and dividends of £2,700 were received during the year.

Required

(a) Calculate the amounts of income tax payable to/repayable by HM Revenue and Customs for each of the quarters ended 30 June 2006, 30 September 2006, 31 December 2006 and 31 March 2007.

(b) Compute the corporation tax payable in respect of the year ending 31 March 2007.

Chapter 11

▷ ACTIVITY 33

Wendy Windows plc

Wendy Windows plc, a 'large' company, has profits chargeable to corporation tax in the year ended 31 January 2007 of £2,400,000.

Required

Calculate the corporation tax liability of Wendy Windows plc for the accounting period to 31 January 2007 and state when this liability is due for payment.

▷ ACTIVITY 34

Universe plc

Universe plc, which has profits of £5 million annually, is preparing its budget for the year ending 30 June 2007.

Required

(a) Prepare a plan of projected corporation tax payments based on its results for the year, stating the amounts due and the due dates.

(b) Advise of any other administrative requirements for corporation tax purposes.

▷ ACTIVITY 35

Corporation Tax Self Assessment

Required

Describe the main features of Corporation Tax Self Assessment covering the filing of returns and the calculations and payment of tax.

Chapter 12

▷ ACTIVITY 36

Bella Ltd

Bella Ltd has an employee, George. He receives wages of £12,480 (gross) per annum. George is provided with a company car and other benefits with a taxable value for 2006/07 of £7,805.

Required

Calculate the total National Insurance contributions for which Bella Ltd should account to HMRC for 2006/07 in respect of George.

▷ ACTIVITY 37 ▷▷▷▷

Pasta Ltd

Pasta Ltd has an employee, Fred. He receives wages of £6,864 (gross) per annum. In addition, he received a £1,200 Christmas bonus.

Fred is provided with taxable benefits for 2006/07 as follows:

Company car, taxable benefit	£6,000
High Street vouchers, taxable amount	£500

Required

Calculate the total National Insurance contributions for which Pasta Ltd should account to HMRC for 2006/07 in respect of Fred.

▷ ACTIVITY 38 ▷▷▷▷

Charles Dickens

Charles Dickens, the Managing Director of CD Ltd receives a salary (gross) of £60,000 p.a.

The company provides him with private medical insurance (cost £200 p.a.) and a company car and fuel for private use (benefits £4,000 for the car and £2,500 for fuel). It also contributes 8% of his salary to an occupational pension scheme.

Required

Calculate CD Ltd's liability to NIC for Charles Dickens for 2006/07.

Chapter 14

▷ ACTIVITY 39 ▷▷▷▷

Manuel Costa (1)

Manuel Costa is a self employed wholesale clothing distributor. His summarised accounts for the year ended 30 June 2006 are as follows:

	£	£
Sales		400,000
Opening stock	40,000	
Purchases	224,000	
	264,000	
Closing stock	(32,000)	
Cost of sales		232,000
Gross profit		168,000

	£	£
Gross profit		168,000
Wages and National Insurance (Note 1)	84,655	
Motor car running expenses (Manuel's car) (Note 2)	2,000	
Lighting and heating	4,250	
Rent and business rates	31,060	
Repairs and renewals (all allowable)	3,490	
Legal expenses (Note 3)	1,060	
Depreciation	3,570	
Profit on sale of office furniture	(60)	
Sundry expenses (all allowable)	5,770	
		(135,795)
Net profit		32,205

Notes to the accounts

(1) Wages

Included in wages are Manuel's drawings of £300 per week, his National Insurance contributions of £109 for the year and wages and National Insurance contributions in respect of his wife totalling £11,750. His wife worked full-time in the business as a secretary.

(2) Motor car running expenses

Manuel estimates that one-third of his mileage is private. Included in the charge is £65 for a speeding fine incurred by Manuel whilst delivering goods to a customer.

(3) Legal expenses

	£
Defending action in respect of alleged faulty goods	330
Defending Manuel in connection with speeding offence	640
Debt collection	90
	1,060

(4) Capital allowances on plant and machinery for the year to 30 June 2006 are £2,480.

Required

Calculate the taxable trade profits for the accounting period to 30 June 2006.

▷ ACTIVITY 39   ▷ ▷ ▷ ▷

Manuel Costa (2)

You are required to complete pages SE1 and SE2 for Manuel Costa's tax return for 2006/07. (See previous question.)

(See over the page.)

Income for the year ended 5 April 2007

Inland Revenue

SELF-EMPLOYMENT

Fill in these boxes first

Name	Tax reference

If you want help, look up the box numbers in the Notes

Business details

Name of business
3.1

Description of business
3.2

Address of business
3.3

Postcode

Accounting period – read the Notes, page SEN2 before filling in these boxes

Start **3.4** / /

End **3.5** / /

- Tick box 3.6 if details in boxes 3.1 or 3.3 have changed since your last Tax return **3.6**

- Date of commencement if after 5 April 2004 **3.7** / /

- Date of cessation if before 6 April 2007 **3.8** / /

- Tick box 3.9 if the special arrangements for certain trades apply – read the Notes, pages SEN11 and SEN12 **3.9**

- Tick box 3.10 if you entered details for all relevant accounting periods on last year's Tax Return and boxes 3.14 to 3.73 and 3.99 to 3.115 will be blank (read Step 3 on page SEN2) **3.10**

- Tick box 3.11 if your accounts do not cover the period from the last accounting date (explain why in the 'Additional information' box, box 3.116) **3.11**

- Tick box 3.12 if your accounting date has changed (only if this is a permanent change and you want it to count for tax) **3.12**

- Tick box 3.13 if this is the second or further change (explain in box 3.116 on Page SE4 why you have not used the same date as last year) **3.13**

Capital allowances - summary

	Capital allowances	Balancing charge
- Car costing more than £12,000 (excluding cars with low CO₂ emissions). (A separate calculation must be made for each car.)	**3.14** £	**3.15** £
- Other business plant and machinery (including cars with low CO₂ emissions and cars costing less than £12,000) read the Notes, page SEN4	**3.16** £	**3.17** £
- Agricultural or Industrial Buildings Allowance (A separate calculation must be made for each block of expenditure.)	**3.18** £	**3.19** £
- Other capital allowances claimed (Separate calculations must be made.)	**3.20** £	**3.21** £
	total of column above	total of column above
Total capital allowances/balancing charges	**3.22** £	**3.23** £

- Tick box 3.22A if box 3.22 includes enhanced capital allowances for environmentally friendly expenditure. **3.22A**

Income and expenses - annual turnover below £15,000

If your annual turnover is £15,000 or more, ignore boxes 3.24 to 3.26. Instead fill in Page SE2

If your annual turnover is below £15,000, **fill in boxes 3.24 to 3.26 instead of Page SE2.** Read the Notes, page SEN4.

- Turnover including other business receipts and goods etc. taken for personal use (and balancing charges from box 3.23) **3.24** £

- Expenses allowable for tax (including capital allowances from box 3.22) **3.12** £

	box 3.24 minus box 3.25
Net profit (put figure in brackets if a loss)	**3.13** £

SA103

TAX RETURN ■ SELF-EMPLOYMENT: PAGE SE1

Now fill in Page SE3

Income and expenses - annual turnover £15,000 or more

You must fill in this Page if your annual turnover is £15,000 or more - read the Notes, page SEN2

If you were registered for VAT, do the figures in boxes 3.29 to 3.64, include VAT? **3.27** ☐ or exclude VAT? **3.28** ☐

Sales/business income (turnover)
3.29 £ _____

	Disallowable expenses included in boxes 3.33 to 3.50	Total expenses
● Cost of sales	**3.30** £	**3.46** £
● Construction industry subcontractor costs	**3.31** £	**3.47** £
● Other direct costs	**3.32** £	**3.48** £

box 3.29 *minus* boxes 3.46 + 3.47 + 3.48

Gross profit/(loss) **3.49** £ _____

Other income/profits **3.50** £ _____

● Employee costs	**3.33** £	**3.51** £
● Premises costs	**3.34** £	**3.52** £
● Repairs	**3.35** £	**3.53** £
● General administrative expenses	**3.36** £	**3.54** £
● Motor expenses	**3.37** £	**3.55** £
● Travel and subsistence	**3.38** £	**3.56** £
● Advertising, promotion and entertainment	**3.39** £	**3.57** £
● Legal and professional costs	**3.40** £	**3.58** £
● Bad debts	**3.41** £	**3.59** £
● Interest	**3.42** £	**3.60** £
● Other finance charges	**3.43** £	**3.61** £
● Depreciation and loss/(profit) on sale	**3.44** £	**3.62** £
● Other expenses	**3.45** £	**3.63** £

Put the total of boxes 3.30 to 3.45 in **box 3.66 below**

total of boxes 3.51 to 3.63

Total expenses **3.64** £ _____

boxes 3.49 + 3.50 *minus* 3.64

Net profit/(loss) **3.65** £ _____

Tax adjustments to net profit or loss

total of boxes 3.30 to 3.45

● Disallowable expenses **3.66** £ _____

● Adjustments (apart from disallowable expenses) that increase profits. Examples are goods taken for personal use and amounts brought forward from an earlier year because of a claim under ESC B11about compulsory slaughter of farm animals **3.67** £ _____

● Balancing charges **3.68** £ _____

boxes 3.66 + 3.67 + 3.68

Total additions to net profit (deduct from net loss) **3.69** £ _____

● Capital allowances **3.70** £ _____

boxes 3.70 + 3.71

● Deductions from net profit (add to net loss) **3.71** £ _____

3.72 £ _____

boxes 3.65 + 3.69 *minus* 3.72

Net business profit for tax purposes (put figure in brackets if a loss) **3.73** £ _____

Now fill in Page SE3

▷ ACTIVITY 41   ▷ ▷ ▷ ▷

Freda Jones

Freda Jones runs a business which provides interior design services and supplies furniture and furnishings. Her summarised accounts for the year ended 31 December 2006 are as follows:

	£	£
Sales of furniture and furnishings (Note 1)		300,000
Cost of sales		(200,000)
		100,000
Design fees		85,000
Gross profit		185,000
Wages and National Insurance (Note 2)	75,000	
Rent and business rates	18,250	
Miscellaneous expenses (all allowable)	12,710	
Taxation (Freda's income tax)	15,590	
Depreciation	2,540	
Lease rental on car (Freda's car) (Note 3)	8,400	
Motor car running expenses (Freda's car) (Note 4)	2,500	
Lighting and heating	1,750	
		136,740
Net profit		48,260

Notes to the accounts

(1)   Sales include £1,000 reimbursed by Freda for furnishings taken from stock. This reimbursement represented cost price.

(2)   Wages. Included in wages are Freda's drawings of £1,000 per month and her National Insurance contributions of £109 for the year.

(3)   Lease rental on car. Freda's car was a BMW costing £30,000. The lease was entered into on 1 July 2005.

(4)   Motor car running expenses. Freda estimates that one-half of her mileage is private.

(5)   Capital allowances for the year to 31 December 2006 are £1,200.

Required

Calculate the taxable trade profits for the accounting period to 31 December 2006.

▷ ACTIVITY 42

Hudson

Hudson has been carrying on a manufacturing business in a South London suburb since 1 January 2003 preparing accounts to 31 December each year. He decided to retire at 31 October 2006, having reached 65 years of age.

During the above periods, the following plant was acquired for cash on the dates shown:

| 1 March 2003 | New plant costing £10,858 |
| 1 March 2005 | Second-hand plant costing £1,000 |

On 10 April 2004, Hudson bought a car costing £12,000 through his business. Three-quarters of his usage of the car was for business purposes and one-quarter for private purposes.

No sale of plant took place during these periods, but at 31 October 2006, when the business closed down, all the plant was sold for £2,450 (no one item realising more than its original cost), and the motor car was disposed of to a dealer, who gave Hudson £7,400 for it.

Required

Calculate capital allowances for Hudson for each accounting period.

▷ ACTIVITY 43

Ethan

Ethan prepares accounts to 31 December annually. In the year to 31 December 2005, he bought three cars for use in his business as follows:

11 January 2005	Purchased car for £14,000 (wholly business usage)
21 June 2005	Purchased car for £8,800 (wholly business usage)
16 September 2005	Purchased car for £11,600 (30% private usage by Ethan)

He had never previously acquired any plant and machinery for his business.

In the following year to 31 December 2006, Ethan sold for £9,500 the car originally purchased on 16 September 2005. The car originally purchased on 11 January 2005 was sold for £10,000 on 12 June 2006. There were no other transactions.

Required

Compute the capital allowances and balancing adjustments for the years ended 31 December 2005 and 31 December 2006.

▷ ACTIVITY 44 ▷ ▷ ▷ ▷

Raj

On 1 November 2004, Raj commenced a small manufacturing business in a rented factory.

He subsequently purchased the following machinery:

		£
2 November 2004	Machinery	4,000
1 February 2005	Car (20% private use)	15,000
1 February 2006	New tool grinder	6,000
2 October 2006	Car for salesman	11,600

Accounts are made up to 30 September in each year.

Required

Compute the capital allowances for each accounting period.

▷ ACTIVITY 45 ▷ ▷ ▷ ▷

John Openshaw

John Openshaw imports kitchen appliances from Europe which he sells to wholesale distributors in the United Kingdom. His trading and profit and loss account for his first year of trading to 30 June 2006 is:

	£	£
Sales		167,400
Purchases	89,200	
Closing stock	(27,700)	
Cost of sales		(61,500)
Gross profit		105,900
Wages and salaries	42,900	
Rent and rates	2,100	
Lighting and heating	1,690	
Entertaining (Note 1)	2,950	
Bad debts (Note 2)	6,750	
Depreciation	5,000	
Motor expenses (Note 3)	8,050	
Sundry expenses (note 4)	4,010	
Legal and professional charges (note 5)	2,040	
		75,490
Net profit		30,410

Notes:

(1)   Travelling and entertaining expenses

	£
Christmas presents for staff	200
Entertaining overseas suppliers	750
Entertaining UK customers	2,000
	2,950

(2)   Bad debts

	£
Trading debts written off	3,250
Provisions against specific debtors	1,800
General provision in view of uncertain trading conditions	1,700
	6,750

(3)   Motor expenses

	£
Employers' van expenses	5,000
Car expenses	3,050
	8,050

All of the car expenses related to John Openshaw. One quarter of his mileage was private.

(4)   Sundry expenses are all allowable trading expenses for income tax purposes.

(5)   Legal and professional charges

	£
Purchase of business premises	1,100
Accountancy fees	270
Legal fees in connection with action by employee for unfair dismissal	220
Debt collection	450
	2,040

The following capital purchases were made:

		£
1 July 2005	Office furniture and equipment	8,250
7 July 2005	Car for use by John Openshaw	9,500
10 July 2005	Van	7,000
18 March 2006	Office furniture	1,000

Required

(a)   Calculate the capital allowances for the year to 30 June 2006

(b)   Calculate the taxable trade profits for the year to 30 June 2006.

▷ ACTIVITY 46 ▷ ▷ ▷ ▷

Eastwood

Eastwood, a manufacturer of mobile phones, prepares accounts annually to 31 December. Accounts for the year to 31 December 2006 showed an adjusted profit of £85,000 before taking account of capital allowances.

As at 1 January 2006 there was the following unrelieved expenditure for capital allowance purposes:

Pool of plant - £42,000
Car costing £7,200 in January 2005 with 30% private use - £5,400

In the year to 31 December 2006 the following purchases and sales of plant were made:

Purchases
10 April 2006	Plastic moulding machine cost £27,500
1 May 2006	Car, cost £10,000 (no private use)
1 September 2006	Car, cost £15,000 (no private use)

Sales
21 August 2006	Plastic moulding machine for £5,500 (original cost £14,000)

Required

(a)   Prepare a capital allowance computation based on the above information, assuming the business is small.

(b)   State the amount of taxable trade profits for the year to 31 December 2006.

▷ ACTIVITY 47 ▷▷▷▷

Joshua

Joshua decided to use his engineering skills and business contacts as a self-employed consultant. He commenced business on 1 July 2005 and made up his first accounts to 30 April 2006. His summarised accounts for the first period of trading were:

	£	£	£
Consultancy fees			49,510
Wife's wages as secretary - Note 1		3,500	
Car expenses - Note 2		3,750	
Depreciation		1,850	
Rent of office		7,000	
Office running costs		2,160	
			(18,260)
Net profit			31,250

Notes:

(1) Wife's wages of £350 were paid on the last day of the month and can be justified as being at a commercial rate.

(2) Joshua purchased a BMW for use in the business. Joshua's business mileage in the period covered by the first set of accounts was 20,000 and his private mileage was 2,000. This proportion is expected to apply for future periods. The car expenses included speeding fines incurred by Joshua of £120.

(3) Capital purchases were made as follows:

		£
July 2005	BMW	15,000
July 2005	Office furniture	1,855
July 2005	Computer	1,500
August 2005	Photocopier	920

No election was to be made to treat any of the assets purchased as short-life assets.

Required

Calculate the taxable trade profits for Joshua's first period of trading.

Chapter 15

▷ ACTIVITY 48

Bob, Carol, Ted and Alice

Bob, Carol and Ted commenced business on 1 November 2002, preparing accounts to 31 October each year and sharing profits equally. On 1 February 2004, Alice was admitted to the partnership and profits continued to be shared equally. On 1 August 2005, Carol retired and on 31 January 2007 the partnership was dissolved.

The taxable trade profits of the partnership, after deducting capital allowances, were as follows:

		£
Year ended	31 October 2003	24,000
Year ended	31 October 2004	30,000
Year ended	31 October 2005	36,000
Year ended	31 October 2006	42,000
Three months to	31 January 2007	12,000

Required

Show the allocation of the taxable trade profits between the partners for each accounting period.

▷ ACTIVITY 49

Roger, Brigitte and Xavier

Roger and Brigitte commenced in business on 1 October 2002 as hotel proprietors, sharing profits equally.

On 1 October 2004 their son, Xavier, joined the partnership and from that date each of the partners was entitled to one-third of the profits.

The taxable trade profits of the partnership are as follows:

		£
Period ended	30 June 2003	30,000
Year ended	30 June 2004	45,000
Year ended	30 June 2005	50,000
Year ended	30 June 2006	60,000

Required

Show the allocation of the taxable trade profits between the partners for each accounting period.

▷ ACTIVITY 50

Anne, Betty, Chloe and Diana

Anne and Betty have been in partnership since 1 January 1995 sharing profits equally. On 30 June 2005, Betty resigned as a partner and was replaced on 1 July 2005 by Chloe. Diana was admitted as a partner on 1 April 2006. Profits were shared equally throughout. The partnership's taxable trade profits are as follows:

		£
Year ended	31 December 2005	60,000
Year ended	31 December 2006	72,000

Required

Show the allocation of the taxable trade profits between the partners for each of the years to 31 December 2005 and 2006.

▷ ACTIVITY 51

Bert and Harold

Bert and Harold have traded in partnership for several years. Their accounts for the year ended 30 September 2006 show taxable trade profits of £16,500. Bert and Harold changed their profit-sharing ratio on 1 July 2006. The old profit-sharing ratio applies until 30 June 2006, and the new ratio applies from 1 July 2006.

	Bert	*Harold*
Old ratio:		
Salaries p.a.	£3,000	£2,000
Share of balance	3/5	2/5
New ratio:		
Salaries p.a.	£6,000	£4,000
Share of balance	2/3	1/3

Required

Show the allocation of the taxable trade profits between the partners for the year to 30 September 2006.

Chapter 16

▷ ACTIVITY 52

Roger

Roger started in business on 1 May 2003. His first set of accounts was prepared to 30 September 2003 and he then retained 30 September as his year end.

Taxable trade profits in the early years were as follows:

	£
1 May 2003 – 30 September 2003	40,500
Year ended 30 September 2004	59,400
Year ended 30 September 2005	72,900
Year ended 30 September 2006	56,700

Required

Show the amounts assessable for all fiscal years affected by these results and calculate the overlap profits arising.

▷ ACTIVITY 53

James

James started in business on 1 January 2003 and prepared his first set of accounts to 30 April 2004. He then continued to make up his accounts to 30 April and his taxable trade profits in the early years were as follows:

	£
1 January 2003 – 30 April 2004	75,600
Year ended 30 April 2005	52,650
Year ended 30 April 2006	56,900

Required

Show the amounts assessable for all fiscal years affected by these results and calculate the overlap profits arising.

▷ ACTIVITY 54

Avril

Avril commenced trading on 1 January 2004. She prepared accounts to 30 June each year. Her taxable trade profits for the first few years of trading were as follows:

Period		£
6 months to	30 June 2004	80,000
Year ended	30 June 2005	100,000
Year ended	30 June 2006	110,000

Required

Calculate the amounts assessable for 2003/04 to 2006/07, and show the overlap profit arising to be carried forward.

▷ ACTIVITY 55

Benny

Benny, a fashion designer, decided to commence his own business on 1 July 2004. He prepared accounts on a calendar year basis and his taxable trade profits for the first few periods of trading are as follows:

Period		£
6 months to	31 December 2004	14,000
Year ended	31 December 2005	36,000
Year ended	31 December 2006	28,000

Required

Show the amounts assessable for 2004/05 to 2006/07, and state the overlap profit to be carried forward.

▷ ACTIVITY 56

Colin

Colin, a pop star, commenced trading on 1 July 2003 and prepared his first accounts to 30 June 2004. 30 June was maintained as the accounting year end. Taxable trade profits in the first few years were as follows:

Period	£
30 June 2004	100,000
30 June 2005	80,000
30 June 2006	120,000

Required

Calculate the assessable amounts based on the above profits for 2003/04 to 2006/07.

▷ ACTIVITY 57

Dana

Dana commenced trading on 1 February 2003 and prepared her first accounts for the 15 month period to 30 April 2004. Thereafter she maintained 30 April as her accounting date. Taxable trade profits for the first few periods were as follows:

Period		£
15 months to	30 April 2004	150,000
Year ended	30 April 2005	120,000
Year ended	30 April 2006	140,000

Required

Show the assessable amounts for 2002/03 to 2006/07 based on the above results and state the overlap profits and period to be carried forward.

▷ ACTIVITY 58

Elle

Elle prepares accounts to 31 May annually. Recent taxable trade profits have been as follows:

		£
Year ended	31 May 2005	22,000
Year ended	31 May 2006	26,000

Elle had overlap profits on commencement of the business totalling £5,000.

Required

Show the assessments for all relevant fiscal years for the following alternative dates for cessation of trading.

(a)   31 May 2007 with taxable trade profits of £27,000.

(b)   31 January 2007 with taxable trade profits of £22,500.

▷ ACTIVITY 59

Bernadette

Bernadette opened a charm school on 1 October 2003. Accounts were prepared regularly to 30 September and her taxable trade profits are as follows:

		£
Year ended	30 September 2004	21,280
Year ended	30 September 2005	24,688
Year ended	30 September 2006	28,816
Year ended	30 September 2007	30,304

She intends to cease trading on 28 February 2008. The forecast taxable trade profits for the period from 1 October 2007 to 28 February 2008 have been estimated at £16,792.

Required

Show the assessable amounts for all fiscal years of the business.

▷ ACTIVITY 60

Bay

Bay, who has been carrying on a manufacturing business in a South London suburb since 1 January 2003, decided to retire at 31 October 2006, having reached 65 years of age. His adjusted profits (before capital allowances) and capital allowances over the life of the business are:

		Profits	CAs
		£	£
Year ending	31 December 2003	19,487	4,343
Year ending	31 December 2004	17,840	3,879
Year ending	31 December 2005	16,928	3,310
Period ending	31 October 2006	18,040	1,326

Required

Compute all the assessable amounts for Bay for the years 2002/03 to 2006/07 inclusive.

Approach to the question

Note that you must proceed in the following order:
* Deduct the capital allowances from the adjusted profits.
* Apply the basis period rules to the profits after the deduction of capital allowances.

▷ ACTIVITY 61

Ranjit

On 1 November 2004, Ranjit commenced a manufacturing business preparing accounts to 30 September in each year. The adjusted profits for income tax purposes but before deducting capital allowances and the capital allowances are as follows:

		Profits	CAs
		£	£
Period ended	30 September 2005	6,106	3,800
Year ended	30 September 2006	8,845	5,000
Year ended	30 September 2007	19,087	9,950

Required

Compute the assessable amounts for each of the years affected by the results and calculate the amount of overlap profits.

▷ ACTIVITY 62

Michael

Michael started in business as a hairdresser on 1 March 2001 and finished on 31 October 2007.

His taxable trade profits were as follows:

		£
Period ended	30.4.02	15,000
Year ended	30.4.03	17,000
Year ended	30.4.04	12,000
Year ended	30.4.05	14,000
Year ended	30.4.06	18,000
Year ended	30.4.07	13,000
Period ended	31.10.07	3,000

Required

Calculate the taxable amounts for all relevant years.

▷ ACTIVITY 63

Partnership assessments

Briefly explain the basis by which partners are assessed in respect of their share of a partnership's taxable trade profits.

Chapter 17

▷ ACTIVITY 64

Bourbon

Bourbon, a married man, has been trading as a self employed biscuit maker for many years. His taxable trade profits or losses are given below.

			Taxable trade Profit/loss
Year to	31 March 2006	Profit	£12,200
Year to	31 March 2007	Loss	£(24,050)
Year to	31 March 2008	Profit	£12,750

Details of other income for Bourbon is as follows:

	2005/06	2006/07	2007/08
	£	£	£
Building society received (gross)	7,250	10,250	5,250

Required

Set out the options available to an established continuing trade for relief of the loss and, together with calculations, advise Bourbon as to the best method of obtaining loss relief.

▷ ACTIVITY 65

Lancelot

Lancelot, a bachelor, started a business on 1 July 2004. His taxable trade profits and losses are as follows:

Year ended	30 June 2005	Profit	6,000
Year ended	30 June 2006	Loss	(30,000)
Year ended	30 June 2007	Profit	8,000

Prior to commencing in business Lancelot had been in salaried employment.

His employment earnings for 2002/03 and 2003/04 were £12,000 and £14,000 respectively. In addition, he receives savings income amounting to £2,000 (gross) each year.

Required

Show how Lancelot will obtain relief for the loss if he makes a claim under S381 ICTA 1988, the special loss relief available to a new business.

▷ ACTIVITY 66 ▷▷▷▷

Lucien Buysse

Lucien Buysse, a single man aged 25, commenced trading as a chiropodist on 1 July 2004. His taxable trade profits and losses were as follows:

		£	
Year ended	30 June 2005	(15,000)	loss
Year ended	30 June 2006	5,000	profit

Lucien had not previously been employed or been in business. He had received a cash legacy in April 2003 which was placed on deposit at the Midshires Building Society and has produced the following savings income (gross).

	£
2003/04	15,750
2004/05	11,250
2005/06	12,500
2006/07	13,750

Required

Show how the loss sustained in the year ended 30 June 2005 can be utilised in the most tax-efficient manner and calculate Lucien's taxable income for the years 2003/04, 2004/05, 2005/06 and 2006/07.

Assume that the personal allowance for 2006/07 (i.e. £5,035) applies to all years in the question.

▷ ACTIVITY 67 ▷▷▷▷

Jaqueline

Jacqueline retired from her 'Do-it-yourself' shop on 31 July 2006 after trading for several years.

Her adjusted profits/losses before capital allowances in recent years are as follows:

		£	
Year ended	31 July 2004	13,000	profit
Year ended	31 July 2005	8,000	profit
Year ended	31 July 2006	3,000	loss

There are overlap profits of £2,500.

The tax written-down value of the 'pool' after the capital allowances claim for the year ended 31 July 2003 was £1,200. There were no further additions. The items in the 'pool' were sold for £75 on 31 July 2006.

Required

(a) Calculate the capital allowances for each accounting period.

(b) Quantify the assessable amounts after the capital allowances for the final three years of assessment before loss relief.

(c) Comment briefly on how the loss of 2006/07 could be relieved.

▷ ACTIVITY 68

Leonardo

Leonardo, an art dealer, commenced to trade on 1 September 2003. His taxable trade profits and losses are:

		£	
01.09.03 to 31.05.04		22,500	profit
01.06.04 to 31.05.05		30,000	loss
01.06.05 to 31.05.06		15,000	loss
01.06.06 to 31.05.07		5,000	profit

Leonardo does not foresee making any appreciable profits in the following two or three years.

Leonardo has not had any other income in any of the years in question.

Required

You are required to show how his trading loss can be utilised most effectively, giving your reasons.

▷ ACTIVITY 69

Caren Montaine

Caren Montaine, the wife of a successful derivatives dealer, has been a fashion consultant for five years. Caren had always made taxable profits and her recent taxable trade profits and losses are as follows:

Year ended	31 August 2005	£5,100	profit
Year ended	31 August 2006	£(11,000)	loss
Year ended	31 August 200	£14,000	profit

Her only other income is in the tax year 2006/07 when she receives building society interest of £2,000 (gross).

Required

(1) State the possible ways in which Caren could obtain relief for the trading loss sustained in the year ended 31 August 2006.

(2) State your recommendations assuming Caren wishes to maximise the relief claimed.

You may assume that the income tax rates and personal allowances figures provided for 2006/07 apply to all years affected.

Chapter 18

▷ ACTIVITY 70

Enquiries

HM Revenue and Customs (HMRC) must give written notice before starting an enquiry into a self-assessment personal tax return.

Required

(a) State the date by which the written notice must normally be given.

(b) State the circumstances under which HMRC can extend the above deadline and the time limits for this extension.

(c) State the three main reasons for the commencement of an enquiry.

(d) Explain the choices available to a taxpayer who is notified of additional liability as a result of an enquiry.

▷ ACTIVITY 71

Income tax self assessment

You are required to state:

(a) The latest date by which income tax returns for the year 2006/07 should be returned to HM Revenue and Customs (HMRC).

(b) The date by which income tax returns for the year 2006/07 should be returned to HMRC if the taxpayer wishes HMRC to calculate his/her liability.

(c) The date by which the taxpayer should notify HMRC that he/she has received income in the year 2006/07 which is liable to income tax where no income tax return has been issued.

(d) The fixed penalties for the late submission of income tax returns and when they apply.

(e) The further penalty which may be imposed when HMRC believe that the initial fixed penalty will not result in the submission of the return.

(f) The maximum penalty for not notifying HMRC of the receipt of income liable to income tax within the time limit in (c) above.

(g) The penalty for the submission of an incorrect income tax return.

(h) The penalty for fraudulently or negligently claiming reductions of payments on account of income tax.

(i) The penalty for failing to maintain or retain adequate records backing up an income tax return.

Chapter 19

▷ ACTIVITY 72

Naomi

Naomi, aged 45, has been self employed for many years.

Her accounting profits always exceed her taxable trade profits.

Required

State the National Insurance contributions payable by Naomi for 2006/07, assuming her taxable trade profits are:

(a) £4,500
(b) £24,500
(c) £44,500

Chapter 21

▷ ACTIVITY 73

RBQ

RBQ Ltd made the following disposals in the year ended 31 March 2007.

(1)   On 11 August 2006, it sold a shop for £15,000. The shop was bought in May 1994 for £8,000.

(2)   On 16 October 2006, it sold a painting which had been purchased for £30,000 in November 1991. Sale proceeds were £25,000.

(3)   On 1 February 2007, it sold a car, a VW Beetle, which was bought in February 1985 for £2,000. By the time of the sale, it had become a collector's item and RBQ Ltd managed to obtain proceeds of £10,000.

(4)   On 3 January 2007, it sold a piece of land for £29,000. It had cost £6,000 in May 1991.

Required

Calculate the total chargeable gains on each of the above transactions in the year ended 31 March 2007.

You should use the following indexation factors:

May 1994 – August 2006	0.366
November 1991 – October 2006	0.463
February 1985 – February 2007	1.175
May 1991 – January 2007	0.495

▷ ACTIVITY 74

Jackson Ltd

During the year to 30 September 2006, Jackson Ltd had the following capital transactions:

(a)   It sold for £27,000 in October 2005 land which it had bought in February 1989 for £14,000.

(b)   It also sold a cottage in December 2005 for £100,000. Out of that the company had to pay legal fees of £1,200. It had originally bought the cottage in March 1988 for £10,500 and extended it in April 1992 for £3,000 and in June 1995 for £4,600.

(c)   In March 2006, Jackson Ltd sold a racehorse for £22,000. It had purchased the horse for £4,000 on 1 December 2000.

Required

Calculate the capital gain chargeable on each of the above transactions in the year ended 30 September 2006.

Use the following indexation factors were appropriate:

February 1989 – October 2005	0.729
March 1988 – December 2005	0.865
April 1992 – December 2005	0.398
June 1995 – December 2005	0.296
December 2000 – March 2006	0.132

Chapter 22

▷ ACTIVITY 75

John

John made the following disposals in the year 2006/07.

(1) On 20 June 2006 he sold his offices for £73,000. The offices were bought in October 1995 for £29,000.

(2) On 12 August 2006 he sold his retail shop. It had been purchased for £30,000 in November 1992. Sale proceeds were £26,000.

(3) On 13 March 2007, he sold his workshop. It was purchased in April 1982 for £15,000. It was sold for £25,000.

All of the assets were used in his business.

Required

Calculate the total chargeable gains (after taper relief) for 2006/07.

You should use the following indexation values:

October 1995 – April 1998	0.085
November 1992 – April 1998	0.164
April 1982 – April 1998	1.006

▷ **ACTIVITY 76** ▷ ▷ ▷ ▷

Jacky

During 2006/07 Jacky, who runs her own business, sold business assets as follows:

(a) She sold for £55,000 in October 2006 a factory which she had bought in February 1988 for £14,000.

(b) She also sold a shop used in her business in January 2007 for £35,000. This had cost £37,000 in July 1996.

(c) In March 2007, Jacky sold a second shop for £52,000. She had purchased it for £44,000 on 1 December 2005.

Required

Calculate the total chargeable gains for 2006/07.

Use the following indexation factors where appropriate:

February 1988 – April 1998	0.568
July 1996 – April 1998	0.067

▷ **ACTIVITY 77** ▷ ▷ ▷ ▷

Rosalind

Calculate the taxable gains for 2006/07 for each of the following:

(a) Rosalind's total chargeable gains during 2006/07 were £8,300 and her allowable losses during that year were £1,000.

(b) Derek had total chargeable gains in 2006/07 of £9,200 and total allowable losses of £300. He also had losses brought forward from previous years of £2,500.

(c) Phil's net gains in 2006/07 were £9,700 and he had losses brought forward from previous years of £500.

Assume in each case that taper relief is not available.

▷ ACTIVITY 78

Hannah

Hannah has the following results from capital transactions during 2006/07:

	£
Indexed gain on a business asset (held for 2½ years)	60,000
Indexed gain on business asset (held for 18 months)	12,000
Loss on business asset	7,000

Losses brought forward from 2005/06 were £2,000. She has taxable income of £29,000.

Required

Calculate the CGT payable for 2006/07.

Chapter 23

▷ ACTIVITY 79

Jerry Ltd

Jerry Ltd sold ordinary 25p shares in Blue plc as follows:

	Number of shares	Proceeds
September 1991	2,000	£9,000
March 2007	2,000	£14,500

At 6 April 1985, Jerry Ltd had 2,600 shares in the FA 1985 pool, with an indexed cost of £6,377 and a cost of £5,000. Purchases were made as follows:

	Number of shares	Cost
July 1987	1,500	£3,200
January 1992	200	£450

Required

Compute the gains arising on all of the following transactions in quoted securities.

Use the following indexation factors as appropriate:

April 1985 – July 1987	0.074
July 1987 – September 1991	0.322
September 1991 – January 1992	0.007
January 1992 – March 2007	0.478

▷ ACTIVITY 80

Sunshine Ltd

Sunshine Ltd sold ordinary 10p shares in Red plc as follows:

	Number of shares	Proceeds
January 1995	1,200	£10,100
February 2007	800	£9,340

At 6 April 1985, it held 1,000 of the shares in the FA 1985 pool, with an indexed cost of £1,161 and a cost of £1,000. In December 1989, 1,000 more shares were bought for £1,870.

Required

Compute the gains arising on all of the transactions in quoted securities.

Use the following indexation factors as appropriate:

April 1985 – December 1989	0.253
December 1989 – January 1995	0.229
January 1995 – February 2007	0.370

▷ ACTIVITY 81

Purple Ltd

On 8 August 2006, Purple Ltd sold 5,000 ordinary shares in Indigo plc for £15,000. The company's previous transactions were as follows.

Balance on 1985 pool at 9 June 1990, 3,000 shares with a qualifying cost of £4,000 and an indexed cost of £5,010.

Transactions from 9 June 1990 were as follows:

12 August 1995	Took up 1 for 3 bonus issue
7 May 2000	Took up 1 for 2 rights issue at 150p per share

The indexed rise from June 1990 to May 2000 is 0.347 and from May 2000 to August 2006 is 0.158.

Required

Calculate Purple Ltd's chargeable gain on the disposal on 8 August 2006.

Chapter 24

▷ ACTIVITY 82   ▷ ▷ ▷ ▷

Taylor

Taylor disposed of his freehold factory on 18 July 1987 for £120,000, realising a gain of £30,000. On 1 December 1987, he invested £115,000 of the proceeds in the goodwill of a business similar to the one he had been carrying on for many years. On 22 December 2006, he sold the goodwill for £320,000.

Required

Compute the amount of Taylor's taxable gains which would be subject to capital gains tax as a result of the above transactions, showing the years in which they would be assessed.

The indexation factor from December 1987 to April 1998 is 0.574.

Assume the annual exemption is £8,800 in all years.

▷ ACTIVITY 83   ▷ ▷ ▷ ▷

Jonald

On 5 June 2006 Jonald, aged 49, gifted his 80% shareholding in Jonald Limited (with a market value of £5 million) to his son Reg. The resulting gain before taper relief for CGT purposes was £900,000. The shares are business assets for taper relief and gift relief purposes.

Required

Assuming all possible reliefs are claimed, compute:

(a)   the amount chargeable on Jonald in 2006/07.
(b)   Reg's base cost in respect of the shares gifted.

▷ ACTIVITY 84   ▷ ▷ ▷ ▷

DRV Ltd (1)

DRV Ltd prepares accounts to 31 March annually.

The company sold the freehold of a factory on 3 March 2007 for £275,000, having previously purchased it as a replacement freehold factory for £190,000 in October 1987. The factory which it replaced was acquired in May 1983 for £65,000 and sold in December 1987 for £130,000.

Required

Calculate the chargeable gains, assuming all available reliefs are claimed. The indexation factors are:

May 1983 – December 1987	0.220
October 1987 – March 2007	0.948

▷ ACTIVITY 85

DRV Ltd (2)

DRV Ltd prepares accounts to 31 March annually.

The company sold the freehold of a factory on 3 March 2007 for £275,000, having previously purchased it as a replacement freehold factory for £115,000 in October 1987.

The factory which is replaced was acquired in May 1983 for £65,000 and sold in December 1987 for £130,000.

Required

Calculate the chargeable gains, assuming all available reliefs are claimed. The indexation factors are:

May 1983 – December 1987	0.220
October 1987 – March 2007	0.936

▷ ACTIVITY 86

Marco

Marco, who has a dry-cleaning business, purchased a building for business use in June 1991 for £60,000. In September 2006, he sold the building for £150,000. Marco had purchased a replacement building to carry on his business in December 2005 for £130,000. Marco claimed any available reliefs.

Required

Prepare computations of the capital gains arising, providing explanations as appropriate and showing the effect of any claims made.

Use the indexation factor from June 1991 to April 1998 was 0.213.

▷ ACTIVITY 87

Columbus

Columbus sold one of his factories on 30 April 2006 for £900,000. The factory had been purchased in September 1983 for £300,000. In March 2006, Columbus purchased another factory for £700,000 and claimed rollover relief on the gain on the factory sold in April 2006.

The indexation factor from September 1983 to April 1998 is 0.889.

Required

You are required to calculate the chargeable gain on the sale of the first factory, the amount of any rollover relief available and the base cost of the second factory.

▷ ACTIVITY 88

Astute Ltd

Astute Ltd sold a factory on 15 February 2007 for £320,000. The factory was purchased on 24 October 1998 for £164,000, and was extended at a cost of £37,000 during March 2000. Astute Ltd incurred legal fees of £3,600 in connection with the purchase of the factory, and legal fees of £6,200 in connection with the disposal.

Astute Ltd is considering the following alternative ways of reinvesting the proceeds from the sale of its factory:

(1)   A freehold warehouse can be purchased for £340,000.

(2)   A freehold office building can be purchased for £275,000.

The reinvestment will take place during May 2007. All of the above buildings have been, or will be, used for business purposes.

Required

(a)   State the conditions that must be met in order that rollover relief can be claimed. You are not expected to list the categories of asset that qualify for rollover relief.

(b)   Before taking account of any available rollover relief, calculate Astute Ltd's chargeable gain in respect of the disposal of the factory.

(c)   Advise Astute Ltd of the rollover relief that will be available in respect of EACH of the two alternative reinvestments. Your answer should include details of the base cost of the replacement asset for each alternative.

Indexation factors are as follows:

October 1998 to February 2007	0.216
March 2000 to February 2007	0.188

▷ ACTIVITY 89 ▷ ▷ ▷ ▷

XY Ltd

XY Ltd made the following disposals in relation to its interests in land and property during its accounting year ended 31 March 2007.

March 2007

Sold business premises for £880,000.

This property had been acquired in March 1993 at a cost of £500,000, and in March 1994 £60,000 was expended on improvements which were immediately reflected in the value of the property and continued to influence that value until the date of disposal.

November 2006

Sold an investment property, not used for the purposes of the trade, for £360,000.

This had been acquired in April 1986 at a cost of £120,000 and in June 1987, £20,000 of expenditure had been incurred in respect of capital improvements.

Indexation factors are as follows:

April 1986 to November 2006	1.035
June 1987 to November 2006	0.951
March 1993 to March 2007	0.439
March 1994 to March 2007	0.406

Required

(a) Compute the amount that will be included in the corporation tax computation of XY Ltd for the year ended 31 March 2007 in respect of capital gains.

(b) The directors are considering investing £1,500,000 in new business premises in July 2009. Advise whether any rollover relief will be available.

▷ ACTIVITY 90   ▷ ▷ ▷ ▷

Roy and Colin

In September 2006 Roy gave his business premises to his son Colin. At that time the premises had a market value of £500,000 and had been purchased by Roy in September 1982 for £100,000. Roy and Colin made a joint claim for any capital gain to be held over.

The indexation factor for September 1982 to April 1998 is 0.987.

Required

Calculate, before annual exemption, the gain assessable on Roy for 2006/07 and the cost which will be available to Colin to set against future disposals.

MOCK EXAMINATION 1
QUESTIONS

Section 1

Data

John and Helen West set up West Consulting Associates (WCA), a partnership, on 1 January 2005.

Information on the profits of WCA

1   The tax adjusted trading profit for the year ended 31 December 2006 has been calculated as £48,750 before capital allowances.

2   This figure has been computed on the same basis as in 2005 but is before deducting motor expenses of a motor car used by an employee. The total expenses amount to £900 – and the employee's mileage is 60% for business and 40% private.

3   John and Helen share profits in the ratio 60 : 40.

Information on assets eligible for capital allowances

The only assets eligible for capital allowances are the following motor cars:

1   Bought in 2005.   £

Written down value at 1 January 2006.

-    Landrover used only by John – private use 10%   16,000
-    Ford – used only by Helen – private use 20%   14,000

2   Bought on 1 August 2006.

-    Vauxhall – used only by employee – private use 40% - cost £11,000.

Section 2

Data

You work for a company, Western Ltd, a manufacturing company, with no associated companies, owned by John and Helen West. It has 10 employees.

For the year to 31 December 2006 the company made a profit before tax of £337,520 on a turnover of £489,860.

The following expenses have been charged in arriving at the above profit figure:

		£
1	Depreciation	32,000
2	Marketing gifts	
	- Bottles of wine costing £8 each	1,200
	- Food hampers to staff £40 each	800
	- Personal organisers with Western Ltd logo costing £15 each	1,500
3	Bad debts	
	- Increase in provision for bad debts	3,600
	- Write off of loan to former employee	2,300
4	Staff bonuses totalling £3,200 have been provided in the accounts and were paid in March 2007.	
5	Interest payable on a debenture issued to individuals for a trading purpose	32,000

In addition, profit includes rental income receivable from an individual of £20,000 and patent royalty income of £15,600 (gross) from another individual for use of a patent registered by Western Ltd in the course of its trade.

For the year to 31 December 2006 the company had the following transactions in fixed assets:

1 Additions of plant

01.03.06 Ford car (includes £165 of Vehicle Licence Duty capitalised) (private use by John West: 30%)	£16,265
28.10.06 Sorting machine	£48,600
01.12.06 Milling machine (This has an expected life of about 3 years)	£18,000

2   Disposals of plant

01.03.06 Vauxhall car (originally cost £11,000)   £2,000

3   Sale of freehold shop for £155,000 on 21 June 2006 incurring solicitor's fees and estate agent's fees of £1,780 and £3,000 respectively. The shop was bought for £30,000 on 1 July 1992 and an extension was added in May 1996 at a cost of £10,000.

Indexation factors:
July 1992 – June 2006	0.418
May 1996 – June 2006	0.287

4   Sale of 10,000 shares in Import Ltd on 16 December 2006 for proceeds of £160,000 (less broker's fee of £220). The shares had been acquired as follows:

2 June 2005	10,000 shares – costing £75,000
23 June 2005	10,000 shares – costing £85,000

The indexation factor from June 2005 to December 2006 is 0.036.

A factory and warehouse was bought new on 1 January 2005 for £80,000. Its residue of expenditure for tax purposes at 1 January 2006 was £76,800.

The tax written down value of plant and machinery at 1 January 2006 was £82,000.

Section 1

Task 1a

Compute the capital allowances for WCA for the year ended 31 December 2006.

WCA
Capital allowance computation

	Private use 10% Landrover £	Private use 20% Ford £	Inexpensive car £	Business %	Allowances £
WDV b/f	16,000	14,000			
Addition					
WDA					
	_____	_____	_____		_____
	_____	_____	_____		_____

Tasks 1b and 1c

Adjust the trading profit of WCA for the year to 31 December 2006 for tax purposes and state the tax year in which the profit is assessable and the amount assessable on each partner.

WCA
Computation of taxable trade profits

	£
Profit as computed	
Less:	
	_____
Taxable trade profits	
	_____

Assessment for   /

	Total	John	Helen
Based on profit of year ended			

Task 2

Deal with the following issues which have arisen:

1   The taxable trade profits for the year ended 31 December 2005 were £32,800. The overlap profits for John and Helen need to be entered in the accounting file of WCA.

2   The following dates need to be entered in the accounting file:

-    the due date of submission of the partnership tax return relating to the accounts for the year ended 31 December 2006;

-    the due dates of the payments on account in respect of the income tax due on the profits for this year;

-    the due date of the balancing payment of income tax in respect of these profits.

3   A letter has been received from the Highgate Business Advisory Group asking for financial information on both Western Ltd and WCA. A note needs to be prepared of the action you will take before replying to this letter.

1   **Calculation of overlap profits**

	Total	John	Helen
Overlap profits			

2   **Filing and payment dates**

3   **Note of action re letter**

Section 2

Task 3a

Compute the capital allowances claimable by Western Ltd for the year ended 31 December 2006.

WESTERN LTD
Capital allowances computation

	FYA	Main pool	Expensive car	SLA	Allowances
	£	£	£	£	£
WDV b/f		82,000			
Additions					
Disposal:					
WDA (%)					
FYA (%)					
FYA (%)					
	_____	_____	_____	_____	_____
		_____			_____
IBA					
					_____

Task 3b

Compute the Schedule D Case I profit of Western Ltd for the year ended 31 December 2006.

WESTERN LTD
Computation of adjusted trading profit

Profit per accounts
Add:

Less:

_____

Capital allowances on plant
IBAs

_____ _____

Schedule D Case I

_____

Task 3c

Compute the chargeable gain or allowable loss on the disposal of the property and of the shares.

WESTERN LTD
Computation of chargeable gain/loss

	Shop	Shares
Net sale proceeds		
Cost		
Extension		
	————	————
Indexation allowance On Cost		
On Extension		
	————	————
	————	————

Task 3d

Prepare the corporation tax computation of Western Ltd for the year to 31 December 2006 showing the tax payable.

WESTERN LTD
Corporation tax computation

Schedule D Case I

————

PCTCT

————

FII

Task 4

Complete the following extract from the Form CT600 for Western Ltd for the year to 31 December 2006.

Turnover

1	Total turnover from trade or profession	**1**	£

Income

3	Trading and professional profits	**3** £	
4	Trading losses brought forward claimed against profits	**4** £	
5	Net trading and professional profits		box 3 minus box 4 **5** £
6	Bank, building society or other interest, and profits and gains from non-trading loan relationships		**6** £
11	Income from UK land and buildings		**11** £
14	Annual profits and gains not falling under any other heading		**14** £

Chargeable gains

16	Gross chargeable gains	**16** £	
17	Allowable losses including losses brought forward	**17** £	
18	Net chargeable gains		box 16 minus box 17 **18** £
21	**Profits before other deductions and reliefs**		sum of boxes 5, 6, 11 14 & 18 **21** £

Deductions and reliefs

24	Management expenses under S75 ICTA 1988	**24** £	
30	Trading losses of this or a later accounting period under S393A ICTA 1988	**30** £	
31	Put an 'X' in box 31 if amounts carried back from later Accounting periods are included in box 30	**31**	
32	Non-trade capital allowances	**32** £	
35	Charges paid	**35** £	
37	**Profits chargeable to corporation tax**	box 21 minus boxes 24, 30, 32 and 35 **37** £	

Tax calculation

38	Franked investment income	**38**	
39	Number of associated companies in this investment or	**39**	
40	Associated companies in the first financial year	**40**	
41	Associated companies in the second financial year	**41**	
42	Put an 'X' in box 42 if the company claims to be charged at the starting rate or the Small companies 'rate on any part of it's profits, or is claimimg marginal rate relief	**42**	

Enter how much profit has to be charged at what rate of tax

Finacial year (yyyy)	Amount of profit	Rate of tax	Tax
43	**44**	**45**	**46** £
53	**54**	**55**	**63** £

63	Corporation tax		total of boxes 46 and 56 **63** £
64	Marginal relief rate	**64** £	
65	Corporation tax net of marginal rate relief	**65** £	
66	Underlying rate of corporation tax	**66** £ . %	
67	Profits matched with non-corporate distrubutions	**67**	
68	Tax at non-corporate disatribution rate	**68** £ p	
69	Tax at underlying rate on remaining profits	**69** £ p	
70	**Corporation tax chargeable**		enter value of box 64 or 65 or the total of boxes 68 and 69 if greater **70** £

79	Tax payable under S419 ICTA 1988	79 £	p
80	*Put an 'X' in box 80 if you completed boxA11 in the Supplementry Pages CT600A*	80	
84	Income tax deducted from gross income included in profits	84 £	p
85	Income tax payable to the company	85 £	p
		total of boxes 70 and 79 minus 84	
86	**Tax payable - this is your self-assessment of tax payable**	86 £	

Tax reconciliation

91	Tax already paid (and not already repaid)	91 £	p
		box 986 minus 93	
92	Tax outstanding	86 £	
		box 986 minus 93	
93	Tax overpaid	93 £	p

Information about capital allowances and balancing charges

Charges and allowances included in calculation of trading profits and losses

		Capital allowances	Balancing charges
105 - 106	Machinery and plant – long-life assets	105 £	106 £
107 - 108	Machinery and plant – other (general pool)	107 £	108 £
109 - 110	Cars outside general pool	109 £	110 £
111 - 112	Industrial buidlings and structures	111 £	112 £
113 - 114	Other charges and allowances	113 £	114 £

Charges and allowances not included in calculation of trading profits and losses

		Capital allowances	Balancing charges
115 - 116		105 £	106 £
117	*Put an 'X' in box 117 if box 115 includes flat conversion allowances*	117	

Expenditure

118	Expenditure on machinery and plant on which first year allowance is claimed	118 £
119	*Put an 'X' in box 119 if claim includes enhanced capital allowances for energy-saving investments*	119
120	Qualifying expenditure on machinery and plant on long-life assets	120 £
121	Qualifying expenditure on machinery and plant on other assets	121 £

Losses, deficits and excess amounts

122	Trade loss Case 1	*calculated under S393 ICTA 1988* 122 £	124	Trade losses Case V	*calculated under S393 ICTA 1988* 124 £
125	Non-trade deficits on loan relationships and derivative contracts	*calculated under S82 FA 1996* 125 £	127	Schedule A losses	*calculated under S392A ICTA1988* 122 £
129	Overseas property business losses Case V	*calculated under S392B ICTA 1988* 122 £	130	Losses Case VI	*calculated under S396 ICTA 1988* 122 £
131	Capital losses	*calculated under S16 TCGA 1992* 131 £	136	Excess management expenses	*calculated under S396 ICTA 1988* 136 £

Task 5

A memo needs to be sent to John West dealing with the following matters in respect of corporation tax:

1   State the amount of corporation tax payable for the year ended 31 December 2006, the date that it is payable and the date that the corporation tax return needs to be submitted.

2   The draft accounts have included expenses estimated by John West. Invoices supporting these expenses have been mislaid by John. It is necessary to emphasise to John the importance of accurate accounts supported by valid invoices. Also state one possible consequence of preparing accounts based on estimated information.

3   Each year, on 31 May, Western Ltd:

-   pays debenture interest net to individuals of £25,600;

-   receives royalty income net from individuals of £15,600.

State the amount of income tax payable in the year 2007 under the quarterly income tax procedures and the due date of payment.

4   In June 2007 Western Ltd will have the option of purchasing a 20 year old factory for £180,000 excluding land. The factory cost £120,000 excluding land when new.

Assuming Western Ltd purchases the factory, advise John regarding:

-   the IBA claimable each year;
-   the claim that Western Ltd could make to defer the gain on the shop sold in June 2006.

M E M O

To:

From:

Date:

Re:

MOCK EXAMINATION 2
QUESTIONS

Section 1

Data and tasks

Fred Bare is a tailor who has recently asked us to deal with his tax affairs. Fred started to trade on 1 January 2003 and ceased to trade on 30 April 2007. We have recently prepared computations of taxable trade profits as follows:

1 January 2003 to 30 June 2003	£12,000
Year ended 30 June 2004	£20,000
Year ended 30 June 2005	£16,000
Year ended 30 June 2006	£14,000
1 July 2006 to 30 April 2007	£18,000

It appears that Fred has not sent any Tax Returns to HM Revenue and Customs and he is coming to see us to discover what his taxable profits are for each of the years of assessment affected by his period of trading.

Fred is considering joining two of his friends, who currently trade in partnership. The intention is that Fred will join as a partner on 1 October 2007 and the partnership will continue to prepare its accounts to 31 March each year. Throughout the relevant periods each partner is paid an annual salary of £20,000. Fred will be entitled to 20% of any balance of profits.

PROJECTED TAXABLE TRADE PROFITS
AFTER CAPITAL ALLOWANCES

	£
Year to 31 March 2008	150,000
Year to 31 March 2009	165,000
Year to 31 March 2010	175,000

Note: The above are before taking account of partners' salaries.

Task 1

Calculate the taxable trade profits assessed on Fred in respect of his period as a sole trader for 2002/03 to 2007/08 inclusive.

FRED BARE
Taxable trade profit assessments

Task 2

Advise Fred of the assessable partnership profits which will be allocated to him for all relevant years of assessment.

FRED BARE (AS PARTNER)
Taxable trade profit Assessments

Section 2

Data and tasks

Afton Drilling Limited, a company with no associated companies, prepared its accounts to 31 July for many years. It has now changed its accounting reference date to 30 April and for the nine months to 30 April 2007 has an accounting profit of £78,000 on trading activities with a turnover of £263,000. It has 15 employees.

The profit figure of £78,000 takes account of the following expenses.

1   Bad debts

	£
Opening provision	(19,000)
Non-trade debts written off	(3,000)
Trade debts written off	17,000
Closing provision	22,000
Per accounts	23,000

2   Professional fees

	£
Legal costs re planning application for factory extension	5,000
Accountancy fees and dealing with corporation tax matters for the year to 31 July 2006	5,000
Professional costs re factory disposal	2,500
Debt collection	1,500
Per accounts	14,000

3   Entertaining

	£
Staff Christmas party for 30 attendees	2,000
Corporate hospitality event for customers	1,500
Per accounts	3,500

4   Motor expenses

	£
Motor expenses include:	
Employees' parking fines	260
Directors' speeding fines	1,750

5   Patent royalties payable

Royalty payments of £30,000 have been charged in the accounts on an accruals basis and are payable for a trading purpose. The company made a net payment to an individual of £27,300 on 28 February 2007.

6   Depreciation

	£
Charge for period	£33,250

Plant and machinery details:

The tax written down values of plant at 1 August 2006 were as follows:

General pool	£93,500
Jaguar	£24,000
Mercedes	£17,000

The company bought a lathe on 15 March 2007 for £12,000 and acquired a BMW car and a Ford car for £28,000 and £5,500 respectively on 12 December 2006.

The Jaguar was sold on 14 December 2006 for £18,000 (original cost £33,000) and various items of plant were sold during the period for £35,000 (no one item sold above cost).

Industrial buildings details:

(1)   The company sold a factory on 1 January 2007 for £400,000. This had been acquired new from a builder on 1 January 1992 for £80,000 and brought into industrial use immediately.

It was used for a qualifying industrial purpose throughout the period of ownership. It had a written down value of £32,000 on 1 August 2006.

The indexation factor from January 1992 to January 2007 is 0.469.

(2)   The company acquired a second-hand factory for £300,000 on 1 January 2007 and put it into industrial use by 30 April 2007. The vendor had acquired it new for £500,000 on 1 January 1992 and had used it continuously for a qualifying industrial purpose.

Other income:

(1)   The company received a dividend of £54,000 on 1 December 2006.

(2)   Patent royalties of £20,000 (gross) were receivable for the period and a net royalty of £20,280 was actually received on 20 September 2006. The rights are held as part of the company's trading activities but have not been included in the profit figure of £78,000.

Other gains:

The company acquired 12,000 £1 ordinary shares in Bridge plc during June 1992 at a cost of £46,000.

The entire holding was sold during January 2007 for proceeds of £60,000. (Indexation factor: 0.43)

Task 3a

Compute the capital allowances available to Afton Drilling Limited for the 9 month period to 30 April 2007.

AFTON DRILLING LIMITED
Capital allowances computation
9 months to 30 April 2007

General pool	£	£	Allowances £
TWDV as at 1 August 2006		93,500	
Additions without FYA			
Disposals			
		————	
WDA			
Additions with FYA			
FYA (%)			
	————		
		————	
TWDV as at 30 April 2007		————	

Expensive cars	Jaguar £	BMW £	Mercedes £
TWDV as at 1 August 2006	24,000		17,000
Disposal			
	————		
Balancing allowance	————		
Addition			
WDA			
		————	————
TWDV as at 30 April 2007		————	————

Calculation of industrial buildings allowance

Disposal

Addition

	————

Total net allowances

	————

Task 3b

Prepare a calculation of Schedule D Case I profits for the 9 month period to 30 April 2007.

AFTON DRILLING LIMITED
Schedule D Case I computation
9 months to 30 April 2007

	£	£
Net profit per accounts before taxation		

Add :

           ————

Less:

           ————

           ————

Schedule D Case I

           ————

Task 3c

(i)   Prepare a calculation of any chargeable gains arising on the disposal of the factory during the 9 month period to 30 April 2007 assuming the directors take advantage of any available capital gains reliefs.

AFTON DRILLING LIMITED
Chargeable gain computation
9 months to 30 April 2007

Disposal of factory

Proceeds
Cost of disposal

           ————

Cost

           ————

Indexation allowance

           ————

Chargeable gain

           ————

(ii) Prepare a calculation of any chargeable gains arising on the disposal of shares by the company.

Disposal of shares

12,000 ordinary shares in Bridge plc

Proceeds (January 2007)
Less: Cost

               _____

Less: Indexation

               _____

               _____

Task 3d

Prepare, for each relevant quarter, a summary of income tax suffered or payable and state the due date(s) of any payment or repayment.

AFTON DRILLING LIMITED
Accounting for income tax
9 months to 30 April 2007

Task 3e

Prepare the corporation tax computation for the period to 30 April 2007 and specify the amount payable and the date before which it ought to be paid to avoid interest charges.

AFTON DRILLING LIMITED
Corporation tax computation
9 months to 30 April 2007

Corporation tax liability

Schedule D Case I

_____

Less: Charges on income

_____

Profits chargeable to corporation tax

_____

'Profits' for small company rate

_____

Task 3f

The directors have requested brief details of the rules concerning the payment of tax by instalments. Prepare a memo to your manager, A Smith, outlining the rules and the companies to which they apply.

	M E M O
To: From: Subject:	

Task 4

Complete the following extract from the CT600 for the company for the period to 30 April 2007.

Turnover

1	Total turnover from trade or profession	**1** £

Income

3	Trading and professional profits	**3** £
4	Trading losses brought forward claimed against profits	**4** £
5	Net trading and professional profits	*box 3 minus box 4* **5** £
6	Bank, building society or other interest, and profits and gains from non-trading loan relationships	**6** £
11	Income from UK land and buildings	**11** £
14	Annual profits and gains not falling under any other heading	**14** £

Chargeable gains

16	Gross chargeable gains	**16** £
17	Allowable losses including losses brought forward	**17** £
18	Net chargeable gains	*box 16 minus box 17* **18** £
21	**Profits before other deductions and reliefs**	*sum of boxes 5, 6, 11 14 & 18* **21** £

Deductions and reliefs

24	Management expenses under S75 ICTA 1988	**24** £
30	Trading losses of this or a later accounting period under S393A ICTA 1988	**30** £
31	Put an 'X' in box 31 if amounts carried back from later Accounting periods are included in box 30	**31**
32	Non-trade capital allowances	**32** £
35	Charges paid	**35** £
37	**Profits chargeable to corporation tax**	*box 21 minus boxes 24, 30, 32 and 35* **37** £

Tax calculation

38	Franked investment income	**38**
39	Number of associated companies in this investment or	**39**
40	Associated companies in the first financial year	**40**
41	Associated companies in the second financial year	**41**
42	*Put an 'X' in box 42 if the company claims to be charged at the starting rate or the Small companies 'rate on any part of it's profits, or is claimimg marginal rate relief*	**42**

Enter how much profit has to be charged at what rate of tax

Finical year (*yyyy*)	Amount of profit	Rate of tax	Tax
43	**44**	**45**	**46** £
53	**54**	**55**	**63** £

63	Corporation tax	*total of boxes 46 and 56* **63** £
64	Marginal relief rate	**64** £
65	Corporation tax net of marginal rate relief	**65** £
66	Underlying rate of corporation tax	**66** £ . %
67	Profits matched with non-corporate distrubutions	**67**
68	Tax at non-corporate disatribution rate	**68** £ p
69	Tax at underlying rate on remaining profits	**69** £ p
70	**Corporation tax chargeable**	*enter value of box 64 or 65 or the total of boxes 68 and 69 if greater* **70** £

79	Tax payable under S419 ICTA 1988	**79** £	p
80	*Put an 'X' in box 80 if you completed boxA11 in the Supplementry Pages CT600A*	**80**	
84	Income tax deducted from gross income included in profits	**84** £	p
85	Income tax payable to the company	**85** £	p
		total of boxes 70 and 79 minus 84	
86	**Tax payable - this is your self-assessment of tax payable**	**86** £	

Tax reconciliation

91	Tax already paid (and not already repaid)	**91** £	p
		box 986 minus 93	
92	Tax outstanding	**86** £	
		box 986 minus 93	
93	Tax overpaid	**93** £	p

Information about capital allowances and balancing charges

Charges and allowances included in calculation of trading profits and losses

		Capital allowances	Balancing charges
105 - 106	Machinery and plant – long-life assets	**105** £	**106** £
107 - 108	Machinery and plant – other (general pool)	**107** £	**108** £
109 - 110	Cars outside general pool	**109** £	**110** £
111 - 112	Industrial buidlings and structures	**111** £	**112** £
113 - 114	Other charges and allowances	**113** £	**114** £

Charges and allowances not included in calculation of trading profits and losses

		Capital allowances	Balancing charges
115 - 116		**105** £	**106** £
117	*Put an 'X' in box 117 if box 115 includes flat conversion allowances*	**117**	

Expenditure

118	Expenditure on machinery and plant on which first year allowance is claimed	**118** £
119	*Put an 'X' in box 119 if claim includes enhanced capital allowances for energy-saving investments*	**119**
120	Qualifying expenditure on machinery and plant on long-life assets	**120** £
121	Qualifying expenditure on machinery and plant on other assets	**121** £

Losses, deficits and excess amounts

122	Trade loss Case 1	*calculated under S393 ICTA 1988* **122** £	124	Trade losses Case V	*calculated under S393 ICTA 1988* **124** £
125	Non-trade deficits on loan relationships and derivative contracts	*calculated under S82 FA 1996* **125** £	127	Schedule A losses	*calculated under S392A ICTA1988* **122** £
129	Overseas property business losses Case V	*calculated under S392B ICTA 1988* **122** £	130	Losses Case VI	*calculated under S396 ICTA 1988* **122** £
131	Capital losses	*calculated under S16 TCGA 1992* **131** £	136	Excess management expenses	*calculated under S396 ICTA 1988* **136** £

State the date before which the CT600 should be submitted if a late filing penalty is to be avoided:

KEY TECHNIQUES
ANSWERS

Chapter 3

△ ACTIVITY 1 △ △ △ △

Tricks Ltd

Adjusted trading profits for year ended 31 March 2007

	£
Net profit	249,250
Add Disallowable expenses	5,900
	255,150
Less Debenture interest receivable	(4,100)
UK dividends (net)	(12,000)
Profit on sale of investment	(2,750)
Adjusted trading profits	236,300

The funds raised by the issue of the debenture were used for the purposes of the trade and the interest is therefore an allowable deduction in computing the adjusted trading profits.

△ ACTIVITY 2 △ △ △ △

Prairie Limited

Adjusted trading profits for year ended 31 March 2007

	£
Profit per accounts	186,499
Add Depreciation	6,344
Gift Aid paid	1,000
	193,843
Less Interest receivable	(2,900)
Dividends received	(11,876)
Profit on sale of investments	(2,543)
Adjusted trading profits	176,524

△ ACTIVITY 3 △ △ △ △

Cricket Limited

Adjusted trading profits for the year ended 31 March 2007

	£
Net profit per accounts	738,101
Add Legal charges re new office premises	1,000
Loan to former employee written off	200
New furniture	7,600
Depreciation	30,000
Adjusted trading profit	776,901

△ ACTIVITY 4   △ △ △ △

Uranus Ltd

1   Running expenses, except for depreciation, are an allowable deduction. The depreciation must be disallowed as this will be replaced by capital allowances. The private use of the car by an employee of a company is irrelevant for profit adjustment purposes. Therefore, add back £6,000.

2   Disallow all entertaining except staff entertaining. Therefore, add back £21,000.

3   Part of this lease cost will be disallowed as the car is expensive (cost over £12,000). The disallowable portion added back is as follows:

$$\frac{\frac{1}{2}\,(£20{,}000 - £12{,}000)}{£20{,}000} \times £6{,}000 = £1{,}200$$

△ ACTIVITY 5   △ △ △ △

Saturn Ltd

1   Gift Aid donations are disallowed and treated as a charge on income. Therefore, add back £616.

2   No adjustment is required. The write-off of a trade debt is allowable. There will be a credit in the following year's accounts, when the £5,000 is recovered, which will be taxable as part of the trading profit.

3   As the warehouse can be put to immediate use in the trade, prior to the repairs being carried out, no adjustment is needed in respect of the cost of the repairs. They will be allowable.

△ ACTIVITY 6   △ △ △ △

OP Ltd

Adjusted trading profit for the year ended 30 June 2006

	£
Profit per accounts	30,410
Disallowable expenses:	
Entertaining suppliers	750
Entertaining customers	250
Non-trade loan written off	3,700
Depreciation	5,500
Adjusted trading profits	40,610

Chapter 4

△ ACTIVITY 7   △ △ △ △

Deni Ltd

Capital allowances	£	Pool £	Expensive car £	Allowances £
Year ended 30.9.06				
WDV b/f		8,822		
Additions (no FYA)			19,600	
Disposal		(1,750)		
		7,072		
WDA @ 25%/restricted		(1,768)	(3,000)	4,768
		5,304	16,600	
Additions (with FYA) (Note)				
Machinery (2,050 + 1,500)	3,550			
FYA (40%)	(1,420)			1,420
		2,130		
WDV c/f		7,434	16,600	
Total allowances				6,188

Note: There is no restriction for private use of the car by the managing director. FYA of 40% is available on both purchases as Deni Ltd is a medium sized business.

△ ACTIVITY 8   △ △ △ △

Zeus Ltd

Capital allowances	£	Pool £	Expensive car (1) £	Expensive car (2) £	Allowances £
Year ended 30.9.06					
WDV b/f		13,212	18,500		
Addition (no FYA)				18,000	
Disposals		(2,700)	(15,000)		
		10,512	3,500	18,000	
Balancing allowance			(3,500)		3,500
WDA @ 25%/restricted		(2,628)		(3,000)	5,628
Addition (with FYA)					
Machinery	3,000				
Less: FYA (40%) (Note)	(1,200)				1,200
		1,800			
WDV c/f		9,684		15,000	
Total allowances					10,628

Note: FYA is 40% as Zeus Ltd is a small company and the machinery is purchased between 1 April 2005 and 31 March 2006.

△ ACTIVITY 9   △ △ △ △

TEN Ltd

Capital allowances	General Pool £	Expensive car £	Allowances £
Year ending 31 December 2005			
WDV b/f	16,000		
Additions (no FYA)			
15 March 2005		13,200	
26 July 2005 (2 x 9,300)	18,600		
Disposals			
30 April 2005 (restrict to cost)	(1,600)		
	33,000	13,200	
WDA (restricted)		(3,000)	3,000
WDA (25%)	(8,250)		8,250
WDV c/f	24,750	10,200	
Total allowances			11,250
Year ending 31 December 2006			
Disposals	(7,600)	(9,000)	
	17,150	1,200	
Balancing allowance		(1,200)	1,200
WDA (25%)	(4,288)		4,288
WDV c/f	12,862	Nil	
Total allowances			5,488

△ ACTIVITY 10   △ △ △ △

Booker Ltd

Capital allowances	Pool £	Short life asset £	Allowances £
Year ended 31 December 2006			
WDV b/f	18,150		
Additions (no FYA)	4,400		
Disposal	(4,900)		
	17,650		
WDA @ 50%	(4,412)		4,412
	13,238		
Additions – qualifying for FYA (Note 1)		6,000	
FYA @ 40% (Note 2)		(3,000)	3,000
WDV c/f	13,238	3,000	
Total allowances			7,412

Notes:

(1) A short life asset election should be made to ensure that a balancing allowance is obtained when the plant is scrapped.

(2) FYA of 50% is available as Booker Ltd is a small company and the plant was purchased between 1 April 2006 and 31 March 2007.

Chapter 5

△ ACTIVITY 11 △△△△

Palmer Ltd

Industrial building allowances

Eligible cost	£
Canteen	2,500
Factory	31,500
	34,000

The cost of the offices is excluded as it cost £16,000 which exceeds 25% of the total cost of the building (£50,000 x 25% = £12,500).

Year ended 31 December 2006
    IBA – WDA @ 4% of £34,000   £1,360

△ ACTIVITY 12 △△△△

Brazen Ltd (1)

Balancing adjustment on the sale of workshop:

	£
Allowable cost	150,000
Proceeds are £210,000, but limited to cost	(150,000)
Net cost	Nil

Since the use of the building has not 'cost' the company anything, any allowances given will be clawed back by HMRC in the form of a balancing charge.

A £24,000 balancing charge therefore arises to claw back all the IBAs given.

Allowances for the purchaser

The remaining qualifying expenditure is £150,000.

The building has been used from 1 June 2002 to 1 December 2006 = $4\frac{1}{2}$ years

The tax life remaining is therefore $20\frac{1}{2}$ years (25 years - $4\frac{1}{2}$ years)

The annual writing down allowance for the purchaser is: $\dfrac{£150,000}{20.5} = £7,317$.

△ ACTIVITY 13 △△△△

Brazen Ltd (2)

Balancing adjustment on the sale of the workshop:

	£
Allowable cost	150,000
Proceeds	(135,000)
Net cost	15,000

Compare net cost with IBAs given:

	£
Net cost	15,000
IBAs given	(24,000)
Excess IBAs given = balancing charge	(9,000)

Allowances for the purchaser

The remaining qualifying expenditure is £135,000.

The remaining tax life of the building is $20\frac{1}{2}$ years.

The annual writing down allowance for the purchaser is: $\dfrac{£135,000}{20.5} = £6,585$.

△ ACTIVITY 14 △△△△

Brazen Ltd (3)

Balancing adjustment on the sale of the workshop:

	£
Allowable cost	150,000
Proceeds	(105,000)
Net cost	45,000

Compare net cost with IBAs given:

	£
Net cost	45,000
IBAs given	(24,000)
Shortfall of IBAs given = balancing allowance	21,000

Allowances for the purchaser

The remaining qualifying expenditure is £105,000.

The remaining tax life of the building is $20\frac{1}{2}$ years.

The annual writing down allowance for the purchaser is: $\dfrac{£105,000}{20.5} = £5,122$.

Chapter 6

△ ACTIVITY 15 △ △ △ △

Mound Ltd

Profits chargeable to corporation tax - ended 31 March 2007

	£
Schedule D Case I (W)	171,724
Schedule D Case III	2,900
Chargeable gain	1,376
	176,000
Less Charge on income	(1,000)
Profits chargeable to comparation tax (PCTCT)	175,000

Working: Schedule D Case I profit

	£
Adjusted trading accounts	176,524
Less Capital allowances	(4,800)
Schedule D Case I	171,724

△ ACTIVITY 16 △ △ △ △

Pitch Ltd (1)

Profits chargeable to corporation tax – year ended 31 March 2007

	£
Schedule D Case I (W)	742,113
Schedule A	3,500
Schedule D Case III	2,400
	748,013
Less Gift Aid paid	(1,000)
Profits chargeable to corporation tax (PCTCT)	747,013

Working: Schedule D Case I profit

	£
Adjusted trading profit	766,801
Less Capital allowances	(24,688)
Schedule D Case I profit	742,113

△ **ACTIVITY 17**

Pitch Ltd (2)

Turnover

1	Total turnover from trade or profession	**1** £	

Income

3	Trading and professional profits	**3** £ 742,113	
4	Trading losses brought forward claimed against profits	**4** £	
5	Net trading and professional profits		box 3 minus box 4 **5** £ 742,113
6	Bank, building society or other interest, and profits and gains from non-trading loan relationships		**6** £ 2,400
11	Income from UK land and buildings		**11** £ 3,500
14	Annual profits and gains not falling under any other heading		**14** £

Chargeable gains

16	Gross chargeable gains	**16** £	
17	Allowable losses including losses brought forward	**17** £	
18	Net chargeable gains		box 16 minus box 17 **18** £
21	**Profits before other deductions and reliefs**		sum of boxes 5, 6, 11 14 & 18 **21** £ 748,013

Deductions and reliefs

24	Management expenses under S75 ICTA 1988	**24** £	
30	Trading losses of this or a later accounting period under S393A ICTA 1988	**30** £	
31	Put an 'X' in box 31 if amounts carried back from later Accounting periods are included in box 30	**31**	
32	Non-trade capital allowances	**32** £	
35	Charges paid	**35** £ 1,000	
37	**Profits chargeable to corporation tax**		box 21 minus boxes 24, 30, 32 and 35 **37** £ 747,013

Chapter 7

△ ACTIVITY 18   △ △ △ △

Osmond Ltd

Corporation tax computation - Year ended 31 March 2007

	£
Schedule D Case I	510,000
Schedule D Case III	8,000
Chargeable gains	7,500
PCTCT	525,500
Corporation tax liability (W)	132,364

Working: Corporation tax liability

	£
PCTCT (I)	525,500
FII $(£18,000 \times \frac{100}{90})$	20,000
Profits (P)	545,500

The FY2006 applies to the year ended 31 March 2007.
'P' is above the lower limit of £300,000; therefore marginal relief applies.

	£
£525,500 x 30%	157,650
Less Marginal relief $\frac{11}{400} \times (£1,500,000 - £545,500) \times \frac{525,500}{545,500}$	(25,286)
Corporation tax liability	132,364

△ ACTIVITY 19   △ △ △ △

Unpretentious Undercurrents Ltd

Corporation tax computation - year ending 31 March 2007

	£
Schedule D Case I	636,250
Schedule D Case III (£1,700 + £2,700)	4,400
PCTCT	640,650
Corporation tax payable (W)	172,886

Working: Corporation tax payable

	£
PCTCT (I)	640,650
FII (£67,500 x 100/90)	75,000
Profit (P)	715,650

'P' is more than £300,000 but less than £1,500,000; marginal relief therefore applies.

	£
£640,650 x 30%	192,195
Less Marginal relief	
$\dfrac{11}{400}$ x (£1,500,000 - £715,650) x $\dfrac{£650,650}{£715,650}$	(19,309)
Corporation tax payable	172,886

△ ACTIVITY 20   △ △ △ △

Pitch Ltd (3)

(a)   **Corporation tax liability - year ended 31 March 2007**

	£
PCTCT (I)	747,013
FII (£4,800 x $\dfrac{100}{90}$)	5,333
Profits (P)	752,346

	£
£747,013 x 30%	224,104
Less Marginal relief	
$\dfrac{11}{400}$ (£1,500,000 - £752,346) x $\dfrac{£747,013}{£752,346}$	(20,415)
Corporation tax liability	203,689

(b) Extracts from CT600 form

Tax calculation

38	Franked investment income	**38** £ 5,333		
39	Number of associated companies in this investment or	**39** 0		
40	Associated companies in the first financial year	**40**		
41	Associated companies in the second financial year	**41**		
42	*Put an 'X' in box 42 if the company claims to be charged at the starting rate or the Small companies 'rate on any part of it's profits, or is claimimg marginal rate relief*	**42** X		

Enter how much profit has to be charged at what rate of tax

Finacial year (*yyyy*)	Amount of profit	Rate of tax	Tax	
43 2 0 0 6	**44** 747,013	**42** 30	**45** £ 224,104	00 p
53	**54**	**55**	**45** £	

			total of boxes 46 and 56	
63	Corporation tax		**63** £ 224,104	00 p
64	Marginal relief rate	**64** £ 20,415 00 p		
65	Corporation tax net of marginal rate relief	**65** £ 203,689 00 p		
66	Underlying rate of corporation tax	**66** £ . %		
67	Profits matched with non-corporate distrubutions	**67**		
68	Tax at non-corporate disatribution rate	**68** £ p		
69	Tax at underlying rate on remaining profits	**69** £ p	enter value of box 64 or 65 or the total of boxes 68 and 69 if greater	
70	**Corporation tax chargeable**		**70** £ 203,689	00 p

79	Tax payable under S419 ICTA 1988		**79** £	p
80	*Put an 'X' in box 80 if you completed boxA11 in the Supplementry Pages CT600A*	**80**		
84	Income tax deducted from gross income included in profits	**84** £		p
85	Income tax payable to the company	**85** £		p
			total of boxes 70 and 79 minus 84	
86	**Tax payable - this is your self-assessment of tax payable**		**86** £ 203,689	00 p

Tax reconciliation

91	Tax already paid (and not already repaid)		**91** £	p
			box 986 minus 93	
92	Tax outstanding		**86** £ 203,689	00 p
			box 986 minus 93	
93	Tax overpaid		**93** £	p

Chapter 8

△ **ACTIVITY 21**   △ △ △ △

Wolf Ltd

Corporation tax computations	Year ended 30 September 2006 £	3 months to 31 December 2006 £
Schedule D Case I (W1)	223,000	52,000
Schedule A (W2)	16,000	4,000
Chargeable gains		25,000
PCTCT	239,000	81,000
Corporation tax liability (W3)	45,410	16,215

Workings

(W1) Schedule D Case I

	Year ended 30 September 2006 £	3 months to 31 December 2006 £
Trading profits time apportioned (12.3)	240,000	60,000
Less Capital allowances	(17,000)	(8,000)
Schedule D Case I	223,000	52,000

(W2) Schedule A

	Year ended 30 September 2006 £	3 months to 31 December 2006 £
Rent receivable time apportioned (12 : 3)	16,000	4,000

(W3) Corporation tax liabilities

	Year ended 30 September 2006 £	3 months to 31 December 2006 £
PCTCT and 'P' (as there are no dividends)	£239,000	£81,000

Financial years	FY05	FY06	FY06
	6m	6m	3m

		Year ended 30 September 2006	3 months to 31 December 2006
Lower limit	Annual	£300,000	
	Three months		
	(£300,000 x $^3/_{12}$)		75,000
Upper limit	Annual		
	Three months	£1,500,000	
	(£1,500,000 x $^3/_{12}$)		£375,000

Corporation tax liabilities

	Year ended 30 September 2006	3 months to 31 December 2006
PCTCT	£239,000	£81,000
	£	£
£239,000 x 19%	45,410	
£81,000 x 30%		24,300
Less $\frac{11}{400}$ x (£375,000 - 81,000)		(8,085)
		16,215

△ ACTIVITY 22   △△△△

Unbelievable Upshots Ltd

(a)   Capital allowances computation - 9 m/e 28 February 2007

	Pool	Expensive car (1)	Expensive car (2)	Short-life asset	Total
	£	£	£	£	£
WDV b/f	102,000	7,000		17,500	
Additions (no FYA)			14,000		
Disposals		(6,000)		(5,000)	
		1,000		12,500	
Balancing allowances		(1,000)		(12,500)	13,500
WDA (25% x $^9/_{12}$)	(19,125)				19,125
(£3,000 (max) x $^9/_{12}$)				(2,250)	2,250
WDV c/f	82,875	Nil	11,750	Nil	
Total allowances					34,875

(b)   Profits chargeable to corporation tax – 9 m/e to 28 February 2007

	£
Adjusted trading profit	270,000
Capital allowances:	
Plant and machinery (Part (a))	(34,875)
Schedule D Case I profit	235,125
Schedule D Case III	13,000
Net Chargeable gain (£50,000 - £20,000 b/f)	30,000
PCTCT	278,125

(c)   Corporation tax - payable - 9 m/e 28 February 2007

	£
PCTCT (I)	278,125
FII (45,000 x $^{100}/_{90}$)	50,000
Profits (P)	328,125

Small company limits (see note)	£
lower limit (£300,000 x $^9/_{12}$ x $^1/_2$)	112,500
upper limit (£1,500,000 x $^9/_{12}$ x $^1/_2$)	562,500

Note: The limits are adjusted due to the 9 month accounting period, and the company has one associated company.

'P' falls in between the limits, therefore marginal relief applies.

	£
FY2006 (£278,125 30%)	83,438
Less: Marginal relief
$\frac{11}{400}$ x (562,500 - 328,125) x $\frac{£747,013}{£752,346}$	(5,463)
Corporation tax payable	77,975

△ ACTIVITY 23 △△△△

Upbeat Ukuleles Ltd

(a) **Capital allowances**

	12m to 31.3.07		3m to 30.6.07
	£		£
Tax WDV brought forward	100,000		75,000
WDA at 25%	(25,000)	WDA x 25% x $^3/_{12}$	(4,688)
Tax WDV carry forward	75,000		70,312

(b) **Schedule D Case I**

		12m to 31.3.07	3m to 30.6.07
	£	£	£
Trading profit (12 : 3)	1,250,000	1,000,000	250,000
Capital allowances		(25,000)	(4,688)
Schedule D Case I		975,000	245,312

(c) **Corporation tax computations**

	12m to 31 March 2007	3 months to 30 June 2007
	£	£
Schedule D Case I	975,000	245,312
Schedule D Case III (12 : 3)	30,000	7,500
Chargeable gains	10,000	-
	1,015,000	252,812
Less Charges on income	(5,000)
PCTCT	1,010,000	252,812
Corporation tax liability (W)	39,900	73,061

Working: Corporation tax liability

			12m to 31 March 2007 £	3m to 30 June 2007 £
PCTCT (I)			1,010,000	252,812
FII				
25 March 2007 (£20,250 x $\frac{100}{90}$)			22,500	
29 June 2007 (£13,500 x $\frac{100}{90}$)				15,000
Profits (P)			1,032,500	267,812
Upper limit	Annual		1,500,000	
	Three months			375,000
Lower limit	Annual		300,000	
	Three months			75,000

	Decision		Marginal relief applies £	Marginal relief applies £
FY2006 (£1,010,000 x 30%)			303,000	
less $\frac{11}{400}$ x (1,500,000 – 1,032,500) x $\frac{£1,010,000}{£1,032,500}$			(12,576)	
FY2007 (assume as for FY06) (£252,812 x 30%)				75,844
Less $\frac{11}{400}$ x (£375,000 - £267,812) x $\frac{£252,812}{£267,812}$				(2,783)
Corporation tax liability			290,424	73,061

△ ACTIVITY 24 △ △ △ △

Unpredictably Uptown Limited

Corporation tax payable - period 30 September 2007

	12 months to 31.03.07 £	6 months to 30.09.07 £
Schedule D Case I (W1)	660,000	330,000
Schedule D Case III	9,000	3,500
	669,000	333,500
Less Charge on income (Gift Aid)	(20,000)	-
Profits chargeable to corporation tax	649,000	333,500
Add FII 17,500 x $\frac{100}{90}$	19,444	-
Profits	668,444	333,500
Corporation tax Liability (W2)	172,497	88,596

Workings

(1) Schedule D Case I

			£
Apportioned	12 months to 31.03.07	$^{12}/_{18}$ x £990,000	660,000
	6 months to 30.09.07	$^{6}/_{18}$ x £990,000	330,000
			990,000

(2) Corporation tax liability

			Year to 31.03.07 £	6 months to 30.09.07 £
FY 2006				
Lower limit	Annual/6 months		300,000	150,000
Upper limit	Annual/6 months		1,500,000	750,000
	Decision		30% less SCMR £	30% less SCMR £
(£649,000/£333,500 x 30%)			194,700	100,050
Less $\frac{11}{400}$ x (1,500,000 - 668,444) x $\frac{649,000}{668,444}$			(22,203)	
Less $\frac{11}{400}$ x (750,000 – 333,500)				(11,454)
Corporation tax liability			172,497	88,596

Chapter 9

△ ACTIVITY 25 △△△△

Eldorado (Birmingham) Limited

Corporation tax computations

Year to 31 August	2005 £	2006 £	2007 £
Schedule D Case I	18,000	Nil	Nil
Schedule A	22,000	22,000	22,000
Chargeable gain	3,000	-	-
	43,000	22,000	22,000
Less S393A current year		(22,000)	(6,000)
S393A carry back	(43,000)		
PCTCT	Nil	Nil	16,000

Loss memorandum	£		£
Loss – ye 31.8.06	81,000	Loss – ye 31.8.07	6,000
Offset: Current year	(22,000)	Offset: Current year	(6,000)
Carry back	(43,000)		
Losses carried forward	16,000		Nil

The losses carried forward can only be offset against future trading profits of the same trade.

△ ACTIVITY 26

Potter Limited

Corporation tax computations

Years ended 30 September		2006	2007
		£	£
Schedule D Case I		Nil	94,000
Less	Losses brought forward (£35,000 - £32,700)	-	(2,300)
		Nil	91,700
Schedule D Case III		11,400	8,400
Schedule A		21,300	21,400
		32,700	121,500
Less	Losses set against profits (S393A)	(32,700)	
		Nil	121,500
Less	Charges on income	(Wasted)	(500)
PCTCT		Nil	121,000

△ ACTIVITY 27

Brian Phillips Ltd

Corporation tax computations

Years ended	31.10.2004	31.10.2005	31.10.2006
	£	£	£
Schedule D Case I	25,000	Nil	12,000
S393(1) carry forward relief			(8,000)
			4,000
Schedule D Case III	6,000	2,000	1,000
Chargeable gains	4,000	5,000	7,000
	35,000	7,000	12,000
S393A(1)(a) current year relief		(7,000)	
S393A(1)(b) carry back relief	(35,000)		
	Nil	Nil	12,000
Gift Aid	Wasted	Wasted	(5,000)
PCTCT	Nil	Nil	7,000

The Gift Aid of £5,000 paid in each of the years ended 31 October 2004 and 2005 is wasted.

Loss memorandum

	£
Year ended 31 October 2005 - Loss	50,000
Current year relief	(7,000)
Carry back relief – year ended 31 October 2004	(35,000)
Carry forward – year ended 31 October 2006	8,000

KAPLAN PUBLISHING

△ ACTIVITY 28   △ △ △ △

Unseen Ultrasonics Ltd

Corporation tax computation - year ended 31 December 2006

	£
Schedule D Case I	2,174,100
Less Schedule D Case I loss brought forward	(567,750)
	1,606,350
Schedule D Case III (£1,500 + £80,000)	81,500
Chargeable gains (W1)	Nil
	1,687,850
Less Charge on income (Gift Aid)	(5,000)
PCTCT	1,682,850
Corporation tax liability (W2)	504,855
Unrelieved amounts – capital loss carried forward	(5,000)

The unrelieved capital loss will be offset against the first available capital gains arising in the future.

Workings

1   Net chargeable gains

	£
Current gain	25,000
Capital loss brought forward	(30,000)
Capital loss carried forward only	(5,000)
Therefore net chargeable gain in the period	Nil

2   Corporation tax liability

	£
PCTCT	1,682,850

As this is clearly more than £1,500,000 the full rate applies

| Corporation tax liability (£1,682,850 x 30%) | 504,855 |

△ ACTIVITY 29   △ △ △ △

Uncut Undergrowth Ltd

Corporation tax computations	Year ended 30.6.05	6 months ended 31.12.05	Year ended 31.12.06
	£	£	£
Schedule D Case I	35,000	25,000	-
Schedule D Case III	-	15,000	22,000
Schedule A	25,000	-	-
Chargeable gains (W1)	-	-	-
	60,000	40,000	22,000
Less: Current year relief			(22,000)
Carry back relief (W2)	(30,000)	(40,000)	
	30,000	Nil	Nil
Less: Non-trade charges	(1,000)	Wasted	Wasted
PCTCT	29,000	Nil	Nil

Balances carried forward

· There is a Schedule D Case I loss at 31 December 2006 to carry forward of £258,000 (W2) under S393(1) CTA 1988.

· Capital losses of £10,000 available for carry forward (W1).

Workings

(W1)   Net chargeable gains

	£
Year ended 31 December 2006	
Gain	30,000
Losses b/f (£40,000)	(30,000)
Net chargeable gain	Nil
Losses c/f (£40,000 - £30,000)	10,000

(W2)   Trading losses

	£
Loss for 12m to 31 December 2006	350,000
Current year relief	(22,000)
Carry back relief – 6 months to 31 December 2005	(40,000)
– 6 months to 30 June 2005	
(£60,000 x $^6/_{12}$)	(30,000)
Carry forward at 31 December 2006	258,000

Chapter 10

△ ACTIVITY 30　　　　　　　　　△ △ △ △

Chappell Limited

Quarterly accounting for income tax

Return period ended	Income tax suffered £	Income tax deducted £	Cumulative income tax £	Income tax payable/ (repayable) £	Date of payment/ receipt
30.06.06	(440)	286	(154)	–	14.07.06
30.09.06	(660)	1,034	374	220	14.10.06
			220		
31.12.06	–	1,100	1,100	1,100	14.01.07
			1,320		
31.03.07	–	440	440	440	14.04.07
	(1,100)	2,860	1,760		
Income tax paid during year				1,760	

△ ACTIVITY 31　　　　　　　　　△ △ △ △

P Ltd

Quarterly accounting for income tax - year ended 31 March 2007

Return period ended	Income tax suffered £	Income tax deducted £	Cumulative income tax £	Income tax payable/ (repayable) £	Date of payment/ receipt
30.6.2006	(8,400) (a)	–	(8,400)	–	N/A
30.9.2006	(4,800) (b)	9,000 (c)	4,200	–	N/A
			(4,200)		
31.12.2006	–	11,400 (d)	11,400	7,200	14.1.07
			7,200		
31.3.2007	(6,200) (e)	–	(6,200)	(6200)	14.4.07
	(19,400)	20,400	1,000		
Income tax paid during year				1,000	

Notes: IT suffered and deducted is calculated at 20/80 for interest or 22/78 as the for royalties net receipts/(payments) have been quoted in the question.

(a)　(29,782 x $^{22}/_{78}$) on 10/5/06　　=　　£8,400

(b)　(17,018 x $^{22}/_{78}$) on 30/8/06　　=　　£4,800

(c)　(36,000 x $^{20}/_{80}$) on 12/7/06　　=　　(£9,000)

(d)　(45,600 x $^{20}/_{80}$) on 24/11/06　=　　(£11,400)

(e)　(21,982 x $^{22}/_{78}$) on 15/1/07　　=　　£6,200

Gift Aid payments are made gross by companies.

△ ACTIVITY 32   △ △ △ △

Pack Ltd

(a)

Quarter ended	Income tax suffered £	Income tax deducted £	Cumulative income tax	Income tax paid/(repaid) £
30.06.06 $4,000 \times {}^{20}/_{80}$	-	1,000	1,000	1,000
30.09.06 $15,600 \times {}^{22}/_{78}$	(4,400)		(4,400) (3,400)	(1,000)
31.12.06 $4,000 \times {}^{20}/_{80}$		1,000	1,000 (2,400)	Nil
31.03.07 No return			-	
	(4,400)	2,000	(2,400)	
Income tax paid during year				Nil

Net income tax suffered (4,400 – 2,000) = £2,400.

(b) Corporation tax payable - year ended 31 March 2007

	£
PCTCT (I)	97,000
FII ($2,700 \times \frac{100}{90}$)	3,000
Profits (P)	100,000
19% x £97,000	18,430
Less Income tax recoverable	(2,400)
Corporation tax payable	16,030

Chapter 11

△ ACTIVITY 33   △ △ △ △

Wendy Windows plc

Corporation tax liability and pay days for the year to 31 January 2007

	£
Corporation tax due (£2,400,000 x 30%)	720,000
Each instalment ($^{1}/_{4}$ x £720,000)	180,000
Due date:	
14 August 2006	180,000
14 November 2006	180,000
14 February 2007	180,000
14 May 2007	180,000
	720,000

△ ACTIVITY 34   △ △ △ △

Universe plc

(a) **Projected corporation tax payments**

Corporation tax liability (£5,000,000 x 30%)   £1,500,000

The accounting period will be subject to self assessment and to the quarterly system of instalments as the company is large and was large in the previous year.

The liability for the year ended 30 June 2007 should be settled by four equal instalments of £375,000 (£1,500,000 ÷ 4).

		£
Instalment 1	14 January 2007	375,000
Instalment 2	14 April 2007	375,000
Instalment 3	14 July 2007	375,000
Instalment 4	14 October 2007	375,000
		1,500,000

(b) **Administrative requirements**

(1) A return, including statutory accounts and computations, must be submitted within 12 months of the accounting period end otherwise penalties will be exacted.

(2) Late payments of tax will give rise to interest charges, which will be deductible under Schedule D Case III.

△ ACTIVITY 35   △ △ △ △

Corporation Tax Self Assessment

Corporation tax self assessment (CTSA) applies to all companies.

Under CTSA it is the company's responsibility to calculate (i.e. self assess) its corporation tax liability. There is no facility to request HM Revenue and Customs (HMRC) to do the calculation (unlike income tax self assessment).

HMRC have 12 months from the due filing date to open an enquiry. If an enquiry is not raised within the time limit the company can assume its assessment is final. However, if the company has provided incomplete or inaccurate information in the return HMRC may be able to raise a discovery assessment after the enquiry deadline has expired. Adequate disclosure in the return is therefore an important issue.

Payment of corporation tax

Corporation tax is payable 9 months and 1 day after the end of the chargeable accounting period, in accordance with the company's self assessment. Interest on unpaid or overpaid tax runs from this 9 month date.

Large companies (i.e. who pay tax at the full rate of 30%) are required to pay their corporation tax liability by four equal quarterly instalments on the 14th day of the 7th, 10th, 13th and 16th months following the start of the accounting period.

As estimates will invariably be required for most if not all of the instalments, there are interest provisions for under and over payments. There are also penalties for negligently understating the amount of an instalment.

Filing of return

HMRC will issue a notice to the company requiring a self assessment return to be filed.

The company must file its corporation tax return and accounts by the end of 12 months after the end of the chargeable accounting period (or 3 months after the issue of the notice if later).

If the period of account is longer than 12 months then the returns must be filed within 12 months of the end of the period of account (or 3 months after the issue of the notice if later).

There are penalties for the late filing of returns.

Chapter 12

△ ACTIVITY 36   △ △ △ △

Bella Ltd

	£
Employer's Class 1 contributions:	
12.8% on the balance above the earnings threshold	
(12,480 – 5,035) x 12.8%	953
Class 1A contributions:	
12.8% on taxable benefits	
(£7,805 x 12.8%)	999
	1,952

△ ACTIVITY 37

Pasta Ltd

There is no upper earnings limit for the employer and therefore NICs must be paid on all of Fred's earnings above the earnings threshold at 12.8%. Vouchers are included in the definition of earnings.

Class 1A NICs are payable on taxable benefits, but excluding the vouchers as they are charged to Class 1 NICs.

	£
Class 1A NICs	
£6,000 x 12.8%	768
Secondary Class 1 NICs	
(£6,864 + £1,200 + £500 - £5,035) = £3,529 x 12.8%	452
	1,220

△ ACTIVITY 38

Charles Dickens

Class 1 secondary contributions are payable by the employer on all earnings above the earnings threshold.

Class 1 = (£60,000 – £5,035) x 12.8% = £7,035

Class 1A NIC is payable by the employer on taxable benefits, but not on pension contributions which are an exempt benefit.

	£
Medical insurance	200
Car	4,000
Fuel	2,500
Total taxable benefits	6,700

Class 1A NIC = (£6,700 x 12.8%) = £858

△ ACTIVITY 39   △ △ △ △

Manuel Costa (1)

Adjustment of profits for 12 months ended 30 June 2006

	£
Net profit per accounts	32,205
Manuel's drawings (£300 x 52)	15,600
Manuel's NIC	109
Speeding fine	65
Motor expenses ($\frac{1}{3}$ of balance)(£2,000 - £65) x $\frac{1}{3}$	645
Legal expenses in connection with speeding offence	640
Depreciation	3,570
	52,834
Less: Profit on sale of office furniture	(60)
Capital allowances	(2,480)
Taxable trade profits	50,294

△ **ACTIVITY 40**   △ △ △ △

Manuel Costa (2)

Inland **Revenue**

Income for the year ended 5 April 2007

SELF-EMPLOYMENT

Fill in these boxes first

Name

Tax reference

If you want help, look up the box numbers in the Notes

Business details

Name of business

3.1 Manuel Costa

Description of business

3.2 Wholesale clothing distributor

Address of business

3.3

Postcode

Accounting period - read the Notes, page SEN2 before filling in these boxes

Start

3.4 01 / 07 / 05

End

3.5 30 / 06 / 06

- Tick box 3.6 if details in boxes 3.1 or 3.3 have changed since your last Tax return   **3.6**

- Date of commencement if after 5 April 2004   **3.7** / /

- Date of cessation if before 6 April 2007   **3.8** / /

- Tick box 3.9 if the special arrangements for certain trades apply - read the Notes, pages SEN11 and SEN12   **3.9**

- Tick box 3.10 if you entered details for all relevant accounting periods on last year's Tax Return and boxes 3.14 to 3.73 and 3.99 to 3.115 will be blank (read Step 3 on page SEN2)   **3.10**

- Tick box 3.11 if your accounts do not cover the period from the last accounting date (explain why in the 'Additional information' box, box 3.116)   **3.11**

- Tick box 3.12 if your accounting date has changed (only if this is a permanent change and you want it to count for tax)   **3.12**

- Tick box 3.13 if this is the second or further change (explain in box 3.116 on Page SE4 why you have not used the same date as last year)   **3.13**

Capital allowances - summary

	Capital allowances	Balancing charge
Car costing more than £12,000 (excluding cars with low CO_2 emissions). (A separate calculation must be made for each car.)	**3.14** £	**3.15** £
Other business plant and machinery (including cars with low CO_2 emissions and cars costing less than £12,000) read the Notes, page SEN4	**3.16** £ 2,480	**3.17** £
Agricultural or Industrial Buildings Allowance (A separate calculation must be made for each block of expenditure.)	**3.18** £	**3.19** £
Other capital allowances claimed (Separate calculations must be made.)	**3.20** £	**3.21** £
	total of column above	total of column above
Total capital allowances/balancing charges	**3.22** £ 2,480	**3.23** £

- Tick box 3.22A if box 3.22 includes enhanced capital allowances for environmentally friendly expenditure.   **3.22A**

Income and expenses - annual turnover below £15,000

If your annual turnover is £15,000 or more, ignore boxes 3.24 to 3.26. Instead fill in Page SE2

If your annual turnover is below £15,000, **fill in boxes 3.24 to 3.26 instead of Page SE2.** Read the Notes, page SEN4.

- Turnover including other business receipts and goods etc. taken for personal use (and balancing charges from box 3.23)   **3.24** £

- Expenses allowable for tax (including capital allowances from box 3.22)   **3.12** £

Net profit (put figure in brackets if a loss)   **3.13** £

box 3.24 minus box 3.25

SA103   TAX RETURN ■ SELF-EMPLOYMENT: PAGE SE1   *Now fill in Page SE3*

Income and expenses - annual turnover £15,000 or more

You must fill in this Page if your annual turnover is £15,000 or more - read the Notes, page SEN2

If you were registered for VAT, do the figures in boxes 3.29 to 3.64, include VAT? **3.27** ☐ or exclude VAT? **3.28** ☐

Sales/business income (turnover)

3.29 £ 400,000

	Disallowable expenses included in boxes 3.33 to 3.50	Total expenses	
● Cost of sales	**3.30** £	**3.46** £ 232,000	
● Construction industry subcontractor costs	**3.31** £	**3.47** £	
● Other direct costs	**3.32** £	**3.48** £	

Gross profit/(loss) | box 3.29 *minus* boxes 3.46 + 3.47 + 3.48
3.49 £ 168,000

Other income/profits | **3.50** £

● Employee costs	**3.33** £ 15,709	**3.51** £ 84,655	
● Premises costs	**3.34** £	**3.52** £ 35,310	
● Repairs	**3.35** £	**3.53** £ 3,490	
● General administrative expenses	**3.36** £	**3.54** £	
● Motor expenses	**3.37** £ 710	**3.55** £ 2,000	
● Travel and subsistence	**3.38** £	**3.56** £	
● Advertising, promotion and entertainment	**3.39** £	**3.57** £	
● Legal and professional costs	**3.40** £ 640	**3.58** £ 1,060	
● Bad debts	**3.41** £	**3.59** £	
● Interest	**3.42** £	**3.60** £	
● Other finance charges	**3.43** £	**3.61** £	
● Depreciation and loss/(profit) on sale	**3.44** £ 3,510	**3.62** £ 3,510	
● Other expenses	**3.45** £	**3.63** £ 5,770	

Put the total of boxes 3.30 to 3.45 in box 3.66 below

Total expenses | total of boxes 3.51 to 3.63
3.64 £ 135,795

Net profit/(loss) | boxes 3.49 + 3.50 *minus* 3.64
3.65 £ 32,205

Tax adjustments to net profit or loss

	total of boxes 3.30 to 3.45
● Disallowable expenses	**3.66** £ 20,569
● Adjustments (apart from disallowable expenses) that increase profits. Examples are goods taken for personal use and amounts brought forward from an earlier year because of a claim under ESC B11about compulsory slaughter of farm animals	**3.67** £
● Balancing charges	**3.68** £

Total additions to net profit (deduct from net loss) | boxes 3.66 + 3.67 + 3.68
3.69 £ 20,569

● Capital allowances	**3.70** £ 2,480
● Deductions from net profit (add to net loss)	**3.71** £

boxes 3.70 + 3.71
3.72 £ 2,480

boxes 3.65 + 3.69 *minus* 3.72
3.73 £ 50,294

Net business profit for tax purposes (put figure in brackets if a loss)

TAX RETURN ■ SELF-EMPLOYMENT: PAGE SE2

Now fill in Page SE3 ➤

△ ACTIVITY 41   △ △ △ △

Freda Jones

Adjustment of profits for 12 months ended 31 December 2006

	£
Net profit per accounts	48,260
Goods for own use (W1)	500
Freda's drawings (£1,000 x 12)	12,000
Freda's NIC	109
Taxation (Freda's income tax)	15,590
Lease rental on expensive car (W2)	5,460
Depreciation	2,540
Motor car running expenses (½ x £2,500)	1,250
	85,709
Less Capital allowances	(1,200)
Taxable trade profits	84,509

Workings

(W1) Goods for own use

Where goods are taken for own use, the proprietor will be taxed on the profit that would have been made, had the goods been sold at market value.

Here, the cost of the goods has already been credited to the profit and loss account, but an additional credit is needed to reflect the *profit* that would have been made.

As no information is given about profit margins, an estimate will have to be used, based on the trading account.

	£
Sales	300,000
Cost of sales	(200,000)
Gross profit	100,000

$$\text{Gross profit as a percentage of cost} = \frac{100,000}{200,000} = 50\%$$

Gross profit on goods taken for own use = 50% x £1,000 = £500

(W2) Lease rental on expensive car

Amount to be disallowed found using the formula:

$$\text{Disallowed amount} = \frac{\frac{1}{2}\,(\text{Retail price when new} - £12,000)}{\text{Retail price when new}} \times \text{Hire charge}$$

$$\frac{\frac{1}{2}\,(£30,000 - £12,000)}{£30,000} \times £8,400 = £2,520$$

The car is also used privately so in addition to the disallowable amount calculated above, the private use element of the balance must also be disallowed.

Balance of expenditure £8,400 – £2,520 = £5,880
Private use element £5,880 x ½ = £2,940

Total amount disallowed:

	£
Expensive car element	2,520
Private use element	2,940
	5,460

△ ACTIVITY 42

Hudson

Capital allowances computation

	General pool £	Private use asset £	Allowances £
Year ended 31 Dec 2003			
Addition – 1 March 2003	10,858		
FYA @ 40%	(4,343)		4,343
WDV c/f	6,515		
Total allowances			4,343
Year ended 31 Dec 2004			
Addition (no FYA)		12,000	
WDA @ 25%	(1,629)	(3,000) 75%	3,879
WDV c/f	4,886	9,000	
Total allowances			3,879
Year ended 31 Dec 2005			
WDA @ 25%	(1,222)	(2,250) x 75%	2,910
Addition – 1 March 2005	1,000		
Less FYA (50%)	(500)		500
	500		
WDV c/f	4,164	6,750	
Total allowances			3,410
10 months ended 31 Oct 2006			
Disposal proceeds	(2,450)	(7,400)	
Balancing allowance	1,714		1,714
Balancing charge		(650) x 75%	(488)
Total allowances			1,226

Note: No WDAs or FYAs are given in the final period of account.

△ ACTIVITY 43   △ △ △ △

Ethan

Capital allowances computation

	General pool £	Expensive car £	Private use asset £	Allowances £
Year ended 31 Dec 2005				
Additions 11 January 2005		14,000		
21 June 2005	8,800			
16 September 2005			11,600	
WDA (25%/restricted/25%)	(2,200)	(3,000)		5,200
WDA (25% (Note 1)			(2,900)	2,030
WDV c/f	6,600	11,000	8,700	
Total allowances				7,230
Year ended 31 Dec 2006				
Disposals		(10,000)	(9,500)	
Balancing charge (Note 2)			800	(560)
Balancing allowance		1,000		1,000
WDA (25%)	(1,650)			1,650
WDV c/f	4,950			
Total allowances				2,090

Notes

(1)   Business portion of WDA = £2,900 x 70% = £2,030
(2)   Business portion of charge = 800 x 70% = 560

△ ACTIVITY 44

Raj

Capital allowances computation	General pool £	Expensive car (80% business) £	Allowances £
11 m/e 30 September 2005			
Additions (No FYA)		15,000	
WDA @ 25% (max £3,000) x $^{11}/_{12}$		(2,750) x 80%	2,200
Additions (with FYA)			
Machinery	4,000		
FYA @ 50%	(2,000)		2,000
WDV carried forward	2,000	12,250	
Total allowances			4,200
Year ended 30 September 2006			
WDA @ 25%	(500)		500
Restricted		(3,000) x 80%	2,400
Additions (with FYA)			
Tool grinder	6,000		
FYA (40%)	(2,400)		2,400
WDV carried forward	5,100	9,250	
Total allowances			5,300
Year ended 30 September 2007			
Additions (no FYA)	11,600		
	16,700		
WDA @ 25%	(4,175)	(2,312) x 80%	6,025
WDV carried forward	12,525	6,938	
Total allowances			6,025

△ ACTIVITY 45

John Openshaw

(a) **Capital allowances computation**

		General pool £	Private use 25% car £	Allowances £
Additions (no FYA)			9,500	
WDA at 25%			(2,375) x $^3/_4$	1,781
Additions qualifying for FYA				
Furniture/equipment – 1.7.05	8,250			
Furniture/equipment – 18.3.06	1,000			
Van – 10.7.05	7,000			
	16,250			
FYA @ 40%	(6,500)			6,500
		9,750		
WDV carried forward		9,750	7,125	
Total allowances				8,281

KAPLAN PUBLISHING

(b) **Taxable trading profit computation - year ended 30 June 2006**

	£
Profit per accounts	30,410
Disallowable expenses:	
Entertaining overseas suppliers	750
Entertaining UK customers	2,000
General bad debt provision	1,700
Car expenses (one-quarter private) (£3,050 x 25%)	762
Legal fees: Purchase of premises	1,100
Depreciation	5,000
	41,722
Less: Capital allowances (see part (a))	(8,281)
Taxable trade profits	33,441

△ ACTIVITY 46   △ △ △ △

Eastwood

(a) **Capital allowances computation**

Year to 31 December 2006	General pool £	Private use asset £	Expensive car £	Total £
WDV b/fwd	42,000	5,400		
Additions (no FYA)				
1.5.06 car	10,000			
1.9.06 car			15,000	
Disposals				
21.8.06 machine	(5,500)			
	46,500			
WDA (25%)	(11,625)			11,625
WDA (25%) (Note)		(1,350)		945
WDA (max)			(3,000)	3,000
Additions (with FYA)				
10.4.06 machine	27,500			
FYA @ 50%	(13,750)			13,750
WDV c/fwd	48,625	4,050	12,000	
Total allowances				29,320

Note: Only 70% of the WDA on the private use asset can be claimed
(70% x £1,1350 = £945)

(b) **Taxable trade profits for the year to 31 December 2006**

	£
Adjusted profits	85,000
Less: Capital Allowances	(29,320)
Taxable trade profits	55,680

△ ACTIVITY 47

Joshua

Taxable trading profits - 1 July 2005 to 30 April 2006

	£
Net profit per accounts	31,250
Add:	
Depreciation	1,850
Speeding fines	120
Car expenses (3,750 – 120) x $^2/_{22}$	
(private use excluding fines)	330
	33,550
Less: Capital allowances	3,983
Taxable trade profits	29,567

Working

Capital allowances computation

	Pool £	Expensive car ($^{20}/_{22}$ business use) £	Capital allowances £
10 months ended 30.4.06			
Additions (no FYA)			
Car		15,000	
WDA @ £3,000 x $^{10}/_{12}$		(2,500) x $^{20}/_{22}$	2,273
Additions qualifying for FYA			
Furniture	1,855		
Computer	1,500		
Photocopier	920		
	4,275		
FYA @ 40%	(1,710)		1,710
WDV c/f	2,565	12,500	
Total allowances			3,983

KAPLAN PUBLISHING

Chapter 15

△ ACTIVITY 48 △ △ △ △

Bob, Carol, Ted and Alice

	Total £	Bob £	Carol £	Ted £	Alice £
Year ending 31 Oct 2003	24,000	8,000	8,000	8,000	Nil
Year ending 31 Oct 2004					
1 Nov 2003 – 31 Jan 2004	7,500	2,500	2,500	2,500	
1 Feb 2004 – 31 Oct 2004	22,500	5,625	5,625	5,625	5,625
	30,000	8,125	8,125	8,125	5,625
Year ending 31 Oct 2005					
1 Nov 2004 – 31 Jul 2005	27,000	6,750	6,750	6,750	6,750
1 Aug 2005 – 1 Oct 2005	9,000	3,000	-	3,000	3,000
	36,000	9,750	6,750	9,750	9,750
Year ending 31 Oct 2006	42,000	14,000	Nil	14,000	14,000
Period ending 31 Jan 2007	12,000	4,000	Nil	4,000	4,000

△ ACTIVITY 49 △ △ △ △

Roger, Brigitte and Xavier

	Total £	Roger £	Brigitte £	Xavier £
Period to 30 June 2003 (9 months)	30,000	15,000	15,000	Nil
Year to 30 June 2004	45,000	22,500	22,500	Nil
Year to 30 June 2005				
1 July 2004 – 30 Sept 2004 (3 months)	12,500	6,250	6,250	-
1 October 2004 – 30 June 2005 (9 months)	37,500	12,500	12,500	12,500
	50,000	18,750	18,750	12,500
Year to 30 June 2006	60,000	20,000	20,000	20,000

△ ACTIVITY 50   △ △ △ △

Anne, Betty, Chloe and Diana

			Anne £	Betty £	Chloe £	Diana £
Year ended 31.12.05						
01.01.05 – 30.06.05	$^6/_{12}$ x 60,000		15,000	15,000		
01.07.05 – 31.12.05	$^6/_{12}$ x 60,000		15,000		15,000	
			30,000	15,000	15,000	
Year ended 31.12.06						
01.01.06 – 31.03.06	$^3/_{12}$ x 72,000		9,000		9,000	
01.04.06 – 31.12.06	$^9/_{12}$ x 72,000		18,000		18,000	18,000
			27,000		27,000	18,000

△ ACTIVITY 51   △ △ △ △

Bert and Harold

Allocation of taxable trade profits

The profit-sharing ratio was changed on 1 July 2006 which is 9 months into the accounting period. The profits will therefore be time-apportioned for allocation as follows:

Old ratio   £16,500 x $^9/_{12}$ = £12,375
New ratio £16,500 x $^3/_{12}$ =   £4,125

Allocation of taxable trade profits

	Total £	Bert £	Harold £
1/10/05 to 30/6/06			
Salaries ($^9/_{12}$)	3,750	2,250	1,500
Balance (3:2)	8,625	5,175	3,450
	12,375	7,425	4,950
1/7/06 to 30/9/06			
Salaries ($^3/_{12}$)	2,500	1,500	1,000
Balance (2:1)	1,625	1,083	542
	4,125	2,583	1,542
Total allocation	16,500	10,008	6,492

Chapter 16

△ ACTIVITY 52   △ △ △ △

Roger

Year of assessment	Basis period		Assessment £
2003/04	1 May 2003 – 5 April 2004	£40,500 + (£59,400 x $^6/_{12}$)	70,200
2004/05	Year ending 30 September 2004		59,400
2005/06	Year ending 30 September 2005		72,900
2006/07	Year ending 30 September 2006		56,700

There are overlap profits of £29,700 (£59,400 x $^6/_{12}$).

△ ACTIVITY 53   △ △ △ △

James

Year of assessment	Basis period		Assessment £
2002/03	1 January 2003 to 5 April 2003	(£75,600 x $^3/_{16}$)	14,175
2003/04	Year ending 5 April 2004	(£75,600 x $^{12}/_{16}$)	56,700
2004/05	Year ending 30 April 2004	(£75,600 x $^{12}/_{16}$)	56,700
2005/06	Year ending 30 April 2005		52,650
2006/07	Year ending 30 April 2006		56,900
Overlap	(01.05.03 - 05.04.04), (£75,600 x $^{11}/_{16}$)		51,975

△ ACTIVITY 54   △ △ △ △

Avril

Year of assessment	Basis period	Assessment £
2003/04	(01.01.04 – 05.04.04) (3 months) Period ended 30.06.04 (6 months) £80,000 x $^3/_6$	40,000
2004/05	Accounting period is less than 12 months therefore use first 12 months Period ended 30.06.04 (6 months) Year ended 30.06.05 - £100,000 x $^6/_{12}$	80,000 50,000
		130,000
2005/06	Current year basis to 30.06.05	100,000
2006/07	Current year basis to 30.06.06	110,000
Overlap	£40,000 (01.01.04 – 05.04.04) + £50,000 (01.07.04 – 31.12.04)	90,000

△ ACTIVITY 55   △ △ △ △

Benny

Year of assessment	Basis period	Assessment £
2004/05	(01.07.04 – 05.04.05) (9 months) Period ended 31.12.04 (6 months) 14,000 Year ended 31.12.05 (3 months) £36,000 x $^3/_{12}$	9,000
		23,000
2005/06	Current year basis to 31.12.05	36,000
2006/07	Current year basis to 31.12.06	28,000
Overlap	(01.01.05 – 05.04.05) from y/e 31.12.05	9,000

△ ACTIVITY 56 △△△△

Colin

Year of assessment	Basis period	Assessment £
2003/04	(01.07.03 – 05.04.04) (9 months)	
	$^9/_{12}$ of year ended 30.6.04 x 100,000	75,000
2004/05	Current year basis to 30.06.04	100,000
2005/06	Current year basis to 30.06.05	80,000
2006/07	Current year basis to 30.06.06	120,000

△ ACTIVITY 57 △△△△

Dana

Year of assessment	Basis period	Assessment £
2002/03	(01.02.03 – 05.04.03) (2 months)	
	First accounts: period ended 30.04.04 (15 months)	
	£150,000 x $^2/_{15}$	20,000
2003/04	No accounting period ending in tax year, so = (6.4.03 – 5.4.04)	
	$^{12}/_{15}$ x period ended 30.04.04 of £150,000	120,000
2004/05	Period ended 30.04.04 (15 months) therefore tax 12 months to accounting period end	
	£150,000 x $^{12}/_{15}$	120,000
2005/06	Current year basis to 30.04.05	120,000
2006/07	Current year basis to 30.04.06	140,000
	Overlap period (01.05.03 – 05.04.04) (11 months)	
	£150,000 x $^{11}/_{15}$	110,000

△ ACTIVITY 58 △△△△

Elle

(a) Cessation of 31 May 2007

Year of assessment	Basis period	Assessment £
2005/06	Current year basis to 31.05.05	22,000
2006/07	Current year basis to 31.05.06	26,000
2007/08	Current year basis to 31.05.07	27,000
	Less Overlap profits	(5,000)
		22,000

(b) Cessation on 31 January 2007

Year of assessment	Basis period	Assessment £
2005/06	Current year basis to 31.05.05	22,000
2006/07	Current year basis to 31.05.06 plus	26,000
	Period to 31.01.07 (cessation)	22,500
	Less Overlap profits	(5,000)
		43,500

△ ACTIVITY 59 △△△△

Bernadette

Year of assessment	Basis period	Assessment £
2003/04	(1 October 2003 – 5 April 2004)	
	$^{6}/_{12}$ x £21,280	10,640
2004/05	(Year ended 30 September 2004)	21,280
	(overlap profits £10,640)	
2005/06	(Year ended 30 September 2005)	24,688
2006/07	(Year ended 30 September 2006)	28,816
2007/08	(Year ended 30 September 2007)	30,304
	Plus period to cessation on	
	28 February 2008	16,792
	Less Overlap profits	(10,640)
		36,456

△ ACTIVITY 60 △△△△

Bay

Year of assessment	Basis period	Assessment £
2002/03	1 January 2003 – 5 April 2003	
	$^{3}/_{12}$ x £15,144 (W)	3,786
2003/04	Year ended 31 December 2003	15,144
	(overlap profits £3,786)	
2004/05	Year ended 31 December 2004	13,961
2005/06	Year ended 31 December 2005	13,618
2006/07	10 months to 31 October 2006	16,714
	Less Overlap relief	(3,786)
		12,928

Workings: Adjusted profits after capital allowances

	Trading profit £	Capital allowances £	£
Year to 31 December 2003	19,487	(4,343)	15,144
Year to 31 December 2004	17,840	(3,879)	13,961
Year to 31 December 2005	16,928	(3,310)	13,618
10 months to 31 October 2006	18,040	(1,326)	16,714

△ ACTIVITY 61

Ranjit

Year of assessment	Basis period	Assessment £
2004/05	01.11.04 – 05.04.05 (5 months of the period to 30.09.05 of 11 months) ($£2,306 \times {}^5/_{11}$)	1,048
2005/06	Accounting period less than 12 months so: 11 months to 30.09.05 plus 1 month to 30.09.06 ($£3,845 \times {}^1/_{12}$)	2,306 320
		2,626
2006/07	Year ended 30.09.06	3,845
2007/08	Year ended 30.09.07	9,137

Overlap profits = (£1,048 + £320) = £1,368

Workings: Adjusted trading profits after capital allowances

	Trading profit £	Capital allowances £	£
Period ending 30.09.05	6,106	(3,800)	2,306
Year ended 30.09.06	8,845	(5,000)	3,845
Year ended 30.09.07	19,087	(9,950)	9,137

△ ACTIVITY 62 △△△△

Michael

Year of assessment	Basis period	Assessment £
2000/01	Actual (1.3.01 – 5.4.01) ($^{1}/_{14}$ x 15,000)	1,071
2001/02	Actual (6.4.01 – 5.4.02) ($^{12}/_{14}$ x 15,000)	12,857
2002/03	12 months to 30/4/02 (1.5.01 – 30.4.02) ($^{12}/_{14}$ x 15,000)	12,857

Overlap relief (1.5.01 – 5.4.02) = $^{11}/_{14}$ x 15,000 = £11,785

2003/04	Current year basis (year to 30.4.03)	17,000
2004/05	Current year basis (year to 30.4.04)	12,000
2005/06	Current year basis (year to 30.4.05)	14,000
2006/07	Current year basis (year to 30.4.06)	18,000
2007/08	(1.5.06 - 31.10.07)	
	Year to 30.4.07	13,000
	Period to 31.10.07	3,000
		16,000
	Less: Overlap relief	(11,785)
		4,215

Total profits assessed	92,000
Total profits earned	92,000

△ ACTIVITY 63 △△△△

Partnership assessments

The partners first divide their adjusted profits after capital allowances between themselves in accordance with their profit sharing agreement for the period concerned. This information is shown on the partnership tax return for the period. Each partner is then assessable on his or her share as if he or she was a sole trader earning that amount of taxable trade profits.

Capital allowances on privately owned assets and privately incurred business expenses must go through the partnership accounts and cannot be relieved separately. The partnership can adjust profit shares to reflect such items. However, the figures for the partnership return must appear unadjusted in the tax returns of each partner.

If a partner joins or leaves the partnership, the opening and closing tax rules will apply in respect of the profit shares just as if the partner was a sole trader commencing or ceasing.

Chapter 17

△ ACTIVITY 64 △ △ △ △

Bourbon

(a) Alternative means of loss relief

(i) Carry forward under S385 ICTA 1988 for set off against the next available taxable trading income from the same business and so continue until the loss is fully relieved.

(ii) Claim under S380 ICTA 1988 against the total income of:
- the fiscal year of loss; and/or
- the preceding fiscal year.

(b) Advice on relief

From the following computations it can be seen that the best method of obtaining relief is for Bourbon to claim relief under S380 ICTA 1988 for 2005/06 to obtain relief as early as possible. A S380 ICTA 1988 claim should be made also in 2006/07 for the balance of the loss, as this will not result in the wastage of any personal allowance.

	2005/06 £	2006/07 £	2007/08 £
Trading profits	12,200	Nil	12,750
S385 Relief	-	-	-
	12,200	Nil	12,750
BS interest	7,250	10,250	5,250
STI	19,450	10,250	18,000
S380 Relief	(19,450)	(4,600)	
STI after loss relief	Nil	5,650	18,000

△ ACTIVITY 65 △ △ △ △

Lancelot

First identify the basis periods and hence the taxable trade profits or losses arising in each fiscal year.

Year of assessment	Basis period	Loss available £	Taxable trade profits £
2004/05	(1 July 2004 – 5 April 2005) £6,000 x $^9/_{12}$		4,500
2005/06	(Year ended 30 June 2005)		6,000
2006/07	(Year ended 30 June 2006)	30,000	
2007/08	(Year ended 30 June 2007)		8,000

2006/07 is the year of the loss.

The loss of £30,000 sustained in 2006/07 will be set off under S381 as follows:

		2003/04 £	2004/05 £	2005/06 £
Employment earnings		14,000	-	-
Taxable trade profits		-	4,500	6,000
Savings income		2,000	2,000	2,000
STI		16,000	6,500	8,000
Less	S381 ICTA 1988 claim	(16,000)	(6,500)	7,500)
Revised STI after loss relief		Nil	Nil	500

Loss memorandum:

		£
S381 ICTA 1988 loss		30,000
Less	S381 claim 2003/04	(16,000)
		14,000
Less	S381 claim 2004/05	(6,500)
		7,500
Less	S381 claim 2005/06	(7,500)
Loss c/f		Nil

△ ACTIVITY 66   △ △ △ △

Lucien Buysse

Identify the loss with the relevant tax year(s) (opening years of business)

Year of assessment	Basis period	£	Loss available £	Taxable trade profits £
2004/05	01.07.04 – 05.04.05 (9 months) £15,000 x $^9/_{12}$		(11,250)	Nil
2005/06	y/e 30.06.05 Less used 2004/05	(15,000) 11,250	(3,750)	Nil
2006/07	y/e 30.06.06			5,000

Income tax computations

	2003/04 £	2004/05 £	2005/06 £	2006/07 £
Taxable trade profits (see (i))	–	Nil	Nil	5,000
Savings income	15,750	11,250	12,500	13,750
STI	15,750	11,250	12,500	18,750
S380 relief	(11,250) (a)	(3,750) (b)		
Personal allowance	(4,500) (rest)	(5,035)	(5,035)	(5,035)
Taxable income	Nil	2,465	7,465	13,715

Loss memorandum

	£
2004/05	(11,250)
S380 relief – 2003/04	11,250
2005/06	(3,750)
S380 relief - 2004/05	3,750

Explanation

2004/05 loss £11,250

- Could be used against STI in 2004/05 and/or 2003/04 under S380. (S381 could have the same effect in 2003/04).

- The use of the loss in 2003/04 is preferred to 2004/05 as it reduces personal allowance wastage and is the earliest use of the loss, taking account of cash flow impact.

2005/06 loss £3,750

- Could be used against STI in 2005/06 or 2004/05 under S380.

- The use of the loss in 2004/05 is preferred as this gives earliest use.

- S381 is not recommended as this would use the loss in 2003/04 and waste the personal allowance.

Neither loss should be carried forward under S385, as this does not utilise the loss fully nor at the earliest opportunity.

KAPLAN PUBLISHING

△ ACTIVITY 67   △ △ △ △

Jacqueline

(a) Capital allowances

	Pool £	Allowances £
Year ended 31 July 2004		
Brought forward	1,200	
WDA – 25%	(300)	300
WDA c/f	900	
Year ended 31 July 2005		
WDA – 25%	(225)	225
WDA c/f	675	
Year ended 31 July 2006		
Disposal proceeds	(75)	
	600	
Balancing allowance	600	600

(b) Trading income assessments

	Profit/ (loss) £	Capital allowances £	£
Year to 31 July 2004	13,000	(300)	12,700
31 July 2005	8,000	(225)	7,775
31 July 2006	(3,000)	(600)	(3,600)

Determine the final assessable amounts for the final three years.

Year of assessment	Basis period	Assessment £
2004/05	Year ending 31 July 2004	12,700
2005/06	Year ending 31 July 2005	7,775
2006/07	Year ending 31 July 2006 (3,600 + 2,500 = 6,100 Loss)	Nil

(c) Utilisation of a terminal loss

The loss of 2006/07 could be relieved as follows:

(i)   against other income of 2006/07 (s380 Relief).
(ii) against other income of 2005/06 (s380 Relief).
(iii) by carry back against the taxable trade profits of 2005/06, 2004/05 and 2003/04 (s388 Relief).

△ ACTIVITY 68

Leonardo

Year of assessment	Basis period		Assessment £
2003/04	01.09.03 – 05.04.04 ($^7/_9$ x 22,500)		17,500
2004/05	01.09.03 – 31.08.04 (22,500 + ($^3/_{12}$ x 30,000 loss))		15,000
2005/06	01.06.04 – 31.05.05	Loss	Nil
2006/07	01.06.05 – 31.05.06	Loss	Nil
2007/08	01.06.06 – 31.05.07		5,000

Years of the loss

		£
2005/06	Year to 31.05.05	30,000
	Less used in 2004/05 opening year rules	(7,500)
	Available loss	22,500
2006/07	Year to 31.05.06 - available loss	15,000

Most effective use of the losses

	£
Loss of 2005/06	22,500
Use under S380 against STI of 2004/05	(15,000)
	7,500
Use under S381 against STI of:	
2002/03 – assume no STI	-
2003/04	(7,500)
	Nil

	£
Loss of 2006/07	15,000
Use under S381 against balance of:	
STI for 2003/04 (17,500 – 7,500)	(10,000)
Carry forward against trading profits of 2007/08	(5,000)
	Nil

Summary of use of the available losses

			2003/04 £	2004/05 £	2007/08 £
Taxable trade profits (before relief)			17,500	15,000	5,000
2005/06	loss:	S380		(15,000)	
		S381	(7,500)		
2006/07	loss:	S381	(10,000)		
		S385			(5,000)
STI after loss relief			Nil	Nil	Nil

△ ACTIVITY 69

Caren Montaine

(1) Options for utilisation of loss

The loss sustained in the accounting period ended 31 August 2006 will be treated as a loss for the fiscal year 2006/07.

Under S380 this loss may be set off against Caren's income from all sources for the year of the loss, 2006/07, and/or income from all sources for the year preceding the year of loss, 2005/06.

In the event that S380 claim(s) are not made or that the income available is insufficient to absorb the losses claimed under S380, a claim can be made under S385 to carry the losses forward against future trading income from the same trade.

(2) Most tax efficient use of the loss

(i) **2005/06**

The total income for the year 2005/06 is £5,100 being the trading profits assessed on a current year basis.

As losses are set off before personal allowances, in this case £5,035, there would be no point in claiming under S380 because the income is almost covered by the personal allowance.

(ii) **2006/07**

There is no trading profit expected for 2006/07 but there is building society interest of £2,000 (gross). This income is already covered by personal allowances so no additional benefit would be gained by making a claim under S380.

(iii) **2007/08**

The income for the year 2007/08 is £14,000 being the trading profits assessed on a current year basis.

If no claim is made under S380, the losses of £11,000 will carried forward under S385 and must be used against the first available trading profit.

The assessment of £14,000 will be reduced by £11,000 (S385) to £3,000. Personal allowances of £3,000 will be used to reduce the taxable income to £nil and there will be unused allowances of £2,035.

As this saves the most amount of tax and relief can be for seen within the next year, it is the recommended method of relief.

Chapter 18

△ ACTIVITY 70 △△△△

Enquiries

(a) HM Revenue and Customs (HMRC) must normally give written notice within 12 months of the filing date (i.e. by 31 January 2009 for the 2006/07 tax return).

(b) HMRC can extend the above deadline by making a discovery assessment to prevent loss of tax. This may be done if HMRC make a discovery which they could not reasonably have been expected to make from the information provided in the return.

This assessment can be made up to five years from the filing date (i.e. by 31 January 2013 for the 2006/07 return) or 20 years in the case of fraud or negligence.

(c) An enquiry is normally commenced due to:

- under-declaration of income.
- overstatement of deductions.
- selection for a random review.

(d) The taxpayer can either:

- accept HMRC's amendment to his return; or
- appeal to the Commissioners within 30 days.

△ ACTIVITY 71 △△△△

IT self assessment

(a) Income tax returns for 2006/07 should normally be submitted by 31 January 2008.

(b) In order for HM Revenue and Customs (HMRC) to calculate the tax liability for 2006/07, a return should be submitted by 30 September 2007.

(c) Notification is due by 5 October 2007 if a new source arises in 2006/07 and a tax return has not been issued.

(d) If a tax return is submitted late, a £100 fixed penalty is charged. If it is still outstanding after 6 months, a further £100 penalty is charged. If the return is still outstanding after 12 months, a penalty of up to 100% of the tax outstanding is charged.

(e) If HMRC feel that further incentives are required to ensure a tax return is submitted, they can apply to the Commissioners to charge a further penalty of up to £60 a day while the return remains outstanding.

(f) The maximum penalty for failing to notify a new source of income on time is 100% of the tax thereon which is unpaid by 31 January following the tax year.

(g) The penalty for submitting an incorrect tax return is 100% of the tax which would be underpaid.

(h) The penalty for fraudulently or negligently over-reducing payments on account is 100% of the tax by which the payments on account have been reduced in excess of the correct reduction.

(i) The penalty for failing to maintain adequate records is up to £3,000.

Chapter 19

△ ACTIVITY 72   △△△△

Naomi

Naomi must pay Class 2 NICs of £2.10 per week. In all cases her accounts profits exceed her taxable profits, therefore they exceed the small earnings limit of £4,465.

She is liable to pay Class 4 NICs as follows:

(a)	Profits do not exceed lower limit, Class 4 NICs	=	£Nil
(b)	Class 4 NICs = £(24,500 – 5,035) x 8%	=	£1,557
(c)	Class 4 NICs = £(33,540 – 5,035) x 8% + £(44,500 – 33,540) x 1%)	=	£2,390

Chapter 21

△ ACTIVITY 73   △△△△

RBQ Ltd

	£
Shop (W1)	4,072
Painting (W2)	(5,000)
Car – exempt	Nil
Land (W3)	20,030
Total net chargeable gains	19,102

Workings

(W1) Shop

	£
Proceeds	15,000
Cost	(8,000)
Unindexed gain	7,000
Indexation allowance (£8,000 x 0.366)	(2,928)
Chargeable gain	4,072

(W2) Painting

	£
Proceeds	25,000
Cost	(30,000)
Allowable Loss	(5,000)

No indexation is available to increase the loss.

(W3) Land

	£
Proceeds	29,000
Cost	(6,000)
Unindexed gain	23,000
Indexation allowance (£6,000 x 0.495)	(2,970)
Chargeable gain	20,030

△ ACTIVITY 74   △ △ △ △

Jackson Ltd

		£	Gains £
(a)	**Land**		
	Sales proceeds	27,000	
	Less Cost	(14,000)	
	Unindexed gain	13,000	
	Less Indexation allowance		
	£14,000 x 0.729	(10,206)	
	Chargeable gain	2,794	2,794
(b)	**Cottage**	£	
	Sale proceeds	100,000	
	Less Legal fees	(1,200)	
		98,800	
	Less Cost (March 1988)	(10,500)	
	Extension (April 1992)	(3,000)	
	Extension (June 1995)	(4,600)	
	Unindexed gain	80,700	
	Less Indexation allowance		
	Cost £10,500 x 0.865	(9,083)	
	Extension £3,000 x 0.398	(1,194)	
	Extension £4,600 x 0.296	(1,362)	
	Chargeable gain	69,061	69,061
(c)	**Racehorse** – exempt asset		Nil
	(wasting chattel)		
	Total chargeable gains		71,855

Chapter 22

△ ACTIVITY 75   △ △ △ △

John

	£
Offices (W1)	41,535
Retail shop (W2)	(4,000)
Workshop (W3)	Nil
Total net indexed gains	37,535

As business assets held over two years the gains are all 25% chargeable.

	£
Chargeable gain (25% x £37,535)	9,384

Workings

(W1) Offices

	£
Proceeds	73,000
Cost	(29,000)
Unindexed gain	44,000
Indexation allowance (£29,000 x 0.085)	(2,465)
Indexed gain	41,535

(W2) Retail shop

	£
Proceeds	26,000
Cost	(30,000)
Allowable loss	(4,000)

No indexation is available to increase the loss.

(W3) Workshop

	£
Proceeds	25,000
Cost	(15,000)
Unindexed gain	10,000
Indexation allowance (£15,000 x 1.006) restricted (Note)	(10,000)
Indexed gain	Nil

Note: Restricted because indexation cannot create an allowable loss.

△ ACTIVITY 76   △ △ △ △

Jacky

Asset	Indexed gain £	Loss in year £	Net gains £	Chargeable %	Chargeable gains £
Factory (W1)	33,048		33,048	25%	8,262
Shop (W3)	8,000	(2,000) (W2)	6,000	50%	3,000
Total chargeable gains					11,262

Workings

(W1) Factory

	£
Sale proceeds	55,000
Less Cost	(14,000)
Unindexed gain	41,000
Less Indexation allowance (£14,000 x 0.568)	(7,952)
Indexed gain	33,048

Business asset, held more than 2 years; therefore gain is 25% chargeable.

(W2) Shop (1)

	£
Sale proceeds	35,000
Less Cost	(37,000)
Allowable loss	(2,000)

The loss can be set off in the most tax efficient manner (i.e. against gains with the highest chargeable percentage first).

(W3) Shop (2)

	£
Proceeds	52,000
Less Cost	(44,000)
Indexed gain	8,000

Business asset, held one complete year; therefore the gain is 50% chargeable.

△ ACTIVITY 77

Rosalind

(a) **Rosalind**

	£
Gains in 2006/07	8,300
Losses in 2006/07	(1,000)
	7,300
Annual exemption	(8,800)
Taxable gains	Nil

(b) **Derek**

	£
Gains in 2006/07	9,200
Losses in 2006/07	(300)
	8,900
Losses b/f	(100)
	8,800
Annual exemption	(8,800)
Taxable gains	Nil
Losses carried forward (£2,500 - £100)	2,400

(c) **Phil**

	£
Net gains in 2006/07	9,700
Losses b/f	(500)
	9,200
Annual exemption	(8,800)
Taxable gains	400

△ ACTIVITY 78 △△△△

Hannah

Step 1: Determine the chargeable percentage of each gain

		£
Business asset	25% chargeable	60,000
Business asset	50% chargeable	12,000
		72,000

Step 2: Allocate losses to gains – and apply taper relief

Indexed gain	Current losses	Losses b/f	Net gains	Chargeable percentage	Chargeable gains
£	£	£	£	£	£
12,000	(7,000)	(2,000)	3,000	50%	1,500
60,000			60,000	25%	15,000

Total chargeable gains	16,500
Annual exemption	(8,800)
Taxable gains	7,700

Step 3: Calculate capital gains tax

Basic rate band available
(£33,300 - £29,000 taxable income = £4,300)

		£		£
CGT:	4,300 x 20%			860
	3,400 x 40%			1,360
	7,700			2,220

Chapter 23

△ ACTIVITY 79 △△△△

Jerry Ltd

	£
Disposal - September 1991	
Proceeds	9,000
Less Cost (W)	(4,000)
Unindexed gain	5,000
Less Indexation (£6,480 - £4,000)	(2,480)
Chargeable gain	2,520
Disposal - March 2007	
Proceeds	14,500
Less Cost (W)	(4,043)
	10,457
Less Indexation (£9,386 - £4,043)	(5,343)
Chargeable gain	5,114

1985 pool working	Number of shares £	Unindexed cost £	Indexed cost £
6 April 1985			
Balance	2,600	5,000	6,377
July 1987			
(i) Indexed rise (0.074 x £6,377)		-	472
(ii) Acquisition	1,500	3,200	3,200
	4,100	8,200	10,049
September 1991			
(i) Indexed rise (0.322 x £10,049)			3,236
	4,100	8,200	13,285
(ii) Disposal	(2,000)	(4,000)	(6,480)
	2,100	4,200	6,805
January 1992			
(i) Indexed rise (0.007 x £6,805)			48
(ii) Acquisition	200	450	450
	2,300	4,650	7,303
March 2007			
(i) Indexed rise (0.478 x £7,303)			3,491
	2,300	4,650	10,794
(ii) Disposal	(2,000)	(4,043)	(9,386)
	300	607	1,408

△ ACTIVITY 80   △ △ △ △

Sunshine Ltd

	£
Disposal – January 1995	
Sale proceeds	10,100
Less Cost (W)	(1,722)
Unindexed gain	8,378
Less Indexation (£2,452 - £1,722)	(730)
Chargeable gain	7,648
Disposal – February 2007	
Sale proceeds	9,340
Less Cost (W)	(1,148)
Unindexed gain	8,192
Less Indexation (£2,239 - £1,148)	(1,091)
Chargeable gain	7,101

1985 pool working

	Number of shares £	Unindexed cost £	Indexed cost £
6 April 1985			
Balance	1,000	1,000	1,161
December 1989			
(i) Indexed rise (0.253 x £1,161)			294
(ii) Acquisition	1,000	1,870	1,870
	2,000	2,870	3,325
January 1995			
(i) Indexed rise (0.229 x £3,325)			761
	2,000	2,870	4,086
(ii) Disposal	(1,200)	(1,722)	(2,452)
	800	1,148	1,634
February 2007			
(i) Indexed rise (0.370 x £1,634)			595
	800	1,148	2,239
(ii) Disposal	(800)	(1,148)	(2,239)
	Nil	Nil	Nil

△ ACTIVITY 81   △ △ △ △

Purple Ltd

Disposal - 8 August 2006 (Sale of 5,000 shares)

	£
Sale proceeds	15,000
Less Cost	(5,833)
Unindexed gain	9,167
Less Indexation (£9,407 - £5,833)	(3,574)
Chargeable gain	5,593

1985 pool working

	Number	Cost £	Indexed cost £
	£		
Balance at 9 June 1990	3,000	4,000	5,010
12 August 1995			
Bonus issue 1 for 3	1,000	Nil	Nil
	4,000	4,000	5,010
Indexed rise to May 2000 (£5,010 x 0.347)			1,738
7 May 2000 Rights issue (1 for 2 x 150p)	2,000	3,000	3,000
Bal c/f	6,000	7,000	9,748

	Number	Cost	Indexed cost
	£	£	£
Bal b/f	6,000	7,000	9,748
Indexed rise to August 2006 (£9,748 x 0.158)			1,540
	6,000	7,000	11,288
8 August 2006 sale $\frac{5,000}{6,000}$ x £7,000/£11,288	(5,000)	(5,833)	(9,407)
Pool c/f	1,000	1,167	1,881

Chapter 24

△ ACTIVITY 82   △△△△

Taylor

Disposal of freehold factory (18 July 1987)

£115,000 has been reinvested in a business asset (goodwill) within three years and therefore part of the gain may be rolled over.

The £5,000 (120,000 - 115,000) proceeds not reinvested is taxed in 1987/88, but will be covered by the annual exemption.

The gain rolled over is £25,000 (£30,000 - £5,000).

Disposal of goodwill (22 December 2006)

	£	£
Proceeds		320,000
Less Cost	115,000	
Less Gain rolled over	(25,000)	
Base cost of goodwill		(90,000)
Unindexed gain		230,000
Less Indexation allowance (£90,000 x 0.574)		(51,660)
Indexed gain		178,340

As a business asset held for more than two years, the gain is 25% chargeable.

	£
Chargeable gain (£178,340 x 25%)	44,585
Less Annual exemption	(8,800)
Taxable gain in 2006/07	35,785

△ ACTIVITY 83 △ △ △ △

Jonald

(a) **Amount chargeable on Jonald in 2006/07**

Gain eligible to be held over = £900,000

The gain assessable in 2006/07 is therefore £Nil.

(b) **Reg's base cost for shares gifted**

Market value at date of gift less gain held over = £5,000,000 - £900,000 = £4,100,000.

△ ACTIVITY 84 △ △ △ △

DRV Ltd (1)

Sale of original freehold factory (purchased May 1983)

	£
Sale proceeds (December 1987)	130,000
Less Cost	(65,000)
Unindexed gain	65,000
Less Indexation allowance (December 1987 – May 1983) 0.220 x £65,000	(14,300)
Indexed gain before relief	50,700
Less Rollover relief upon purchase of replacement factory in October 1987	(50,700)
Chargeable gain - year ended 31 March 1988	Nil

Sale of replacement factory

	£	£
Sale proceeds (March 2007)		275,000
Cost (October 1987)	190,000	
Less Rolled over gain	(50,700)	
		(139,300)
Unindexed gain		135,700
Less Indexation allowance (March 2007 – October 1987) 0.936 x £139,300		(130,385)
Chargeable gain (Note)		5,315

Note: DRV Ltd may be able to roll this gain over if it makes a further qualifying purchase in the qualifying time period.

△ ACTIVITY 85   △ △ △ △

DRV Ltd (2)

Sale of original freehold factory (purchased 1983)

	£
Sale proceeds (December 1987)	130,000
Less Cost	(65,000)
Unindexed gain	65,000
Less Indexation allowance (December 1987 – May 1983)	
0.220 x £65,000	(14,300)
Indexed gain (as above)	50,700
Less Rollover relief (balancing figure)	(35,700)
Chargeable gain - year ended 31 March 1988 (Note)	15,000

Note: Not all of the sale proceeds are reinvested. Therefore, the chargeable gain arising now is the sale proceeds not reinvested: £130,000 - £115,000.

Sale of replacement factory

	£	£
Sale proceeds (March 2007)		275,000
Cost	115,000	
Less Rolled over gain	(35,700)	
		79,300
Unindexed gain		195,700
Less Indexation allowance (March 2007 – October 1987)		
(0.936 x £79,300)		(74,225)
Chargeable gain		121,475

△ ACTIVITY 86   △ △ △ △

Marco

Gain on disposal of the building

	£
Sale proceeds	150,000
Cost	(60,000)
Unindexed gain	90,000
Indexation allowance (£60,000 x 0.213)	(12,780)
Indexed gain	77,220

Qualifying time period for reinvestment

Sale: September 2006 } Within 12m before disposal
Purchase: December 2005 } therefore qualifies for rollover relief

The amount reinvested is as follows:

	£
Sale proceeds	150,000
Amount spent	(130,000)
Sale proceeds not reinvested	20,000

Chargeable now			
= lower:	(1)	Sale proceeds not reinvested	20,000
	(2)	Gain	77,220

Therefore £20,000 indexed gain before taper relief is taxable in 2006/07.

As a busines asset held for more than 2 years, the gain is 25% chargeable.

	£
Chargeable gain (£20,000 x 25%)	5,000

Base cost of the replacement asset

	£
Cost	130,000
Less Gain rolled over (77,220 – 20,000)	(57,220)
Revised base cost	72,780

△ ACTIVITY 87 △△△△

Columbus

Disposal of first factory

	£
Proceeds	900,000
Less Cost	(300,000)
Unindexed gain	600,000
Less Indexation allowance (300,000 x 0.889)	(266,700)
Indexed gain	333,300

Indexed gain taxable in 2006/07:

Lower of		
(1)	Sale of proceeds not reinvested (900,000 - 700,000)	200,000
(2)	Indexed gain	333,300

As a business asset held of more than 2 years, the gain is 25% chargeable.

Chargeable gain in 2006/07 (200,000x 25%)	50,000
Rollover relief is therefore (333,300 - 200,000)	133,300

Base cost of second factory

		£
Cost		700,000
Less	Gain rolled over	(133,300)
Base cost		566,700

Note that the accrued taper relief on the gain rolled over is lost. On the subsequent disposal of the factory taper relief runs from March 2006.

△ ACTIVITY 88   △△△△

Astute Ltd

(a) **Conditions for rollover relief**

  (i)   The reinvestment must be within the period starting 12 months before the disposal and ending 36 months after the date of disposal of the original asset.

  (ii) The original asset and the replacement asset must be qualifying business assets used for a trading purpose by the taxpayer.

  (iii) The replacement asset must be brought into use by the taxpayer for a trading purpose on acquisition.

(b) **Disposal of the factory – 15 February 2007**

		£
Proceeds (320,000 – 6,200)		313,800
Less	Cost (24.10.98)	(164,000)
	Extension (March 2000)	(37,000)
	Legal fees of purchase	(3,600)
Unindexed gain		109,200
Less	Indexation allowance	
	on cost:(164,000 + 3,600) x 0.216	(36,202)
	on extension: (37,000 x 0.188)	(6,956)
Chargeable gain		66,042

(c) **Alternative reinvestments**

  (1) *Freehold warehouse costing £340,000*

      As the full sale proceeds have been reinvested, the company can claim to rollover the gain in full.

      The base cost of the warehouse becomes £273,958 (£340,000 - £66,042).

  (2) *Freehold office building costing £275,000*

      As less than the full proceeds have been reinvested, only part of the gain can be rolled over.

The proceeds not reinvested of £45,000 (£320,000 - £275,000) results in a gain of £45,000 remaining chargeable (see notes).

The balance of £21,042 (£66,042 - £45,000) is rolled over.

The base cost of the office building becomes £253,958 (£275,000 - £21,042).

Note

HMRC allow the 'proceeds not reinvested' to be calculated as the difference between the **net** sale proceeds i.e. after selling costs) and the purchase cost (including purchase expenses) of the replacement asset.

In (c) (2) this would mean only £38,800 (£313,800 - £275,000) of the gain remaining chargeable. However, you may not be expected to know this and would not be penalised either way.

△ ACTIVITY 89 △△△△

XY Ltd

Chargeable gains

	March 2007 £	November 2006 £
Sales proceeds	880,000	360,000
Cost	(500,000)	(120,000)
Enhancement	(60,000)	(20,000)
Unindexed gain	320,000	220,000
Indexation allowance		
500,000 x 0.430	(215,000)	
60,000 x 0.398	(23,880)	
120,000 x 1.035		(124,200)
20,000 x 0.951		(19,020)
Chargeable gain	81,120	76,780

Total chargeable gains (81,120 + 76,780) = £157,900

(b) **Availability of rollover relief**

Provided that the business premises were occupied by XY Ltd, rollover relief will be available on it disposal. However, there will be no such relief on the gain on the disposal of the investment property, as only business assets qualify.

When a business asset is disposed of, rollover relief is available when a qualifying asset (e.g. land, buildings and fixed plant and machinery) is purchased within 12 months before or 36 months after the disposal. When all the proceeds are reinvested, the cost of the replacement is reduced by the chargeable gain.

The gain of £81,120 can therefore be rolled over against the cost of the new business premises. The base cost will be (£1,500,000 - £81,120) = £1,418,880.

△ ACTIVITY 90   △ △ △ △

Roy and Colin

Roy

	£
Deemed disposal proceeds	500,000
Cost	(100,000)
Unindexed gain	400,000
Indexation allowance (0.987 x £100,000)	(98,700)
Gain eligible for gift relief	301,300

If a joint claim for gift relief is made, there will be no chargeable gain arising on Roy in 2006/07.

Colin

The cost Colin can set against future disposal of the shares is (£500,000 - £301,300) = £198,700.

Note that the indexed gain (before taper relief) is deferred. Any accrued taper relief by Roy is lost. On the subsequent disposal Colin will be entitled to taper relief based on ownership since the date of the gift (September 2006).

MOCK EXAMINATION 1
ANSWERS

Section 1

Task 1a

Compute the capital allowances for WCA for the year ended 31 December 2006.

WCA
Capital allowance computation

	Pool £	Private use 10% Landrover £	Private use 20% Ford £	Business %	Allowances £
WDV b/f		16,000	14,000		
Addition	11,000				
WDA – limit		(3,000)		x 90%	2,700
WDA – limit			(3,000)	x 80%	2,400
WDA	(2,750)			-	2,750
WDV c/f	8,250	13,000	11,000		
Total allowances					7,850

Task 1b and 1c

WCA
Computation of taxable trade profits

	£
Profit as computed	48,750
Less: Motor expenses – fully deductible	(900)
Capital allowances	(7,850)
Taxable trade profits	40,000

Assessment for 2006/07

	Total £	John £	Helen £
Based on profit of year ended 31.12.06	40,000	24,000	16,000

Task 2

1   Calculation of overlap profits

Year of assessment	Basis period	Total £	John £	Helen £
2004/05	1.1.05 – 5.4.05			
	32,800 x 3/12	8,200	4,920	3,280
2005/06	y/e 31.12.05	32,800	19,680	13,120
Overlap profits			4,920	3,280

2   **Filing and payment dates**

Y/e 31 December 2006 is assessment in 2006/07

Tax return for 2006/07 – submission – date 31.1.08

Payments on account – 31.1.07 and 31.7.07

Balancing payment – 31.1.08

3   **Note of action re letter**

Action on letter – obtain permission from John and Helen West to supply information to the Highgate Business Advisory Group.

Agree with John and Helen what information you may disclose.

Task 3a

WESTERN LTD
Capital allowances computation

	£	Main pool £	Expensive car £	SLA £	Allowances £
WDV b/f		82,000			
Additions (no FYA)					
Motor car (Note)			16,100		
Disposal:					
Motor car		(2,000)			
		80,000			
WDA 25%		(20,000)	(3,000)		23,000
Additions (with FYA)					
Sorting machine	48,600				
Milling machine				18,000	
FYA (50%)	(24,300)				24,300
		24,300			
FYA (50%)				(9,000)	9,000
WDV c/f		84,300	13,100	9,000	
Total allowances					56,300
IBA (4% x 80,000)					£3,200

Note: Private use of the motor car by an employee of the company is not relevant.

Task 3b

WESTERN LTD
Computation of adjusted trading profit

		£
Profit per accounts		337,520
Add: Depreciation		32,000
Marketing	- wine	1,200
	- organisers – under £50 so allow	-
Bad debt	- write off of loan to	
	former employee	2,300
		373,020
Less: Rental income		(20,000)
Licence for Ford	– wrongly capitalised	(165)
		352,855
Less: Capital allowances (Task 3a)		(56,300)
IBA (Task 3a)		(3,200)
Schedule D Case I		293,355

Task 3c

WESTERN LTD
Computation of chargeable gain/loss

	Shop		*Shares*
	£		£
Net sale proceeds	150,220		159,780
Cost	(30,000)	$(\frac{10}{20} \times £160,000)$	(80,000)
Extension	(10,000)		
	110,220		79,780
Indexation allowance:			
On cost (30,000 x 0.418)	(12,540)	(£80,000 x 0.036)	(2,880)
On extension (10,000 x 0.287)	(2,870)		
	94,810		76,900

Task 3d

WESTERN LTD
Corporation tax computation

	£
Schedule D Case I	293,355
Schedule A	20,000
Capital gains (£94,810 + £76,900)	171,710
PCTCT (I)	485,065
FII	Nil
Profits (P)	485,065

Profits fall between the small company rate bands. The company is therefore a small marginal relief company.

			£
Corporation tax	- FY 05 (3 months)	£121,266 x 30%	36,380
	- FY 06 (9 months)	£363,799 x 30%	109,140
			145,520
Less: Marginal relief			
$(1,500,000 - 485,065) \times {}^{11}/_{400}$			(27,911)
Corporation tax payable			117,609

Turnover

1	Total turnover from trade or profession		**1** £ 489,860

Income

3	Trading and professional profits	**3** £ 293,355	
4	Trading losses brought forward claimed against profits	**4** £	
5	Net trading and professional profits		box 3 minus box 4 **5** £ 293,355
6	Bank, building society or other interest, and profits and gains from non-trading loan relationships		**6** £
11	Income from UK land and buildings		**11** £ 20,000
14	Annual profits and gains not falling under any other heading		**14** £

Chargeable gains

16	Gross chargeable gains	**16** £ 171,710	
17	Allowable losses including losses brought forward	**17** £	
18	Net chargeable gains		box 16 minus box 17 **18** £ 171,710
21	**Profits before other deductions and reliefs**		sum of boxes 5, 6, 11 14 & 18 **21** £ 485,065

Deductions and reliefs

24	Management expenses under S75 ICTA 1988	**24** £	
30	Trading losses of this or a later accounting period under S393A ICTA 1988	**30** £	
31	Put an 'X' in box 31 if amounts carried back from later Accounting periods are included in box 30	**31**	
32	Non-trade capital allowances	**32** £	
35	Charges paid	**35** £	

		box 21 minus boxes 24, 30, 32 and 35
37	**Profits chargeable to corporation tax**	**37** £ 485,065

Tax calculation

38	Franked investment income	**38** £ 0
39	Number of associated companies in this investment	**39**
	or	
40	Associated companies in the first financial year	**40** 0
41	Associated companies in the second financial year	**41** 0
42	*Put an 'X' in box 42 if the company claims to be charged at the starting rate or the Small companies 'rate on any part of it's profits, or is claimimg marginal rate relief*	**42** X

Enter how much profit has to be charged at what rate of tax

Finacial year (*yyyy*)	Amount of profit	Rate of tax	Tax	
43 2 0 0 5	**44** 121,266	**45** 30%	**46** £ 36,380	00 p
53 2 0 0 6	**54** 363,799	**55** 30%	**56** £ 109,140	00 p

			total of boxes 46 and 56
63	Corporation tax		**63** £ 145,520 00 p
64	Marginal relief rate	**64** £ 27,911 00 p	
65	Corporation tax net of marginal rate relief	**65** £ 117,609 00 p	
66	Underlying rate of corporation tax	**66** £ . %	
67	Profits matched with non-corporate distrubutions	**67**	
68	Tax at non-corporate disatribution rate	**68** £ p	
69	Tax at underlying rate on remaining profits	**69** £ p	enter value of box 64 or 65 or the total of boxes 68 and 69 if greater
70	**Corporation tax chargeable**		**70** £ 117,609 00 p

79	Tax payable under S419 ICTA 1988	**79** £ p
80	*Put an 'X' in box 80 if you completed boxA11 in the Supplementry Pages CT600A*	**80**
84	Income tax deducted from gross income included in profits	**84** £ p
85	Income tax payable to the company	**85** £

		total of boxes 70 and 79 minus 84
86	**Tax payable - this is your self-assessment of tax payable**	**86** £ 117,609 00 p

Tax reconciliation

91	Tax already paid (and not already repaid)	**91** £ p
92	Tax outstanding	box 986 minus 93 **86** £ 117,609 00 p
93	Tax overpaid	box 986 minus 93 **93** £ p

Information about capital allowances and balancing charges

Charges and allowances included in calculation of trading profits and losses

		Capital allowances	Balancing charges
105 - 106	Machinery and plant – long-life assets	105 £	106 £
107 - 108	Machinery and plant – other (general pool)	107 £ 53,300	108 £
109 - 110	Cars outside general pool	109 £ 3,000	110 £
111 - 112	Industrial buidlings and structures	111 £ 3,200	112 £
113 - 114	Other charges and allowances	113 £	114 £

Charges and allowances not included in calculation of trading profits and losses

		Capital allowances	Balancing charges
115 - 116		105 £	106 £
117	Put an 'X' in box 117 if box 115 includes flat conversion allowances	117	

Expenditure

118	Expenditure on machinery and plant on which first year allowance is claimed	118 £ 66,600
119	Put an 'X' in box 119 if claim includes enhanced capital allowances for energy-saving investments	119
120	Qualifying expenditure on machinery and plant on long-life assets	120 £
121	Qualifying expenditure on machinery and plant on other assets	121 £ 16,100

Losses, deficits and excess amounts

		calculated under				calculated under
122	Trade loss Case 1	S393 ICTA 1988 122 £		124	Trade losses Case V	S393 ICTA 1988 124 £
125	Non-trade deficits on loan relationships and derivative contracts	S82 FA 1996 125 £		127	Schedule A losses	S392A ICTA1988 122 £
129	Overseas property business losses Case V	S392B ICTA 1988 122 £		130	Losses Case VI	S396 ICTA 1988 122 £
131	Capital losses	S16 TCGA 1992 131 £		136	Excess management expenses	S396 ICTA 1988 136 £

Note: Box 107 includes short life assets.

MEMO

To: John West

From: Accountant

Date: 19.6.07

Re: Corporation Tax

I have set out below some information on matters which require to be dealt with:

1 The corporation tax payable for the year ended 31 December 2006 is £117,609. This is payable on 1 October 2007 and the tax return in respect of the year has to be submitted by 31 December 2007.

2 The draft accounts have been prepared based on some estimated figures and the invoices supporting these payments were mislaid. This is not acceptable to HM Revenue and Customs and, if they challenge the accounts, and we are unable to support our figures an enquiry into the accounts could result.

3 Income tax will be payable to HMRC as follows:

Quarter to 30.6.2007

	£
- income tax retained (£25,600 x 20/80)	6,400
- income tax suffered (£15,600 x 22/78)	(4,400)

Therefore, £2,000 income tax is payable by 14.7.07

4 IBA for a used factory.

Eligible cost = lower of £180,000 (purchase price) or £120,000 (original cost)

A WDA is available which spreads the eligible cost over the remaining tax life. As it is a 20 year old factory the remaining tax life is 5 years.

WDA = (£120,000 ÷ 5) = £24,000 p.a.

The capital gain on the sale of the shop could be rolled over as the purchase price of the factory, £180,000, exceeds the proceeds from the sale of the shop.

MOCK EXAMINATION 2
ANSWERS

Section 1

Task 1

FRED BARE
Taxable trade profit assessments

Year of assessment	Basis period		Assessment £
2002/03	01/01/03 – 05/04/03	($^3/_6$ x £12,000)	6,000
2003/04	01/01/03 – 31/12/03	(£12,000 + ($^6/_{12}$ x £20,000))	22,000
2004/05	Year to 30 June 2004		20,000
2005/06	Year to 30 June 2005		16,000
2006/07	Year to 30 June 2006		14,000
2007/08	1 July 2006 to 30 April 2007		18,000
	Less: Overlap profits (see below)		(16,000)
			2,000

Overlap profits	£
01/01/03 – 05/04/03	6,000
01/07/03 – 31/12/03	10,000
	16,000

Task 2

FRED BARE (AS PARTNER)
Taxable trade profit Assessments

		£	£
2007/08	01/10/07 – 31/03/08		
	Profits for 12 months to 31/03/08	150,000	
	Profits for 01/10/07 – 31/03/08 (6m)	75,000	
	Less: Salaries	(30,000)	
	Profits to be allocated	45,000	
	Fred		
	Share of profits ($^1/_5$)	9,000	
	Salary ($^6/_{12}$ x £20,000)	10,000	
	Assessable profit		**19,000**

		£	£
2008/09	01/04/08 – 31/03/09		
	Profits for 12 months to 31/03/09	165,000	
	Less: Salaries	(60,000)	
	Profits to be allocated	105,000	
	Fred		
	Share of profits ($^1/_5$)	21,000	
	Salary	20,000	
	Assessable profit		**41,000**
2009/10	01/04/09 – 31/03/10		
	Profits for 12 months to 31/03/10	175,000	
	Less: Salaries	(60,000)	
	Profits to be allocated	115,000	
	Fred		
	Share of profits ($^1/_5$)	23,000	
	Salary	20,000	
	Assessable profit		**43,000**

Section 2

Task 3a

AFTON DRILLING LIMITED
Capital allowances computation
9 months to 30 April 2007

General pool

	£	General pool £	Allowances £
TWDV as at 1 August 2006		93,500	
Additions without FYA		5,500	
Disposals		(35,000)	
		64,000	
WDA (25% x £64,000 x 9/12)		(12,000)	12,000
Additions with FYA	12,000		
FYA @ 50%	(6,000)		6,000
		6,000	
TWDV as at 30 April 2007		58,000	
Allowances on general pool			18,000

Expensive cars

	Jaguar £	BMW £	Mercedes £	Allowances £
TWDV as at 1 August 2006	24,000		17,000	
Disposal	(18,000)			
	6,000			
Balancing allowance	(6,000)			6,000
Addition (no FYA)		28,000		
WDA (restricted to £3,000 x 9/12)		(2,250)	(2,250)	4,500
TWDV as at 30 April 2007		25,750	14,750	
Allowances on expensive cars				10,500

Calculation of industrial buildings allowance

Disposal

The building is sold for more than original qualifying cost, therefore all the IBAs originally given are clawed back as a balancing charge.

	£	Allowances £
Original eligible cost	80,000	
TWDV b/f	(32,000)	
Allowances claimed to date	48,000	
Balancing charge		(48,000)

Addition

The qualifying cost of a second hand factory is the lower of original cost and the purchase price, i.e. £300,000.

The tax life of the building commenced 1 January 1992 and expires 31 December 2016. Afton acquired the building on 1 January 2007 at which time the unexpired life was 10 years.

The qualifying cost is written off equally over that period.

Industrial buildings allowance in the current 9 month period is therefore:

	Allowances £
WDA = £300,000/10 x 9/12	22,500
Total net allowances on industrial buildings (– 48,000 + 22,500)	(25,500)

Total capital allowances	£
General pool	80,000
Expensive cars	10,500
Industrial buildings	(25,500)
	3,000

Task 3b

AFTON DRILLING LIMITED
Schedule D Case I computation
9 months to 30 April 2007

			£	£
Net profit per accounts on trading activities				78,000
Add :	Depreciation		33,250	
	Legal fees	(Note 1)	7,500	
	Motor expenses		1,750	
	Entertaining		1,500	
	Patent royalty income receivable		20,000	
Less:	Bad debts	(Note 2)	3,000	
				67,000
				145,000
Less:	Capital allowances (Task 3a)			(3,000)
Schedule D Case I				142,000

Note 1: Disallowable legal fees

	£
Planning application	5,000
Disposal of factory	2,500
	7,500

Note 2: Disallowable bad debts

	£
Non-trade debts written off	3,000

Task 3c

AFTON DRILLING LIMITED
Chargeable gain computation
9 months to 30 April 2007

(i)   Disposal of factory

	£
Proceeds	400,000
Cost of disposal	(2,500)
Net sale proceeds	397,500
Cost	(80,000)
Unindexed gain	317,500
Indexation allowance (£80,000 x 0.469)	(37,520)
Chargeable gain	279,980

A new factory was purchased at a cost of £300,000. Rollover relief can be claimed with the chargeable gain being restricted to the lower of the proceeds not reinvested and the actual gain.

Proceeds not reinvested amounted to £100,000 and this is the amount of the chargeable gain in the 9 m/e 30 April 2007.

(ii) Disposal of shares

12,000 ordinary shares in Bridge plc

	£
Proceeds (January 2007)	60,000
Less: Cost	(46,000)
Unindexed gain	14,000
Less: Indexation (to January 2007) (see Note)	
(46,000 x 0.43) restricted	(14,000)
Chargeable gain	Nil

Note: Full indexation allowance is £19,780 but this is restricted to £14,000 being the amount required to reduce the chargeable gain to nil. This restriction is made since indexation allowance cannot be used to create a capital loss.

Task 3d

AFTON DRILLING LIMITED
Accounting for income tax
9 months to 30 April 2007

Quarter to	Income tax deducted £	Income tax suffered £	Cumulative income tax £	Income tax paid (repaid) £	Due date
30.09.06 (Note 1)	-	(5,720)	(5,720)	-	
31.03.07	7,700	-	7,700	1,980	14.04.07
Income tax paid in accounting period (Note 2)			1,980		

Note:

(1) Afton Drilling Ltd will not obtain a repayment in the quarter to 30.09.06 as no income tax has been paid in the CAP. It will recover the tax suffered by set off in the quarter to 31.03.07. Instead of paying £7,700 to HMRC on 14.04.07, the company will only pay £1,980.

(2) There is no offset of income tax against the corporation tax liability as income tax retained exceeded income tax suffered.

Task 3e

AFTON DRILLING LIMITED
Corporation tax computation
9 months to 30 April 2007

Corporation tax liability

	£
Schedule D Case I	142,000
Chargeable gain	100,000
	242,000
*Less:*Charges on income	Nil
Profits chargeable to corporation tax	242,000
Dividend received (£54,000 x $\frac{100}{90}$)	60,000
'Profits' for small company rate	302,000

Corporation tax chargeable in:

	£
Financial year 2006 at 30% (£215,111 at 30%)	64,533
Financial year 2007 at 30% (£26,889 at 30%)	8,067
	72,600

*Less:*Marginal relief:

Financial year 2006 (£1,000,000 - £268,444) x £215,111/£268,444 x $\frac{11}{400}$ (16,121)

Financial year 2007 (£125,000 -   £33,556) x   £26,889/ £33,556 x $\frac{11}{400}$ (2,015)

Corporation tax payable	54,464

Corporation tax is payable 1 February 2007.

Task 3f

M E M O

To: A Smith
From: Accounting Technician
Subject: Payment by Instalments

I refer to your recent enquiry.

Payment of corporation tax by instalments

This was introduced as part of Corporation Tax Self Assessment and has applied for several years. The broad principle is that a large company should settle its corporation tax liability for an accounting period by the payment of 4 equal quarterly instalments commencing in month 7 of the accounting period in question.

The company has to estimate its liability for the year from month 7 onwards as at least 3 and probably 4 of the payments will fall due before the CT liability is finalised. HM Revenue and Customs will expect to see evidence of how estimates were made (management accounts etc) if the company has significantly under-estimated, so record keeping is important.

As stated above, these rules only apply to large companies which are companies which pay corporation tax at the full rate of 30%. This requires taxable profits for a company with no associates to be £1,500,000 or more – companies with chargeable profits less than that will continue to pay their corporation tax liability nine months after the year end.

Task 4

Company tax calculation

Turnover

1	Total turnover from trade or profession	**1**	£ 263,000

Income

3	Trading and professional profits	**3**	£ 142,000
4	Trading losses brought forward claimed against profits	**4**	£
5	Net trading and professional profits	**5** box 3 minus box 4	£ 142,000
6	Bank, building society or other interest, and profits and gains from non-trading loan relationships	**6**	£
11	Income from UK land and buildings	**11**	£
14	Annual profits and gains not falling under any other heading	**14**	£

Chargeable gains

16	Gross chargeable gains	**16**	£ 100,000
17	Allowable losses including losses brought forward	**17**	£
18	Net chargeable gains	**18** box 16 minus box 17	£ 100,000
21	**Profits before other deductions and reliefs**	**21** sum of boxes 5, 6, 11 14 & 18	£ 242,000

Deductions and reliefs

24	Management expenses under S75 ICTA 1988	**24**	£
30	Trading losses of this or a later accounting period under S393A ICTA 1988	**30**	£
31	Put an 'X' in box 31 if amounts carried back from later Accounting periods are included in box 30	**31**	
32	Non-trade capital allowances	**32**	£
35	Charges paid	**35**	£
37	**Profits chargeable to corporation tax**	**37** box 21 minus boxes 24, 30, 32 and 35	£ 242,000

Tax calculation

38	Franked investment income	**38**	£ 0
39	Number of associated companies in this investment or	**39**	
40	Associated companies in the first financial year	**40**	0
41	Associated companies in the second financial year	**41**	0
42	*Put an 'X' in box 42 if the company claims to be charged at the starting rate or the Small companies 'rate on any part of it's profits, or is claimimg marginal rate relief*	**42**	X

Enter how much profit has to be charged at what rate of tax

Finacial year (yyyy)	Amount of profit	Rate of tax	Tax	
43 2 0 0 6	**44** 215,111	**45** 30	**46** £ 64,533	00 p
53 2 0 0 7	**54** 26,889	**55** 30	**56** £ 8,067	00 p

63	Corporation tax	**63** total of boxes 46 and 56	£ 72,600 00 p
64	Marginal relief rate	**64** £ 18,136 00 p	
65	Corporation tax net of marginal rate relief	**65** £ 54,464 00 p	
66	Underlying rate of corporation tax	**66** £ . %	
67	Profits matched with non-corporate distrubutions	**67**	
68	Tax at non-corporate disatribution rate	**68** £ p	
69	Tax at underlying rate on remaining profits	**69** £ p	enter value of box 64 or 65 or the total of boxes 68 and 69 if greater
70	**Corporation tax chargeable**	**70** £ 54,464 00 p	

79	Tax payable under S419 ICTA 1988		**79** £		p
80	*Put an 'X' in box 80 if you completed boxA11 in the Supplementry Pages CT600A*	**80**			
84	Income tax deducted from gross income included in profits		**84** £		p
85	Income tax payable to the company		**85** £		
			total of boxes 70 and 79 minus 84		
86	**Tax payable - this is your self-assessment of tax payable**		**86** £ 54,464		00 p

Tax reconciliation

91	Tax already paid (and not already repaid)		**91** £		p
			box 986 minus 93		
92	Tax outstanding		**86** £ 54,464		00 p
			box 986 minus 93		
93	Tax overpaid		**93** £		p

Information about capital allowances and balancing charges

Charges and allowances included in calculation of trading profits and losses

		Capital allowances	Balancing charges
105 - 106	Machinery and plant – long-life assets	**105** £	**106** £
107 - 108	Machinery and plant – other (general pool)	**107** £ 18,000	**108** £
109 - 110	Cars outside general pool	**109** £ 10,500	**110** £
111 - 112	Industrial buildings and structures	**111** £ 22,500	**112** £ 48,000
113 - 114	Other charges and allowances	**113** £	**114** £

Charges and allowances not included in calculation of trading profits and losses

		Capital allowances	Balancing charges
115 - 116		**105** £	**106** £
117	*Put an 'X' in box 117 if box 115 includes flat conversion allowances*	**117**	

Expenditure

118	Expenditure on machinery and plant on which first year allowance is claimed	**118** £ 12,000	
119	*Put an 'X' in box 119 if claim includes enhanced capital allowances for energy-saving investments*	**119**	
120	Qualifying expenditure on machinery and plant on long-life assets	**120** £	
121	Qualifying expenditure on machinery and plant on other assets	**121** £ 5,500	

Losses, deficits and excess amounts

122	Trade loss Case 1	*calculated under S393 ICTA 1988* **122** £	124	Trade losses Case V	*calculated under S393 ICTA 1988* **124** £
125	Non-trade deficits on loan relationships and derivative contracts	*calculated under S82 FA 1996* **125** £	127	Schedule A losses	*calculated under S392A ICTA 1988* **122** £
129	Overseas property business losses Case V	*calculated under S392B ICTA 1988* **122** £	130	Losses Case VI	*calculated under S396 ICTA 1988* **122** £
131	Capital losses	*calculated under S16 TCGA 1992* **131** £	136	Excess management expenses	*calculated under S396 ICTA 1988* **136** £

Date before which the CT600 should be submitted if a late filing penalty is to be avoided:

30 April 2007

SPECIMEN PAPER QUESTIONS

This examination paper is in TWO SECTIONS. You have to show competence in BOTH sections. You should therefore attempt and aim to complete EVERY task in EACH section.

You should spend about 90 minutes on Section 1 and 90 minutes on Section 2.

Section 1

Data

You work in the tax department of a firm of Chartered Accountants. One of your colleagues, Samantha, who works in the Small Business Accounts department, has contacted you about a new client, Joe Dunn.

He commenced trading on 1 January 2004, but has not prepared any accounts. Samantha has completed the accounts for the period ended 30 June 2004 and the two years ended 30 June 2005 and 2006. She asks you to carry out tax work for Joe Dunn for all tax years up to and including 2006/07.

Samantha supplies you with the following information:

1   Adjusted trading profits, before deducting capital allowances:

	£
Period ended 30 June 2004	27,055
Year ended 30 June 2005	30,645
Year ended 30 June 2006	30,207

2   Fixed assets additions and disposals:

ADDITIONS		£
January 2004	Plant and machinery	26,400
February 2004	Motor car, no private usage	11,600
February 2004	Motor car, 30% private usage	10,000
June 2004	Plant and machinery	13,640
November 2004	Computer	6,400
May 2005	Motor car, no private usage	13,000

DISPOSALS		
December 2004	Plant and machinery	4,600

3   Joe Dunn has paid no National Insurance Contributions since he started trading.

4   Joe Dunn wants to take his brother into partnership to help him run the business, from January 2007.

Task 1.1

Calculate the capital allowances for all relevant years.

Task 1.2

Calculate the taxable trade profits for each accounting period

Task 1.3

Calculate the taxable profits for all tax years, from commencement of trade to 2006/07, clearly showing the dates and amount of overlap profits.

Task 1.4

Calculate the total amount of NIC Class 4 payable by Joe Dunn for 2006/07.

Task 1.5

Explain the implications on Joe Dunn of his failure to:

· Notify HM Revenue and Customs of his chargeability to taxation

· Complete and submit his tax returns by the due dates, stating what the due dates are.

Task 1.6

Outline the key points that you would like to make to Joe Dunn regarding the taxation implications of a business being operated as a partnership.

Section 2

Data

You work for a company, Delta Ltd, preparing their tax information prior to it being entered in the CT600 tax form. The company has traded for many years, using a year end of 31 December. However, it has now changed its year end to 31 March.

The Chief Accountant for Delta Ltd has supplied you with the accounts for the 15 month period ended 31 March 2007.

The profit and loss account shows:

	£	£
Gross profit		1,131,950
Profit on the sale of shares (Note 3)		23,800
General expenses (Note 1)	425,380	
Impaired debts (Note 2)	5,850	
Salaries and wages	280,645	
Depreciation	125,630	
		(837,505)
Net profit		318,245

Note 1: General expenses includes:

	£
Entertaining customers	2,300
Parking fines paid for employees	650
Gifts to customers (100 bottles of wine)	1,000
Staff Christmas party (20 people)	600

Note 2: Impaired debts are made up of:

		£
Debts written off	– trade	3,300
	– Employee loan	2,400
Increase in provision for impaired debts		500
Bad debts recovered	– trade	(350)
		5,850

Note 3: Profit on the sale of shares

In January 2007, Delta Ltd sold 30,000 shares in Alpha Ltd for £58,500. These shares had been acquired as follows:

	No. of shares	£
June 1996	20,000	12,000
November 2000	10,000	16,000

In May 1997, Alpha Ltd made a bonus issue of 1 for 10.

Additional information:

1   You have already calculated the capital allowances for the plant and machinery at £35,060 for the year ended 31 December 2006, and £10,400 for the period ended 31 March 2007.

2   In September 1989, Delta Ltd had acquired a new industrial building for £250,000. The building had been in industrial use throughout the period of ownership.

3   Delta Ltd has no associated companies.

4   For calculating the capital gain on the Alpha Ltd shares use the following indexation factors:

    June 1996   – November 2000   0.125
    November 2000   – January 2007   0.160

Task 2.1

Calculate the capital gain arising from the disposal of the shares in Alpha Ltd.

Task 2.2

Calculate the adjusted trading profit, before capital allowances, for the 15 month period ended 31 March 2007.

Task 2.3

Show the PCTCT (profit chargeable to corporation tax) for the two periods of the year ended 31 December 2006, and the period ended 31 March 2007.

Task 2.4

Calculate the Corporation Tax payable for the 12 month period ended 31 December 2006.

Task 2.5

Calculate the Corporation Tax payable for the three month period ended 31 March 2007.

Task 2.6

Data

The Chief Accountant tells you that he anticipates that Delta Ltd will make a loss in the year ended 31 March 2008. He has asked if you could advise him about the tax implications of such a loss.

Using the headed paper below, write a memo to the Chief Accountant, setting out the options available to Delta Ltd for the set-off of the potential loss.

MEMO	
To: **Chief Accountant**	**Date:** **1 August 2007**
From: **Accounting Technician**	**Ref:** **Corporation Tax Losses**

SPECIMEN PAPER ANSWERS

Section 1

Task 1.1

Capital allowances

		Pool £	Exp Car £	Car with PU £	TOTAL £
6 m/e 30/06/04					
Additions (no FYA)					
Cars		11,600		10,000	
WDA @ 25% x 6/12		(1,450)		(1,250) (70%)	2,325
		10,150		8,750	
Additions with FYA					
P&M	26,400				
@ 40%	(10,560)	15,840			10,560
P&M	13,640				6,820
@ 50%	(6,820)	6,820			
WDV c/f		32,810		8,750	
Total allowances					19,705
Y/e 30/06/05					
Disposals		(4,600)			
		28,210			
Additions (no FYA)			13,000		
WDA @ 25%		(7,053)	(3,000)	(2,188) (70%)	11,585
		21,157	10,000	6,562	
Additions with FYA					
Computer	6,400				
@ 50%	(3,200)	3,200			3,200
WDV c/f		24,357	10,000	6,562	
Total allowances					14,785
Y/e 30/06/06					
WDA @ 25%		(6,089)	(2,500)	(1,640) (70%)	9,737
WDV c/f		18,268	7,500	4,922	
Total allowances					9,737

Task 1.2

Taxable trading profits

	Adjusted profit £	CA £	Taxable trade profits £
P/e 30/06/04	27,055	(19,705)	7,350
Y/e 30/06/05	30,645	(14,785)	15,860
Y/e 30/06/06	30,207	(9,737)	20,470

KAPLAN PUBLISHING

Task 1.3

Taxable profits for all years

Year of assessment	Basis period	Assessment £
2003/04	01/01/04 – 05/04/04	
	3/6 x £7,350	3,675
		———
2004/05	01/01/04 – 31/12/04	
	P/e 30/06/04	7,350
	6/12 x £15,860	7,930
		———
		15,280
		———
2005/06	Y/e 30/06/05	15,860
2006/07	Y/e 30/06/06	20,470
		———

Overlap profits
01/01/04 – 05/04/04	3,675
01/07/04 – 31/12/04	7,930
	———
	11,605
	———

Task 1.4

Class 4 NIC liability - 2006/07

(£20,470 - £5,035) x 8%   £1,235

Task 1.5

Administration

1   Failure to notify the chargeability to tax – this will incur a maximum penalty of an amount equal to the tax remaining unpaid on 31 January following the end of the tax year.

2   A £100 fixed penalty is charged if the tax return is submitted late, with a further £100 fixed penalty if the tax return is more than six months late. If the tax return is more than 12 months, as in this case, an additional penalty may be charged of up to 100% of the tax liability for the year.

3   The due dates for the filing of a tax return are 30 September following the end of the tax year, for taxpayers who want HM Revenue and Customs to calculate their tax liability, or 31 January following the end of the tax year, for taxpayers who have calculated their own tax liability.

4   In addition there is a £100 penalty for traders who have not registered to pay Class 2 NIC within 3 months of commencing to trade.

Task 1.6

Key points relating to trading as a partnership

1 The taxable trade profits and losses are calculated in the same way as for an individual.

2 The taxable trade profit or loss is split between the partners in the agreed profit sharing ratio.

3 Each partner is assessed individually.

4 Each partner is responsible for his own tax liability.

Task 2.1

Disposal of Alpha Ltd shares

FA 1985 pool:	No. of shares	Cost £	Indexed cost £
June 1996	20,000	12,000	12,000
May 1997 Bonus issue	2,000	Nil	Nil
	22,000	12,000	12,000
November 2000			
IA (£12,000 x 0.125)			1,500
			13,500
Addition	10,000	16,000	16,000
	32,000	28,000	29,500
January 2007			
IA (£29,500 x 0.160)			4,720
			34,220
Disposal	(30,000)	(26,250)	(32,081)
Pool to c/fwd	2,000	1,750	2,139

	£
Proceeds	58,500
Cost	(26,250)
Unindexed gain	32,250
Indexation allowance (32,081 – 26,250)	(5,831)
Chargeable gain	26,419

Task 2.2

Adjusted trading profit before capital allowances

	£	£
Net profit		318,245
Add:		
Entertaining	2,300	
Gifts	1,000	
Employee loan written off	2,400	
Depreciation	125,630	131,330
		449,575
Less:		
Profit on sale of shares		(23,800)
Adjusted trading profit		425,775

Note: Although fines and penalties are not usually deductible, HM Revenue and Customs will allow an employee's parking fine provided it is incurred whilst parking the employer's car on employer's business. However, such fines are never allowed if incurred by a director.

Task 2.3

Profits chargeable to corporation tax

	12 months to December 2006	3 months to 31 March 2007
	£	£
Adjusted Profit (split 12/3)	340,620	85,155
Capital allowances	(35,060)	(10,400)
IBA (£250,000 x 4%)/3 months	(10,000)	(2,500)
Schedule D Case I	295,560	72,255
Chargeable gain (Task 2.1)	-	26,501
PCTCT	295,560	98,756

There is no FII in either period therefore PCTCT = Profits.

Task 2.4

Corporation tax payable - y/e 31 December 2006.

Profits fall below £300,000 therefore corporation tax is charged at 19%.

	£
£295,560 x 19%	56,156

Task 2.5

Corporation tax payable - 3 m/e 31 March 2007

Profits fall between the upper and lower limits for a three month period (see below), therefore marginal relief applies.

	£
CT @ 30% : (£98,756 @ 30%)	29,627
Less marginal relief	
(375,000 − 98,756) x 11/400	(7,597)
Corporation tax payable	22,030

Small company rate limits:	£300,000 x 3/12	=	£75,000
	£1,500,000 x 3/12	=	£375,000

Task 2.6

MEMO

To:	**Chief Accountant**	Date:	**1 August 2007**
From:	**Accounting Technician**	Ref:	**Corporation Tax Losses**

There are two basic alternatives regarding the corporation tax loss that you are anticipating:

1   To carry the loss forward under s393(1) ICTA 1988 and relieve against future trading profits.

2   To relieve the loss under s393A(1) against total profits. This means that the loss is set against all other profits arising in the year of the trading loss.

3   If (2) is opted for, the company may also, under s393A(1), carry the loss back against the total profits rising in the 12 months prior to the loss making period.

I hope this answers your query.

INDEX

KAPLAN
PUBLISHING
FOULKS LYNCH

AAT Order Form

Swift House, Market Place, Wokingham, Berkshire RG40 1AP, UK.
Tel: +44 (0) 118 989 0629   Fax: +44 (0) 118 979 7455
Order online: www.kaplanfoulkslynch.com
Email: publishing@kaplanfoulkslynch.com

To order books, please indicate quantity required in the relevant box, calculate the amount(s) in the column provided, and add postage to determine the amount due. Please clearly fill in your details plus method of payment in the boxes provided and return your completed form with payment attached.

For assessments in 2006/07		Study Text		Workbook		Pocket Notes		Total
Unit		Price £	Order	Price £	Order	Price £	Order	£
30	Introductory accounting	21.00	☐	21.00	☐	8.00	☐	
1, 2 & 3	Receipts, payments and an initial trial balance	21.00	☐	21.00	☐	8.00	☐	
		Study Text & Workbook						
Unit		Price £	Order					
4	Supplying information for management control	16.00	☐					
5	Maintaining financial records and preparing accounts	16.00	☐					
6	Recording and evaluating costs and revenues	21.00	☐			8.00	☐	
7	Preparing reports and returns	21.00	☐			8.00	☐	
8 & 9	Performance management, enhancement of value and planning & control of resources	21.00	☐			8.00	☐	
10	Managing systems and people in the accounting environment	21.00	☐			8.00	☐	
11	Drafting financial statements	21.00	☐			8.00	☐	
15	Cash management and credit control	16.00	☐			8.00	☐	
17	Implementing auditing procedures	21.00	☐			6.00	☐	
18	Business taxation (FA05)	15.00	☐					
18	Business taxation (FA06)	21.00	☐			8.00	☐	
19	Personal taxation (FA05)	15.00	☐			6.00	☐	
19	Personal taxation (FA06)	16.00	☐			8.00	☐	
21, 22&23	Working with computers, personal effectiveness and health & safety	16.00	☐			8.00	☐	
31	Accounting work skills	16.00	☐			8.00	☐	
32	Professional ethics	16.00	☐			8.00	☐	
33	Management accounting	16.00	☐			8.00	☐	
							TOTAL	

Postage, Packaging and Delivery (per item):   **Note:** Maximum postage charged for UK orders is £15

Study Texts and Workbooks	First	Each	Pocket Notes	First	Each Extra
UK	£5.00	£2.00	UK	£2.00	£1.00
Europe (incl Republic of Ireland	£7.00	£4.00	Europe (incl Republic of Ireland and	£3.00	£2.00
Rest of World	£22.00	£8.00	Rest of World	£8.00	£5.00

Product Sub Total £................   Postage & Packaging £................   Order Total £..................... (Payments in UK £ Sterling)

Customer Details

☐ Mr ☐ Mrs ☐ Ms ☐ Miss Other

....

Initials:................................ Surname:...........................

....

Address:

....

....

Delivery Address – if different from above
Address:

....

....

..

Delivery please allow:-   United Kingdom   - 5 working days

Europe   - 8 working days

Payment

1 I enclose Cheque/Postal Order/Bankers Draft for £.................
Please make cheques payable to **'FTC Kaplan Limited'.**

2 Charge MasterCard/Visa/Switch/Delta no:

Valid from: ☐☐☐ Expiry date: ☐☐☐

Issue no: (Switch only) ☐☐☐   3-digit security code on back of card ☐☐☐

Declaration

I agree to pay as indicated on this form and understand that FTC Kaplan Limiteds Terms and Conditions apply (available on request).

Signature: ....   Date: ....

Notes: All orders over 1kg will be fully tracked & insured. Signature required on receipt of order. Delivery times subject to stock availability. A telephone number or email address is required for orders that are to be delivered to a PO Box number

Kaplan Publishing Foulks Lynch
Swift House
Market Place Wokingham
Berkshire RG40 1AP
UK

PUBLISHING

FOULKS LYNCH

Thank you for choosing this Kaplan Publishing Study Text/Workbook for your AAT qualification. As we are constantly striving to improve our products, we would be grateful if you could provide us with feedback about how useful you found this publication.

Name: ....

Address: ....

....

Email: ....

Why did you decide to purchase this Study Text/Workbook?

Have used them in the past ☐

Recommended by lecturer ☐

Recommended by friend ☐

Saw advertising ☐

Other (please specify) ....

....

How do you study?

At a college ☐

On a Distance Learning Course ☐

Home study ☐

Other (please specify) ....

....

Within our AAT range we also offer Distance Learning Courses and Pocket Notes. Is there any other type of service/publication that you would like to see as part of the range?

CD Rom with additional questions and answers ☐

A booklet that would help you master exam skills and techniques ☐

Space on our website that would answer your technical questions and queries ☐

Other (please specify) ....

During the past six month do you recall seeing/receiving any of the following?

Our advertisement in Accounting Technician magazine? ☐

Our leaflet/brochure or a letter through the post? ☐

Other (please specify) ....

Overall opinion of this Study Text/Workbook

	Excellent	Adequate	Poor
Introductory pages	☐	☐	☐
Standards coverage	☐	☐	☐
Clarity of explanations	☐	☐	☐
Clarity of definitions and key terms	☐	☐	☐
Diagrams	☐	☐	☐
Activities	☐	☐	☐
Quick quiz questions	☐	☐	☐
Key technique questions	☐	☐	☐
Answers to key technique questions	☐	☐	☐
Mock exams/skills tests	☐	☐	☐
Layout	☐	☐	☐
Index	☐	☐	☐

If you have further comments/suggestions or have spotted any errors, please write them on the bottom of the next page.
Please return this form to: Briony Wastell, Kaplan Publishing Foulks Lynch, FREEPOST NAT 17540, Wokingham RG40 1BR

Other comments/suggestions and errors

. . . .
. . . .
. . . .
. . . .
. . . .
. . . .
. . . .
. . . .
. . . .
. . . .
. . . .
. . . .